STAR-SPANGLED CANADIANS

JEFFREY SIMPSON

STAR-SPANGLED
CANADIANS

Canadians Living the American Dream

HarperCollins*PublishersLtd*

STAR-SPANGLED CANADIANS:
CANADIANS LIVING
THE AMERICAN DREAM
Copyright © 2000 by Jeffrey C. Simpson Publications Inc.
All rights reserved. No part of this book may be used
or reproduced in any manner whatsoever without prior
written permission except in the case of brief quotations
embodied in reviews. For information address
HarperCollins Publishers Ltd,
55 Avenue Road, Suite 2900,
Toronto, Ontario, Canada M5R 3L2

www.harpercanada.com

HarperCollins books may be purchased for
educational, business, or sales promotional use.
For information please write:
Special Markets Department,
HarperCollins Canada,
55 Avenue Road, Suite 2900,
Toronto, Ontario, Canada M5R 3L2

First HarperCollins hardcover ed.
ISBN 0-00-255767-3
First HarperCollins trade paper ed.
ISBN 0-00-639132-X

Canadian Cataloguing in Publication Data

Simpson, Jeffrey, 1949–
Star-spangled Canadians :
Canadians living the American dream

Includes bibliographical references and index.
ISBN 0-00-255767-3

1. Canadians – United States – Attitudes.
2. United States – Public opinion.
3. National characteristics, Canadian.
4. National characteristics, American.
5. Canada – Relations – United States.
6. United States – Relations – Canada.
I. Title.

FC95.4.S55 2000   971   C00-931175-0
F1021.2.S55 2000

00 01 02 03 04 HC 5 4 3 2 1

Printed and bound in the United States
Set in Electra

Good fences make good neighbors,
Robert Frost, "Mending Wall," 1914

CONTENTS

As I snoop around my old town I do not find evidence that the urge toward success has been chastened since my time. I heard a good deal about people I grew up with, and most of it concerns how they married an American millionaire, or made it big as a geologist for Standard Oil, or tour the country every year giving piano recitals, or have become contractors in Calgary, bankers in Victoria, newspaper publishers in Regina, teachers or doctors or executives somewhere else. — Wallace Stegner, Wolf Willow

INTRODUCTION

AUTHORS of fiction are counselled to write what they know; that is, what they understand of the human condition from the perspective of the environment in which they live. Although not a work of fiction, this book about Canadians in the United States follows the fiction writer's guidance, in a manner of speaking. Through an accident of birth and the citizenship laws of the day, I was born an American, but have lived most of my life in Canada as a Canadian citizen. As a result, the similarities and differences between the two countries have always fascinated me.

As the Canadian ex-patriate writer and broadcaster Robert MacNeil observed when we spoke in New York City, a Canadian brain is programmed with gigabytes of knowledge about the United States, whereas an American brain knows little or nothing about Canada. The physical border separating the two countries, to quote Canadian author Margaret Atwood, is a "one-way mirror" through which Canadians see the United States but Americans do not see Canada.

Canadians and Americans, in the millions, have crossed that border to live in each other's country. The migrations began long before the political creation of Canada and the United States, when North America was a collection of British and French colonies. With a few exceptions, north-to-south migrations have eclipsed the reverse movement.

Immigration policies today make resettlement much more difficult than it was fifty or a hundred years ago. What politicians, on ceremonial occasions, love to call the "world's longest undefended border" was also a highly permeable one until recent decades, so permeable that hundreds and hundreds of thousands of Canadians crossed it with impunity to take up residence in the United States.

Canada's population of 30 million might today be 40 or 50 million had so many Canadians not migrated to the United States, or had so many immigrants to Canada stayed put rather than passing through Canada *en route* to their eventual destination: the United States.

The vast majority of migrants resettled in times of peace, but some changed countries to seek refuge in times of war. William Lyon Mackenzie, Louis-Joseph Papineau, and Louis Riel all fled south after their respective rebellions failed in Canada, although each subsequently returned. Canadians by the thousands volunteered for duty in the Union armies during the U.S. Civil War; others joined the American military during the Vietnam War.

Between 60,000 and 100,000 Loyalists (estimates vary wildly) trekked north during and after the U.S. War of Independence. They preferred the British Crown to the American Republic, although some of them subsequently returned to the United States. Thousands of "skedaddlers," as they were called in the United States, avoided enlistment in the Civil War armies by slipping across the border. During that war, thousands of black Americans made their way to Canada via the Underground Railroad. Tens of thousands of Americans uprooted to Canada during the Vietnam War to escape military duty or to register a personal protest against U.S. policy.

My own father crossed the border not to flee military duty, but eventually to seek it. The son of an upstanding middle-class family from Yonkers, New York, my father decided in 1940, after the Nazi armies had overrun France, that the United States should enter the Second World War. American public opinion, however, remained rooted in isolationism. President Franklin D. Roosevelt made no secret of his desire to assist the beleaguered British, and designed the Lend Lease policy to show it, but the president knew his people too well to force an active U.S. military commitment.

My father spent his whole life despising FDR, the roots of his dislike having been sunk before 1940. My father idealized his uncle, a big-shot New York State Republican who had made a pile of money and actively supported Herbert Hoover and other Republican worthies at the state and national level. Decades after the war, my father would rail against FDR for his economic policies and his political cowardice in not bringing the United States earlier into the struggle against the Nazis.

My father was living in Canada with his first wife, an Englishwoman, when war broke out in 1939. Always possessed of a rebel streak, he tried to enlist in the Canadian army, as did thousands of other Americans between the time of the Nazi invasion of Poland and Pearl Harbor. He somehow talked himself into the office of Billy Bishop, Canada's First World War flying ace, who doubted whether the Canadian forces wanted foreign nationals but referred him to the proper place for a medical examination. There, as my father subsequently related, his career in the Canadian military ended before it began.

While playing football at Brown University in Providence, Rhode Island, my father had suffered a severe back injury that hobbled him until a subsequent spinal-fusion operation. In my father's recounting of the story to me, the Canadian army medical examiner told him to strip to his underwear, took one look at his injured back, and promptly declared him unfit for military duty.

Undaunted, my father stayed in Canada, met a few folks, and started working in the troop-entertainment business in Toronto, the beginning of his lifelong career in radio, television, and advertising. He became acquainted with some of Canada's leading lights of music and radio, a handful of whom became his enduring friends, such as Mart Kenney, the bandleader known especially in Western Canada. Some of my fondest early Canadian memories are of Mart playing the piano in our living room while his wife, the marvellous Norma Locke, sang and other friends of Dad's from the entertainment world joined in.

After the collapse of his first marriage in Toronto, my father met my mother, a woman born in Winnipeg who was living in Toronto. They moved soon after the marriage to New York City, where my father began his career in advertising. In those days, a mother's nationality counted for nothing in determining a child's citizenship. Although my mother was a Canadian, and fiercely proud of it, the geographic fact that I joined the world in New York City, born of an American father, meant, by definition, that I was an American and nothing else.

At the age of nine, I was uprooted with my family to Montreal, where my father's U.S. advertising agency had decided to open an office. Casting about for an employee who knew something about Canada, the higher-ups asked my father to go. He gladly accepted, having become quite attached to Canada. Two years later, he moved again, to the firm's Canadian headquarters in Toronto, where he ended his career and died many years later.

I was sixteen when my father decided to become a Canadian citizen, a more consequential decision then than now, because in the mid-1960s U.S. law stipulated that an American who acquired another citizenship automatically lost U.S. nationality. In the quaint words of U.S. law, anyone who swore allegiance to another country, with "foreign kings or potentates"—the Queen of the United Kingdom and Canada included—abandoned U.S. citizenship.

Things were slightly different for me. Americans presumably could not conceive of why anyone would forgo the privileges and glories of U.S. citizenship at a young age. Therefore, those opting for another citizenship could hold two passports until the age of twenty-one in case they came belatedly to their senses. At the age of twenty-one, however, a choice was required: allegiance to the flag of the United States and to the republic for which it stands, or to one of those "foreign kings or potentates." I chose Canada, not because I had anything against the United States, but because my parents were now both Canadians, I was happy in Canada, and, if the truth be known, I did not wish to run the slight risk of finding my name on a draft list. I have never regretted the decision. Canada has been wonderful to me and for me, and although I sometimes grieve, as concerned citizens do, about the country's hang-ups and missed opportunities, I at least have had the outlet of the national-affairs column in *The Globe and Mail* to criticize and contemplate the Canadian condition.

People who resettle on the other side of the border take along cultural baggage, as the Canadians in this book explain in their own words. How much baggage they take and whether they ever fully shed it are questions that have always intrigued me, given the many observable similarities of daily life in Canada and in the United States, especially for those with English as their mother or acquired tongue.

A cross-border move requires a process of acculturation, often more difficult for Americans who have an inbred sense of their country's superior way of doing things. Canadians who move south already understand plenty of American cultural signals, courtesy of travel; proximity to the U.S. border; the omnipresence of American popular culture; and the vastly greater size, power, and influence of the United States.

Canadians habitually grumble about how little Americans know about Canada—the one-way mirror—but Americans can perhaps be excused their indifference or ignorance. The United States is so vast, so distant from the rest of the world, and so successful that its self-fascination blocks out much room for thinking about others. Only in the last half-century has the United States been engaged militarily, politically, and economically around the world. Even in today's global economy, the share of the U.S. gross national product dependent upon foreign trade ranks far below that of other major industrialized countries, including Canada. A country founded by people determined to be different, forged in a revolutionary war, separated by long distances from other continents, and still acutely proud of its own accomplishments and vast power is not one instinctively curious about other places.

I had my share of acculturation problems, although some merely related to my being young and therefore needing to learn lots of new things anyway. For example, I could barely skate upon arriving in Montreal, despite my Canadian mother's earnest efforts to instruct me on the ice sheet at Rockefeller Center in New York City. I wanted desperately to play hockey, not just to fit in with schoolmates and neighbours, but because my father, hooked on hockey from his Canadian years, had often taken me to the old, smoky Madison Square Garden to watch the sad-sack New York Rangers. My hockey hero then, and for years thereafter, was Lorne "Gump" Worsley, Rangers' goalie of barrelled belly and cracker-barrel wisdom who, when once asked which National Hockey League team gave him the most trouble, replied, "the Rangers."

What were my new Canadian friends to do with a wobbly-skating import? I had played lots of Little League baseball and innumerable games of stickball in concrete schoolyards in my New York City neighbourhood, so I could catch better than they could. The obvious answer presented itself. Thus began an altogether undistinguished career as a goaltender, and the start of that acculturation process through which immigrants pass.

Growing up, I experienced once in a while the same kind of tug from my American past that many of my Canadian ex-patriate interlocutors in this book recounted having felt occasionally from their Canadian upbringing. For years after moving to Canada, I continued to attend summer camp in the United States, where the philosophy was learning through competing—the American way, we might say. If you wanted to learn how to hit a backhand or swim the crawl (or shoot a target rifle—a distinctly American twist), you took instruction in a group, then divided into teams for a competition under the watchful eye of counsellors-cum-coaches.

This seemed so perfectly natural that I tried introducing learning through competition at the Canadian camp where I worked for one summer. This attempt lasted about a week, until the camp director pulled me up short by explaining that the "Canadian way" involved competing against nature and oneself, not against others.

A lifetime spent growing up in both countries—much more in Canada than in the United States—has persuaded me of the virtues of both countries and the futility of trying to argue that one is somehow inherently superior to the other. A Canadian, however, measures Canada inevitably and overwhelmingly against the United States, whereas it would occur to only the occasional American to measure the United States against Canada. This Canadian measuring produces a kaleidoscope of reactions, ranging from envy to anger, from inferiority complex to moral superiority, from doubt to defiance.

Several generations ago, many English-speaking Canadians used the United Kingdom as the touchstone for comparison, but those days are now long gone. Apart from the monarchy and the parliamentary form of government, little remains of the British connection in Canada. Ex-patriates in this book who left Canada in the 1950s described a Canada that would scarcely be recognizable to today's generation, in part because the British influences they remembered have vanished. (France, by the way, has inspired comparisons for a few francophone Quebeckers, but for most of them the French connection pales in contrast with the American one.)

Apart from first-generation immigrants to Canada who can compare their homeland with their adopted one, Canadians have only one comparative yardstick: the United States, with which Canada does 84 per cent of its trade and whose popular culture saturates every aspect of Canadian life. Canadians, whether they like or acknowledge it, have never been more like Americans, and Canadian society has never been more similar to that of the United States. If the two countries are becoming more alike, and they are, this drawing together does not arise because Americans are changing. Canadians are the ones whose habits of mind, cultural preferences, economy, and political choices are becoming more American—without being American.

Right there lies the crucial distinction, and the question around which much private and political discussion turns in Canada. In a North American continent never more integrated, and in a global economy never more entwined, how can a country such as Canada retain some elements of distinctiveness adjacent to the American giant? Much public debate is devoted in Canada, directly or indirectly, to answering that question about how and whether to preserve, or where possible to enhance, some margin for Canadian manoeuvre in a world where pressures for integration and harmonization have never been more intense.

Every Canadian grows up with stereotypes about the United States. Being born or becoming a Canadian confers, to use an American expression, two "inalienable" rights: to enjoy the benefits of Canadian citizenship and to hold opinions about the United States. Canadians arguably know more than any other foreigners about the United States, and certainly more than Americans know about them. But these bromides are self-satisfying and self-defeating because Canadians do not know as much as they think they do about the United States, nor as much as they need to know.

One way of testing stereotypes against reality is suggested by this book about "Star-Spangled Canadians." What better group to compare Canada with the United States than those Canadians who have voluntarily resettled there? They took to their new country their Canadian baggage, which includes those ever-present stereotypes. If any group could discern the similarities and differences between the two countries, it would be people who had left one country for the other. Why they left, and what they have found, are the central questions explored in this book. Shelves groan with weighty tomes about Canadian–American foreign policy, relations between prime ministers and presidents, bilateral trade, case studies of this or that bilateral event—books about the great and the good in Canadian–U.S. relations. Some excellent surveys are available about the history of Canada and the United States. These are all top-down books, whereas *Star-Spangled Canadians* tries to examine issues from the bottom up, as it were, with a few observations from the top of the writer's head.

Star-Spangled Canadians was researched and written during one of Canada's periodic spasms of disquiet about the "brain drain." The migration of Canadians to the United States has been going on for generations, as I said earlier, but concern about the exodus has only occasionally flared into public debate. For the last three or four years, scarcely a week has gone by without an article or television report describing the experience of Canadians living in the United States. Various Canadian institutions, from think-tanks to House of Commons committees, from industry groups to trade unions, have weighed into the "brain drain" debate, usually drawing from the movement of Canadians to the United States conclusions that suit their public-policy agenda in Canada. A rounded picture of the "brain drain," such as *Star-Spangled Canadians* aspires to provide, has therefore been hard to find because the subject has been either treated episodically in the media or weighed down by political agendas.

Even a book-length treatment such as this one crashes against certain inescapable limitations. About 660,000 Canadian ex-patriates are reckoned to live in the United States. I could have given up my day job and spent the rest of my life ferreting out these Star-Spangled Canadians without finding more than a fraction of them. Similarly, the U.S. Bureau of Census estimates that about 120,000 Canadians are living illegally in the United States, and such people by definition are hard to find because they keep their nationality well hidden.

I tried to find, however, as representative a sample as possible of these Star-Spangled Canadians, knowing that I was probably missing plenty of fascinating people. I set out to cover as many major occupational groups as possible and to spread my interviews across the United States. The vast majority of interviews were conducted face-to-face, a few over the telephone. Striving for geographic inclusion, I travelled to New York City (four times); New Jersey; Buffalo; Rhode Island; Boston; Michigan; Washington, D.C.; Raleigh–Durham; Tampa; Orlando; Dallas; Houston; Minneapolis–St. Paul; Denver; Seattle (twice); San Francisco/Silicon Valley; and Los Angeles (twice).

Although *Star-Spangled Canadians* is studded with some easily recognizable names of successful Canadians living the American Dream, I wanted to find ex-patriates without a public profile, people just going about their business and living their lives. The stories of these less-publicized individuals perhaps offer more relevance to ordinary Canadians than do the experiences of the famous. So I interviewed cooks and crooks, brokers and bankers, homemakers and hardwaremen, artists and architects, lawyers and low-lifers, anchormen and accountants, Nobel laureates and nurses, preachers and poets.

Three warnings are in order. Finding Canadian ex-patriates in the United States is not difficult, there being so many of them, but those located for this book represent only a tiny fraction of the whole. They are exceptional cases, by definition, because they had identified themselves as Canadians in some public manner. The vast majority of ex-patriates do not identify themselves as Canadians sufficiently for an author/journalist and his sources to discover. For every Canadian I interviewed, I am aware that five? ten? fifteen? ex-patriates have so ingrained themselves in the United States that their Canadian identity is vestigial. A whole swath of them left Canada for whatever reasons, breathed a sigh of relief, and never looked back or returned. Canada means nothing to them but bad memories or a place on a map where they were born and raised by an accident of birth. They would be insulted by the description of themselves as Star-Spangled Canadians, because they are Star-Spangled Americans and damned proud of it. This book then runs the risk of exaggerating the degree of attachment that ex-patriates in the United States feel for Canada, and readers should be acutely aware of this possibility/probability.

We also know that some Canadians return from the United States after living there for a time. I did not interview any of them, this book being an already sprawling project. Whether their views would dissent from or corroborate those of Canadians who remained in the United States, I do not know.

I conducted these interviews from January 1998 to January 2000. Undoubtedly some of those with whom I spoke subsequently moved on to other jobs or places. A few may even have returned to Canada. It was impossible to keep track of so many people, so I opted for describing them as they were when they spoke to me. For all I know, some of their opinions and experiences will have changed between the time of our conversations and my reporting of them in this book.

My deepest debt of gratitude goes to the nearly 250 people who gave freely of their time to recount their experiences and offer their opinions. They invited me into their homes, offices, clubs, labs. Some stood me to lunches and dinners, a reflection of their generosity and perhaps their understanding of how costly the United States can be for a traveller on the enfeebled Canadian loonie. I could not quote every one of them for reasons of space, but each of them taught me something about being a Canadian in the United States. The whole damned project was terrific fun, although a heap of grinding work, because it afforded me windows into the United States I would never have otherwise enjoyed. A journalist, I have always believed, should wear out shoe leather. And so I watched *Saturday Night Live* live. I toured art galleries and television studios. I entered palatial homes and walked filthy streets. I saw movie sets and software designers' offices, university classrooms and hospitals, the Denver Broncos' training room, Houston's Petroleum Club and that city's air pollution, the tenements of Brooklyn, the soft hills of New England, the outline of the Rockies, the surf of Santa Monica, the plains of the Midwest, the Golden Gate Bridge, Puget Sound, homeless people and beggars, wealthy folk and poor, the affluently indifferent and the actively engaged, the amazing energy but also sometimes the dispiriting lassitude with which Americans tackle their challenges; and after each trip I returned, I think, a little wiser about the sprawling diversity that is the United States. I was also glad each time to be home.

I owe a special acknowledgment to people who put me up: cousin Janet Kuenne in Princeton; cousin Diana Sheridan on Bainbridge Island; niece Kelly Simpson in Los Angeles; Dr. Bill Leliever in Cary, North Carolina; Bob Minzesheimer and Mary Murphy in New York City; my Queen's roommate and dear friend Andy Duncanson in Minneapolis. I am grateful to personnel at various Canadian consulates in the United States, especially Gerry Foley, Jon Swanson, Kevin O'Shea. Two editors-in-chief at *The Globe and Mail*—Norman Webster and William Thorsell—sustained me as national affairs columnist on the editorial page. My happy collaboration with HarperCollins that now stretches over three books is due to Iris Tupholme, whose unfailing good cheer helped the project along. I thank professors John Helliwell and Don DeVovetz for their comments. Since the research quite often took me away from home, and made huge demands on my time while at home, my family was forced to display once again the forbearance they had shown during previous books. To them this book is dedicated, and to my wife, Wendy, I repeat: you remain *sine qua non* thirty years after we first met. May my wonderful children—Tait, Danielle and Brook—grow up to be proud of their country but alive to the virtues of others.

Ottawa, 1997–2000

*America. How many dreams and fears and contradictions were tied
up in that single word, a word which conjured up a world, like a
name uttered at the dawn of creation, even while it broke another,
the one of village and home and family. — Nino Ricci,* Lives of
the Saints

HISTORY

HOW many times has an adult Canadian heard or sung "O Canada"?
Hundreds of times? thousands?

In the United States, schoolchildren usually know that Francis Scott
Key wrote "The Star Spangled Banner." But how many Canadian young-
sters are taught that Calixa Lavallée wrote "O Canada"? How many adults
subsequently learned about Lavallée and how he came to write Canada's
national anthem? Chances are, not many.

It can be fairly said that Canadians do not know their country's history,
so Lavallée languishes in obscurity in his native land, where, during his
lifetime, he was less celebrated than in his adopted one, the United States.
Like hundreds of thousands of other Canadians in the nineteenth century
and later, in the twentieth, Lavallée became a "Star-Spangled Canadian,"
an emigrant lured south in part by better opportunities to pursue his musical craft.

Lavallée left Quebec in 1857 for New Orleans at the age of fifteen, an
impressive young musical talent with an appetite for adventure. Victory
in a musical competition in New Orleans led to a tour of South America,
the West Indies, and Mexico as piano accompanist for a famous Spanish
violinist.

Lavallée chose sides at the outbreak of the U.S. Civil War. He headed north and signed on as a musician with the Fourth Rhode Island Regiment, formed in a state already attracting tens of thousands of French-Canadian emigrés. At Antietam, the bloodiest of all Civil War battles, Lavallée was wounded in the leg and given an honourable discharge from the Union army.[1]

Lavallée was among the thousands of Canadians (or British North Americans, since Confederation did not occur until after the Civil War) who enlisted to serve the Northern cause. Canadian public opinion may have been split between pro-Union and pro-Confederate sentiments — most of the country's Conservative press was hostile to Yankee ways and took its lead from the pro-Southern elements of the British press — but Canadians who enlisted overwhelmingly did so in the Union army.

How many Canadians enlisted? Estimates used to range from 40,000 to 100,000, until the most thorough study suggested that many fewer had enlisted, a maximum of perhaps 20,000. Some of those signed up only to grab the enlistment bonus before scooting back across the Canadian border.[2] Born horse-traders, many Canadians enlisted, deserted, and re-enlisted, collecting a bounty each time. The Americans eventually caught on to this Canadian fraud and began to execute the illegal bounty-collectors — the record-holder went to his death with twenty-three enlistments.

Other wars have propelled people across the Canada–U.S. border. Canadians signed up to fight for the United States in the Vietnam War; Americans came north to enlist in the Canadian armies in the two world wars. Americans headed to Canada to escape military service in the Vietnam War; Canadians went south to avoid military service in the First World War.

Lavallée returned to Canada after his discharge, but stayed for only three years, writing, composing, and performing to little public acclaim, before returning to the United States. Bad luck plagued him there and he returned to Montreal, then spent two years in Paris before again returning to Montreal. He was becoming well known in Quebec's musical circles when a committee asked him to plan the music for the national convention of French Canadians organized by the Société Saint-Jean-Baptiste of Quebec City. Taking the words to the poem "O Canada," Lavallée wrote music that evoked a tremendous ovation from the audience. One observer of the scene noted that "everyone stood up, not out of politeness, but electrified by an overwhelming impulse. Never had French Canadians felt flowing in their veins such streams of patriotic exaltation."[3]

French Canadians immediately adopted "O Canada" as their national song. It was first sung in English in 1901, then did musical battle with patriotic songs in the rest of Canada until, on July 1, 1980, "O Canada" became the country's official national anthem, a century after Lavallée composed it.

Although his song became famous in Canada, Lavallée did not. Unable to make a decent living in Quebec, he went south again, never to return to Canada permanently. In Boston, Lavallée became a choirmaster at a Catholic cathedral and a professor of music at a local university. Lavallée was considered a bit of a hero in U.S. musical circles. His music was often performed, and his reputation grew. He became a member of the prestigious Music Teachers' National Association and organized in Cleveland what was believed to be the first public concert dedicated solely to the works of American composers.

In 1887, Lavallée was elected by 700 delegates to be president of the association and represented the United States at the first international musicians' convention in London in 1888. He died at the age of forty-eight in Boston, respected and admired in the country of his adoption, remembered dimly in the country of his birth. Forty-two years after his death, his remains were finally brought back to Canada to be buried in Côte-des-Neiges Cemetery in Montreal.

Canadians like to believe that immigrants built their country, although aboriginal people would demur from that belief. People arrived on Canadian shores from around the world, mostly from Europe and the United States, from the first settlements until the 1960s, and thereafter from Asia, Latin America, the Middle East, the Caribbean, and Europe. In the late 1980s and throughout the 1990s, Canada accepted more legal immigrants in relation to its population than any other country on earth—more than 200,000 per year, the vast majority coming from non-European countries of origin.

Nobody bothered with language about "mosaic" and "diversity" and "multiculturalism" until perhaps the 1970s, when the source countries of immigration changed dramatically. Before the 1970s, immigrants received no formal government support for their languages or traditions and kept these alive as best they could through their own efforts. Since the 1970s, however, multiculturalism has been placed on the high altar of national mythology. The concept even found formal expression in the Charter of Rights and Freedoms.

One crack has always appeared in the national myth of Canada as a land of immigrants. In one crucial respect, Canada has always been a land of emigrants—to the United States. With three exceptions—the Loyalist migration north during the American Revolution, during the period 1896–1910, and during the Vietnam War—Canada sent two to three emigrants to the United States for every American who came north. The American Dream has danced on the horizon for generations of Canadians, a wagon or train trip away in earlier times, a car or plane ride in more recent times.

No one can calculate precisely what Canada's population might be today without this emigration. The U.S. net gain from Canada stands in the millions since the earliest days of settlement, but how many children these Canadian emigrants produced, and how many of them in turn had children who remained in the United States, must be counted a mug's game. Canada's population today stands at about 30 million. Who can say with assurance what it might have been without emigration to the United States? All that can be asserted is that Canada would be a more populous, and perhaps even more prosperous, place had the country been only a land of immigrants without the open vein of emigration to the United States.

Thomas Jefferson, like other founders of the American Republic, believed that sooner rather than later the British North Americans would join the emerging United States. In 1775, Jefferson wrote, "the delegates of Canada will join us in Congress and complete the American Union." Article XI of the Articles of Confederation provided that, on application, "Canada shall be admitted into and entitled to all the advantages of the union." Letters from Congress invited the "oppressed inhabitants" north of the border to share in the "Transcendent Nature of Freedom."[4]

Jefferson would not be the last American politician or writer who predicted the eventual swallowing-up of Canada. Throughout the nineteenth century, scattered U.S. politicians called for or dreamed about annexation. Henry James, the famous writer, said of Canada in 1871, "I suppose no patriotic American can look at all these things [the unique dimensions of Canada], however idly, without reflecting on the ultimate possibility of their becoming absorbed into his own huge state." The poet Walt Whitman wrote that "it seems to be a certainty of time, sooner or later, that Canada shall form two or three grand States, equal and independent, with the rest of the American union. The St. Lawrence and the lakes are not for a frontier line, but a grand interior or mid-channel."[5]

For more than two centuries, Canadians have resisted becoming Jonah in the American whale. The Americans never tried annexing Canada, although as the acerbic Canadian writer Goldwin Smith observed in the late nineteenth century when hundreds of thousands of Canadians were heading south, even if the United States was not annexing Canada, it was annexing Canadians.

The revolution Jefferson and others launched against British rule para-
doxically reinforced the determination of those living north of the border
to remain apart from the United States, since an estimated 60,000 residents of the British colonies south of the border trekked north rather than
live in the new, revolutionary country. Some of those "loyalists" who fled
north eventually returned to the United States, and some even went back
to Britain, but the majority who stayed reinforced the British, anti-American character of British North America.

The Loyalists were not the first flotsam cast adrift by the vagaries of eigh-
teenth-century French–English wars fought on North American soil. That
tragic distinction belongs to the Acadians, victims of British military and
political decisions. In 1755, as relations were worsening with the French,
Governor Charles Lawrence of Nova Scotia made the fateful decision to
expel French speakers from the colony. As two historians wrote, "The residents were summoned from the farms and herded together in the village
churches; their fate was declared to them and then they were transferred
to the waiting ships. Crops that had been harvested were destroyed, the
livestock confiscated, and all but a few buildings standing on remote farms
were burned."[6] The Acadians were cruelly dispersed among various
British colonies in the West Indies and Louisiana so that their French-
speaking identity might be lost forever, a fate those who returned to
Canada's Maritime provinces ultimately avoided. Acadians relocated to
Louisiana found that keeping French alive was a hard and ultimately losing struggle within the American Dream. Today's Cajun communities are
folkloric remembrances of a particle of the French fact in North America,
celebrated in song and cuisine rather than in daily life.

Assimilated in fact, Acadians also became absorbed into U.S. popular
mythology courtesy of Henry Wadsworth Longfellow's "Evangeline," published in 1847. Longfellow, who never visited Nova Scotia, produced a
poetic reconstruction that immediately ran through five editions and gave
part of Canada a romantic literary image that found later echoes in U.S.
fictionalized portrayals of Canada. In Uncle Tom's Cabin, author Harriet
Beecher Stowe gave the name "Evangeline" to one of the daughters, and
held Canada out as a better land than the United States.[7]

Replacing the Acadians with more trustworthy citizens became the
avowed intention of British policy. Publicity campaigns were organized in
New England, touting the availability of land. By 1760, ships carrying
loyal, English-speaking settlers arrived from Salem, Boston, Plymouth,
Providence, and New London, and townships sprang up bearing English
names: Cornwallis, Horton, Falmouth, Annapolis, Granville, Liverpool.

To these settlements and others later came the "loyalists" in flight from the American Revolution.

This two-staged migration north—New Englanders replacing the dispossessed Acadians; Loyalists fleeing the war—was one of the few occasions in Canadian–American history that people heading north eclipsed in number those going south. For four decades after the British surrender and the establishment of the United States, the border was, for all intents and purposes, just a line on a map. People moved back and forth at will, settling on one side or the other in merry disregard of flags or nationality, although, of course, the movements halted during the War of 1812–14. Americans crossed the border to buy land or start businesses; Canadians headed south for land or jobs, needing only to satisfy U.S. officials of their identity. Philemon Wright of Woburn, Massachusetts, was among the first of what became in subsequent decades a flood of U.S. entrepreneurs. By the early nineteenth century, Wright had started a thriving lumber business in the Ottawa valley opposite the site of the Parliament buildings, the first U.S. lumber baron to exploit the timber resources there. Americans, portrayed so cuttingly by Nova Scotian writer Thomas Haliburton's character Sam Slick, were considered aggressive and somewhat uncouth, but the locals loved their money.

What had been an even exchange of people across the border began tilting in the United States' favour following the 1837 rebellions in Upper and Lower Canada. Some of the rebels left for good—Louis-Joseph Papineau and William Lyon Mackenzie fled south but returned—and the economic panic of 1837–38 drove others south. A thousand people a week were reported crossing the Niagara River into New York State in July 1838. From Upper Canada, hundreds per week flooded across the border at Detroit, heading for the U.S. Midwest. When the British lowered lumber tariffs in 1842 and 1846, trade from the Atlantic provinces slumped, pushing people south in search of work.[8] The southward emigration from Atlantic Canada to what Maritimers called the "Boston states" ebbed and flowed but never fully stopped. Young Nova Scotian women established a reputation in Boston society as polite, hard-working, and obedient maids.

Precise emigration figures are impossible to ascertain, given the sometimes rudimentary record-keeping by Canadian and American authorities and the porous nature of the nineteenth-century border, but in sheer numbers the movement of Canadians to the United States was staggering from the end of the rebellions until 1900. The best estimates suggest that more than 1.5 million people migrated from Canada to the United States between 1840 and 1900. An estimated 427,000 Maritimers emigrated to the

"Boston states"; 582,000 Quebeckers moved to New England and the Midwest; 521,000 people left Ontario for New York, Michigan, the Ohio Valley, and the Midwest.[9]

The emigration of about 1.5 million people equalled approximately half the increase in Canada's population, since in 1851 the Canadian census showed 2.4 million people living in Canada, compared with a population of 5.3 million in 1901. Put another way, Canada's population grew by about 3 million people from 1850 to 1900, and the emigration during that same period was about 1.5 million. In 1850, the ratio of the United States' population to that of Canada stood at 9.5:1; by 1900, the ratio was 14:1, a widening gap caused by the greater attractiveness of the United States for arrivals to North America and by the emigration of Canadians. Obviously, not all Canadians who emigrated remained in the United States. The return migration of Canadians, although not quantified, must have been appreciable since, despite the departure of more than 1.5 million people, by 1900 the U.S. census showed 1.2 million Canadians living in the United States.

By 1900, then, about one in five native-born Canadians was living in the United States, compared with one in ten in 1850. In that same year, 1900, only Germans and Irish were more numerous in the United States than Canadians. Canadians represented 11 per cent of the U.S. foreign-born population. Ten per cent of Detroit's population was reckoned to be Canadian-born; 9 per cent of Boston's; 5 per cent of Buffalo's and Seattle's. Fifty thousand Canadians were living in Boston, 35,000 in Chicago.

The New England textile industry attracted tens of thousands of French Canadians, who made up 15 to 20 per cent of the population of such centres as Fall River, Lowell, and New Bedford, in Massachusetts; Central Falls and Woonsocket, in Rhode Island; and Manchester and Nashua, in New Hampshire. In these and dozens of other New England communities, French Canadians tried to replicate the lives they'd had in Quebec and to speak their own language.

The vast majority of English-speaking Canadians, however, melted into the American mainstream, "hidden immigrants" then as now. Curiously, perhaps, only a small minority of the first generation of Canadian emigrants took out U.S. citizenship, another pattern that continues today. In a few locations where Canadian émigrés congregated, they published newspapers such as the *Canadian-American* of Chicago, or formed social clubs. After one Dominion Day celebration in 1880, a Michigan newspaper observed that it seemed as if "half the population of Canada has arrived here during the last month."[10]

Americans, of course, did emigrate to Canada but in much smaller numbers. Whereas 1.2 million Canadians were living in the United States in 1900, only 127,000 Americans resided in Canada. Given that Canada was much less populous, the U.S.-born accounted for 18.6 per cent of Canada's foreign-born population.

One small stream of northbound U.S. emigration from 1840 to 1865 consisted of black people attempting to escape slavery, many of them on the so-called Underground Railroad. Canadians' attitudes to this black flight were mixed: a certain pride that Canada (or British North America, as it then was) should be a haven for the oppressed was coupled with a distaste for blacks. (The first black people had arrived in Canada with the Loyalists and settled largely in Nova Scotia.)

Canadians remained ambivalent or hostile to black Americans crossing the border in large numbers. Blacks who sent letters inquiring about emigration to Canada were offered discouraging official replies. When the celebrated U.S. black leader W.E.B. Du Bois complained about this Canadian attitude, his complaints drew an official Canadian response: "There is nothing in the Canadian immigration law which disbars any person on the ground of color, but since colored people are not considered as a class likely to do well in this country [where] regulations respecting health, money etc. are strictly enforced ... it is quite possible that a number of your fellow-countrymen may be rejected on such grounds."[11] American farmers, tradesmen, entrepreneurs, and investors were welcome in Canada; blacks were not.

Canada's net loss through emigration slowed around 1896 and somewhat more encouraging migration patterns lasted until the outbreak of the First World War. The Canadian government was opening up the prairies, populating them with immigrants from Europe, but, as the country tried to draw European immigrants, word of available land on the Canadian prairies, especially in Alberta and Saskatchewan, spread through the U.S. Midwest. American authorities were still permitting massive immigration to their country from Europe, adding new states to the Union as territories filled up. Thousands of these new immigrants made it to the upper Midwest; coupled with the westward drift of the existing U.S. population, this caused a scarcity of cheap and available land, and emboldened some Americans to head north across the porous border. Canadian authorities actively encouraged this movement, sending immigration officials to the Midwest, while railways offered special deals for the transportation of American emigrants and their livestock. Estimates suggest that perhaps 243,000 people from the upper Midwest headed to Canada between 1896 and 1914, although no one will ever know how many returned. Despite this northbound movement, however, Canadians heading south still outnumbered Americans moving to Canada during some of the period, but the Americans left their imprint on the prairies, especially Alberta, which early in its history became known as the most "Americanized" part of Canada.

The United States entered the First World War late. American soldiers participated in the grand total of two major battles, but the prospect of hundreds of thousands of U.S. soldiers augmenting the Allied forces persuaded the Germans to sue for peace. With Europe exhausted from four years of bloodshed, and the Soviet Union, as it had become, engaged in a civil war, the entire European continent fell into an economic slump. The United States, by contrast, emerged from the war to enter the "roaring twenties," with its economy robust and its people barely scathed by the tragedy of war.

Canada, by contrast, had entered the war as a colonial reflex once the Mother Country declared war on Germany. The Canadian contribution was heroic, but costly in men and money for a young country with a small population situated far from the conflict. During the late stages of the war and afterwards, nothing galled Canadians more than hearing Americans brag—a long-standing American reflex—about how they had won the war. Harold Innis, later to become one of the titans of Canadian economics, wrote to his family after watching U.S. celebrations on July 4, 1918: "The Americans ... never get tired of talking about the things they do or the things they are going to do ... I never heard such a line of bragging and boasting in all my life. It was really disgusting at least to Canadians. Personally I should have liked to have had the opportunity to tell them how long it took them to get into the war and if they were doing so much why there were so many young men on the streets. Some of them think they have won the war."[12]

During the war, some Americans tried to enlist in the Canadian Armed Forces. Conversely, a dirty secret of the Canadian war effort was how many Canadians slipped over the border to avoid entanglement in the Canadian forces. Canadian emigration to the United States jumped in the war years: 86,139 in 1914; 82,215 in 1915; 101,551 in 1916; and 105,399 in 1917. In 1918, the end of the war eliminated the need to flee Canada to escape military service, so the number of emigrants dropped precipitously, to 32,452.[13]

The postwar economic slump in Canada, coupled with boom times in the United States, provided a magnetic attraction for emigrants, despite the intellectuals who bemoaned the Americanization of Canada and politicians who tried to make political hay from these departures. In 1918, the numbers starting rising again: 57,782 in 1919; 90,025 in 1920; 72,317 in 1921; 46,310 in 1922; 117,011 in 1923. The rise in emigrant numbers in 1919 and 1920, followed by the fall in 1921 and 1922, followed in turn by an upsurge in 1923 and the early months of 1924, also resulted from potential emigrants' fears of changing American attitudes towards immigration.

Canadians thinking about taking the road south after the First World War could read in their newspapers or hear by word of mouth that unrestricted immigration, a hallmark of U.S. policy from the founding of the republic, was under political siege. Just what the U.S. Congress would do in response to public unhappiness with the scale of pre-war immigration remained unclear. But some political response to the pressure seemed inevitable, with consequences no would-be Canadian emigrant could predict.

Congress did indeed respond in 1921, passing legislation that limited immigration on the basis of nationality. Using the 1910 census, Congress set a quota of 3 per cent of each nationality group already established in the United States—but only from Europe. No numerical ceiling was applied to western-hemisphere countries, so Canadians could breathe easily again. The 1921 law, however, did not stop agitation for tougher measures, and this agitation received considerable attention in Canada, creating fears that perhaps the U.S. border might be partly or wholly shut.

In 1924, Congress acted again, this time by passing the second Immigration and Naturalization Act, lowering the quota to 2 per cent of those nationalities in the United States as of 1890, as opposed to 1910 in the previous act. The act clearly discriminated against immigrants from Southern and Eastern Europe, whose numbers had swelled after 1900. Once again, however, immigrants from western-hemisphere countries were excluded from the quotas, removing doubts about difficulties for Canadians to emigrate. The border remained porous, and stayed that way until the 1960s.[14]

The 1920s, and particularly the first half of the decade, featured the first of the three national spasms of concern in Canada (the others came in the late 1950s and early 1960s, and the last half of the 1990s) about the extent of emigration and what it portended. (French Canadians had been worried about the exodus of their numbers for decades before the rest of Canada's first spasm during the 1920s.) Intellectuals, journalists, business leaders, and politicians all drew attention to the losses. Whereas the massive flows of previous emigrants had largely been labourers and farmers, to these traditional occupational groups were added in the 1920s people of higher education. *MacLean's* (spelled with a capital "L" in those years) discovered that, between 1919 and 1926, 11 per cent of University of Toronto graduates, 15 per cent of the University of Western Ontario's graduates, and 36 per cent of Acadia University graduates had moved south. In 1927, 600 Canadians taught in U.S. universities. Observers naturally read into the emigration their own recipes for slowing down the flow, so that emigration became one of the staples of parliamentary discourse throughout the 1920s.

Arthur Meighen, the Conservative leader, repeatedly seized on the emigration figures to chastise Prime Minister Mackenzie King's Liberal government. "The United States immigration figures show that the population of this country is going over to the United States at a rate which is increasing every month," he told the Commons on February 1, 1923. "That was the case throughout 1922; in the later months the figures run up to almost eight thousand per month ... Unemployment has gone down because the artisans of Canada have gone across to American cities where they are getting work that they cannot obtain in this Dominion."[15]

His Conservative colleague Thomas Church, a former mayor of Toronto, opined that "in Canada, we sing 'O Canada' and then weep over the procession of our sons as they leave their home land to find work in the United States." Later, he added that "too many Canadians are being driven to travel along the road that ends in a life under the Stars and Stripes."

Joseph Harris, another Conservative, read into the record a poem from an unnamed (and not very talented) poet. Entitled "Lament for a Canuck," it read:

> I am sitting and a thinking of the
>   days that's gone before,
> For I'm leaving this my country and
>   my heart feels sick and sore;
> There's a hundred thousand others,
>   and their plans are kin to mine,
> For they're leaving home and country
>   to migrate across the line.
>
> Sure I've tried to stick it longer
>   but my bank account is low,
> Though I hate to leave the homestead,
>   still I know I've got to go;

For while politicians sidestep
   and declare the times are fine,
I have got to leave my birthplace
   and migrate across the line.

They say our neighbors over there
   appreciate our worth,
And welcome sons from Canada,
   the richest land on earth
I'm doing what I think is best,
   and I sure don't want to whine,
But conditions here have forced me
   to migrate across the line.

I've made my plans to settle
   in that land across the way,
And if I like the country
   you can bet your life I'll stay;
But I'll watch your progress over here,
   and I hope you'll all do fine,
But me, I'm through with Canada,
   I'm bound across the line.

Joseph Shaw, an Independent MP from Calgary, recounted evidence of the migration from southern Alberta. "An examination of the railway figures indicating the emigration through the port of Kingsgate, which is one only of the avenues of exit from the province of Alberta to the States," he said, "shows that in the three months ending December 31st last, there has been an excess of emigration over immigration of approximately 5,000 persons."

Hermas DesLaurier, a Liberal, recalled the emigration of French Canadians — "between 1865 and 1890, more than 400,000 of our people have crossed the border" — and offered evidence that the departures were continuing. "A few months ago, a paper published in the United States, *Le Messager*, of Lewiston [Maine], stated that during the year 1922, for the period of July, August and September, 5,000 Canadian families, that is to say 25,000 people, had crossed to the frontier. In one parish in the Richelieu Valley, in the space of a few weeks only, 126 people went over to the American side. In one of the northern parishes, seven families, in a week's time, sold their furniture at auction and purchased railway tickets to the United States."

The great J.S. Woodsworth, the first Independent Labour Party MP and future leader of the Co-operative Commonwealth Federation, noted that, "in my constituency of Center Winnipeg, I think there have been thousands of people during the past year who have been forced to go south of the line in order to get work. Among these people there were the very best mechanics to be found in this country, and to such an extent that we are now told there may be a shortage."

Milton Campbell, a Progressive MP, echoed Woodsworth's lament about the loss of skilled workers. He read from a newspaper clipping about the emigration at Windsor: "Lured by high wages, hundreds of young Canadians are emigrating to the United States. According to the railway and ferry companies, no fewer than eighty families a day are entering the States at Detroit. On one train arriving here this afternoon from the East there were forty-five young men who said they were on their way to Michigan industrial centers. A majority of them came from Toronto, Hamilton and other cities of eastern Ontario. Lack of work and prospect of high wages, they explained, induced them to leave the Dominion. More than half of the 45 are mechanics connected in some way with the building trades."

William Lucas, a Progressive MP, added more specific evidence. "I can give the figures for the little village in which I live and the immediate vicinity. From that district 113 people left last fall, and among them are many of our good Canadian-born men whom I have known from boyhood and who understand farming conditions as well as any man."

Inevitably, emigration became part and parcel of wider partisan controversies. Conservatives and Progressives blamed the Liberal government's economic policies for accelerating out-migration. High taxes, insisted the Conservatives, drove people from Canada, an argument reminiscent of debates seven decades later.

Conservative H.H. Stevens echoed a familiar Tory complaint when he insisted that "one of the reasons why people are leaving Canada, one of the reasons why there is such hard times in the industrial world, is because of heavy taxation and, in some regards … unfair taxation."

Progressives and some Conservatives from rural ridings blamed the exodus on low wheat prices, inadequate government support for farmers, and, in the Progressives' case, the high tariff that made purchasing of farm machinery and implements ruinously expensive.

Some Conservatives, by contrast, argued that an even higher tariff would stimulate domestic employment, thereby raising wages and encouraging would-be emigrants to remain in Canada. Conservatives added that it was absurd to bring so many immigrants from Europe when many of them treated Canada as a way station *en route* to the United States. "Canada," thundered Conservative Charles Dickie, "cannot afford to be a preparatory school for people from European countries whose ultimate destination will be with our neighbors to the south."

If fewer Canadians emigrated, argued the Conservatives, then fewer immigrants would be needed, especially of the unskilled and difficult-to-assimilate variety. "We in British Columbia," said Brigadier-General John Clark, MP, "have a very good illustration of the sort of immigrants we cannot assimilate, in the Orientals who have been allowed to come into the country. And the people in the East, I believe, have also had an example of people whom it is impossible to absorb into the population in those immigrants who go into the city of Montreal, for instance, and work in the sweat shops, thus driving out our best labor from the manufacturing industries and forcing them to seek employment elsewhere."

The Liberals, placed on the defensive by the emigration figures, adopted the classic government response: things were improving, the Opposition exaggerated, and the fault lay with either the policies of previous governments or world events over which the government had no control.

Charles Marcil, a Liberal minister, noted that "this exodus from Canada to the United States has existed at all times ... Some of them make a success of their trip. Others were there for a time, but the majority of them have come back, because there is a lure of the home land which cannot be found elsewhere."

Finance minister Henry Fielding predicted better times ahead. "We are so near to the United States, and it is so easy for our people to cross the border, that when things are somewhat dull over here, and high wages are offered in the United States, there would naturally be such an exodus as there has been during the recent months," he explained. "But this, I believe, is only a temporary condition. I believe they will come back. Experience has shown that the United States are usually ahead of us by a few months, perhaps a year, in the change of condition ... This experience justifies us in believing that history will repeat itself in this respect."

Ernest Lapointe, Mackenzie King's Quebec lieutenant, fingered the Opposition as responsible for the out-migration. "Reference has been made to the fact that a number of our population have left the country," he said. "It is unfortunate that it should be so, but I do not hesitate to say that if men are leaving this country, those who are primarily responsible for it are the whisperers of death, the preachers of blue ruin, the men who say that Canada is today a land of desolation, taxes and debts. The young

Canadians of today will never forgive those who have been slandering their country."

As for Mackenzie King, he would build a long political career on blaming everything but his own government's performance. So, of course, the emigration was the fault of the previous Conservative government that had neglected what he called the "machinery of immigration." What conceivable link existed between immigration policy and the outflow of migrants was testimony only to the fertility of King's peculiar reasoning. Like other Liberals, King insisted up to 60 per cent of those who departed returned to Canada, a figure spawned by the prime minister's robust imagination.

Samuel Jacobs, a Liberal MP, wondered just what Canada could do. "People [in the United States] who have been accustomed to receiving hundreds of thousands of workmen find that they cannot get them any longer, and where do they turn?" he said. "They turn to the north, and in that way our people are being drawn off the farms and from the cities in order to supply the demand for people in the United States ... I am told that in some of the border cities of the United States carpenters receive from $12 to $20 a day as wages. How is it possible for us to keep our people in this country when they are attracted by such enormous wages on the other side of the line?"

The media reflected and abetted parliamentary concerns. Newspapers reported individual stories about departing Canadians; editorialists weighed in with their opinions, usually echoing the partisan line established by the political parties they supported. *Canadian Forum* noted glumly that "there is not a man in Canada under fifty years of age who would not pack up and move to the States tomorrow if he got a good business offer."

MacLean's pursued the emigration issue in its pages. In February 1922, the magazine published a long article by John Stevenson entitled "Is Canada an Immigration Sieve?" It began with an admirably arresting lead: "Mr. Samuel Johnson once said that the finest view in Scotland was the high road into England, and today it seems as if the roads and railways southward across the international boundary are the most attractive objects that many Canadian eyes can see."[15]

Stevenson usefully reminded readers that emigration had served as political fodder for the Liberals, just as it now provided ammunition for Conservatives. Liberal orators of the 1890s painted gloomy pictures of "the trails southward out of Manitoba worn bare by settlers fleeing in disgust from the consequences of a Tory regime," Stevenson reported. He went on to place emigration in a historical perspective but noted that "the cult of pessimism about Canada's future has spread far and wide and its fruits are reflected in an accumulation of evidence that a southward exodus on an alarming scale has been in progress for the last six months."

Stevenson offered some calculations that were extensively referred to in parliamentary debates. He concluded that emigration had cost Canada almost 1.7 million people: "In 1911, the population was officially estimated at 7,206,463. In the succeeding decade 1,975,000 people entered our gates and the natural increment should normally have been 1,800,000. Making the fullest allowance for losses of the war, the census of 1921, if Canada had retained all her native born increment and her immigrants, should have reached a total of ten and a-half millions. But the actual figure as given by the Bureau of Statistics is 8,769,489."

A sluggish Canadian economy, higher wages in the United States, the unwillingness of British immigrants to live on the Canadian prairies, and the failure of the government to assist the farming communities were among the reasons Stevenson advanced for what he called the "exodus."

MacLean's continued to follow the emigration issue, publishing a three-part series in 1927 called "Can We Stem the Exodus?" The series was based, in part, on a survey sent to 1,000 Canadian ex-pats living in the United States, 203 of whom responded. Asked why they left, 57 per cent replied: for "economic advantage"; 20 per cent: for "better opportunities for advanced education and a wider field for the specialist"; 9 per cent: for "health and climate"; 5 per cent: for "family and personal reasons"; 5 per cent: for objections to "political, social and intellectual conditions in Canada"; 2 per cent: for "lure of the unknown"; 2 per cent: for miscellaneous reasons — responses that would not surprise today's generation of Star-Spangled Canadians.

MacLean's observed that "the seriousness of our loss through export of our brains is emphasized by the number of outstanding successes recorded among those of the exiles who have been in the United States for a number of years." In response after response, participants in the MacLean's survey complained about limited prospects in Canada, narrow-minded attitudes in the business and academic communities, and, of course, higher wages in the United States. Income taxes, inextricably linked to the emigration debate of the 1990s and early twenty-first century, were hardly a factor in the 1920s. Income taxes were low and had been introduced as only a "temporary" measure to help finance the war effort.

The Great Depression that began in 1929 and did not end until the start of the Second World War accomplished what no amount of political rhetoric, exhortations, or colonization schemes in Canada could achieve: It dramatically slowed emigration to the United States. The Depression brought hardships to Canadians everywhere, and had those hardships been confined to Canada they would certainly have pushed Canadians south. But the United States, too, fell into a severe depression, souring the American Dream for millions of its own citizens and would-be emigrants north of the border. Moving from the parched prairie of Saskatchewan to the dust bowl of the U.S. Great Plains, or trading the struggles of rural Quebec for those of the creaking textile mills of New England, some of which were closing as employers moved to the U.S. South, hardly constituted an improvement in life's lot.

The issue of emigration to the United States that had roiled Canadian politics throughout the 1920s, entwining itself with issues such as immigration, freight rates, tariff policy, and agricultural prices, disappeared from public debate, not to reappear for another three decades. Still, the 1930 U.S. census found almost 1.3 million Canadian-born residents in the United States. The Canadians represented the third-largest group of foreign-born, after Germans and Italians.[16] Canadian-born people comprised 9.1 per cent of the foreign-born population of the U.S. in 1930. That 1.3-million-person figure represented the equivalent of 12.4 per cent of Canada's own population.

The Depression pushed U.S. authorities to tighten immigration controls on western-hemisphere countries, including Canada. Canadians had to enter the United States through designated "points of entry," and the U.S. Department of Immigration began to deport those foreign-born who became public charges. The U.S. crackdown, coupled with terrible economic conditions, caused more than 100,000 Canadians to return to Canada between 1930 and 1936, briefly reversing the usual trend of more Canadians going south than Americans coming north.[17] From 1920 to 1929, emigration from Canada to the United States had ranged from 46,810 to 200,690 yearly; from 1932 to 1939, it dropped from 6,187 to 14,404 yearly.

The Second World War demanded the fullest participation from military personnel and civilians in countries engaged in the struggle. Industry hummed in Canada. Farmers' produce was everywhere in demand. Women left home to work in factories, while men served overseas from 1939 to 1945. During the war years, emigration followed the pattern of the 1930s, averaging about 10,000 per year.

The war gave the U.S. economy its mightiest boost in the twentieth century, catapulting the country out of the Depression. The war devastated Europe and large parts of Asia, but left the U.S. homeland unscathed. The Canadian homeland, too, had emerged intact, so that Canada also became a magnet for Europeans seeking a better life. In the immediate postwar years, Europeans flocked to Canada, a third of them as refugees, or "displaced persons" as they were usually called. That Canadians were simultaneously resuming their emigration to the United States seemed of little immediate concern with so many arrivals from Europe, especially Britain, Germany, and Holland. As soon as the war ended, emigration to the United States more than tripled from the levels of the Depression, ranging from 21,344 in 1946 to 25,880 in 1951.

By the mid-1950s, however, European immigration had waned, but Canadian emigration to the United States accelerated, sparking another eruption of concern about population losses, this time colloquially known as the "brain drain." Canada borrowed the phrase "brain drain" from Britain, where it was coined after the war to describe the flow of talented and educated people leaving that war-shattered island for the United States. Canadians, more attuned then than now to British expressions, appropriated the phrase to describe Canada's postwar emigration. By 1956, the number of Canadian-born emigrating annually reached 30,000. Added to that number were another 12,000 emigrants who had lived in Canada but were not born there. They were using Canada as a postwar stepping stone to the United States. The resulting yearly exodus of about 42,000 people, Canadian-born or otherwise, rekindled the political debate of the 1920s about why so many were leaving.

Canadian Business magazine asked in March 1955, "What's the bait across the border?" and answered its own question with the well-rehearsed answer: more money and greater opportunities. "If you're a professional man or woman," wrote *Canadian Business*, "you'll go in the knowledge that you are joining a large group of people who have become the subject of innumerable speeches and editorials bemoaning the exports of human brains and energy from Canada to the United States."[18]

The number of departing Canadians crept up during the next decade: 42,363 in 1956; 46,668 in 1960; 50,509 in 1963; 50,035 in 1965. Sixty to 75 per cent of these were native-born Canadians; many of the rest were people in effect passing through Canada from Europe to the United States, reopening the question asked in the 1920s by *MacLean's* magazine about Canada being an "immigration sieve" for the United States. Nobody knew in the government of either country how many Canadians were moving illegally to the United States, since the border in those days was much more permeable than today's. Some estimates suggested one illegal emigrant for every legal one, but those estimates were probably far too high, since admission to the United States, although not automatic, was reasonably easy for those with education or considerable work experience. Whatever the official numbers of the day, they undoubtedly underestimated total emigration.

The nature of the debate changed from that of the 1920s. The earlier debate had centred upon the sheer number of emigrants, but the one from the mid-1950s to the mid-1960s swirled around both the volume and the occupational skills of the departing. Some of the "best and the brightest" in terms of education had always left Canada, but these had been dwarfed in number by the less educated, such as farmers, artisans, mechanics, and factory workers. French Canadians in New England, for example, were among the lowest-paid and least-skilled immigrant workers in the United States. But, by the mid-1950s, it had become clear that the portion of emigrants from Canada with considerable education and training had risen sharply, and newspapers, magazines, politicians, intellectuals and business leaders began to trumpet concerns about the "brain drain."

The concerns, although sometimes overstated, were not misplaced. One study discovered that, from 1957 to 1961, 29.8 per cent of all Canadian graduates with their first degree in science or engineering had gone to the United States. Canada was accordingly the number-one provider of immigrant scientific and engineering talent for the United States, followed by the United Kingdom and Germany. The study properly noted, however, that some of those who left did return and that Canada was also importing scientific and engineering talent from other countries. The authors, economists themselves, noted parenthetically that the same southward migration had occurred in their profession. They found that there were as many U.S.-born economists teaching in Canada as Canadian-born ones teaching in the United States, a rather startling figure, given the difference in size between the two countries.[19]

Another study, this one of total emigration from 1955 to 1968, discovered that those who departed were indeed better educated than the average Canadian. Almost twice as many had university degrees compared with the Canadian average — 12.6 per cent compared with 6.5 per cent. The later the emigrant group had departed, the higher its level of education. The group from 1960 to 1964 had higher levels of education than the one from 1950 to 1954. A snapshot of all Canadians living in the United States based on the U.S. census data of 1961 found 27.3 per cent had some college education or a university degree, compared with only 6 per cent of Canadians at home. The concern about the "best and the brightest" leaving, then, was not entirely misplaced. In that 1955–68 period, health-care professionals (the largest component of whom were nurses) led the way, followed by engineers and teachers.[20]

Why did they go? A group called the Canadian Medical Scientists in the U.S. explained the departure of medical researchers: "The multitude of interrelated factors which attract basic medical scientists to the United States can be summed up in the word 'opportunity.' Opportunity for rapid career advancement, opportunity to take on added responsibility, to test one's ideas with enlightened and stimulating colleagues, to reach for a goal, and in some cases simply to work."[21]

The Canadian economy was doing well enough, but it still lagged behind that of the United States. In 1965, personal disposable income of Canadians was only 74 per cent that of Americans. One student of the "brain drain" compared the incomes of Canadian-born in the United States who left between 1955 and 1968 with those who remained in Canada within the same occupational groups and found the incomes of those who departed 10 to 25 per cent higher. When he factored in all Canadian-born living in the United States, he concluded, "an average increase of 50 per cent in earnings is to be expected."[22] Real wages for those employed in manufacturing were almost 50 per cent higher in the United States than in Canada.

And yet emigrants returned to Canada despite the apparent economic advantages available south of the border. It was hard to estimate just how many came back, but reputable estimates suggested perhaps as many as 35 per cent. By coupling these returnees with the immigrants arriving from other countries, some experts concluded that the "brain drain," although real, was not as serious a problem as alarmists suggested, a harbinger of the arguments advanced in the late 1990s by those who debunked a serious "brain drain" of Canadians to the United States.[23]

Experts could argue about the seriousness of the loss of talented Canadians, but the popular press believed in the "brain drain" and sought to explain it. Editorialists lamented the problem, university presidents drew attention to it, businesses groused about it, and authors such as the celebrated magazine writer Christina McCall Newman set out to find out why. Then a staff writer for *Maclean's* (as of October 24, 1931, spelled with a small "l"), she revisited the issue that had been addressed by the same magazine in the 1920s.

"The exodus of Canadian brains to the United States has gone on so

steadily for so long that it has become a kind of national joke and its meaning has ceased to sting us," she wrote. "Yet the issue has never been more
important than it is now." About 130 people per day were "packing their
bags" and moving south. She continued with growing alarm: "It's not hard
to find examples of the first-class citizens we have lost; it's harder to decide
whom to leave out of any list."[24]

Eight hundred graduates of the University of Toronto were teaching at
U.S. universities, she wrote. Fifty Canadians served on the medical faculty
of Johns Hopkins University; at least twenty held positions at the Mayo
Clinic. The suffragan bishop of New York City, the mayor of Seattle, the
winner of the Pulitzer Prize and the National Book Award, the manager
of Project Gemini, the president of Sarah Lawrence College, the former
editor of the *Journal of the American Medical Association*, the first foreign-
born head of the American Medical Association, cosmetician Elizabeth
Arden, and brushman Arthur Fuller were all Canadian-born. So, too, in
the business world were the heads of the U.S. Communications Satellite
Corporation, ABC Television, Harper and Row, Continental American
Life Insurance, and Otis Elevator, and senior executives at such companies as S.S. Kresge, Westinghouse, U.S. Rubber, Bank of America, and
RCA.

"I just had to get out" was a phrase McCall Newman reported that she
had heard repeatedly from the ex-patriates. They gave her three main reasons for leaving: higher salaries, more stimulating work, better jobs. Strong
on description and shot through with mild despair, the article offered next
to nothing by way of solution, except a mild remonstrance that Canadian
authorities did not keep track of those who left, and therefore were unable
even to try to lure ex-patriates home.

The year of McCall Newman's article, 1963, 50,509 emigrants left
Canada. Soon thereafter the concern about the "brain drain" vanished as
suddenly as it had after the onset of the Depression in 1929. Not for
another three decades did it re-emerge as a staple of Canadian public discourse. Two factors—a drastic change in U.S. immigration law, and the
Vietnam War and accompanying turbulence that beset U.S. society in the
late 1960s—ended "brain drain" worries.

In 1965, the U.S. Congress amended the Immigration and Naturalization Act, wiping out preferences for western-hemisphere immigration.
The new provisions, went into effect in 1968, slapping an annual quota of
120,000 immigrants for the entire western hemisphere where previously
no limits had applied. A year later, a further amendment imposed a limit
of 20,000 immigrants on any country, including those in the western

hemisphere. Canadians, who had passed through a permeable border throughout the nineteenth and early twentieth centuries, and a quite porous one thereafter, suddenly found the United States a much more difficult country to enter as immigrants. The new law did not derive from any spite against Canadians. It was intended to broaden the scope for potential immigration to the United States, rather than being specifically aimed at reducing Canadian immigration. The numbers of emigrating Canadians reflected the change: from 50,035 people leaving in 1965, the year of the law's enactment, to 18,592 departing in 1972.

The numbers also dropped because the United States was floundering in the bloody quagmire of the Vietnam War. Violent race riots rocked U.S. cities. Demonstrations, social protests, civil disobedience, and the onset of "stagflation," the dreaded economic combination of slow growth and high inflation, mocked the American Dream. Emigration from Canada was down to only 11,215 in 1975, the lowest number since the Second World War. From an object of envy, the United States became one of scorn, even ridicule, its president the glowering and awkward Richard Nixon, a pathetic contrast in the eyes of many Canadians to the trendy, trenchant bachelor Prime Minister Pierre Trudeau. For arguably the first time in Canadian history, Canadians felt they were no longer wallflowers next to the boisterous, bragging Americans.

Millions of Americans, too, despaired of their country's plight, locked in an increasingly unpopular war abroad, rocked by social tensions at home. As the war intensified and demands for young Americans to serve in Vietnam grew, hundreds, then thousands, of Americans slipped across the border seeking to avoid military service: the so-called draft dodgers. Thousands of others left for a variety of motives rooted in dismay at the condition of the American Dream. Canada, near if not familiar, seemed the most obvious place to take refuge. For one of the few times in 200 years, the number of Americans coming north exceeded that of Canadians emigrating south. (The other two post-Confederation periods were 1898 to 1914 and a brief time during the early years of the Depression.) From 1970 to 1979, 179,585 Canadians emigrated, but 193,111 Americans moved to Canada, a reversal of the traditional two- or three-to-one ratio. By contrast, in the 1950s, 353,169 Canadians emigrated to the United States compared with 97,687 Americans who emigrated to Canada.[25]

The Canadian government took the position that the "draft dodgers" were not political refugees and granted them landed-immigrant status. The government said, in officialese, that "an individual's status with regard to compulsory military service in his own country has no bearing upon his admissibility to Canada either as an immigrant or as a visitor; nor is he subject to removal from Canada because of unfilled military obligations in his country of citizenship." Some of the "draft dodgers" entered Canada illegally, but little was done to chase them down. Perhaps 30,000 Americans were "draft dodgers" or deserters, and some Canadian politicians decried their presence. Vancouver mayor Tom Campbell wanted the War Measures Act invoked against them. In Parliament, some Conservative politicians demanded stern action against the deserters. A 1968 public-opinion poll found only 28 per cent of Canadians wanted to allow in the "draft dodgers," but opinion became more favourably disposed to their admittance as the war's unpopularity grew in Canada.[26] *The Globe and Mail* probably captured the national mood—not something the paper has always reflected—in asserting that "political sanctuary is being extended and the principle is one Canada must not reject."[27]

Some of those who had fled the United States returned under an amnesty offered by President Jimmy Carter in 1977. The United States recovered its equilibrium, and Canadian emigration doubled: from 11,439 in 1976 to 23,495 in 1978. For the next decade, 15,000 to 20,000 Canadians per year emigrated, two to three times the number of Americans who took up residence to Canada. The traditional south-to-north pattern, in other words, reasserted itself, although the aggregate numbers of emigrating Canadians was much lower than for most of the previous century and a half, courtesy of the 1965 changes to U.S. immigration laws. Canada, a country with one-tenth the population of the United States, was continuing to lose people not just in absolute terms on a bilateral basis but quite staggeringly when the two countries' populations were considered. That U.S. laws constrained Canadian emigration was easily observed when the United States twice announced lotteries for green cards. The demand from Canada was overwhelming.

The United States' gain was Canada's loss, just as it had always been during 200 years of southbound emigration. Little was said about the emigration in the 1980s, although Canada's relations with the United States dominated the 1988 election over free trade, a debate that touched one of Canada's most sensitive nerves: whether Canada could continue to maintain a society of sufficient distinctiveness in North America in an age of crunching economic and cultural integration.

In all the fury over free trade, and its extension to include Mexico, almost no attention was paid to a provision easing the movement of people from one country to another to work. "Temporary" visas were indefinitely renewable, however, and thousands of Canadian began securing them, thereby availing themselves of a back-door entry to the United States. The number of these visas quadrupled to 27,000 between 1990 and 1998. Visas did not equate to emigration, because many people went back and forth across the border two or three times on short-term contracts. But up to half of these visas represented people who had found full-time work in the United States, and as long as they retained their jobs the visas could be renewed each year.

This back-door emigration contributed to a renewed debate about the "brain drain" in the 1990s, a debate that will continue as continental economic integration proceeds. The "brain drain" debate revolved around certain issues directly related to statistics, but there were deeper questions involved. Did closer economic integration also mean intensified pressures for emigration? Why had Canada performed much worse in unemployment, taxes, growth, and personal disposable income than the United States since the 1970s? Was Canada becoming in all spheres more like the United States, to the point where Canadians were increasingly kidding themselves about their distinctiveness vis-à-vis the Americans? Did the emigrants leaving for the United States constitute a serious economic problem, or were their departures offset by immigrants coming to Canada from abroad, so that Canada in fact enjoyed a "brain gain" rather than a "brain drain"? And if there were appropriate measures to close the economic gap, and perhaps stem the population losses, would these also inexorably shrink Canadian–American differences, thus making Canada a clone of the United States, separated only by a flag and an anthem? Did these people go south because they were pushed from Canada for lack of opportunity, or pulled to the United States, or both? Did they go for reasons different than those that had sent hundreds of thousands of Canadians south for a century and a half? Were their departures a harbinger of even further economic integration, and perhaps eventually political integration? Would flags be rearranged to follow people rather than the other way around? Canadians asked these questions, nervously and publicly, at century's end when they read about so many of their once fellow citizens—including sometimes their own sons and daughters, brothers and sisters, friends and colleagues—heading south to pursue the American Dream and, like so many who had preceded them, becoming Star-Spangled Canadians.

In order to catch the real trend of American thought, you have to get your ear down to the soil to listen—Frederick Philip Grove, A Search for America

DIFFERENCES

DOUGLAS Leatherdale grew up on a farm southwest of Winnipeg in a part of Manitoba where he still owns land. Great-West Life Assurance was headquartered in Winnipeg when Leatherdale joined the company—the company's U.S. operations are now concentrated in Colorado—and, from Winnipeg, Leatherdale travelled across the United States in the early years of his career. He got to know the United States well, so that his acculturation was easy when he first moved to Minneapolis–St. Paul. Today, as president of the huge insurance conglomerate, the St. Paul Companies (13,000 employees worldwide; shareholders' equity in 1997 $4.6 billion), Leatherdale is well positioned to note differences between Minnesota and Manitoba.

"I've thought about that a lot. I'm not sure that there is anything deeply fundamental that is different," he said in his top-floor office, with the city of St. Paul spread out below. "People do think a little bit differently. The values are sometimes a little different. But they're all kind of small things. It's not quite as much of a contrast between here in Minnesota and living in Manitoba. If we were sitting in Alabama, then the gulf would be much wider.

"I think the differences in regions in this country are greater—if you exclude Quebec and the French fact—than they are in Canada. You go into the Deep South and into that culture and that value system, and contrast that to Seattle or southern California or New York City, the differences are huge.

"When we try to assimilate people from around the United States into corporate home office here, for example, it's very difficult sometimes. It would be easier to move somebody from Toronto or Winnipeg or Calgary or Vancouver here and assimilate them that it would be to move somebody from New York."

Fred Corrigan, head of the Minnesota Transportation Alliance (a group that lobbies for public investments in highways), would agree. Corrigan's company transferred him from Toronto to the Twin Cities in 1975. He intended to stay for a while before returning to Ontario. He never did go back.

"You come from southern Ontario to Minnesota, and the only thing that's different, frankly, is that it's colder here. The culture is the same. The sports are the same: they play a lot of hockey here. There are a lot of Canadians here, especially Western Canadians," he said. "So it's really not a tough move. It's not like moving to the South or the West or New York City. It didn't feel like we'd had much of a change."

Harold Brandt, originally from Edmonton, shared Corrigan's intention to return to Canada after being transferred to the United States. He had worked in banking and real estate across Canada and the United States before settling in the Twin Cities, where, in the 1970s, the Canadian firm Oxford Development Co. had made massive investments in downtown Minneapolis. Along the way, he spent six years in Kentucky.

"For a long time I thought I'd go back to Canada. I always identified myself as a Canadian. I observed Canadian holidays," Brandt said. "I'd go to events here and see all these Yanks singing the national anthem and doing all the stuff that they do, and say, 'My God, What's this all about?' I thought Canadians were quite superior to Americans.

"I don't think that now. I think that it changed as I took a harder look at how people live in the U.S. and spent some time here. I just became impressed with the diversity of this country, and how much there is here … In Minneapolis, you change the accents a little and, for all intents and purposes, you're in a Canadian city.

"I don't find Minneapolis to be very different from Toronto in many respects. The people are honest. The values are the same in a lot of ways. There's a high moral standard here. The work ethic is very strong. When you go to Kentucky, it's a different deal. In Minneapolis, the present isn't so entwined with the past. It doesn't seem to dictate as much. In Kentucky, the past has an astounding way of influencing the future."

Lyle Wray, with a PhD from the University of Manitoba, runs the Citizens League of Minnesota, an umbrella group for dozens of community and civic-action groups across the state.

"I grew up in Medicine Hat, Alberta, which is halfway like growing up in the United States. The school superintendent was a PhD from UCLA. We were surrounded by Americans and American influences. So we never felt that the U.S. was all that foreign. It wasn't like New Brunswick," Wray said.

"I kept driving to Chicago each year for a conference. I would drive from Winnipeg to the Twin Cities, then from the Twin Cities to Chicago the second day. I thought, 'Gee, this is pretty nice. It's clean. It works. It looks good. It's progressive. It seems like it's a bigger community. There's more going on.' So I kind of got seduced into Minnesota.

"It wasn't so much the U.S. It was more focused. It's green and well run. It's part of a Midwestern belt. Just as we had prairie reform efforts in Canada, they had [Progessive Republican Senator Robert] La Follette in Wisconsin and [Farmer-Labor Governor Floyd] Olson in Minnesota. This is a progressive, good-government region. If you look at North Dakota versus Minnesota or Minnesota versus Manitoba, it's not all that clear. People work in similar ways. There are similar ethnicities. Similar values."

Jennifer and James Hamilton both completed their master's degrees at the University of Waterloo, worked for a while at IBM in Toronto, then joined more than 100 Waterloo graduates at Microsoft in Redmond, Washington, a satellite city near Seattle. Both had travelled extensively in the United States before moving to Washington.

"We spent so much time travelling across the U.S. that we had no stereotypes really. It's a 280-million-person country. It differs geographically," James observed. "A big centre has a different flavour than a small centre, and Texas has a diffcrent feel from Oregon, that in turn has a different flavour than Raleigh, North Carolina."

Jennifer echoed her husband's observation: "I grew up in Victoria, then we went to Toronto. Toronto is a wonderful city, but when we moved to Seattle, I felt like I was coming home, because the Pacific Northwest is its own little region ... I find Vancouver, Seattle, and Victoria to be very much the same." James added: "The differences across the country may be greater than the differences across the border in some respects."

Another ex-patriate from the University of Waterloo noted the same phenomenon. Said Paul Larson, a former Waterloo professor and now senior researcher at Microsoft, "One thing that I underestimated is the magnitude of regional differences in the U.S. The U.S. is not homogeneous at all. There are lots of places in the U.S. where I simply couldn't live. There are other areas of the U.S. that seem very reasonable ... The difference between regions in the U.S. is as great as differences between Canada and some parts of the U.S., including this one that is very much like Canada."

Graham Hill was raised in Montreal before moving to Vancouver. He then made his way to Seattle, where, with his Canadian cousin, he founded an outstandingly successful Web-site company, Sitewerks. Hill had lived therefore in both eastern and western North America, and observed: "Because of the geographical location, I don't feel there are a lot of differences between Seattle and Vancouver ... The American stereotypes don't come from Seattle. They come from Texas or the Midwest. Here, because most of the people I associate with are generally well educated, I don't feel much like an outsider. My accent has gone a little bit. Very often people don't know I'm a Canadian."

His Sitewerks colleague Korina Jane Brown, a British Columbia native, emphatically agreed: "There's a lot more similarity between Vancouver and Seattle than there is, say, between Vancouver and eastern parts of Canada. The weather is the same; the general attitude is the same."

Minnesota and Washington are border states. Washington and British Columbia think of themselves as part of Cascadia, a fancy name for the Pacific Northwest. So perhaps the similarities noted by Star-Spangled Canadians in border states such as Minnesota and Washington are not too surprising. But Colorado is a very long way from Canada, and yet Star-Spangled Canadians there repeatedly commented on the similarities between their adopted state and Western Canada.

"Denver and Calgary are clones," said Rolf Abt, who came to Denver from Winnipeg to work for Great-West Life and has no intention of returning to Canada. "I've been to Calgary numerous times. I know many people down here that moved during the oil boom, stayed during the bust, became real-estate agents or whatever, and to a person they can't believe when they go back how much Calgary reminds them of Denver," Abt said. "I've had people come down from Calgary, and to them it's just like home ... When I cross from North Dakota to Manitoba, or Manitoba to North Dakota, there's no difference. I reach over to flip my speedometer to go to kilometres. That's it."

David Thompson, originally from Alberta and at one stage of his career an official in Prime Minister Pierre Trudeau's office, is a senior executive with Great-West's real-estate division. He had spent fifteen years working and travelling extensively in the United States. "I can't see the differences between Canada and the States. It's at the margin for me

... I have foreclosed on loans across the country and I travel every week of the year. I think a person from Boston will find more uncomfortableness in San Diego or San Jose than ... in Virginia or Toronto."

Terry Wasley is president of Rocky Mountain Insurance in Denver. He grew up in Moose Jaw, played hockey there for three years in the Western Junior B League, worked for the Royal Bank in various small Saskatchewan towns, then moved to California. He didn't like either southern California or banking, so moved back to Canada with Great-West Life. He travelled throughout both countries but jumped at the chance to relocate to Denver when Great-West decided to put its U.S. headquarters in the city. In 1992, Wasley left Great-West and founded his own successful insurance business.

"Are there differences? I think they are fairly small. I find Denver very similar to Western Canada. A lot of people here are from other places. There are not many home-grown people," Wasley said.

"There are a lot of Canadians here. I run into them a lot. But I wouldn't live in the eastern part of the United States on a bet. To go to New York or Philadelphia or Boston or Chicago—they're wonderful places to visit. I wouldn't move back to Los Angeles. There are just so many people, and it's so crowded and fast.

"I would say there are greater differences between Denver and New York City than between Denver and Calgary or Winnipeg. Absolutely. Like I won't go to Florida any more, because the last time I went there all there was were big-mouth people from New York talking all the time and demanding this or that."

Rhonda Rubinstein, originally from Montreal but educated at the Nova Scotia College of Art and Design, worked for twelve years in New York City as a magazine-design specialist, launching her career with *New York* magazine. She went to San Francisco to work for another magazine, but switched jobs to redesign the renowned, although small, magazine of the U.S. political left, *Mother Jones*.

"San Francisco is more similar to Vancouver than to New York. New York is not similar to anything else in the States, let alone the world," she said. "I had worked on a project basis in Vancouver on and off for six months, and when I came to San Francisco I was amazed at how similar it was to Vancouver. The mentality here is very West Coast. You may be committed to your work, but you live in this wonderful place and you want to leave at 5 p.m. The thinking is very different than in New York and the East Coast, where it's work, work, work."

Mike Wadsworth grew up in Toronto, played football for the Toronto

Argonauts, practised law in Toronto, worked from 1981 to 1984 in New Hampshire, and even served a stint as Canadian ambassador to Ireland. For more than five years, Wadsworth has been athletics director at University of Notre Dame, in South Bend, Indiana, and anybody who understands the importance of athletics at Notre Dame—a university with an excellent academic reputation, too—will appreciate Wadworth's significance in the Notre Dame hierarchy. He's lived, therefore, on both sides of the border in states close to Ontario and he just doesn't see many differences between areas on contiguous sides of the border.

"I think there are cultural differences that are real, but I'm not sure that they're really as pronounced as some people might think," he told me before a Notre Dame–Michigan State football game in East Lansing, Michigan. "They are the same kind of differences that you would find between Nova Scotia and Saskatchewan, or between Maine and Alabama.

"There are regional differences in the United States, as there are regional differences in Canada. Seen in that context, I don't think the differences between Canadians and Americans are that large."

Joe Medjuk, an immensely successful Hollywood producer originally from Fredericton, New Brunswick, said: "There are cultural patterns that run north–south. The people in Vancouver have more in common with people in Seattle. People in Toronto so suck up to New York, it's unbelievable."

David Frum, a conservative journalist and author who lives in Washington, D.C., and writes for publications on both sides of the border, says that "what we have here is one large, English-speaking North American culture with a number of components, of which Ontario is one, Western Canada is another. It's true that you can get in a car at Anchorage and drive diagonally southeast until you hit Miami and speak the same language, use the same credit card, pump gas the same way. I think you'd be struck much more by the similarities than the differences. And the places where you would notice the dissimilarities would not match the border."

Joel Garneau, an editor at *The Washington Post*, had some fun with this idea of regional similarities that are not defined by national political boundaries. Garneau also made a rather serious if provocative point in *The Nine Nations of North America*, published in 1981, slightly less than a decade before the Canada–U.S. free-trade agreement.[1]

Suppose, wondered Garneau, history had written its story differently in North America. Look at the map of the continent. Study its geography: water systems, mountain ranges, coasts, prairies. Parse its industries. Listen to how people speak. Watch what they eat. Now imagine that national political borders did not exist, because, with one exception, the borders do not conform to economic, geographical, sociological, or linguistic realities. Borders are political creations and are therefore important, but, he argued, they are also artificial.

Garneau divided North America into nine regions, within which he suggested that people share more in common than they share with people in other regions. His regions bore no resemblance to existing political boundaries, except for Quebec, the continent's French-speaking enclave.

Ecotopia, he called the slice of coastal geography running from Alaska to just north of Los Angeles. *The Empty Quarter*, he named the vast territory from the Canadian Arctic running down through Alberta, western Saskatchewan, the rest of British Columbia, and the U.S. Rocky Mountain states. *MexAmerica* encompassed Mexico and the U.S. Southwest. *The Breadbasket* took in the Canadian and U.S. Plains, and the corn-growing areas of Iowa, southern Illinois, and southern Indiana. *The Foundry* included the Great Lakes states, southern Ontario, and the industrial states of New Jersey, New York, and Pennsylvania. *Dixie* was the U.S. South. *New England* swept up the six small northeastern U.S. states and Canada's four Atlantic provinces.

Garneau correctly observed that "Canada, unlike the United States, has migraines about losing its 'identity'." Canada, he argued, "shares five perfectly respectable and different identities with the northern United States."

"Of course, the oil-rich 'sheikdom' of Alberta defies Ottawa," he wrote. "Economically and philosophically, Calgary is far more akin to Fairbanks, Salt Lake City or Denver than it is to Ontario. It's part of *The Empty Quarter*. By the same token, the grain belt of the north, centered on Winnipeg, is visibly and temperamentally part of *The Breadbasket*. The industries of Windsor, Toronto and Ottawa are part of *The Foundry*. Vancouver shares far more with Seattle than it does with Halifax, Nova Scotia. And the poor but proud Maritimes are in the same boat as New England."[2]

Garneau, of course, stretched the argument to augment its shock value, but perhaps his conclusion is no longer so arresting two decades after the book's publication. Canadians are far more likely to move within their country than to the United States, and, as Canadian economists John McCallum and John Helliwell have demonstrated, the intensity of trade within Canada is greater than that with the United States once distances are considered. But more than a decade of free trade has intensified north–south trade links, increased pressure for economic harmonization, and caused Canadians to think more about American markets, American culture, and American ways of doing things than ever before, even if Canadians' southward fixation is met by scarcely a northward glance from their American neighbours.

Each year, the premiers of Canada's Atlantic provinces meet the governors of the New England states. Canadian premiers regularly attend the yearly conference of the U.S. Governors Association. Parti Québécois premiers regularly underline how their province trades more with the United States than with the rest of Canada. Premier Lucien Bouchard was even given the honour of addressing the Maine legislature. Premier Mike Harris of Ontario boasted that his province was now locked into an economic embrace with Great Lakes states and periodically pointed to the work of economist Thomas Courchene, who argues that Ontario now conducts itself like a "nation-state" within North America. Only a quarter of Ontario's trade is now with other provinces, compared with one-half twenty years ago. Western Canadian premiers have worked hard to intensify their ties with governors of border states in the U.S. Midwest and West.

Star-Spangled Canadians I interviewed would not be shocked by Garneau's description of North America as a continent of nine "nations." Time and again, interviewees such as those already mentioned underlined the similarities they experienced between where they had landed in the United States and the closest parts of Canada. The exceptions came among those interviewees who had emigrated to the U.S. South, which stands to reason given its distance from Canada and its distinctive history within the United States. Those Canadians living in the border states, and even those in the central swath of the United States, looked north and found at least as many similarities, and in many cases more, than they felt existed with other parts of the United States.

Their observations spoke to something generally misunderstood by Canadians, or at least not properly appreciated: the abiding regional differences within the United States. It may be, as many U.S. writers have argued, that these differences within the country are blurring, that the South has never been more like the rest of the nation, that television and other forms of modern communications have shrunk regional variations, that the population flows of people from the North and East to the South and West have created a more homogeneous republic. Indeed, anyone driving across the United States, with its Identikit suburbs, copy-cat clusters of fast-food franchises, and patriotic symbols everywhere, can easily miss the entrenched attachment to place that is the hallmark of local identity. The genius of the U.S. political system—it has its oddities, too—lies in the reconciliation of regional and state-based identities with an abiding national sentiment. The powerful U.S. Senate, with two members from each state regardless of population, and the federal system itself both speak to the state-based element of American life. The presidency and the Supreme Court reflect the national dimension of political and judicial leadership.

The United States is such a flag-waving, deeply nationalistic country that its regional differences and local identities can easily be obscure to those observing the country from outside its border.

Jeffrey Dworkin, a senior executive at CBC Radio in Toronto, was required to visit member-stations across the United States after becoming vice-president (news) for National Public Radio in Washington, D.C. "One has this kind of Disney-like view of the United States as this kind of cultural monolith based on patriotism. It doesn't exist," Dworkin said. "This is a very regional country, and astoundingly so. People are rooted in their locality in a way that really surprised me."

Most of the U.S. political news Canadians consume comes from Washington, the economic news from New York, the entertainment news from Los Angeles, because Canadian correspondents are based there, and U.S. media outlets abound in those markets. If Canadians travel as tourists to the United States, chances are they go regularly to one or two spots: Saskatchewan farmers head to Arizona; British Columbians and Edmontonians, to Hawaii; Ontarians and Quebeckers, to Florida. There are exceptions, of course, but when Canadians confidently assert that they "know the United States," they probably "know" only a few slices of it, and likely small ones at that. Canadians will declare that they know more than any other people on earth about the United States, but they invariably know less than they think about such a diverse country, and a good deal less than they need to know, given Canada's overwhelming inter-dependence with the United States.

"All politics is local," a Speaker of the U.S. House of Representatives once quipped, and it is that local dimension of U.S. politics that Canadian observers frequently misunderstand. Canadians are much more accustomed to the highly centralized parliamentary system in which a prime minister with a majority exercises far more unfettered power than a U.S. president does within the U.S. political system. The apparent messiness of the U.S. system—with its institutionalized checks and balances, swarming lobby groups, sometimes weak party discipline—leaves Canadians bewildered, but the system is a reasonable reflection not just of the original intentions of the Founding Fathers but of the sprawling, diverse, restless United States of today.

It may come as a shock to those Canadians who define themselves largely as "not being American" to learn that, for many of the Star-Spangled Canadians, that particular self-comforting (or deluding) generalization needs at least one important qualification. Depending upon where you live in Canada or the United States, the differences across the border are small, as between Minnesotans and Manitobans, British Columbians and Oregonians, Nova Scotians and Mainers, Albertans and Coloradans. At a high level of generality, Canadians can wrestle with what differentiates them from Americans; at a more local, cross-border level, those differences are much smaller than the "We're not American" line of thinking would suggest.

The one substantial exception within the United States remains the South, and perhaps the Southwest with its growing Hispanic influence. Americans have always been on the move in search of opportunity and their slice of the American Dream. No government programs exist such as those in Canada to foster regional development in slow-growth areas, programs anchored by the thin rope that jobs should be created for people where they live, rather than the more American attitude that people should move to where jobs exist.

In recent decades, a substantial migration has occurred from the North and East to the South and West of the United States. This shift can be illustrated by the official centre in 1991 of U.S. population — Steelville, Missouri, ninety-five miles southwest of St. Louis.[3] The "official centre" means a statistician's mythical fulcrum point for a perfectly level map of the United States, assuming every resident of the country weighed the same. It's just a device to measure population flows, but an intriguing one because, in 1981, the official centre was still east of the Mississippi River. The official centre moved because, from 1980 to 1989, eight of the top ten states gaining from migration as a share of their previous populations were in the South or West (in order: Nevada, Florida, Arizona, New Hampshire, California, Georgia, Alaska, Texas, Virginia, Washington). Six of the largest U.S. cities are now west of the Mississippi. Cities with the fastest-growing rates of population from 1980 to 1989 were: Fresno, Sacramento, Austin, San Diego, San Jose, Phoenix, Tucson, Los Angeles, El Paso, San Antonio, Jacksonville, and Fort Worth.[4]

In the 1980s and 1990s, another migration wave sent white Californians flocking from their state north to Washington, Oregon, and Idaho, then to Utah, Colorado, Arizona. An estimated 1.5 million Californians left their state, yet the state's population kept rising, thanks to immigration from

Mexico (and other Central American countries) and Asia. Those departing Californians, plus arrivals from the East, made the large but sparsely
populated states of the so-called New West among the fastest growing in
the 1990s, especially Utah, Colorado, and Arizona. To the list of expanding cities of the 1980s would then be added larger urban/suburban areas
such as Salt Lake City and Provo, Utah; Tucson, Arizona; Boulder, Colorado; and even Boise, Idaho. The sprawling suburbs around these cities
were part of a nationwide trend documented by the 1991 census. That census found that, for the first time, the largest number of Americans lived in
census districts defined as suburban, where crime rates and taxes were low,
single-family housing prevailed, ethnic minorities were rare, Republican
voting patterns were established, and the car drove everything before it. So
vast was the suburbanization, and apparently so unstoppable, that urba-
nologists invented a name for the new sprawl—"exurbia." Increasingly,
suburbanites had little to do with inner cities, except as places of periodic
entertainment, because they commuted to other suburban or ex-urban
locations to work.

Southern, western, and suburban—that's the growing United States,
and it's quite a different one from the more liberal country dominated
politically by the northern-tier states that Canadians know better. Canadians may holiday disproportionately in the U.S. South courtesy of the warm
climate, but they tend to be more familiar, through family and business
ties, with nearby northern states. Part of Canada's misunderstanding of the
United States grows, then, from not appreciating the southern and western dimensions of U.S. life. The new United States wants lower taxes,
even less government intervention in the economy, and no new social programs. The South, in particular, is home to religious evangelicalism, one
dimension of the far greater religiosity of Americans, compared with
Canadians. Indeed, on a scale of differences between the two peoples, religion ranks as the largest single difference. More Americans, by far, than
Canadians attend church, believe in God (and the Devil), and describe
themselves as religious. Evangelical movements are powerful throughout
the U.S. South, and they have carved for themselves an influential niche
within the Republican party. Nothing remotely similar exists in Canada,
and for those Star-Spangled Canadians living in the U.S. South, the influence of religion is something disconcerting.

John Kennedy was the last elected U.S. president from a northern
state, and he won the election in 1960. His successors have been South-
erners—Lyndon Johnson and George Bush from Texas, Jimmy Carter
from Georgia, and Bill Clinton from Arkansas—or Westerners, such as

Richard Nixon and Ronald Reagan from California. (Gerald Ford
hailed from Michigan, but he simply filled out the remainder of Nixon's
second term.) In the recent congresses, Southern Republicans have
filled many of the important posts.

Broadly speaking, Canadian emigrants have tracked the Americans'
own migration patterns. A study of Canadians in the United States, based
on the 1980 U.S. census, showed the largest concentrations in Northern
or Pacific-Western states and Florida. More recent surveys show them
heading to fast-growing cities such as Raleigh–Durham, Dallas, San Jose,
Phoenix, Denver. Statistics Canada's survey of 1995 Canadian graduates
in the United States found half of them wound up in a handful of states:
Texas, 16 per cent; California, 11 per cent; New York, 10 per cent (the
Wall Street factor); Florida, 8 per cent. Presumably, as these Canadians
spread out through the rapidly expanding parts of the United States, their
home country's appreciation of these vital regions will increase, because
messages and impressions will be relayed north. But for now the Southern and Western dimensions of U.S. society remain somewhat blurred in
Canadians' minds.

Mark Snyder offers a penetrating view of the differences, real or imagined,
between Canadians and Americans. Snyder grew up in Montreal, graduated from McGill, did a PhD in the United States, but could not find a
job in Canada (a familiar story?) upon graduation in 1972. Snyder found
one, however, at the University of Minnesota, where he is now head of the
psychology department. He visits relatives several times a year in Montreal. His perspective is that of a psychologist, a resident at various times of
both countries, and a member of two minority groups (a Jew from Quebec, a Canadian in the United States).

"Living here, I have been struck by how people have state-based identities. The people of Minnesota and the culture of Wisconsin really look the
same. Yet I am aware that this is an outsider's perspective on things.

"I understand what the people of Minnesota are saying when they say
that they are Minnesota people. These are genuine feelings of some difference in the context of great similarity. The same model applies to the
U.S. and Canada.

"If you step back, it's very hard in objective terms to plot out what are
the true differences between Canadians and Americans. Yet there are psy-
chic benefits that come from having a sense of identity ... Identities are
constructed anyway. Humans have a strong capacity to construct identities
for themselves. It's largely a social process of construction. Some of it is

taking small differences and making them seem bigger. A lot of it comes not from the differences, but from feelings of a sense of identity.

"It may not matter how strong the basis for it actually is if people can derive some sense of who they are, what makes them who they are, what makes them different from other people."

Having lived on both sides of the border, Snyder believes the Canadian identity does stem largely from being "not American."

"It's tough to find things on which to hang an identity for all the English-speaking Canadians," he continued. "It's not really a language that makes them distinct. It only makes them distinct from French-speaking Canadians. It makes them more like the U.S. to focus on language.

"Food doesn't work very well because, by and large, food in Canada is the same as food in the United States. What are you left with? Well, there's geography. It's clear that if you live in Canada as opposed to the U.S., there's a border between the two. There aren't a lot of things onto which you can pin a distinctively Canadian culture, other than growing up and learning that you're Canadian and not American.

"It's identity by negation rather than affirmation. But I think identity is as much what we are not as what we are. Identity says who we are and sets up the boundaries between ourselves and other groups. Being a Canadian may not be much more than learning that you're not an American and that you live in this country and you know something about its history and you know what its sports teams are, its political process. But then you stop thinking about it.

"One of the things about identities is that the longer we hold them, the less able we are to recite the reasons why we have them. It's like a vegetarian who chooses an identity partly for a negative reason — 'I don't like meat.' People at the beginning can cite a list of reasons. Ten years later, you haven't thought through the reasons and someone asks you why you don't eat meat and you say, 'Because I'm vegetarian.' 'Well, why are you a vegetarian?' 'Because, that's just the way I am.' Gone are all the reasons that supported and justified the identity."

Phil Migicovsky, a Montrealer who studied at McGill and the Harvard Business School, left Canada for good in 1979. Migicovsky "loves Dallas," where he is a successful consultant for a firm that specializes in advising universities where to invest endowments. (He mentions *en passant* that, of his sister's three children, "one has moved to the States, one would like to move, and one is there for good.") Still, Migicovsky admires the country he left, and he offers an interesting bit of pop psychology about Canadians vis-à-vis Americans.

"I have this analogy of Canadians to Americans as being like the second child to the first. The first child is the great athlete, good-looking, funny," he said. "The second child is a damn good athlete, pretty damn smart, funny although maybe not as funny. He's good-looking, but he's got a pimple or two and just never could come to grips with the fact that he's the second. Instead of revelling in all his assets, which in Canada are huge, he bitches and moans about how suffocating the older brother is."

On a sea of clichés have floated earnest attempts to differentiate Canadians from Americans, but what struck me in asking Star-Spangled Canadians about those differences — people such as Mark Snyder and Phil Migicovsky aside — were their stumbling, inarticulate answers. They were overwhelmingly well-educated people, making comfortable lives for themselves in their adopted country. They spoke intelligently about a range of subjects, especially their work, impressions of the United States, or reasons for leaving Canada. But when it came to defining why they still felt Canadian in the United States, assuming that they did, the answers often turned folkloric, banal, unfocused. Sometimes, it appeared that in defining what it meant to be a Canadian they had been asked to parse a sentence in Japanese or unravel a mathematical formula. That many of them still felt an attachment to Canada and considered themselves Canadian no listener could doubt. But a bit like the Canadian identity itself, why they felt as they did frequently proved indefinable for them. Invariably, although perhaps not unreasonably, since they were living in the United States, they created their sense of being Canadian by contrasting it to their sense of what it was to be an American. There were *sui generis* references to things Canadian — hockey (it came up all the time), snow, stronger beer, a different health-care system, pieces of geography — but the definitional description of their "Canadianness" usually emerged from contrasting Canada to the United States, the Mark Snyder approach of perceiving an identity through contrast.

Munroe Eagles, for example, is a professor of political science at the State University of New York at Buffalo. He's been in the United States for eight years, having left his native Nova Scotia. Asked to define what it was that still made him feel Canadian, Eagles said: "I don't know. I don't identify as an American. I don't know. It's not home. Obviously, the U.S. has been very good for me. I don't know. I can't pin it down. I've an affiliation with Canada that's emotional, non-rational. I discovered referendum night that it was a very harrowing event for me. It was a cataclysmic event. I was out of the country. I couldn't have done anything about it, but it was a very emotional time for me. I don't know why."

Marc Mayer is an exceptionally articulate man. He's now moved back to Canada to run the Power Plant contemporary art gallery in Toronto, but when I spoke to him Mayer was curator of the Albright–Knox Gallery in Buffalo, one of the best in the United States courtesy of the philanthropy of the Knox family, whose members owned the Marine Midland Bank and married into the Woolworth family fortune. Eloquent about everything else, Mayer struggled to define why he felt Canadian: "I don't know why. I can't put my finger on it. It's something that I am very conscious of, being Canadian, just in the sense of feeling a different attitude towards life in general. It's hard to put your finger on it. There are cultural differences, there really are. I think it's something that all of a sudden becomes part of you. As a Canadian, you're given a certain inherent sense of distinctions."

Craig Fiander from Fredericton, New Brunswick, graduated from Princeton University in 1993 and still lives and works in the town of Princeton, New Jersey. "There's probably a minimal chance that I'll wind up settling down with a family and working in Canada," he said. "But that Canadian pride is still there. And I hate it when some of my good friends back home say, 'Well, Craig's an American now.' It drives me crazy. The United States has treated me well and I enjoy it, but I'm a Canadian and I have Canadian pride. What is Canadian pride? I can't quantify it. I don't know how to explain it."

Harold Shapiro, Princeton's president, has spent most of his adult life in the United States and yet still feels a tug from Canada for reasons he cannot easily articulate: "It's an emotional thing. I don't have any rational explanation for it. I felt then, as I do now, a strong emotional attachment."

Sparkle Hayter, an excellent writer of crime novels, makes her living with words, but she too struggled with defining why she felt Canadian. "You do feel like you're in a strange country sometimes, even though you feel like you're an American," she said. "I mean we're so like Americans in so many ways, and yet there's something different about us. You know, I haven't been able to put my finger on it … I was trying to articulate it the other day and I just had a really hard time for finding the words to describe what it is that makes me feel Canadian … I guess it's the whole cultural and historical thing."

Not all Star-Spangled Canadians believe any fundamental differences in values or attitudes distinguish Canadians from Americans. What links them as North Americans from democratic, industrialized countries exceeds what differentiates them. Compared with any bilateral subset of nations in the Western world, Canadians and Americans are the most alike in terms of how they see the world, the role of government, the protection of rights, and societal attitudes. International surveys show Canadians and Americans are not the same, but similar. And yet, those who feel themselves still Canadians, although living in the United States, point to something many of them struggle to define, something that might be a stronger social conscience.

"You don't appreciate Canada until you are away from it," said Laurie Lithwick, a Montrealer working for Microsoft in Redmond, Washington. "There's something I haven't exactly put my finger on, whether it's a concern for others in the community that I find more in Canada than I do in Seattle, or the general American ethos: each individual for yourself and if you can't pull yourself up by the bootstraps, then it's not necessarily my responsibility to help you out. We don't do everything just because it gains the most money."

Don Carty, American Airlines chief executive officer and a native of Montreal, isn't sure how long Canada's more extensive social programs can last, because of their deadening impact on economic development. But he does note a difference between Canadians and Americans.

"The whole perception of wanting more fairness, more equality in society, perhaps a more reasonable approach to how people get treated. You see pockets of very similar views in the U.S. ... But Canadians are less individualistic and more focused on the greater whole," he said.

"At the heart of what Americans believe about themselves and what makes them special is the sanctity of individual rights. We obviously don't teach our children in Canada, and don't talk as extensively, about that as Americans do. So, at the very earliest part of education in the U.S., there is this overwhelming importance on individuality, which of course has served America terribly well. On the other hand, certainly for me and for a lot of other Canadians, there are some limits to that."

Margot Blacker served eight years on the city council in Bellevue, Washington, an affluent suburb of Seattle. Her grandfather was one of the architects of Medicare in Saskatchewan, although the family later split with the Saskatchewan CCF and became more conservative.

"I like a lot about Canada. I like their attitude towards land use. They are more community-oriented. The public weal is more important in Canada than in the U.S. To me, the United States has gone too far in individual rights. Canada is more balanced between the public good and the individual good ... I've always been teased down here that I am the Canadian socialist on the Bellevue city council with all these right-wing Republicans.

I do think that, because of my upbringing in Canada, I have a different balance between public and private good."

Caroline Birks, trying to break into New York's art world after studying in Chicago, attended Queen's and grew up in Toronto and Montreal.

"To me the difference is ideology. I think the States is much rougher and meaner. It's a more cruel society. Canada is more socially oriented, and my politics tend to lean that way. I see Canada changing, and I feel badly about that," Birks said.

"We complain about Americans so much. It's part of our pastime. When I first came here, I was appalled. Chicago is so segregated. You have two American cultures side by side, black and white, and I hadn't been exposed to that in Toronto. The poverty is worse here. For me, capitalism here is more pure and ideological. So many people fall through the cracks of capitalism here, whereas in Canada there is more of a safety net for these people."

Val Azzoli used to manage bands in Canada before coming to New York City and, within an astonishingly short period of time becoming president of Atlantic Records, the largest company of its kind in North America.

"It's much, much, much more competitive down here," he told me. "It's truly the strong will survive. I've never been in a more competitive — I don't want to say 'cutthroat' — place. But whatever it takes to win, one will do. It was never like that in Canada."

Azzoli works in New York City, arguably the most dog-eat-dog city in a competitive country. Does he fear the competitive environment? I asked him. "It's certainly not to be feared," he replied. "It's something to be taken advantage of. We could use a bigger dose of that. You really become a better businessman. You know that song, 'If you can make it here, you can make it anywhere.' It's very true. As you look around, there's 20 million people here [in the New York City area]. There's all fighting for a piece of something, and that piece is getting smaller and smaller, so you become better at what you do. You don't take anything for granted … Down here, you really have that sense that no one is going to look after you … You have to become more self-sufficient and more aware that you are the architect of your own future."

Rick Marin, a reporter with the Style section of *The New York Times*, suggested a variation on the American-as-aggressive theme: "They are great believers in their own country and in self-improvement. You wouldn't believe how many courses they take … and they're not afraid of that ambitious side of themselves. They're very aggressive. People in Toronto are sort of passive-aggressive. And in a way, there's something very refreshing about

Americans. Canadians are ambitious, too, but Americans are more honest about it."

Witold Rybczynski, a professor at the University of Pennsylvania and one of the most respected writers on architecture and urban planning in North America, had written often about the United States before he left McGill University. "Because we had visited the United States, and because we'd been told that there wasn't much of a difference between Canada and the United States, we thought that moving would not be such a big deal. And it was an enormous big deal. It's an absolutely different place," he said. "As an individual, you're much more on your own in a way that's simply not true in Canada, which is somehow built around the individuals, whereas here the individual is responsible for himself ... It took us a long time to get used to that, especially since we weren't expecting it."

A study for the Carnegie Endowment for International Peace, using data from the U.S. Census Bureau, attempted to answer the question: How likely are immigrants to become U.S. citizens?[5] The researchers looked at immigrants to the United States from a representative sample of twenty countries in 1977 to determine what portion of those who remained in the United States in 1995 had become U.S. citizens. They found that, of immigrants from these twenty countries, Canadians were the second least likely to have become citizens after eighteen years in the United States.

They estimated that only 18.1 per cent of Canadians had been naturalized eighteen years after arriving in the United States; only Germans had a lower rate, at 16.8 per cent. To put the Canadian number in context, it's important to know that citizens of developed countries (Italy, the United Kingdom, Germany) and those from contiguous countries (Canada, Mexico) were less likely to have become naturalized Americans than those from underdeveloped countries, such as Haiti or Jamaica or Guyana, or those far away, such as China, the Philippines, or Greece. At the risk of purveying pop sociology, it would seem that immigrants to the United States from underdeveloped countries or Communist ones (Cuba, the Soviet Union) were extremely anxious once they had arrived in the country to become citizens—because they did not expect to return home and they wanted as quickly as possible to grasp, quite literally, a passport to what they hoped would be the American Dream.

The Carnegie study corresponded precisely with results of a joint analysis published in 1990 by the U.S. Bureau of Census and Statistics Canada. That analysis found that, of those who had emigrated to the United States prior to 1960, 80 per cent had become American citizens. Thereafter, however, the rate of naturalization dropped: 35.9 per cent for those who left between 1960 and 1964; 25.4 per cent, between 1965 and 1968; 18 per cent, between 1970 and 1974.[6] A more up-to-date survey by the U.S. Bureau of Census in 1997 revealed broadly comparable findings.[7] Canadians in the United States over sixty-five years of age were five times more likely to have taken out U.S. citizenship than not. Those forty-five to sixty-four years old were slightly more likely not to have become Americans; those below age forty-five were overwhelmingly Canadian.

Canadians are now quite blasé about becoming American citizens, even though Canada has allowed, and continues to allow, dual citizenship. A Canadian who takes out U.S. citizenship gives up nothing back home. He or she remains a Canadian, at least for legal purposes. So there is no price to be paid by Star-Spangled Canadians who become Americans. And yet the majority do not become U.S. citizens, even after considerable success in the United States.

"Nope. I never have and probably never will [become a citizen]. I don't know the reasons other than sloth, because it's a bureaucratic procedure that doesn't really change anything except that you get a piece of paper and you can vote. But who would want to vote in the U.S. these days anyway?" said Bruce McCall, a writer and illustrator at *The New Yorker*. "I never think of myself as an American. Somehow, it's important to me to retain that distinction, with all the baggage it brings. It's essentially a kind of underdog position. I think that's one of the reasons I cling to it.

"There's no getting around the fact that my family were very staunch nationalists—United Empire Loyalists, very proud of being of British stock—and that was drummed into me in a thousand ways when I was a kid. There's a part of me that has a deep respect and affection for all that would, and it would, be sundered if I signed a piece of paper saying I was an American. I'm trying to have it both ways, I suppose."

Rob Burgess, president of Macromedia, a San Francisco high-technology company, is frustrated by what he sees as the impediments to doing business in Canada. And yet: "I have never thought about becoming an American. I'm a Canadian. I don't see myself ever changing my identity. I'm a well-known Canadian down here. Half the members of the [company's] senior executive team are Canadians—friends I have brought down, business acquaintances, people affectionately known as 'cold wind from the north.' It's two different things in my mind between being an American and wanting to live down here. Canadians are similar to Americans in many ways, but in many ways they are different."

Douglas Leatherdale, president of a Fortune 500 insurance conglomerate, left Canada more than three decades ago and has been for many years one of the Twin Cities' most prominent business leaders (and also one of the driving forces behind St. Paul getting a National Hockey League expansion franchise, the Minnesota Wild). And yet: "I'm still a Canadian citizen. I still have a Canadian passport. I'm a green-card–carrying alien. First, I take my Canadian heritage very seriously. Second, I'm an ardent monarchist. If I became an American citizen, I'd have to stand up and renounce the Queen … It's a small point, but it's important to me. Third, a lot of my family live in Canada. Four, I'm a big landowner there. I have as many friends in Canada as I probably do in the United States.

"This job requires me to travel constantly around the world. Quite frankly, Canadian passports are frequently better received at crossing points than American ones."

Jill Seidel, a Nova Scotian, has been in the United States for fifteen years, living for most of that time in Washington State. She's married to an American, and her two children are therefore American, but "I can't quite bring myself to do it. I feel so strongly about being Canadian. I just feel so passionately about it. I've always said to my husband that if either one of our children needed their mother to be American—if that was required to become President of the United States—I would probably do it. But being Canadian is such a big part of me that I don't feel any compulsion to take out American citizenship."

Amanda Touche had written a newspaper article in Canada about how her children were poorly received at summer camp in Alberta because they were Americans. The article stirred a small debate in the letters-to-the-editor section. Touche said she sent her children north from Dallas because she wanted them to stay in touch with her own Canadian roots. "You can love the country you're in but you still retain inside of you the kind of moral structure that you grew up with," she said over coffee in her kitchen in Highland Park, an affluent Dallas suburb. "I haven't taken out American citizenship. I still like being Canadian. I haven't fully committed to being American. I love living here. I like the quality of life, the opportunities. I love the people, but I am a little on the outside. I can't vote. I view things with different eyes."

Gordon Leighton, who grew up in Dundas, Ontario, and studied at McMaster University and the University of Western Ontario, underlined how not taking out U.S. citizenship represents a kind of internalized statement to oneself.

"I've been here twenty-one years, but I haven't taken out citizenship," said Leighton, who works in public relations for North States Power Co.

in Minneapolis. "I have a theory about it. The two countries are in so many ways alike. One of the ways we can differentiate ourselves from the U.S. is to retain our citizenship."

Rick Marin's work as is a highly accomplished journalist takes him to intriguing niches of American society, including to such venues as Hugh Hefner's Playboy mansion for a story on parties thrown by the aging philanderer. And yet, Marin says, "no matter how much you have benefited from or admired the values of America that have made you successful here—a kind of ruthlessness, a go-after-it mentality and competitiveness— you still value those things that form part of the Canadian side of you: a deferential quality, a politeness, a niceness. You don't want to feel that you have abrogated all of those Canadian things to become an American. You feel like there are these qualities that are involved in being a Canadian that you can't quite articulate, that you would be giving up or renouncing in a way if you became an American citizen."

David Card is professor of economics at the University of California at Berkeley. He's one of the leading labour economists in the United States and the former winner of the John Bates Clark Medal for the best young economist in the United States under forty years of age. He left Canada in 1978 after graduating from Queen's and has never returned. And yet, U.S. citizenship for Card "didn't seem like any pressing need. You find that's really common ... I probably think that, like most Canadians, the United States [is] a little bit odd. American politics is very strange to me. When you live among Americans you realize that they are very nationalistic. You're never going to fit in if you're not an American. Canadians still think of themselves as Canadians, not Americans. You'll be sitting at a cocktail party and it will be reinforced and you'll say to yourself, 'I'm not really one of these guys.' Also, the benefits of citizenship? I'm not sure what they are. The one serious issue arises when people get into their fifties and have to start planning their estate."

Noted conservative columnist and author David Frum told me he does not believe as a matter of principle in dual citizenship.

"It's not something you change like a shirt. I think one needs to be clear on something like this," he said. "I don't think dual citizenship is a good phenomenon ... This is a big, beautiful, borderless world ... But [citizenship's] not something you change. I think it's something you're born with." I asked Frum, a Canadian living in the United States but writing for publications in both countries, whether he felt more American or Canadian. "I feel comfortable in different ways," he replied. "Suppose you have a family that drives you a little crazy, which I do not, and you have friends with whom you can talk about the things that really interest you. With whom do you feel more at home? With friends in some ways you have much more in common and you can speak more freely, talk about more things in the way you want to, but they're still friends. Canada is my family. It's the place where I grew up."

For some hold-outs against taking U.S. citizenship, then, there is the tug of memory and roots and family. For others, the reluctance represents a kind of statement to self, an internal definitional message that the person is *in* the United States but not *of* the United States. Between two peoples who share so much in common, the positive act of not becoming an American signals a desire to retain a margin of distinctiveness. The margin may be small. It may even be shrinking as Canada becomes more like the United States, but the margin remains for those who make the positive act. They cling to it with a stubborn intensity even in the face of their own success and comfort in the United States, although U.S. citizenship for some eventually makes sense as a practical matter.

I met a variety of Star-Spangled Canadians in their mid-fifties who took out citizenship on the advice of their accountants. Under U.S. estate-tax law, the spouse of a deceased alien, even a green-card holder, is taxed more heavily than a citizen. So it makes sense to become a U.S. citizen for estate-planning reasons.

Then there are others whose public profile suggested to them that U.S. citizenship made sense.

Harold Shapiro took out U.S. citizenship after becoming provost of the University of Michigan. "Nobody ever asked me about it, [but] I began to feel that if I'm going to have a position like this, I just should finally do it."

The most commonly stated reason for taking out citizenship, however, was an expression of gratitude for the opportunities offered by the United States, a reason elegantly expressed by broadcaster and author Robert MacNeil.

"The attempts to particularize nationality are getting weaker and weaker in some ways. I'm an example of that," he said. "After resisting for thirty-five years, I became an American citizen eighteen months ago. Why? I had that visceral reluctance to give in to what seemed to be the great force sucking everybody here.

"But then I had to acknowledge that this country had given me enormous opportunities and rewards that I didn't get in either Britain or Canada. Not to slight Britain or Canada, but it just worked out that way. Three of my four children are American citizens. My wife is American. I live here nine months of the year. I thought I owed something to this country because it has been extraordinarily generous to me."

Keith Radford anchors the highest-rated newscast in Buffalo for station WKBW. He had been working in the United States for about fifteen years when he decided to take out citizenship.

"I was really grateful to be here. I knew so many people in Canada who were dying to get into the States and they couldn't get in," he said.

"One July 4, about four or five years ago, I became a citizen. On July 4, they had a ceremony on one of the battleships that docked down here. Of course, we had to shoot it and put it on the news. They thought that this was a great opportunity to show that 'he's an American.' So they shot it and made a news story of it."

John Kieser emigrated from Ottawa, where he had worked for the National Arts Centre Orchestra. In the early 1980s, he took a senior administrative position with the San Francisco Symphony and a decade later became a citizen. "It seemed the right thing to do. I'd been down here for ten years," he said. "Part of me said I owed some allegiance to this country. This country has been very good to me. It's given me a lot of opportunity."

Gordon Legge is Distinguished University Professor at the University of Minnesota. He left Ontario after high school to study in the United States and never returned. "I did identify for a long time primarily as a Canadian living in the United States," he said. "Then, very slowly and eventually, by 1993, I decided my roots were in the U.S. and that I was at least partly an American. I realized that I could become an American and have dual citizenship so I didn't have to renounce Canadian citizenship. I guess I felt I've been living in this country for twenty years. I've been treated very well in this country. My family is here. My son has grown up here. I belong more here than in Canada. It makes sense for me to be an American, to vote. It took a long time to reach this point."

The Canadian immigrant experience in the United States is unique. At least for the native English-speakers among them, Canadians are the classic hidden immigrants. They can, if they wish, sew a maple leaf on their clothes or make a special point of affixing "eh" to the end of every sentence, but none of them does. They may be proud of their roots, but they blend into the United States, unless they speak with a pronounced French-Canadian accent, in which case the Americans probably think of them as being from France.

Star-Spangled Canadians do not stand out by distinctive skin colour, different language, dress code, or religious roots. An Englishman or a Guatemalan woman or a Hmong refugee is immediately earmarked as being from somewhere else. African Americans quickly recognize people from the Caribbean or Africa; Canadian blacks appear to U.S. blacks as essentially the same. Canadians do not cluster, although French Canadians once did, in Little Canadas. No "Canadatown" exists in any U.S. city. No restaurants advertise "Canadian" cuisine, unless a Canadian consulate has bribed them as part of a trade promotion. Americans see Canadians as "just like us," so that little, if anything, distinguishes them. Canada as a country has such a blurred or non-existent image in the United States that there are few, if any, top-of-the-mind stereotypes to signal to Americans that someone is Canadian.

David Frum remembered being asked shortly after arriving at *The Wall Street Journal* to write an editorial on immigration. "The chief editorial writer came over and said, 'This is today's topic and would you do something on it?'" Frum recalled. "I tried to beg off. I said, 'I've got an immigration petition being considered right now and I do not think it's appropriate [the *Journal* is very pro-immigration] that I be expressing pro-immigration views when I myself am petitioning.' He looked at me as if I were absolutely nuts. And he said, 'As far as I am concerned, you are from Wisconsin.' That is every Canadian's fondest wish and worst nightmare."

Only the occasional tic of an accent can give a Canadian away, but the Canadian accent in, say, the Deep South, is hard to distinguish from those found in the Northern states. Since the United States has many more pronounced regional accents than does Canada, a Canadian accent may strike a U.S. ear as just another one from some other part of the United States. When Canadian television reporters head south, for example, their accents are never a barrier, because the Canadian accent is so hard to distinguish from many in the United States.

Occasionally, Canadian emigrants explained that they had deliberately changed the way they spoke.

John Fotheringham, brother of the renowned Canadian columnist Allan, began his teaching career in Washington State, where he spent his career and retired as superintendent of a school district south of Seattle.

"I purposely spoke American. I can remember an incident when I was student-teaching. We had a spelling lesson. The word I was giving was 'shone.' In Canada they say the 'the sun shone yesterday,' with a soft 'o.' Down here, they say 'shone' with an open 'o.' These kids didn't know what I was talking about. So I purposely made sure that I used the American pronunciation. I never did, after that, talk like a Canadian," he said.

Harold Wright, an insurance executive in Denver, recalled his first days in Texas.

"Finally, after several months, my supervisor called me in and said his eighteen-year-old daughter could sell insurance better. He said the problem was that, with that accent, people were listening to how I said things rather than what I was saying," Wright recalled. "So he gave me a tape of someone speaking in a Texas accent, and I learned the accent and prospered. But I had a tough time unlearning it when I returned to Winnipeg."

Dimitri Pantazopoulos, who had worked for the Reform Party before moving to Washington as research director for a marketing-research company, felt his accent needed a trim.

"It's important in this business, because you talk to a lot of people. You're trying to get people's opinions in a focus group, and if you're sitting around with some local yokels trying to engage them in conversation and you say 'I've been to Topeka, eh?' they're not going to respond in the same way as if they can't tell where you're coming from."

Accent aside, Canadians are difficult to distinguish in the United States. This blending offers an option available to no other first-generation immigrant group in the United States. Canadians, already heavily Americanized before they arrive and hard to distinguish after they do, can hide their original nationality if they choose. That option is not available to other foreigners whose language, accent, dress code, and other symbols signal, at least to American eyes, that they come from somewhere else.

Canadians, therefore, can acculturate themselves into the United States far more easily than any other immigrant group. They may completely disappear as Canadians, as many of them do by burying their background. They do not have to wait until the second generation to lose their identity as immigrants. Upon arrival in the United States, they can become fully Americans in every sense of the term, except for legal documents, and few of their American friends will know, and only a few of those who do will care. American historians who write about the waves of immigrants that arrived in the late nineteenth and early twentieth centuries discuss Jews, Galatians, Poles, Russians, Germans, Scandinavians, Irish, and all other manner of other Europeans, but few of them even mention the hundreds of thousands of Canadians who arrived. Even today, when American journalists and scholars tackle the subject of immigration, their eyes turn to Latin Americans, Asians, or people from the Caribbean. Canadians are ignored, perhaps because they do not seem "foreign" at all.

Star-Spangled Canadians may, if they wish, take the attitude of Don Gillmor, a retired professor of journalism at the University of Minnesota who was born in Fort Frances, Ontario: "It's a strange thing about being a Canadian. Perhaps it's that 'little brother' complex, something of an inferiority complex in a collective sense, but I always take great pains to tell people that I'm a Canadian."

They do not need other Canadians for cultural support or tangible help, although the occasional informal network develops among Canadians already settled in an area to assist new arrivals in finding their way around. This ease of acculturation perhaps explains why formal networks of Canadians are so weak. Dennis Andersen, a software designer at Microsoft in Redmond, Washington, for some years organized Watpub, a Friday-night get-together for the many former Waterloo students working for the company. It "sort of fizzled out" around 1990, he said. "Canadians are good assimilators everywhere. The ones I know down here, they all seem to fit in anywhere."

Canadian consulates will compile lists of Canadians they know in their geographical areas and organize occasional "Canadian" events such as a reception on July 1. These are seldom well attended, given the number of Canadians living throughout the United States. A few cities have long-established Canadian clubs that organize luncheons or Maple Leaf balls, but these, too, attract only a tiny fraction of the Canadian expatriate community. In cities such as Los Angeles or San Francisco, clutches of Canadians will organize an annual outing to a professional hockey game. (It's not at all unusual to see a smattering of Maple Leafs or Canadiens or Oilers sweaters at NHL games in Denver, Phoenix, San Jose, or Los Angeles.)

As "hidden immigrants" and usually well trained upon arrival, Canadians do not live the classic U.S. immigrant story of climbing up the ladder of U.S. society. They land on the middle or upper rungs of that ladder, and upward mobility is the norm because of the skills they bring. Under U.S. immigration law, it is difficult to emigrate to the United States without considerable education; and only those with university or advanced college training are eligible for the increasingly popular NAFTA "temporary" visas. Almost by definition, therefore, Canadians who emigrate have "brains," and in a country that prides itself (sometimes wrongly) on being a meritocracy, a premium is placed on brains and energy. Not one single Star-Spangled Canadian I interviewed reported that being a Canadian had impeded his or her career. None of them had faced the slightest discrimination by virtue of being an immigrant. At worst, being a Canadian had been irrelevant; at best, it had helped their careers. Americans may know little about Canada, but what they do know is overwhelmingly positive, an image that assists any Canadian who emigrates. It also helps that the U.S. economy is so strong, with a national unemployment rate hovering around 4 per cent and large pockets of the country crying for skilled people. The oft-felt resentment against immigrants who arrive to "take" locals' jobs is not present for well-trained Canadians who land in a country that has been experiencing its longest postwar economic boom. Indeed, public-opinion data show that the U.S. public feels a great deal of trust for Canada; Americans' trust in Canadians outweighs distrust by a ratio of 16:1. Canadians trusted Americans by a ratio of 3.5:1.[8]

"Nobody hates Canadians. To many people 'Canada' means we don't have any baggage. You're one of those middle powers," said Douglas Smee, a senior executive at Citibank in New York. "There are Canadians who have been here so long you'd never know they were Canadian. You only find out by indirect means."

Don Carty runs an airline whose very name bespeaks the Stars and Stripes: American Airlines. Being a Canadian (he took out U.S. citizenship in the late 1980s) has never been a problem.

"Most people think of me as a Canadian. If asked what I am, I say I'm a Canadian. People introduce me as a Canadian. People like Canadians in the U.S. There's no discomfort. It's only from the most extreme American nationalists that you'd hear any kind of reaction. I've never had any kind of hostility."

Bruce McCall, *The New Yorker* illustrator and writer, offers another explanation. "Americans are so used to assimilation that everyone comes from somewhere else here in New York," he said. "There's no great difference if you're a Canadian because they are so much like Americans compared to Senegalese or Australians or Brazilians. They're very blasé about it. They're an immigrant society."

Favio Savoldelli, now working at Merrill Lynch in New York, puts his finger on one reason ex-patriates think their nationality provides an advantage working in the United States, a reason echoed repeatedly in my conversations.

"What does it mean to be a Canadian? It's a different way of viewing the world … Within Merrill, the head of Global Debt, the head of Derivatives—the number of Canadians is amazing," he said. "It's a curious blend because you have an understanding of different cultures. When American business went international there was a real lack of that, whereas at least Canadians knew some French and understood that other cultures existed. That's proven to be a big plus. It's surprising how many Canadians you'll find in positions all around the Street [i.e., Wall Street] which have some international bias. They're like Americans who understand what it's like not to be American."

That more internationalist perspective may be Canadians manifesting their moral superiority, a touchstone of many Canadians' sense of self vis-à-vis the United States. Canadians are hardly as internationalist as they think, but everything is relative, and, for an ex-patriate such as Douglas Leatherdale, that relatively more open perspective on the world has helped in business.

"I've found that it has been an advantage in terms of my business career, especially because anybody who runs a company of this size [the St. Paul Companies] today necessarily is involved on a global basis," Leatherdale said. "And my Canadian background makes it easier for me to deal with, assimilate, and understand business and cultures and environments you deal with.

"Our major place of operations outside the United States is the United Kingdom. I go to London. I intuitively understand the parliamentary system, the institutions. I understand how they work. I take executives from here and they don't quite understand because the American education systems are so insular ... It's easier for me. I find it easier dealing internationally as a Canadian. I don't carry American baggage. I don't carry quite as inward-looking [a] focus as most Americans. I'm more tolerant. I think I understand intuitively and I ask better questions."

Peter Duncan, a geophysicist originally from the Maritimes who had worked in Western Canada before emigrating to Houston, found that being a Canadian was helpful to his business career in Texas.

"In my end of the business, I find that it's an advantage being Canadian," he said at the city's Petroleum Club. "I find that I am given the benefit of the doubt because I'm Canadian, more than perhaps I should be. The general perception in the business I'm in is that Canadians are better educated than perhaps we are, more competent—and I'm not sure that we are ... We're getting the benefit of the doubt ... The sample the Texans see tend to be well educated, well spoken, and can fend for themselves."

Ashleigh Banfield, a Fox news anchor in Dallas, worried about how her local audiences would react to a Canadian having such a high public profile.

"I was really worried when I came down that Texans were very xenophobic and that I would be cast aside," she admitted. "It hasn't been like that at all. Most people get a kick out of it. Most people think we're so cute. I've never had anyone say anything negative."

Canadian nurses in some U.S. states are highly prized because of their excellent training. The same applies for Canadian physicians, especially in specialty areas. As Dr. Marc Caron, a Howard Hughes Fellow and professor of cell biology at Duke, commented: "Americans hold Canadians in higher esteem than just about anybody else in the world. We're looked at quite favourably. It's not been an impediment in my career."

Jeffrey Dvorkin left the Canadian Broadcasting Corporation (CBC) to become Vice-President (News) of National Public Radio (NPR) in Washington, D.C. His Canadian background and CBC experience led NPR to try, successfully, to lure him south.

"Being Canadian was a huge asset, because Canada as a country is deeply admired, because of those '60s and '70s values that Americans still think exist there. To some extent they do, but Americans are as out of touch with the reality of Canada as they are with the reality of most other countries," he said. "Canadians are admired. The CBC as an institution is admired. People in the public-broadcasting community, and even in private broadcasting, when they hear I've spent twenty years at the CBC they are incredibly impressed. People still talk about the National Film Board down here as if it still had cultural import, which of course it doesn't. It's irrelevant."

Mike Seller, like others who gained experience in the Canadian banking system, then emigrated to work in the regional banks of the United States, believes his Canadian training more than adequately equipped him for his job with the People's First Bank in Altamonte Springs, Florida.

"Americans don't like to hear that they're not a forerunner in technology and on the cutting edge. But what I've seen in Central Florida is that the banks are years behind the Canadian banks," Seller said.

Daniel Langelier found the same thing when he moved two decades ago to Tampa after working for two of the large Canadian banks.

"When I came down here twenty years ago, the Canadian banking system was more competitive. The Canadian banking system was doing things that the American banking system has only been doing for the last five years or so," he said. "There was a concentration of banking in Canada at that time; the concentration of banking in the United States had just started. In terms of competence, back then the Canadian bankers were substantially better generalists, more knowledgeable about the economy and the banking market than [were] American bankers."

Real estate was another industry where Canadian talents were sought after in the United States—although the collapse of the prominent firm Olympia and York dented Canada's reputation in that field. (Olympia and York, it should be remembered, was hailed for building the World Trade Center in New York City at a time when that city's economy was deteriorating.) Canadian companies invest massively in the U.S. real-estate market today, but there was a time not long ago when they were deemed to have some special abilities to develop central cities creatively.

Harold Brandt of Brookfield Management, in Minneapolis, remembers those days.

"There was a time in the U.S. when urban renewal was a big deal ... It was generally believed, through some decent marketing and maybe by default, that Canadians had a better feel for a way of dealing with downtowns than Americans did," he said.

"There were a lot of U.S. cities that were in pretty bad shape. Canadian cities were in better shape, but we hadn't had as much time to screw them up ... Canadian developers were very sought after ... The Canadians were sort of heralded as the kind of people who could save you."

Canadians who emigrate may not fully appreciate the strength of local attachment and regional difference that pervades the United States, but they do know something about U.S. patriotism. No Canadian with the slightest acquaintance with the United States can fail to notice the flag-waving south of the border. Any student of U.S. history is struck, at least from a Canadian perspective, by the U.S. sense of exceptionalism, its millennial political rhetoric, its sense of being still a "city on a hill," a light among the nations—attitudes that have withstood the Civil War, economic downturns, the defeat in Vietnam, and massive internal upheavals. American patriotism remains sturdier than ever, especially since the United States has become the world's only superpower. This robust and sometimes aggressive patriotism often grates on some Canadians, whose own country's patriotism (outside Quebec) is deep but not of the same in-your-face variety. Canadian ex-patriates immediately notice the patriotism around them, and react with a mixture of admiration and irritation.

"Canada has always had an identity problem," observed Mike Seely, an ex-patriate banker in Florida. "You ask an American, and he or she knows right away. What are the things people don't like about Americans? They stick their noses into other people's business. They think they're the world's policeman. They get dragged into regional conflicts. But they've never been afraid to say who they are and get in somebody's face if it was contrary to their interests. 'Right or wrong'—I think that's the saying down here—'an American first.' I would love to see some of that in Canada."

Keith Radford, the Buffalo newscaster, agrees.

"Amercians, in my opinion, are so much more patriotic ... They'll wave the flag at the drop of a pin. They don't need an excuse, whereas, in my whole life in Canada, I found Canadians very reserved, quiet. They didn't wave the flag. They actually loved to criticize the government, criticize the country, criticize everything. You have to do that, too, but there's a feeling in the States that these people really love this place and they don't make any secret about it, whereas in Canada, when I lived there, it wasn't spoken about."

More frequent was the kind of observation offered by Lyle Wray, president of the Citizens League of Minnesota: "I think there's a lot of noisy nationalism here that makes Canadians squeamish." Or as Joe Medjuk, the Hollywood producer, put it: "I keep saying this thing to Americans, and they look at me as if I'm a complete idiot, which is that I find Thanksgiving really scary in this country, because it's a strange mixture of politics and religion. They find it really weird that we have Thanksgiving in Canada. What do we have to give thanks for? We're not American. What they're giving thanks for is being American. It's sort of weird."

Almost universally accepted as positive additions to the United States, already highly Americanized when they arrive, skilled and motivated, largely disguised as immigrants, Canadians can inhabit the *demi-monde* of living and working in the United States, pursuing the American Dream, rejoicing in the opportunities afforded by the United States while still considering themselves, if only to themselves, as not quite *of* the United States.

"That's the Canadian condition. We are stuck in a halfway culture. Halfway history. Halfway culture. Halfway everything," said Johnathan Hausman, an exceedingly articulate ex-patriate at a major U.S. investment firm.

"Everybody feels like they're an outsider here. That's the culture. I have a lot of French friends here," he said. "They're American. They just got here last year ... The only people I meet in New York who feel different are Canadians.

"They are the people who say, 'Oh, it's so American.' Nobody else says that with the same amount of glee. The Canadians say it because they know these people. I, as a Canadian, know these people.

"It's sort of like you can see the difference between you and your brother much more closely than anyone else. We're brothers. We're the little brother; they're the big brother. And we need to feel different. We need to feel that there is something that keeps us apart ... This is the thing we always have to guard against—this sense of superiority vis-à-vis Americans. Because we think we're better. But the little brother always has an inferiority complex. He always feels he'll be against the grain and sometimes he feels a little diffident, and that's the Canadian condition. The little brother will come up with all sorts of ideas about how he's the adventurer and the pioneer, but really it's the older brother who has already done everything."

"Halfway." Or, as Marc Mayer, the art-gallery curator in Buffalo, called it, the "Canadians' inherent sense of distinctions."

Rhonda Rubinstein, who's lived in New York and San Francisco, understands what Mayer means.

"The differences are subtle in how we see things. Even growing up in Canada, you're so inundated by American culture that it's part of who you are, but because of that at some point you realize that this is not you," she said.

"I remember watching all this American TV and I finally realized that this was a different culture from me. This was not just farther away in Canada. When you realize that this is a different culture, you start to see the differences. That's what makes Canadians much more observant between the two cultures. They are more able to comment on American culture because they've spent so much time cataloguing the differences."

John Kapelo, an ex-patriate actor in Los Angeles, describes this in-but-not-of positioning for Canadians in the United States.

"When I first got to understand Canada was when I went to Scotland, because it sort of sits over England with this bemused attitude. They're outnumbered but they're not outwitted," he said. "Having been raised in a Canadian family with an American mother, I could just see this spar-ring match going on all the time, because Canadians get infuriated that Americans have so much ignorance about the country, whereas Ameri-cans really don't care. Thery're like the older brother who has the '56 Chevy. Canadians tend to be more ironic, self-deprecating. You develop an acute sensitivity, I suppose. There is that ability to fit in without really being a part of it."

Canadian federal and provincial governments spend millions of dollars a year trying to lure U.S. tourists north. They organize seminars to entice U.S. investment north. Canadian consulates busy themselves through-out the United States attempting to raise the profile of Canada. The traf-fic in goods and travellers across the border is unparalleled in the world.

And yet, as Canadian writer Margaret Atwood suggested, the relationship is a one-way mirror through which Canadians see the United States but Americans see next to nothing. Even when Hollywood or New York producers shoot their films or programs in Canada, they change everything required to make the setting look like the United States.

In March 1999, the Canadian Department of Foreign Affairs paid Sage Research Corp. to conduct focus groups in Baltimore and Atlanta to test Americans' awareness of Canada. Those selected were deemed to be "politically active"—in the previous three years, they had attended a public meeting, participated in the activities of a political party, or worked for a candidate; or, at some point in their life, they had run for local, state, or national office. Those selected were, therefore, among the most politically sophisticated Americans. And they knew next to nothing about Canada.

"The overall level of knowledge about Canada was generally low across the participants in both Baltimore and Atlanta," reported Sage Research. "This lack of knowledge was evident in *all* aspects of the group discussion." Asked for "top of the mind" associations to Canada, or anything they liked or disliked about Canada, "most people had little to say." On specific issues, "the majority response with respect to Canada was typically 'don't know'." Canada was seen as the second-closest ally of the United States, after Britain. Despite the economic relationship between the two countries—the largest bilateral trade in the world and all that—only three of twenty-seven focus-group participants ranked Canada as the United States' largest trading partner, and only one-third placed Canada as one of the top three. "When we informed participants that Canada is the U.S.'s largest trading partner, there was a great deal of surprise," Sage Research reported.[9]

One explanation among many for the lack of knowledge, let alone interest, in Canada is the U.S. media's widespread disregard for things Canadian. No U.S. television network has a correspondent in Canada, nor do any radio stations. Among newspapers, the number of U.S. correspondents based in Canada continues to fall. *The Detroit News*, *Boston Globe*, *Los Angeles Times*, and *Chicago Tribune* are among the U.S. newspapers that have closed bureaux in Canada. Only *The Washington Post* and *Wall Street Journal* maintain correspondents in Canada. At the very moment, then, when the ties between the two countries have become the most intense in history, the U.S. media's coverage of Canada has hit a nadir.

The New York Times had two Canadian correspondents until the 1980s. Then the paper reduced that staff to one, based in Toronto. In

1999, *The Times* withdrew its correspondent altogether. Citing high Canadian taxes, *The Times* announced that its "Canadian" correspondent would henceforth be located in Denver, Colorado. *The Times* complained all the way to the Prime Minister's Office that Canadian taxes were driving the paper from Canada, because whatever extra money the newspaper gave the correspondent to compensate for higher Canadian taxes was taxed, and whatever *The Times* offered as compensation for these additional taxes was also taxed, and so on.

No doubt *The Times* felt the sting of Canadian taxes, but the newspaper faces the same "topping up" challenge in other countries where taxes are higher than in the United States. It nonetheless maintains foreign correspondents in cities with far higher costs than Toronto, such as any in Europe, Tokyo, Beijing, and Shanghai. *The Times*, however, would never dream of closing a bureau in London or Moscow or Tokyo for reasons of cost. But Canada? The country just isn't worth it. A hint of *The Times'* attitude came in the December 22, 1998, memo to staff inviting applications for the Canada post from *Times* editor Andrew Rosenthal. "It's a tough assignment in some ways," wrote Rosenthal. "Canada is relatively big and right next door, which means that it's (a) important, (b) unimportant, or (c) all of the above." *The Times*, insisted Rosenthal, was "strongly committed to our coverage of Canada. Witness the front-page play given recently to the Quebec elections, which were actually leading the paper for about an hour before the impeachment story blew up again." For one hour, then, a Canadian story led the paper. The country is important/unimportant. Hardly an endorsement to make a would-be correspondent hungry for the assignment.

That Americans know little about Canada recurred repeatedly in conversations with Star-Spangled Canadians, and it naturally offended some of them. As Rolf Abt, a Winnipegger now living in Denver, remarked, "The insularity of Americans. That is one disappointment I have with American culture and society. Everything in America has to revolve around America. Turn on the evening news locally. They don't cover a story of national merit unless there's a Colorado connection. Yes, insular, myopic. If it's outside their border, they don't care." In this respect, however, the United States is no different from other superpowers in their time. All dominant countries exhibit a certain narcissism, a feeling that the country's position in the world arises from its inherent superiority so that the very idea that it might have something to learn from others seems preposterous. Canada does not threaten vital U.S. interests. Bilateral disputes, when they arise, tend to be narrowly economic or environmental. In the bulky memoirs of such U.S. luminaries as Presidents Ronald Reagan and Jimmy Carter, or Secretaries of State Henry Kissinger, James Baker, or George Schultz, the word "Canada" seldom appears. The one recent exception was the memoirs of former president George Bush, who developed a deep personal friendship with Prime Minister Brian Mulroney.[10]

To be charitable to Americans, why should they know much about Canada? The country has one-tenth the population of the United States, and no military ambitions (and few capabilities); poses no security threat to U.S. interests; and acts mostly as a compliant, quiet, friendly neighbour and ally. Yes, Canada is the leading trading partner of the United States, but much of that trade is conducted by multinationals shipping parts and finished products from one plant to another, or resource-extraction companies sending logs, oil, natural gas, potash, or hydro-electric power silently across the border. Most of the talented Canadian artists in the field of popular culture are already in Hollywood and New York making money producing U.S. products for U.S. audiences. Canada is not thought of as foreign, interesting, or relevant. For example, when *The New York Times* Sunday magazine decided to ask writers from around the world to offer their impressions of the United States, Canadians were not approached, the thinking being perhaps that no American would want to read something from a writer in Wisconsin North or Michigan East.[11]

This American inwardness noticed by Canadians living in the United States has also been reflected in the media since the Cold War ended. Various studies have tracked the decline in foreign news on the U.S. television newscasts. U.S. newspapers, with some honourable exceptions such as *The New York Times, The Washington Post, The Wall Street Journal*, and a few others, are relentlessly regional or local. So Canada is not being singled out for special treatment. Apart from a handful of quality papers, the U.S. media ignore most of what is happening in the world that does not directly involve the interests of the United States. As Jeffrey Dvorkin, who left CBC Radio for National Public Radio, commented, "Every survey we did at the CBC, what did they value most? National and international news. Here, they want national news. They want quality productions, but they want international news only if there's a crisis. There's less interest in international affairs here than in Canada."

The acculturation of Canadians in the United States has never been easier because Canadians have never been more like Americans. Certainly, car licences must be changed, documents filled out, local shopping areas and entertainment locations scouted, commuting patterns established, new friendships made, local politics understood. But there will be at least as much that is familiar as is strange.

The acculturation experiences of those Star-Spangled Canadians who emigrated long ago contrast substantially with those of more recent arrivals. Those who arrived forty years ago left a very different Canada, an English-speaking nation that was much more British and Protestant, and a French-speaking Canada heavily under the influence of the Catholic Church. The contrast between the Canada they left and the United States eclipsed anything emigrants experience today.

"I left Canada as one of that generation that was very glad to get out. This was in 1955," recalled author and broadcaster Robert MacNeil. "I wanted to be a writer of plays and novels. I had gotten degrees at Dalhousie and Carleton while working for the CBC, and the moment Carleton gave me my diploma, I grabbed it from them and ran for the boat, because it just seemed that nothing was happening there."

Bruce McCall, the author of the brilliantly bittersweet memoir *Thin Ice*, about growing up in Ontario in the 1940s and 1950s, described an Ontario that would be barely recognizable to anyone who lived there in the 1980s and 1990s. For him, the leap was from a backwater to a "go-ahead country with more interesting people."[12]

John Kenneth Galbraith, one of the world's best-known economists, grew up in a small town along the north shore of Lake Erie among Scots families like his own, but left Canada for a teaching position at Harvard. In a memoir of those years, he captured the essential Britishness of his birthplace. "Patriotism was inculcated by a rendering of 'God Save the King' at the beginning of each day as well as 'The Maple Leaf Forever.' (The more or less official anthem was 'O Canada' but at this time there was still grave uncertainty as to the words.) And from time to time we had talks on the virtue and beneficence of the Royal Family to which the Scotch were rightly thought to be very indifferent," he wrote in *The Scotch*. "Much of this latter instruction was undertaken by the school inspector, Mr. Taylor, who visited us twice a year. A staunch imperialist, it was his view that the Prince of Wales was a particularly compelling figure for Canadian youth."[13]

Don Gillmor, retired professor of journalism, remembers his first experiences as a boy when visiting the United States from his home in Fort Frances, Ontario. "My childhood recollection of going across the border was of going into a golden country because the restaurants were better, the movie theatres were better. Young teenagers could drink in any of the fifty-two bars in International Falls. There were slot machines on the sidewalks. It was, even then, a more affluent society."

MacNeil recalls Canadians carrying a chip on their shoulders about Americans. "My father had been in the RCMP, then the Canadian navy, and there was always, while recognizing the enormous power of the Yanks, this little thing: 'Well, they aren't as smart when they march, and they're always whining about needing their own ice cream and Coca-Cola.' There were strong undercurrents of that."

That anti-American chip has disappeared for many of today's Canadians, or at least has shrunk in size. Jack Granatstein, the distinguished Canadian historian who did his PhD at Duke, has written the most comprehensive history of anti-Americanism in Canada, an attitude that once coloured Canadians' sense of self.[14] Granatstein wrote about his own upbringing. "When I was a child in the 1940s, the Loyal Orange Order's parades in Toronto were massive demonstrations of Protestant power and solidarity—Up with King Billy and To Hell with the Pope! ... In many ways, the same transformation has occurred in the power of Canadian anti-Americanism in this century." After studying several hundred years of Canadian attitudes towards the United States, Granatstein concluded that, "with all its hatred, bias and deliberately contrived fearmongering, anti-Americanism was once the Canadian way of being different. Now it has faded away, and good riddance to it."

That Canadians distinguished themselves from Americans, in part, by what Mark Snyder called the "not being American" sense of identity still remains within Canada. Star-Spangled Canadians sense it sometimes when they return to Canada. They meet friends and relatives who envy their opportunities in the United States but that chip—the "little brother syndrome"—has not entirely disappeared.

"There's still an underlying current in Canadians' attitudes, an insecurity about Americans, somewhat of a resentment towards the success of America," said Bonnie Cavanaugh, born in Edmonton, now married and living in Seattle. "I feel it among my own relatives. They speak kind of down about Americans and I don't like that at all, because until you experience them, I don't think you can make that kind of judgment. People are people wherever you go."

Amanda Touche, living in Dallas, returns occasionally to visit relatives and friends in Calgary.

"Canadian attitudes towards the U.S. are very negative, yet Canadians borrow hugely from the U.S. I detect jealousy. I have a standard of living that my girlfriends who have husbands in equally high-paying jobs do not have," Touche said. "When I go back to Calgary I just get this feeling that there is this 'above you' kind of thing."

Many Star-Spangled Canadians contrasted the perceived individualism of Americans with a greater sense of collectivity in Canada.

Lendre Kearns works for a major booking agency in Minneapolis–St. Paul, where she also worked for the famous Guthrie Theater, one of the best regional theatres in the United States. "I find that the kind of Darwinian survival of the fittest is not very comfortable for me. I'm okay living in Minnesota, but there's other states I'm not so sure of," she said. "America celebrates success in a very different way. I can't criticize that because, in my own field, I'm part of that success. I certainly take advantage of it, but at the same time there's a part of that success that doesn't feel quite right."

Wallace Weylie, a lawyer in Indian Rocks Beach, Florida, established a successful law practice after emigrating from Ontario in 1980. He loves his corner of the United States—the sunny weather, the lower taxes, and the opportunities offered by his adopted country. But, Weylie said, "this is a hard society. This society is very competitive. You better do well here or you're not going to survive. They'll just go right over you. I say this to people who come here and ask whether they'll make it here.

"I have a standard speech and it goes like this: 'First, don't underestimate the American. He works hard. He's very competitive. On the other hand, if you have a good product and if you work hard, you'll do great.' The big difference between here and there is the market. If you've got a good thing here, and you work at it, because the market is here, you will survive in spades. On the other hand, there are people who get rolled over here because they can't handle the competition."

Weylie adds an observation that tempers some Canadians' rose-coloured view of the American Dream.

"The perception is that Americans are rich. Americans aren't rich. There are an awful lot of poor people in the U.S. There's a lot of rich people, but the poor here are poor. That's what I meant about the hard society. If you're not making it, you ain't making it, and you're suffering. There isn't the safety net as we have in Canada. All the goodies there are for people in Canada. By golly, there are some awfully poor people here, and nobody gives a shit."

Anthony Ekonomides, the son of Greek immigrants to Toronto, left Canada to study law in the United States and now practises with his brother in Tampa. He echoes Weylie's observation: "If you're not going to take a risk, don't come here. This is not a good land for someone who doesn't want to take a certain amount of risk."

Annalee Luhman, originally from Smithers, British Columbia, has been a human-relations consultant to many companies in and around Seattle during her thirty-year career. Sitting in her home in affluent Bellevue, a Seattle suburb, she reflected on her experiences of the American workplace.

"There's an undercurrent of worry and wanting to make sure one has enough in the States—and I don't know whether it comes from the tradition of not having the social safety net that exists in Canada—but Americans work really, really hard. That's an observation I made almost immediately after coming here," Luhman said.

"I still see people with very good jobs with little businesses on the side. I see a real trend in the States that we're going to have a nation of independent contractors. I don't pass judgment on that. I just think it's had a big impact on how people see themselves and their lives.

"There's a fundamental view here that the strong survive and hard work pays off. People take responsibility here. They put lots of lines in the water in case one doesn't pan out. But I see an undercurrent of fear here, coupled with the sense that if you work hard you'll be successful. I see people very, very driven. I see people afraid to take a vacation. They're afraid their job won't be there when they come back. It's my observation as a consultant and a trainer who goes into a wide spectrum of companies—high-tech, engineering, law firms—I see people absolutely killing themselves. I see people making bundles of money but only being able to take a long weekend for their vacation."

John Fotheringham spent his career in education in the Pacific Northwest, supposedly among the most laid-back parts of the United States. But not according to Fotheringham: "The work ethic is significantly greater [than in Canada]. My brother, when he lived in Washington, D.C., used to say that Americans are crazy the way they work. The work ethic, for whatever reason, seems to be significantly different."

Harold Wright, president of his own insurance company, grew up in British Columbia, worked in Manitoba and Dallas, but settled eventually in Denver.

"At certain levels, there's not a whit of difference [between Canadians and Americans]. A university graduate working for himself or for somebody else, there's hardly any difference," Wright said over lunch at the famous Brown's Hotel. "If he's a card-carrying union guy, there's a big difference ... Culturally, people are more willing here to think that the dream is still possible for them, on their own, whereas in Canada there always seemed to be the impression that if you did it on your own and you're successful, they're going to be very jealous of you, that you probably stepped on somebody's hand or head to get yours."

Bruno Freschi, who grew up in Trail, British Columbia, had a booming architecture practice in Vancouver. He designed the master plan for Expo 86 in Vancouver as well as that city's Expo Centre, and Science Museum. But he left in 1989 for the State University of New York at Buffalo and an association with a global firm of architects.

"What I've learned is that the United States is not Canada, and the similarities aren't as real as we think they are. This is my tenth year, and I am always amazed, stunned at the differences ... The fundamental difference is the American democratic project. It is unbelievable," Freschi said.

"The degree to which this country in 200 years has evolved these democratic ideals, outrageous democratic principles. 'We're the world's best' kind of American bravado can get you down, but in fact the democratic project here is different than in Canada. Canadians are less participatory, less demanding."

At one level—voter turn-out—Freschi is wrong, since rarely do more than half of eligible Americans vote in national elections, whereas in Canada more than 70 per cent of voters cast ballots in most elections, and in provincial elections the participation rate is sometimes above 80 per cent. The two political systems are structured differently and based on different concepts of how best to protect liberty, although the adoption of the Charter of Rights and Freedoms has married the "right-based" discourse and muscular role for courts into the parliamentary system, thereby making political attitudes in Canada much more like those in the United States.

Freschi and many other Star-Spangled Canadians also exaggerate the degree of Canadians' dependence upon the state, the major difference between the two peoples underscored in Seymour Martin Lipset's examination of both countries, *Continental Divide*.[15] Since the mid-1980s, Canadian federal and provincial governments have whittled away at state programs through outright privatizations of Crown corporations, joint ventures with the private sector for the delivery of public services in everything from emergency legal aid to highway construction, scaling back existing programs, withdrawing subsidies from failing industries, or trimming social programs such as unemployment insurance and social welfare. The old Canada that many Star-Spangled Canadians left in the 1960s, 1970s, and even the 1980s is not the Canada of the 1990s. What exists today is a somewhat leaner state and, of greater significance, what Canadians pollsters, from Michael Adams at Environics Research to Angus Reid of the Angus

Reid Group, to Allan Gregg, formerly of Decima Research, have discovered to be attitudes of increasingly lesser dependence upon government. The Cánadian state still takes more of the country's GNP than does the U.S. state, a difference magnified if defence spending is discounted, but still smaller than decades ago.

The Canadian state is more evident—as are higher Canadian taxes—but American society provides services in other ways.

Lyle Wray has found himself in an excellent position to observe the difference. His state, Minnesota, is not necessarily representative of the United States because it has always been among the most "progressive," with a long tradition of activist government. Wray is president of the Citizens League of Minnesota, an umbrella group that represents community groups across the state. He came to Minnesota with a PhD from the University of Manitoba, having grown up in Medicine Hat, Alberta. A committed New Democrat, Wray worked for a cabinet minister in Premier Ed Schreyer's NDP government.

"The parliamentary system is a cleaner system in some ways in the sense that you can have a referendum on a subject and go and do it," he said. "Here, with the separation of powers, it's a lot untidier, and things tend to be incremental and bottom-up. The contrast is that, in Canada, historically citizens didn't have much power. I don't know when we started the semantic shift from 'subject of the Crown' to 'citizens,' but it's a major semantic shift.

"This country has always had citizens, which meant that they had inalienable rights. Their counties in which they live—even though they are creatures of the state government—governors know better than to mess with them. So it's a grass-roots, citizen-empowered model. That's not just Alexis de Tocqueville. It's real."

Minnesota, Wray said, has 30,000 non-profit groups for 4.2 million people. "They're vigorous and dynamic and highly varied. And that's an exciting situation. Yes, there's a United Way and there's this and that, but I didn't see the same dynamism in that sector in Canada."

Americans, Wray observed correctly, are somewhat schizophrenic about government. "In good times, we get this market triumphalism. Then when the market crashes and burns, whether through some speculative excess or whatever, then we pound our fist on the table and say 'Where was government? Why weren't they involved'?

"Public services in this country work extremely well, despite all the yapping. The post office runs extremely well. The roads get cleared. Things are done on bid and low budget. There are exceptions, but things work.

People expect a level of service that is fairly high, even though they despise it. It's a weird kind of mix."

Wray's experience with civic activism in Minnesota did not match what Pat Cooper found in Denver, where she runs the outstanding Children's Museum. Both are cities with large well-educated populations, but Colorado lacks Minnesota's "progressive tradition." Pockets of activism exist in "red" Boulder, home of the University of Colorado, in the pricey ski resorts west of Denver and in parts of the big city, but the rest of Colorado is traditionally sceptical of "big government."

"The majority of people here are so busy making money, they don't really care about public services. People really don't want to run for public office. You get a very poor showing. Most of the candidates for school board have no competition. Public office is really not something Americans aspire to," Cooper said.

"The women's movement down here is really not very active. It may have started in the U.S., but maybe it didn't have the energy of the great leaders. The power of the Canadian women's movement was people like me and my friends who were used to hundreds and thousands of hours of volunteer work, writing briefs, sticking with it.

"Do you know that the YWCA closed here? The YW had been here for 103 years. I'm an old YWer. I was on the YWCA Canada board. I was president of the YWCA in Calgary, where we built a shelter for battered women. I got here and said, 'Oh, there's a YW. I'll charge right over there. I asked somebody about it and they said it closed."

It is an observable irony of American life that so many of the country's heroes—men (mostly) after whom cities have been named, monuments erected, and mountains sculpted—contributed in the sphere of government, and yet Americans have always been decidedly ambivalent about the appropriate role of government in their national life. The ambivalence is as old as the Republic itself, beginning in the first debates between Federalists and Anti-Federalists from the Continental Congress through the Bill of Rights and beyond. Americans today turn out in smaller numbers to vote in national elections than in any advanced industrialized democracy, yet, at the opposite end of the participatory spectrum, New England annual town-hall meetings to approve budgets and chew over issues are not just memories captured in Norman Rockwell paintings but alive-and-well institutions. The U.S. market is so large that it can support an enviable range of literate magazines: *The New Yorker, The New Republic, The Weekly Standard, The Public Interest, Commentary, Harper's, The Atlantic Monthly, The New York Review of Books, The Nation,* and the on-line magazine *Slate*. Canada offers nothing comparable. As with almost every-thing else in the United States, however, trash is also everywhere apparent, as an attentive ear cocked to open-line radio will soon discover. Howard Stern, the shock-jock in New York, gained notoriety in Canada when sta-tions in Montreal and Toronto began picking up his show, but as soon as the notoriety faded, so did Stern. He was too offensive for Canadians' tastes, but, more important, too offensively stupid for Canadians.

Americans may be more sceptical of government, but they are more philanthropic, in part because some of them trust philanthropic institu-tions more than government, and in part because U.S. tax laws encourage giving. U.S. and Canadian tax laws are based on different premises. Canada will tax a citizen heavily when he is alive; the United States, when he dies. The United States therefore has estate taxes, which Canada does not, but an enormous industry of lawyers and accountants exists there to advise wealthy Americans how to arrange their affairs in order to avoid or minimize estate taxes. This scramble encourages some wealthy Americans to create philanthropic foundations. There is also social pressure in some parts of the United States. In Minneapolis–St. Paul, for example, it has been a decades-old tradition that corporations devote 1 per cent of their pre-tax incomes to philanthropy.

The widespread Canadian stereotype about Americans' scepticism for Big Government needs modification, because in some areas Americans have been, and continue to be, more accepting of Big Government than are Canadians. Military spending is the obvious example. If the first pri-ority of the state is to provide security to its people, then the U.S. state obvi-ously does that better since the United States spends lavishly on defence, whereas Canada does not. Indeed, a dirty secret of Canadian defence pol-icy has always been an implicit acknowledgment that Canada can take a bit of a free ride on defence because, in a crunch, the Americans would never permit their security to be imperilled by allowing Canada to fall into hostile hands.

This willingness to spend public funds beyond what Canadians do extends into civic society, too. Americans generally spend more on roads, environmental protection, agricultural subsidies, publicly financed research, and universities. In 1996, the ten jurisdictions in North America paying the highest welfare rates were all U.S. states. This may have changed since "welfare reform" gave the states more latitude to decide their own welfare programs, but in 1996 the ten jurisdictions paying the highest welfare rates (in Canadian dollars) were: Hawaii; Alaska; Con-necticut; Massachusetts; Washington, D.C.; Rhode Island; New York;

New Jersey; California; and New Hampshire. Ontario, the top Canadian jurisdiction, ranked twelfth.[16] Indeed, the so-called welfare state itself began in the United States under the New Deal, elements of which were then copied in political desperation by Prime Minister R.B. Bennett. The United States spends about as much of its GNP on publicly financed health care as does Canada, but then adds a much larger private-sector component. Canadians in the 1980s used to beat up on American governments for acid-rain emissions—and with good reason—but the U.S. Clean Air Act preceded anything comparable in Canada, and several of the worst-emitting plants were in northwestern Ontario. The thrust for "affirmative action" policies, ostensibly designed to assist traditionally underrepresented groups, was imported from the United States into Canada, and even included in the Charter of Rights and Freedoms, a constitutional document and philosophy of rights protection heavily influenced by American practice. Canadian aboriginals have frequently, if somewhat bizarrely, pointed to what they consider superior treatment of U.S. Indians flowing from the nineteenth-century U.S. Supreme Court's decision that Indians are "domestic, dependent nations."

On balance, however, Canada remains a slightly "kinder, gentler" society, with lower aggregate crime rates, less infant mortality, more generous unemployment-insurance payments, longer maternity leaves, universal health care, regional development agencies for poorer provinces and constitutionally entrenched, government-funded equalization. That program, in particular, finds no echo in the United States. American federal and state governments have adopted particular policies to assist disadvantaged areas, the classic examples being the Tennessee Valley Authority, rural electrification, and massive public works (dams, canals) carried out by the U.S. Army Corps of Engineers. But the United States fundamentally believes people should move to jobs and not that government programs or funds should be injected into areas with high unemployment. The differences are starkly apparent between New England and Atlantic Canada. Both areas lost population for generations: New England to the rest of the United States; Atlantic Canada to other parts of Canada and the United States, especially to what Maritimers once called the "Boston states." Rural electrification and the U.S. interstate highway system greatly assisted New England, but neither was specifically designed for that part of the country. None of the New England states, including the poorest, such as Vermont, New Hampshire, and Maine, ever received "equalization" funds from Washington. No federal agencies with alphabet-soup names poured funds into the region to create jobs. New England has experienced some very rough times. Even in the early 1960s, after fifteen postwar years of surging economic growth in the United States, the region's economy was still sagging. Food stamps were prevalent in small towns and rural communities. Today, however, Vermont and New Hampshire are thriving (Maine still struggles), with unemployment rates below the national average of about 4 per cent, rates that would make any government in Atlantic Canada cry for joy. It may be that Canada's regional-development programs illustrate the country's "kinder, gentler" approach, but the history of Atlantic Canada and New England suggests the Canadian approach, in the long run, may not have been necessarily smarter.

This "kinder, gentler" Canada—but also this Canada with a 25 per cent lower per-capita income—is what Star-Spangled Canadians most reflect upon when thinking about their old country. For some, the memory of the "kinder, gentler" Canada makes them feel slightly uneasy with American attitudes; for others, the higher taxes, the 25 per cent income gap, and the more limited opportunities pushed them south to make a better living for themselves and their families. Whether Canadians will want to continue to be "kinder, gentler" but also poorer and less economically dynamic is their country's most difficult—and most important—issue for the twenty-first century. Or, to put the dilemma another way, how can Canadians still be "kinder, gentler"—shorthand for Canada's distinctiveness in North America—while becoming more economically dynamic in an age of continental integration?

*Living across the river from Canada as a kid, I used to go down
and sit and look at Windsor, Ontario. Windsor represented Europe
to me ... For black people, you see, Canada was a place that
treated you better than America, the North. For my father, Detroit
was better than the South; to me, born in the North, Canada was
better ... Canada represented for me something foreign, exotic,
that was not the United States.* — Jazz saxophonist Donald Byrd

RACE, ETHNICITY

WHEN Ashleigh Banfield arrived in Dallas from Calgary, having worked
her way across Ontario and Western Canada as a television journalist, she
thought she understood something about the racial divide within the
United States.

"I knew it, but I didn't realize how stark the reality was. I knew that a lot
of people had bars on their windows. I just didn't know how divided it is.
People don't become accustomed to it because they don't venture," she
said during lunch in a restaurant near central Dallas.

Star-Spangled Canadians are apparently like most white Americans
who might work with black Americans, and perhaps even count a few as
friends, but usually live far from concentrations of black people. Race
permeates American history and present-day reality, but it is entirely possible for white Americans and ex-patriate Canadians to remove themselves
physically and psychologically from the racial front lines. For Banfield,
the aggressive Fox TV anchor in Dallas, such removal was not an option.

"Here, there's no such thing as a pocket. There's a dividing line. There's
the border. I should take you for a quick drive and show you some of
South Dallas's neighbourhoods," she said, sweeping her hand towards the
southern part of the city.

"We can go into Cracktown USA just over the bridge, and you can see
mattresses all over the fields where people are doing crack or hanging out

at night. You notice how the houses and lots are in complete disarray. The city doesn't manicure any of the boulevards down there. There's garbage everywhere that's never picked up, and bars on every single window. We're talking about homes that aren't even worth burglarizing. Gas stations with chain-link fences."

Dallas's racial divide also struck Chuck Scullion, a Harvard Business School graduate from Toronto working for the Boston Consulting Group.

"The integration in Dallas is a lot lower than it is in Toronto. The poor and the rich are split," he said. "There are areas in Canada that have people who are well off and poor and generally not living next to each other, split by a highway or river. But here, coming from the wrong side of the tracks really means coming from the wrong side of the tracks."

The racial divide splits the city geographically, but sociologically too. "It's not overt racism. If people are in a bar and the bar is mixed, no one stops the music and says, What's going on here?" Scullion observed. "But there is a kind of Old South culture that still exists right here. I haven't seen activities that bothered me, per se. I haven't seen behaviour that I find offensive. It's just that things are so split up and I can't necessarily see why. It just seems that that's the way it is."

Emigrating from a country where blacks form a tiny portion of the population to areas of the United States where they form the largest minority racial group requires an adjustment for ex-patriate Canadians. Caroline Birks from Montreal went to Chicago to study and was shocked at the segregation she observed in that northern city. Skye Page, an account executive in Tampa, loved the move from Edmonton to Atlanta, a city she considered beautiful and exciting. "But one of the first things that hit me was the racial problem they have. Coming from Edmonton to Atlanta, that was something I noticed right away. They have a lot of baggage and a lot of history with it, so it's very difficult for someone who doesn't have that baggage to understand what's going on. I found the racial divide deep and complex."

Deep and complex. Jennifer Rees, a nurse from Orillia working at the Duke Medical Center in Raleigh–Durham, North Carolina, quickly discovered when she received supervisory responsibility how touchy and politically sensitive the question of race can be in a work environment.

"It was a culture shock for me," she recalled. "A lot of people I work with are lazy and they're very quick to cry prejudice. They are reprimanded for a behaviour that was inappropriate, and the first thing they say is that it's because 'I'm black.' You have to be very cautious how you approach them, especially if it's a nurse's assistant and you're the RN and you have to reprimand them. You have to be very diplomatic how you do it, because the last thing you want is for your supervisor to come up and say you were disrespectful or prejudiced because they've put in a complaint."

Unless they live in a few large cities, white Canadians may encounter few blacks, let alone socialize or work with them. Only in the last quarter-century has Canada's long-standing but small black community been augmented by black immigrants (or refugees) from the Caribbean and Africa. These new communities are different from the older ones in everything, from accent to customs and social hierarchies. Pockets of blacks live in certain Canadian cities—Toronto, Montreal, and Halifax—but their presence is but a fraction of the demographic presence of black people in the United States. That presence shapes the pattern of U.S. urban neighbourhoods, the funding formulas for school boards, Congressional districts, educational curriculum, homicide rates.[1]

Ex-patriate Canadians with children learn upon arrival in U.S. cities, or shortly thereafter, which neighbourhoods are safe and, critically, which school districts offer the best education, because the gaps in the quality of public-school education are generally larger in the United States than in Canada. Only recently have some U.S. states—under court orders or political pressure, or both—begun to address the imbalances in resources among school districts. New laws that attempt to redistribute revenues from affluent to poor districts have often been bitterly resented—opponents of the Texas law call it the "Robin Hood law." In Kentucky, for example, the state supreme court ruled the entire state public-school system unconstitutional because of glaring inequalities among school districts and ordered the legislature to devise a new funding formula. A similar edict came from the Vermont courts.

Vermont has one of the smallest black populations in the United States, so not all these inequalities arise from race, but many of them do, especially in urban areas. Affluent white suburbanites, having voted with their feet by leaving inner-city areas, are reluctant to see their tax dollars spent in other school districts. The same resentments can flare within cities through transfers either of money or of pupils through court-ordered busing schemes. Canadian ex-patriates, the overwhelming majority of whom are white, parachute into urban areas and must quickly discern which schools or school districts to avoid or frequent, often with the advice of real-estate agents or new colleagues, in a kind of process of initiation to the essential undercurrents of American life.

Jeff Andrews, a doctor who left his practice in Mississauga to emigrate to North Carolina, found himself in the middle of one debate over race and education, a microcosm of debates throughout the United States.

"There's a big racial issue here, whether people recognize it or not. Coming from where I did, there's still a lot of issues on both sides about race here. You land in the middle of it because you have white skin. You clearly belong to one race, and a lot of these ancient issues get ascribed to you," he said during a chat at the Duke Medical Center.

"Within the Durham school system, it's divided between a city and a county system, and they had just agreed to merge those two system when we came. The city schools, as you can imagine, were 95 per cent black, and the county schools were flipped the other way. They couldn't decide how to deal with the issue and were talking about busing as a form of redistricting, which didn't make a lot of sense to me.

"I was aware of the 'magnet school' concept, so I became involved in politics … and became the author of the 'zone-innovative plan,' which was a magnet plan. That sets up a special program in a city school that will attract people who will come by choice rather than forcing people who live on a certain street to go to a certain school and be bused there."

The "magnet school" idea foundered when the county commissioner refused to ante up more money, not an unusual reaction in North Carolina, which, for all its growth and high-technology glitter, ranks forty-eighth in the United States in per-student spending. As for Jeff Andrews, he followed the path to a better school district, in affluent Chapel Hill, home to the University of North Carolina.

Pat Cooper lives in the Colorado equivalent of Chapel Hill, the prosperous Denver suburb of Cherry Creek. Originally from Calgary, Cooper had been an active Liberal, journalist, women's rights activist, and vice-president of the Canadian Advisory Council on the Status of Women. Her job at Denver's Children's Museum offers a unique perspective on the city, its races, and education.

"I was just shocked by the inequalities in the education system," she said. "My youngest is at Cherry Creek High School, rated number ten in the nation, right up there with the privates. It has a calendar as large as a Canadian junior college, by way of courses. She could have taken advanced Chinese at her high school."

"But right over there," she continued, motioning from her office to nearby downtown neighbourhoods, "it's about as bad as you can get. The inequality is profound. There's no other word to describe it … Right up there on this hill, we have two elementary schools, sitting right on that hill over there. Each has 700–800 students. Ninety-five per cent of them are below the poverty line. Being poor in the United States is really being poor." Colorado, she added, had passed legislation to transfer some resources among school boards, but the impact, she believed, had been minimal.

Blacks in Calgary are as rare as critics of the oil industry, so her move to Denver took some adjustment to U.S. racial realities. Denver's black population is only 3 per cent of the whole, but the mayor is black and so are a disproportionate number of civic employees. The children of Denver's diverse communities stream daily into Pat Cooper's museum.

"You had the Civil Rights Act. You had the attempt to integrate blacks into everything. And the reality is that they go to their own colleges or, when they're in a mixed campus, they stick together. There have been tons of articles that demonstrate that," Cooper said.

"Then you began to see Black History month. You see all kinds of black or Asian courses in the colleges, and you see them stick together. When I went to Canadian universities with my daughter, you saw these enormous groups of mixed cultures sitting around having their conversations in the cafeteria.

"Certainly in my neighbourhood, here, you have the African-American families. In my upper-middle-class-whitey neighbourhood, we ask them to every single party, but they don't want to integrate. It's a lack of comfort ... So the melting pot isn't really happening."

My impression from raising the race issue with many ex-patriate Canadians is that their perspective depends in part on how long they've been in the United States. The ones who have emigrated more recently — say, in the last decade — are more sensitive to the country's racial divide than those who have lived longer in the United States; their sharp initial impressions have not yet faded into a more blended view. They cannot remember the racial divide as it was longer ago, and therefore do not measure the progress the United States has unquestionably, if sometimes painfully, made in racial reconciliation.

Geneviève Darrow, a nurse who emigrated from Bramalea, Ontario, to Raleigh–Durham, North Carolina, has felt the improvement quite personally.

"Race relations have gotten much better over the years. My first husband was black. When I was first working at Rex Hospital [in Cary, a suburb of Raleigh] ... everybody was very open and welcoming until they met the man I was marrying, who happened to be black," she recalled. "Then a wide gap emerged. It wasn't an issue for me, but there were those who accepted him and those who didn't. I'd say it [the race question] is pretty marginal now. There's more angry black people than twenty years ago ... when there were a lot of angry white people."

Don Carty, the president of American Airlines, has been in the United States for eighteen of the last twenty years. "Race relations remain obviously one of the most troubling aspects of the U.S. But when I look at Dallas, I see twenty years of too slow but nonetheless progress. It's better today by far than twenty years ago, and it will be better twenty years from now than today. I just have no doubt about it," he said.

Martin Luther King, Jr., the U.S. civil-rights icon, was asked by the Canadian Broadcasting Corporation in Canada's centennial year, 1967, to deliver the Massey Lectures. In one of them, King described how American "Negroes," as he called them, had viewed Canada:

> Canada is not merely a neighbor to Negroes. Deep in our history of struggle for freedom Canada was the north star. The Negro slave, denied education, de-humanized, imprisoned on cruel plantations, knew that far to the north a land existed where a fugitive slave if he survived the horrors of the journey could find freedom. The legendary underground railway started in the south and ended in Canada. The freedom road links us together. Our spirituals, now so widely admired around the world, were often codes. We sang of "heaven" that awaited us and the slave masters listened in innocence, not realizing that we were not speaking of the hereafter. Heaven was the word for Canada and the Negro song of the hope that his escape on the underground railroad would carry him there. One of our spirituals, "Follow the Drinking Gourd," in its disguised lyrics contained directions for escape. The gourd was the Big Dipper, and the north star to which its handle pointed gave the celestial map that directed the flight to the Canadian border.[2]

Such a panegyric would undoubtedly flatter Canadians, for they have come to believe that the Underground Railroad symbolized their country's racial kindness. During Black History Month, a direct import from the United States, Canadian schoolchildren are taught all about the stream of American blacks who fled north to escape slavery. In contrast to the U.S. treatment of black people, Canadians feel smug about their racial tolerance. Whether that self-congratulation is deserved is quite another matter, but many black American writers, poets, and pamphleteers, and white supporters of black emancipation and progress, had idealized Canada long before King's Massey Lectures.

Few people can offer sharper insights into the treatment of blacks in both countries than black ex-patriate Canadians. They are, by definition, double minorities: part of the Canadian diaspora in the United States and automatically, if wrongly, lumped by their new fellow citizens into the African-American minority community. Black Canadian ex-patriates move from a country where blacks are few in number (2 per cent of the total population) to one where they form the country's largest racial minority, at 13 per cent of the U.S. population. Race is the American Dilemma; race in the Canadian story is eclipsed by French–English relations and aboriginal concerns.

"I haven't lived in Canada for fifteen years, and I think a lot has changed. Certainly, when I lived in Canada, the level of obsession with race was not there," said Malcolm Gladwell, the exquisite essayist for *The New Yorker*, who is originally from a small town near Elmira, Ontario.

"It wasn't until I got here that I even thought about the issue. Mind you, I moved to Washington, D.C., which is one of the most race-obsessed cities in America, so I was moving to a somewhat artificial environment. It was really striking to me how much it was part of everyday life. It was always on people's minds. They were always seeing racial motives in things. You can't have a conversation in Washington about any policy issue without discussing the racial dimension. I had never conceived of a world where race was on the tip of everyone's tongue at all times."

Race, as defined by black–white relations, only occasionally surfaces as a public issue in Canada. Race gets commingled with language, as with French-speaking Haitians in Montreal, or with region, as with blacks in Nova Scotia. Even the recently arrived West Indians are divided up into smaller communities based on their original Caribbean island nations.

"Canada's great obsession is, of course, Quebec," explained Gladwell. "Everyone has to have some kind of obsession about division and difference. You only have a limited amount of space in your brain for these kinds of arguments, and Canadians have chosen to fill that space with what I would categorize as an even more absurd debate, which is about language. I just don't think people have the energy left to think about skin colour when they are consumed with this debate about language."

Gladwell, who talked to me in his tiny, cluttered office at *The New Yorker*, is the offspring of a white father, and a black Jamaican woman educated, as Gladwell said, "at schools more English than the English schools." He has written in *The New Yorker* about the gradations among blacks in New York City, wherein West Indian immigrants try to make everyone aware of their ethnic background lest they be lumped in with

U.S. blacks.[3] "There are the constant divisions and subdivisions within dis-enfranchised groups to separate out good blacks from bad blacks, which is very marked here because you have different blacks from different parts of the world," he observed. "So the better-off minority groups become com-plicit in this attempt to separate themselves from the worse-off, so there's extraordinary, almost absurd distinctions that are made."

In Toronto, the city in Canada with the largest concentration of blacks, West Indian immigrants are placed near the bottom of the economic lad-der and accorded less status than other immigrant groups by the majority of the city's population. Torontonians, argued Gladwell, "had no bad blacks to contrast with the newcomers, no African Americans to serve as a safety valve for their prejudices, no way to perform America's crude racial triage." In New York City, by contrast, immigrants from West Indian countries are immediately sensitized to the unfavourable stereotypes whites often hold about U.S. blacks. The West Indians struggle therefore to put distance between themselves and U.S. blacks, and are accorded a more favourable set of stereotypes by the rest of the population.

The stereotypes about blacks in the United States, and the racial ten-sions that still beset U.S. society, struck black actress Gloria Reuben, who grew up in London, moved to Toronto, then to Los Angeles, seeking star-dom, which she found as the IIIV-infected physician's assistant in the hit television series *ER*. Her reactions mirrored those of recently arrived white Canadian ex-patriates who seem more shocked by racial tensions that ex-patriate Canadians who have lived for a longer time in the United States.

"From Day One, it's [racial tensions] been that way since I moved here," she told Graham Fraser of *The Globe and Mail*. "I don't know if it's escalated more because of certain events, and in a large way the media has a major role. The riots. It wasn't just African-American looting, but what did you see on television? … Canada has its problems, of course, but it doesn't have the history America does. It's almost like the polarization is getting great. I think about this a lot."[4]

George Elliott Clarke, a gregarious and articulate poet and professor of English at Duke, comes from a black Nova Scotia family whose ancestors arrived in Canada during the War of 1812 after they were captured by the British. He wrote his doctorate contrasting English-Canadian and African-American writing.

"English Canadians, whether they like it or not, have been historically in some senses a minority on this continent, and so have African Ameri-cans, so they take minoritarian perspectives vis-à-vis the United States and the mainstream American culture," Clarke said during a conversation at

Duke University, where he teaches. "We have viewed it with a kind of love–hate relationship ... African Americans, like English Canadians, have at least paid lip service to a semi-socialist way of organizing the economy and government."

Just as white Canadian ex-patriates often maintain a certain inner distance from American patriotism and political causes, Clarke finds himself living as a black in the United States but not as a U.S. black.

"Down here I cannot automatically join up with African-American agendas, even though I can say intellectually that I agree with this or that, or I think this makes sense for you as a people in this state within this particular power structure," he explained.

"But in an emotional sense I find it more difficult to join up, because there is a distance there, greater caution, a greater attempt to understand how authority works ... In terms of racial politics in the United States, it's very simple. It's us against them. It's black versus white. It's class-oriented.

"Blackness is a more abstract quality in Canada than it is here, because here if you are black you are ingrained with an understanding of your place in the United States, both positively and negatively, that goes back to the founding of the Republic. Your history is part and parcel of the national history. Your culture is American culture. Black culture is American culture ...

"As a black Canadian, I'm in a whole different situation in Canada. My culture does not define Canadian culture. My culture is not recognized. Most Canadians don't even know there's a black population in Nova Scotia that's been there for 200 years. My culture is very much a marginal and set-aside culture."

A child of an old Canadian family, Clarke grew up in a family that loved the Queen and things British, since after all the family ancestors had been liberated from the plantations of Maryland by the invading British. But alongside those British affections were influences imported from U.S. black society. Black American heroes and cultural currents became those of Canadians: Martin Luther King, Jr., writers Eldridge Cleaver and Richard Wright, black musicians. Racism existed in Clarke's Nova Scotia, but the fight against it differed from the U.S. struggle.

"Racism in some ways is worse in Canada. What I mean is this: Whether white Americans like black Americans or not is beside the point. Black Americans help to define this place. They're in the constitution. The fundamental laws of this country were at least partly promulgated around black-American issues, and they remain the main ethnicity against which all other ethnicities measure themselves," Clarke said.

"Given this reality, racism is a fundamental fact of American life, and black Americans constantly challenge it, face, it, deal with it, expose it, fight against it.

Race is the topic in the U.S. that Quebec is in Canada. It's a way of talking about everything else. Racism happens but you have lots of support for dealing with it, fighting against it, and punishing perpetrators of racism.

"In Canada, it's entirely the opposite, so that a person who experiences racism is pretty much on their own. Because it's historically always been a little less obvious in Canada, it's been more difficult to fight."

Nobody in U.S. theatre bothers any more to produce Israel Zangwill's 1908 play, but nobody has forgotten the title either. The ideal of cultural fusion and ethnic amalgamation inspired Zangwill, a Jewish immigrant from England, to write *The Melting Pot*, the play that gave a name to a U.S. national mythology.[5]

Zangwill's United States had been accepting millions of immigrants from Europe for several decades before *The Melting Pot* made its Broadway debut. Fifteen years later, nativist pressures slammed the door on immigration from Europe, a door that did not reopen wide until the 1960s, allowing people from the four corners of the earth to pour in. Europeans and Canadians continued to arrive, but they were outnumbered by immigrants from Asia, Central and Latin America, the Caribbean, the Middle East, and, to a lesser extent, Africa. Still, the national myth of America as a melting pot endured, celebrated by political rhetoric and other patriotic exhortations.

That the United States is a "melting pot," whereas Canada is a "multicultural" country, are contrasting clichés that have inspired a thousand bilateral comparisons. The United States, with its stronger sense of national identity, proclaims as its motto "e pluribus unum"—from many into one. Canada not only rhetorically celebrates multiculturalism, but has placed the concept in the Charter of Rights and Freedoms and designed government programs to give money to multicultural groups.

No standard political speech of the July 1st variety would be complete without obligatory references to Canada's "diversity," which differentiates the country from the "melting pot" approach of the United States. The comparisons between the "melting pot" of the United States and the "multiculturalism" of Canada, dubious as reflections of the past, are almost certainly false today. Indeed, it could be argued that, if anything, Canada is the classic "melting pot" society today, whereas the United States is the "multicultural" society. That is certainly how Star-Spangled

Canadians overwhelmingly understand the country they left and the one they adopted.

To put matters another way, somewhat of a dichotomy exists between the official "e pluribus unum" rhetoric in the United States, with its stark assimilating philosophy, and the reality on the ground. American society has changed hugely since the civil-rights struggles of the 1960s and the subsequent Civil Rights Act. The anti-discrimination measures in that statute have been extended to apply to women, but more profoundly the political affirmation of an African-American identity has been picked up by many of the groups arriving in recent decades in the United States. The assertion of group identity, be it in local politics, on university campuses, or in the workplace, is now very much part of American society, and not just for African Americans. Groups that do not feel themselves reflected today or in the history books as part of the American mainstream culture — a mainstream reinforced by strong national symbols — must break free from the "melting pot" model. A dreadful culinary metaphor — that of a "stew" — has become the politically acceptable description for U.S. society among some of these Americans chafing for more group recognition.

Canada welcomed millions of immigrants, but until recent decades no government programs promoted "diversity." The immigrants who peopled the Canadian prairies, for example, kept alive their traditions, although not their languages, without any government help. Immigrants were expected, just as in the United States, to find their own way, to blend in, to accommodate themselves to the prevailing mores and institutions of their adopted society, which was in every sense of the term a "melting pot." Canadians, until recent decades, grew up with diversity, but they never turned it into a national mythology, as political leaders have now done.

Immigration from non-European sources has changed Canada profoundly, so that Canada has now adopted "multiculturalism" as part of its official mythology. But in Canada, with a weaker sense of national identity than the United States and fewer assertive national symbols, the reverse dichotomy has occurred. Ethnic-group identity (francophone Quebec and aborignals excepted) has been officially sanctioned, but practically buried, except for folkloric purposes. Very few political debates turn on ethnicity, few campuses are bothered by ethnic assertiveness, and strong pressures are at work throughout English-speaking and French-speaking Canada for newcomers to blend into the respective cultural mainstreams. It's almost as if Canada, lacking the powerful national identity and symbols found in the United States, can accept with greater equanimity the demands of diversity because these do not threaten any "e pluribus unum" philosophy. Like the monarchy in Canada, "multiculturalism" is part of "official" Canada, to which few Canadians, including immigrants themselves, pay much attention.

The best academic study of Canadians' and Americans' attitudes towards race and ethnicity revealed few noticeable differences, despite the rhetoric and official policies towards "multiculturalism" and "diversity." Jeffrey Reitz and Raymond Breton examined a welter of studies on both sides of the border and concluded: "Our comparison of the Canadian mosaic and the American melting pot reveals that the differences between them are not overwhelming. At any rate, they do not appear to be large enough to justify the distinction implied by the choice of metaphors."[6] Differences in rates of assimilation and economic mobility were small. A series of studies in the 1970s found that more immigrants to Canada than to the United States identified primarily with their new country. That finding led Reitz and Breton to conclude that "the evidence definitely does not warrant the conclusion that Canada is 'multicultural' and the United States is a melting pot. If anything, they suggest that Canada is the melting pot, since the percentage of respondents who define themselves in national terms—that is, as Canadian or American—appears to be higher in Canada than it is in the United States."

Irene Bloemraad, a Canadian PhD candidate at Harvard, confirmed the Reitz/Breton thesis. She examined census data on immigration in both countries and found that immigrants to Canada were much more likely to become citizens, and faster, than those to the United States. Specifically comparing immigrants to Massachusetts and Ontario, Bloemraad discovered that, of those who had lived in these jurisdictions for ten years, only 18 per cent of the Portuguese in Massachusetts had become citizens, compared with 53 per cent in Ontario. Italian immigrants had naturalized at 13 per cent in Massachusetts and 58 per cent in Ontario; immigrants from the People's Republic of China at 42 per cent and 85 per cent, respectively; Vietnamese at 50 per cent and 90 per cent. Bloemraad argued that Canadian multiculturalism policies and a more generous welfare state made integration easier into Canada than into the United States, where immigrants depend upon community organizations and "bottom up" initiatives.[7]

That Canada is a more integrationist country than the United States, despite political rhetoric to the contrary, is also shown by public-opinion surveys. Asked in 1989 whether immigrants should be encouraged to "change their distinct culture and ways to blend with the larger society," 61 per cent of Canadians said yes, compared with 51 per cent of Americans. In a 1992 survey, 52 per cent of Canadians, but only 41 per cent of Americans, agreed with the statement "People from different racial and cultural backgrounds would be better off if they became more like the majority instead of keeping their own cultures."[8]

Canadians do believe themselves more racially tolerant; however, studies reveal that Canadians' attitudes to race are only slightly more tolerant than those of Americans. Few objective observers, for example, could argue that Canadian aborginal people are significantly better off than American Native people. Canadians treated their Japanese population as harshly during the Second World War as Americans did their Japanese population. Canada also apologized later. A 1990 survey by Decima Research found that Canadians were only slightly less overtly racist than Americans. The least one can say is that Canadian and American attitudes towards race and ethnicity are much closer than the country's two misleading mythologies would suggest, even though Star-Spangled Canadians invariably thought of themselves and their native country as more tolerant than their adopted one.

Douglas Leatherdale, an executive living in Minneapolis–St. Paul, grew up southwest of Winnipeg, where he lived with neighbours from many different ethnic backgrounds.

"Some aspects of my Canadian upbringing have served me well. One of the things that I have done in this company since I became chairman and CEO is drive home as one of our basic values a strong recognition of diversity," he said.

"I think it was easier for me to get there in some respects than it was for Americans. I may be wrong about this because I grew up with an appreciation of two cultures and the fact that, in Canada, it's quite the opposite of the American melting pot, where everybody is poured in and says you're an American. I think that, with my understanding of that kind of cultural background, it was easier for me to embrace the need to build up a much more diverse workforce."

Minnesota, like the Canadian prairies, initially attracted large numbers of European immigrants, mostly Scandinavians and Germans, but in recent years Hispanics and Asians, including Hmong refugees from Cambodia, have arrived in Minneapolis–St. Paul. People of Anglophone stock are now a minority in the city of St. Paul, and these new immigrants, like so many in the United States, have insisted on a more public affirmation of their cultural specificity. "In the last fifteen years," Leatherdale observed, "there has been a very noticeable increase in hyphenated Americans."

The hyphenation of Americans can be seen most evidently in universities. U.S. universities have altered their curricula to make them more sensitive to race and ethnicity. Separate dormitories for blacks, Hispanics, Asians, and other groups are now *de rigueur* at institutions as varied as Stanford and Colgate. Battles over "political correctness" have raged on dozens of campuses and in the wider American society, as groups that consider themselves marginalized by mainstream Americans struggle to protect and promote their identities. Universities these days are the antithesis of the "melting pot," as administrators, teachers, and students wrestle with loudly declared diversity.

Munroe Eagles, a Nova Scotian teaching political science at the State University of New York at Buffalo, has been struck by these struggles, which he believes find few echoes on Canadian campuses.

"It's absolutely true that sensitivities have been heightened in the last ten years. To graduate from the university, you need a course in American pluralism and one on world civilization. These are 'sensitivity-raising' courses," he said.

"There is a strong sense in which there is resegregation among the student body. I think you could reproduce that on almost any campus. There's an incredible climate of political correctness that has to be honoured, respected ... This is a fairly recent phenomenon where people have carved out, institutionally and juridically, niches for protection of minority cultures. You see it in districting in the political realms, in dormitories, in the media ... I don't know what the future of that is. The legal guarantees for affirmative action are under attack."

Harold Wright, a successful insurance company president in Denver, emigrated more than twenty years from Winnipeg, where he had worked for Great-West Life. He returns often to Canada and has noticed the two societies moving in opposite directions.

"When we lived in Winnipeg, which had a lot of ethnic groups, there were different festivals, but there was never the feeling that we were all Canadians under the skin. But in the last twenty-five years or so, that seems to have done a complete flip. Now, there's more of a sense that they're Canadians first, and whatever their ethnicity is comes second," he said.

"That's not the case in the U.S. We see and hear it a lot because Hispanics are the largest ethnic group in Denver, and there are demands for bicultural and bilingual teaching in the schools. It's a big issue."

These Canadian ex-patriates find it hard to reconcile their admiration for U.S. patriotism with the political battles around ethnicity they observe in politics and university circles. These battles do not fit stereotypes about the assertive American sense of self, something they feel Canada lacks. They fear a certain weakening of that robust, if sometimes overwhelming, sense of Americanness. They are not alone in these fears, which have manifested themselves in many U.S. political debates over bilingual education, university curricula, and, of course, affirmative-action policies.

Malcolm Gladwell, who has tackled shadings of U.S. sociology in some of his *New Yorker* articles, thinks the fears of ex-patriates and Americans are overblown. For him, the United States as "melting pot" still works beneath the public hullabaloos about diversity.

"There's a moment when new immigrant groups tend to resemble blacks in terms of their position in society, but it passes. They get assimilated. The melting pot works. It does exist for everyone except blacks," he said.

"To the extent that Hispanics identify themselves as a kind of distinct, separate ethnic group, that is something driven entirely by Hispanic political elites. Bilingual education is not supported by Hispanic rank-and-file voters. It's the last thing they want. It's only supported by a small elite constituency that has political motives. These people want to be part of mainstream American society ...

"People will use the hyphen because it's a fashionable, short-term way of identifying yourself, but over time it ceases to have the same meaning. It may take a generation ... I think we're in a phase where it matters. I think it's going to matter a lot less. If you look at kids under the age of seventeen, their attitudes towards matters ethnic and racial is very postmodern. They're not hypenating any more. It's past with them. They're just merging and mixing." Just like officially "multicultural" Canada.

The United States is just across the lake, of course, and on clear
days you can almost see it — a sort of line, a sort of haze ...
Strange, and more dangerous — that much is clear — and maybe
because of that, superior. — Margaret Atwood, The Robber Bride

CRIME

CANADIANS prefer to think of their country as virtue incarnate, its cup of tolerance running over. They endlessly recycle the cliché about Canada the "peaceable kingdom" in large part because it makes them feel so good about themselves. Canadians are peacekeepers abroad, peaceful citizens at home.

Nothing puffs out Canadians' chests more than a comparison between Canadian and U.S. crime rates, no matter how misleading that comparison. Asked to delineate differences that made Canada a better place to live than the United States, Star-Spangled Canadians in interview after interview underscored crime rates, attitudes towards guns, and the general violence of U.S. society, although, curiously and revealingly, very few of them had ever experienced a criminal act in the United States. The United States, they insisted, is a more violent society, but few of them knew that their statement was only partially correct. None of them mentioned that Canadian crime rates are higher than those in Western Europe and Japan — and, for some crimes, higher than American rates.

Canadians also believe that those who head south are among the country's "best and the brightest," emigrés with energy and vision, education and civic-mindedness, citizens from a "kinder, gentler" society. Canadians choose to forget, however, that crooks and criminals of every age are as much a part of the Canadian landscape as spruce trees and maple syrup. Canada has its pimps and prostitutes, fraud artists and con men, shady dealers and drug pushers.

Some Canadians launder money, especially through the United States. One of Al Capone's right-hand men was a Canadian who helped him with the bootlegging trade during Prohibition. Bank robber Alvin Karpis, a Canadian, became a U.S. "Public Enemy Number One." In 1999, Canadians Andrew Fedorowicz and Ferosa Bluff were convicted in Utah of felony murder, second-degree felony child abuse, and second-degree felony sexual abuse in the grisly beating and murder of the Bluffs' three-year-old child.

Although certainly not criminals or shady dealers, Canadian porn stars have made it big in the United States. So have Canadian Playboy bunnies, three of whom lived in varying states of connubial bliss with *Playboy*'s founder Hugh Hefner. *Playboy* featured on its cover a former Miss Canada, Danielle House of Newfoundland, after she slugged another woman in a bar-room altercation and lost her title. Seeking an acting career, House attempted to capitalize on her fleeting fame by moving to Hollywood and getting herself an agent, a Canadian ex-patriate.

It would be strange, therefore, if some of Canada's less savoury characters did not slide across the border to seek their slice of the American Dream. A number of them—about 1,000 at any one point—wind up in U.S. jails. In mid-1999, for example, 1,438 Canadians were either in U.S. prisons, on bail, or living with certain restrictions on their movements. Of these, 67 were serving life sentences. (By contrast, about 150 Americans are usually in Canadian jails.)

Richard Dowdell, a native of Lethbridge, is among those Canadians serving life in prison. Dowdell was already serving consecutive life sentences at the Wyoming State Penitentiary for first-degree murder when he went on trial for premeditated murder of a prison guard whom he stabbed repeatedly and whose skull he smashed with a fire extinguisher during an escape attempt. For that grisly crime, Dowdell had another life sentence tacked on the other two. Concerned that Dowdell might face retribution from other inmates or from prison guards, he was transferred to Nevada in 1991.

Cherie and Paul Pilipow—she from Yorkton, Saskatchewan; he from nearby Melville—were charged with first-degree murder in 1999. Apprehended in Colorado, they were charged with the grisly murder of a woman in Arizona, whom, it is alleged, the Pilipows sprayed with Mace, gagged with duct tape, beat over the head, ran over with her own motor home, then doused with lighter fluid and set aflame. Arizona is one of the thirty-seven states where the death penalty is in use, and state prosecutors are seeking it for the Pilipows.[1]

In the last three years, four Canadians found themselves on death row in the United States. Fortunately for Patrick Jeffries, an aboriginal from British Columbia, his sentence was reduced in 1998 from death to life in prison at the Walla Walla prison in Washington State.

The most publicized recent case of this sort was that of Stanley Faulder, convicted in Texas in 1981 of the death of Inez Phillips, the matriach of a wealthy oil family who kept jewellery and money in a safe in her house. Phillips was found lying bound and gagged on her bed, her skull smashed in and a kitchen knife plunged into her chest.

Faulder signed a confession after a four-day interrogation by Texas police and was convicted of murder. An appeal court quashed that conviction because Faulder did not have access to a lawyer during the interrogation. At a subsequent trial, however, he was again convicted of murder and sentenced to death. Although supporters questioned whether Faulder committed the murder, he said in a television interview: "I don't say I shouldn't be here. I should say that the death row should not exist."

Nine times, Faulder dodged his date with execution, courtesy of a battery of appeals. His case excited attention in Canada, where the death penalty was abolished in 1976. The Canadian embassy in Washington, the Canadian consul-general in Dallas, the minister of foreign affairs, and groups opposed to the death penalty on both sides of the border appealed for clemency to Texas Governor George W. Bush, to no avail.

Faulder finally ran out of appeals and was executed by lethal injection on June 17, 1999, the first Canadian to be executed in the United States since a Toronto man died in the gas chamber at San Quentin in 1952.

Two other Canadians therefore remain on death row — Ronald Smith and Michael Kelly Roberts. Their cases remind us that not all Canadians who live in the United States want to be there. Smith and Roberts sought, in a perverse manner of speaking, better lives for themselves in the United States but wound up facing one major difference between the two countries — the death penalty.

Their lives underscore that not all Canadians living in the United States are those virtuous, tolerant, peace-loving, kind, generous types that Canadians see when they collectively look into the national mirror. The thousand or so Canadians incarcerated at any particular time in the United States illustrate that the "peaceable kingdom," too, has its share of low-lifers and crooks, some of whom get exported to the United States along with all those doctors and nurses, Nobel scientists and bankers, business leaders and film directors.

On August 4, 1982, Ronald Smith, a Canadian with a long criminal record, slipped across the Alberta border into Montana at night and began hitch-hiking south with two Canadian companions.

Just beyond Glacier National Park, two Indians from the nearby Blackfoot Reserve—twenty-year-old Thomas Running Rabbit, Jr., and twenty-four-year-old Harvey Mad Man, Jr.—offered the Canadian trio a lift.

Shortly thereafter, the Canadians ordered the car to a halt, intending to steal it. They marched the two Indian men into the nearby woods, where Smith—"liquored up," as he puts it—killed them with rifle shots to the head. He had been in the United States for only eight hours. He has been there ever since, on death row.

The trio fled in the stolen vehicle, then subsequently went their separate ways. Three weeks later, Smith was arrested in Wyoming, returned to Montana for trial, and charged with first-degree murder; he pleaded guilty at trial in March 1983. Smith asked for the death penalty—"I stood up in court and said I'm guilty as hell, give me the death penalty"—and the judge obliged.

Ronald Smith still awaits execution by lethal injection in a special room designed for that purpose adjacent to the maximum-security unit of the Montana State Penitentiary in Deer Lodge, an hour west of the state capital of Helena. But appeals have stayed his execution, and he has undergone a change of heart since the trial at which he demanded his own death.

Smith wants his sentence commuted to life in prison without parole, served in Canada, a country from which he once fled in fury and confusion but to which he now wants desperately to return.

An eight-hour drive away, at the Washington State penitentiary in Walla Walla, Canadian Michael Roberts faces a similar fate.

In 1994, Roberts walked out of the Ferndale correctional institution in British Columbia and with a friend crossed the border by foot near Osoyoos. They made their way to Edmonds, Washington, a fishing village near Seattle where Roberts had previously spent time while wanted in Canada for earlier crimes.

The two men went to the home of Eli Cantu, whom Roberts had befriended during his previous stay in Edmonds. They commandeered Cantu's car to drive farther south and tied him to a chair so that he could not phone the police.

Stories differ about what happened next. Roberts insists he was in the car outside, unaware that his companion, Thomas Cronin, was murdering Cantu by strangulation and stabbing. Cronin asserted the reverse at trial: that Roberts had committed the murder.

The duo headed south in Cantu's stolen Chevrolet Blazer. At Salem, Oregon, they committed a robbery at a pharmacy, were spotted, tracked by Oregon state police, chased down the freeway and a side road, surrounded, and apprehended.

At trial in 1997, Michael Roberts was charged and convicted with aggravated murder in the first degree, found guilty, and sentenced to death. His accomplice, Thomas Cronin, was given a life sentence without parole. Appeals are under way against Roberts's death sentence.

"My attorneys tell me five to seven years," Roberts says. "That's it. If I don't get any relief on this in five to seven years, I will be executed."

Since 1977, following the U.S. Supreme Court's ruling the previous year allowing states to reinstitute the death penalty, 530 persons have been put to death by lethal injection, hanging, gassing, electrocution, or firing squad in the United States. In 1998, the death penalty claimed 68 persons; in 1997, 74 persons; in 1996, 45 persons. Texas has led the United States in executions. Montana, where Ronald Smith faces the death penalty, has used it only twice (1995 and 1998); Washington, where Roberts is incarcerated, three times (1993, 1994, and 1998).

The Smith and Roberts cases differ in one crucial sense. Ronald Smith does not deny that he committed murder on U.S. soil, whereas Roberts does. But, in other respects, the cases of the two men are eerily similar. Both were severely troubled youths and adults, intermittently plagued by drug and alcohol abuse.

They left behind them in Canada a trail of crimes that resulted in multiple convictions and prolonged stays in Canadian correctional institutions, from which they were released only to commit further crimes in Canada. Their lives of repeated crime are enough to cause any reasonable Canadian, including the most generously inclined towards the accused, to wonder about a Canadian parole system that kept releasing back into society individuals who went right on committing crimes. In any event, what they now both seek is to avoid the death penalty and return to Canada to serve life sentences without parole under the extradition treaty between Canada and the United States. But appeals against the death penalty, strung out over years, even decades, are becoming harder since Congress in 1996 passed the Anti-Terrorism and Effective Death Penalty Act that allows the U.S. Supreme Court to hear an appeal against the death sentence only once.

Ronald Smith has been a model prisoner. Montana prison officials acknowledge his good behaviour; Smith's election as the maximum-security prisoners' representative on the prison's inmate council would tend to confirm it. When I spoke to him in 1999, Smith, then forty-two, had been on death row for sixteen years, never denying his guilt but feeling terrible remorse for his crime.

"I've grown up. I'm more mature. When I came in, I was extremely immature. It was all about blaming everybody else for me being here. It took a long time for me to realize that pretty much I'm the one who put myself here, and I don't have anybody to blame besides myself," he said.

"Once I came to that realization, I started to grow and become more of a — I hate to use the word 'citizen' because I'll never be a 'citizen' — but a more normal member of society."

Smith lives in an 8-foot-by-10-foot cell with a solid door. He has a ghetto blaster and a television in his cell.

"We get the CBC down here, which we pick up off satellite. I watch 'Marketplace,' 'This Hour Has 22 Minutes,' comedy shows. I haven't been away from Canada for so long that I don't get most of the jokes," he explained. Every Saturday, as part of his fixed routine, he watches "Hockey Night in Canada." An Albertan by birth, he grew up supporting the Edmonton Oilers. "I'm still a big fan of Gretzky," he said.

As the only Canadian in the maximum-security portion of the prison, Smith is "constantly" kidded about his nationality. "We seem to be the butt of all humour down here, everything from the way we talk to living in igloos to beating up baby seals."

Each day, Smith is allowed out of his cell for one and a half hours to work out in what is called a "day room" within the maximum-security building. Whenever Smith leaves the cell block, to greet visitors or attend an inmates' council meeting, he must don bright orange overalls and have his hands placed in manacles. Visitors he greets in an interview room split by a pane of glass. He is well-spoken, showing flashes of good humour. He appears in good health, only a touch overweight, with his hair neatly pulled back into a ponytail.

When Smith first arrived in the town of Deer Lodge, he was placed temporarily in the county jail. He escaped, but only for thirteen minutes. Escape would be impossible from the Montana state prison, set three miles from Deer Lodge, ringed by the usual barbed-wire fences, watchtowers, and walls.

"Every now and then I touch on the idea, because if I was to get away and get back across the border, then I wouldn't have to worry about the death sentence," he says. "There's no way the Canadian government would ship me back if I was to get another death sentence … But it's been a long time since I've actually sat around and thought and planned it."

Smith had a Grade 9 education when he arrived at Deer Lodge. He finished his high-school diploma in prison and completed a bachelor's degree in psychology. He would like to do further university studies. The academic work keeps him busy—"I work at it every day"—and gives him a sense of pride, and signals how he has straightened out his life, even in prison. It also helps him to think about things other than death. He knew the fellow prisoner executed in the adjacent building last year, and tries not to think about his own possible fate.

"I don't know that you do come to terms with it. I don't dwell on it. You'll make yourself nuts if you do dwell on it. You can't sit around and wonder, 'Oh God, am I running out of time?' because you'll just make yourself crazy," he said.

"I've got my school work, workouts, music, television. You stay focused on anything but your time, and for me that works.

"It's the same as dwelling on the crime itself. The more you can stay away from it, the better you're going to be. If I was to spend too much time dwelling on the fact that, if I wasn't executed, I'm going to spend the rest of my life in prison, that would drive me crazy.

"I stopped being a criminal some years ago. Guys sit around and plot and plan and scheme about what they're going to do when they get out. [They say] 'I've got this or that score set up.' For me, I ponder, if I did get out what would I do? Go out and get a job, kick back, spend time with my grandkids, my daughter. I don't even consider criminal activities any more. The criminal aspect of my mentality has dried up."

For most of his teenage and adult life before Deer Lodge, however, Ronald Smith spelled trouble. He grew up in Red Deer, and from his early high-school days began compiling a criminal record: burglaries, car thefts ("penny-ante stuff") that landed him in a series of institutions. He ticked them off in order: Drumheller, Bowden, Drumheller, Prince Albert, Edmonton, Drumheller, Bowden.

Crime became, in his words, a "way of life." He admits: "I was a major idiot. I was major into drugs and alcohol when I was younger, on top of being immature. Drugs and alcohol acted in a detrimental way to make me even more immature."

Besides the drugs and alcohol, Smith quarrelled with his parents—with whom he has since been reconciled. He found prisons in some respect easier to cope with than normal life. "I found a place where I belonged and it basically became my second family—prison—and it developed from there. I developed closer ties in prison than I ever did on the street," Smith said.

In 1976, nineteen years old and briefly out of prison in Canada, he had a daughter, who has since lived with her mother in British Columbia. He did not meet his daughter until she was five years old. He saw her a few times in his early years at Deer Lodge, but then the visits stopped because "she was at an age where she could realize where I'm at." Relations were "rocky" during her teen years, but Smith said they spoke monthly by phone. His daughter has given birth to two children, whom he has never seen.

Thinking about his daughter and family turned Smith some years ago from wanting to die to desiring to live. At trial, "I dared the judge to give me a death sentence, and he did. It was just sheer stupidity. Bravado. Being an idiot was all it was. I wasn't stopping to think of anybody but myself," he recalled.

Smith has already tried once, unsuccessfully, to have his sentence commuted from death to life imprisonment.

"I've never denied my guilt. At no point in time. We tried to show how somebody like me could wind up in that situation and commit that kind of crime, [to] show the processes that made me into a killer at that point. I have never tried to make excuses for my crime," he says.

"Just in my last sentencing hearing, I spoke to the families and I said to them that the person who committed the crime was not me. I'm not that person … It was a completely different person who did that. The judge took that and said, 'Well, he's not accepting his responsibility, so he's got to have another death sentence.'

"To me, that's a miscarriage, because I've never denied my guilt. I've never tried to make excuses for what happened, or to put it off on anybody else. I just don't think I deserve to die for it."

His lawyers, anti–death-penalty advocates in Montana, remain confident that his appeals will succeed and that some day he will be extradited to Canada to serve the rest of his life in prison.

"As a Christian, part of their whole philosophy is against the crime of murder," Smith says. "The death sentence, that's all it is. I don't care what kind of crime you commit, you shouldn't be put to death for it. Because murder is murder. State-sanctioned murder. Murder that I committed. Accidental killing. Killing someone for whatever reason is wrong. That's what Christians are supposed to believe."

Smith welcomes publicity for his case in Canada. "That's why I'm talking to you. I want to keep it out in the public eye. I want the public to understand that, contrary to the crime I committed, I am not a menace to society. Putting me to death really doesn't achieve anything, especially after almost twenty years. Then, it's just vindictiveness. It's not punishment any more. It's just vindictiveness. It's vengeance and retribution."

Facing the death penalty in Montana, it's perhaps understandable why Smith wants eagerly to return to Canada. He claims, however, that there was more to his desire for repatriation. "Going back to Canada is the only thing I'm looking at right now. If I was looking at getting my death sentence commuted and staying here, I would have to give serious thought to not commuting my death sentence."

Beneath the surface of collegiality—president of the prisoners' council and all that—lurks something else, the flash of intense difference, resentment perhaps of a patriot prisoner combined with the knowledge of Montana's death-penalty law. "I'm not in the least interested in staying in the United States any longer than I absolutely have to. I'm tired of Americans. There's no problem or anything around here, but I'm just fed up with Americans," Smith insists.

"I want to go home. I want to get back with my own people, my family. I don't know if I've developed a sense of nationality, but I'm fed up with the jokes. I'm fed up with the United States.

"The country is going to hell in a hand-basket. You can't deny it. I mean you've got a president who is too stupid to keep his dick in his pants, and he's one of the better ones. You've got people gunning themselves down in the streets, kids taking guns to school, and while you do have that in Canada to some degree, it's still not a big thing. We're basically a small community and that's what I want to get back to. If I was figuring on staying here in the United States, I wouldn't bother."

Michael Roberts enters the interview room at the Washington State prison in Walla Walla, wearing the requisite bright orange overalls. Unlike Smith, who has already spent sixteen years under a death sentence in Montana, Roberts arrived at Walla Walla on June 19, 1997.

Roberts, like Smith, speaks articulately, and willingly recounts in considerable detail his life's story. He seems, at least during our hour-long conversation, nothing like someone who amassed a lengthy, grisly track record of crime. He is slim and fit, with neatly parted black hair. Everyone in prison knows he is Canadian.

"I've learned from people I've been around that we tend to have a totally different mentality. We tend to be more easygoing, friendly, and polite than the average American ... I had lived in the United States from 1988 to 1990 and it was the same. People know within minutes of talking to me that I'm Canadian. They tell me I have an accent that's maybe Irish-English."

Roberts dropped out of school in Grade 9 but finished his high-school diploma while serving time in Canada. He is allowed two books a week from the Walla Walla prison library. He recently discovered Buddhism: "I find it helps me through this. When everything is just getting too much, I can just sit down and meditate and clear my mind and block everything out."

How does he deal with the possibility of death? "I go in spurts. At times I get very depressed. I see the psychiatrist here. He puts me on anti-depressants. I go into states where for four or five days I don't get out of bed. I don't eat or sleep.

"I think about it, and then there are times when I block it out of my mind. I say it isn't going to happen, and I just put it out of my mind and don't even deal with it."

As a resident of the Intensive Management Unit, Roberts must spend twenty-three hours a day in his cell. For one hour, he is allowed into the exercise room, where he can also use a telephone to call family members, including his wife in British Columbia.

Roberts describes the routine of leaving his cell: "The officers come to my cell. One stands at the window. They open a small patch in the door. I strip off down to my underwear. They go through my clothes to make sure I don't have anything in them. They pass them back to me. I put them back on. I turn around and stick my hands through, and they handcuff me behind my back. When that's done, the two of them escort me to the yard or the day room, lock me inside. I stick my hands through the door and they take the restraints off and I have my hour." Five days a week, he says. Not seven.

Roberts landed in Walla Walla prison after the murder of Eli Cantu in Edmonds, Washington, and a trial in which he was convicted of first-degree murder and sentenced to die. Before Roberts's troubles in the United States, however, his Canadian criminal record stretched back more than two decades. It included shooting a police officer in Nova Scotia and slaying a fellow inmate. There were also robberies, car thefts, long stretches in prison or lesser correctional institutions, periods of rehabilitation, intermittent drug use, and occasionally too much alcohol, hardly the life of a model Star-Spangled Canadian.

Born in Pembroke, Ontario, Roberts moved with his family from Petawawa, Ontario, to Nova Scotia, to Trenton, Ontario. He attended high school in Belleville, but found trouble with the law in his teens. "I'm forty-five years old. I've spent twenty-four of that incarcerated," he says. The list of Canadian institutions in which he served time is depressingly long: Birch Rapids, Guelph Reformatory, Millbrook Reformatory, county jail in Amherst (Nova Scotia), Barrie, Warkworth, Collins Bay, Joyceville, Dorchester, Millhaven, Collins Bay (again), Abbotsford, Elbow Lake, Mission, Ferndale.

Roberts admits he found life in prison more manageable than life on the street.

"At a very young age, I became institutionalized. I promised my parents I wouldn't talk about my upbringing, [but] it wasn't a very peaceful environment," Roberts says. "My running away from home was running away from my parents, and at a young age prison became my home, my family. I was safe there. I knew how to deal with anything that went on there."

In 1974, Roberts began a three-year prison term after robbing an Ontario Provincial Police Credit Union in Barrie. "I walked in with my hands in my pockets and said I had a gun and told them to give me the money. They gave me $3,000. I was a nineteen-year-old kid. I thought I was on top of the world," he recalls.

Seventeen days after his release, however, Roberts found trouble again.

"I went to Ottawa, where I had a friend who was a little older than myself and had been released a little before me. I moved into the same apartment as him. I had a normal inmate attitude. I wanted to catch up on all the things that I had missed while I was incarcerated—the booze and the drugs," he says.

"I ended up pretty drunk one night, and we wound up driving to Hamilton to look up some enemies of his. We got into a fight in a bar in Hamilton. It was a pretty nasty fight. We headed back to Ottawa. I was driving and intoxicated.

"Someone phoned the police and we got arrested on the freeway. We went to court in Ottawa for stealing the car. My parole was violated, a year was added to my sentence, and I went back to jail."

A year later, released from prison, things began briefly looking up for Roberts. His father found him a job at a tool-and-die factory in Trenton. But on a hot August morning, he and a fellow worker who had also served time were discovered sharing a beer during coffee break. They were fired immediately. Roberts's habit of flaring up in the face of adversity reappeared, only this time it led to extremely serious trouble—the shooting of a police officer.

"We left Ontario and drove to Nova Scotia. We did two or three armed robberies. Every time we ran out of money, we did a robbery," he recalls.

"We had two young females with us who used to hang out at the local tavern, not very reputable women, just women who wanted to party, get drunk, get high and screw ...

"In Nova Scotia, we pulled into a gas station. My crime partner was driving the car. We filled up the tank. We had money because we'd just robbed a Kentucky Fried Chicken.

"When the young guy finished filling up the car, he puts the cover back on, he turns to put the hose back, but my crime partner started the car and we went away. He didn't pay for it.

"The young guy managed to get our licence-plate number. We managed to get eight or nine miles down the freeway, and here comes a RCMP cruiser the other way. [He] spots us, turns around, and on come the lights.

"We had two shotguns in the car, a .22 revolver, and we were just young and crazy. We pulled off the freeway onto what we thought was a dirt road. It turned out to be a mobile home. There was a man and his wife with a small baby in her arms.

"We jumped out of the car, grabbed the guns, and told them to get into the house. We went into the house. The RCMP guy came in the yard. He called for back-up. He got out of the car. He knows we're armed. He came out with his revolver to the door, and as soon as he tried to come in we shot through the door ... He was blown completely off the steps.

"He was a young kid, twenty-two years old. He got up, ran into the woods. He made it through the bush to the Trans-Canada, but he passed out on the guardrail.

"He was hit with birdshot from the shotgun. He had pellets in his arms, his chest, his stomach. The doctor testified that the only reason he didn't die was because he had a traffic-ticket book in his breast pocket covering his heart. It had seventeen pellets in it."

Roberts and his accomplice forced the man in the mobile home to drive them to the Maine border, but U.S. authorities soon apprehended them. Roberts received a twenty-five-year prison sentence for attempted murder.

The uninitiated might believe that, with a conviction record of robberies, car thefts, and attempted murder of a police officer, Roberts would have spent most of the rest of his life in jail for the demonstrated reason that he was a menace to society. Such an impression would ignore the laxities of the Canadian parole system. Not too many years later, Roberts was on the street again, resuming the trail of crime that led eventually to Walla Walla.

In Collins Bay penitentiary, Roberts developed what he calls a "bad pill habit"—drugs smuggled in by girlfriends of inmates—that in turn led to even more serious trouble.

Believing another inmate had stolen his drugs, Roberts set out to find him. Roberts succeeded, "and when I confronted him over stealing the drugs from my cell, he got belligerent. He got up. I carried a home-made knife when I was high on pills. I pulled my knife out and wound up stabbing him three times. He died on the spot."

For this crime—second-degree murder—Roberts received a life sentence with ten-year parole eligibility. At this stage of his life, therefore, Roberts had already been convicted of, among other crimes, murder and attempted murder with a life sentence and a twenty-five-year sentence. By 1988, however, Roberts was out of prison.

Roberts had taken psychiatric counselling, maintained a good record in prison and was serving time in a minimum-security penitentiary in British Columbia. Angry that prison authorities would not release him, despite what he says were psychiatric recommendations in favour of release, Roberts escaped and headed for the U.S. border.

Roberts pawned some jewellery, hitch-hiked to Oregon, got a job selling Christmas trees, then another hawking No Soliciting signs, wandered down to Los Angeles, then came north—to Edmonds, Washington, where he met the subsequently ill-fated Eli Cantu, a retired Chicago police officer. Roberts—he had changed his name in 1989 from Jerry Dowe—fished and made a few friends, none of whom knew about his past. On July 29, 1990, however, Roberts received a frightening shock.

"I'm sitting in my apartment, watching 'America's Most Wanted.' All week long they've been advertising that they're going to do their first program showing Canadian fugitives. I'm sitting there watching it, and there I am. They portrayed the incident in Nova Scotia …," he recalls.

He grabbed some personal effects, jumped onto his 1985 Yamaha motorcycle, and drove as far from Canada as he could—to San Diego. He had an eerie sense people recognized him from the television program. When Roberts phoned Canada, he discovered people, including former fishing buddies in Washington, had been calling the RCMP, saying they had seen him. Figuring the game was up, Roberts hitch-hiked back to British Columbia and turned himself in, hoping that the gesture might minimize the prison time before parole. He had been gone for twenty-one months.

Roberts underwent more psychiatric counselling, got turned down for parole, but was later transferred to Ferndale minimum-security penitentiary, which allowed him eight hours on the street each day. He had been married in 1988 but was experiencing marital problems and seemed estranged from his youngest daughter. He started drugs again: marijuana, then heroin. An old friend, recently released after seven years in prison, began urging him to leave, and after a while those entreaties stoked his anger at not being released.

"Finally, I said, 'Okay, let's go.' I knew how to cross the border. I knew how to live in the States."

Shortly thereafter, Eli Cantu was murdered—by his accomplice, not himself, Roberts insists—and Roberts wound up living in the United States all right. But unless his appeals are successful, the United States will be Roberts's final resting place, although it was also a haven, if only briefly.

"The U.S. has been good to me, other than being incarcerated and facing the death penalty for a crime I didn't commit. The twenty-one months I lived in the United States were the best years of my life," he says.

"I actually felt like a human being, like a part of society, after fifteen years in jail. I don't have much faith in the justice system. I see people being executed all over the United States for crimes they didn't commit. People getting off death row after years and year ... But I look back on those twenty-one months as the best months of my life. If nothing else, I have that memory."

Roberts, as the interview ends, begins to choke up a bit. "I'm very sorry that this man lost his life. This guy was a friend of mine. He wasn't very well off and I helped him at different times. I really feel bad for what happened to him. It bothered me that I wanted to get up and tell the family members that during the sentencing phase."

The jury believed, however, that Roberts and not his partner, Thomas Cronin, had murdered Cantu with premeditation, so he languishes in Walla Walla prison, protesting his innocence while awaiting the outcome of appeals that might prevent his execution—a Star-Spangled Canadian, like Ronald Smith, caught in an American cage.

Prime Minister Jean Chrétien loved playing golf with U.S. President Bill Clinton almost as much as he did telling Canadians how much better their country was than the United States. Down there, the Prime Minister would say, you cannot walk in the parks at night. Crime was rampant, he insisted, and Canadian gun laws were eminently preferable to the Wild West attitudes in the United States.

Catherine Côté believed those stereotypes when she moved from Montreal to work for Boeing in Everett, Washington. Her stereotypes were reinforced soon after she arrived.

"My stereotypes were about violence, about wackos walking the street.

I still have that stereotype because somebody at my office gave me a knife to protect myself. I still have it. It's a key knife with a light. It's a real cool knife, very sharp," she recalled. "Also, my girlfriend gave me pepper spray. Another friend of mine asked me to go with him and shoot a pistol because he said I needed to know how to use a gun."

Monica Green, a pediatric nurse, got quite a shock when she took a job at the Duke Medical Center in Raleigh–Durham, North Carolina.

"There are a lot of gangs in the area. To me, pediatrics is not knife and gun wounds. Last summer, for about three weekends in a row we got knife and gunshot wounds to the heads of fourteen- or fifteen-year-olds. That's very bizarre. That's not pediatrics to me," she said. "That's not the kind of pediatrics I would have seen in London, Ontario."

Louise Masse, an assistant professor of behavioural science at the University of Texas school of public health in Houston, remembered her first impressions. "It's hard to go to the supermarket and see a security agent with a gun at the entrance," she said. "When you buy a house here … whether or not to buy an alarm system isn't a question. You can't get house insurance if the house doesn't have a system. We're very aware of crime," she said, "although I haven't been affected directly by it. The way they talk about it all the time on television means I don't watch television any more. At 6 p.m., it's 'Crime Time News.'"

Indeed, it is. Crime dominates U.S. local news in a way startling to any Canadian ex-patriate. The local news is often a collection of "blood sheets," the more spectacular the crime the better, and the more of them the better. Various U.S. media critics have deplored the fixation with crime that permeates local news throughout the United States, but crime news apparently sells, driving up or maintaining ratings in markets experiencing a proliferation of channels and fragmented audiences. The superficial absurdities of Court TV or former New York mayor Ed Koch presiding over televised trials demonstrate the dreary depths to which television producers will sink in their quest for lowest-common-denominator shows. In the world's most litigious society, the fascination with court proceedings in the media knows few limits.

Television's reporting of crime obscures a statistical fact: violent crime has been declining in the United States since 1993, a trend mirrored in Canada. Of all the things that startled me in interviewing Star-Spangled Canadians, I was most surprised by how little they mentioned crime (apart from those quoted above). Only a couple of them had personally experienced a criminal act, and these crimes were of a rather petty nature—a radio swiped from a car, an occasional home break-in—similar to the kind

experienced in Canadian urban centres. Very little of what I heard confirmed the stereotype widely believed in Canada that the United States is
chronically violent compared with "peaceful, safe" Canada.

Dimitri Pantazopoulus, a native of Ottawa, moved to Washington,
D.C., at the age of twenty-six. His reaction to U.S. crime—imagined and
real—is perhaps typical.

"I probably had some stereotypes with regard to the crime rate. Moving
down here to Washington, which was once the murder capital of the
world, I started to think 'Boy, we're going to have to drive around with our
doors locked and keep our windows up and have bullet-proof glass
installed and not go out at night'," he said. "I don't feel that insecure. It's
fortunate for me—but unfortunate for society, probably—a lot of that
crime is confined to certain income areas of the city. There may be an
average of one crime a day, but it ain't where I'm living.

"Where I live there tend to be a lot more petty crimes—kids coming
around and stealing stereos out of cars. Well, I had my car broken into a
couple of times—in Ottawa and Calgary. So has my stereotype about
crime changed? I would say yes. I'm a lot less concerned about crime than
I was going into it as a Canadian."

International statistics may provide one reason so few Star-Spangled
Canadians mentioned crime.

The table below is based on the International Crime Victimization Survey from 1996. It's a random-sample survey in which respondents were
asked about their experiences of crime during the previous twelve months.

Percentage of the Population Victimized Once or More, 1996

	Violent Offences	Theft of Property	Household Burglary
Canada	6	6	5
England/Wales	8	5	6
France	5	4	4
Sweden	6	5	2
United States	7	4	5

International Crime Victimization Survey, 1996, cited in Sandra Besserer, "Criminal Victimization: International Perspective," *Juristat* 18/6. (Ottawa: Statistics Canada, Canadian Centre for Justice Statistics).

Another table illustrates Canadian and U.S. crime rates.

Crimes Rates (per 100,000 population)
for Canada and the United States, 1998

	Canada	United States
Murder and non-negligent manslaughter	1.8	6.3
Robbery	96	166

Aggravated assault	132	363
Burglary	1,156	855
Larceny	2,352	2,713
Motor-vehicle theft	547	456

Source: Slyvain Tremblay, "Crime Statistics in Canada, 1998," *Juristat*, 19/9. (Ottawa: Statistics Canada, Canadian Centre for Justice Statistics, 1999); Federal Bureau of Investigation, *Preliminary Release of Uniform Crime Reports* (Washington, D.C.: U.S. Government Printing Office, 1999).[2]

Americans, as the tables show, are more likely to be victims of a violent crime such as murder, manslaughter, or aggravated assault. Only two U.S. states (New Hampshire and South Dakota) had lower homicide rates than the Canadian rate of 1.8 per 100,000 individuals. The state with the highest incidence, Louisiana, had a shocking rate of 17.5, followed by Nevada at 13.7, Maryland at 11.6, New Mexico at 11.5, Mississippi at 11.1, Alabama at 10.4, and Illinois at 10.0. Homicide rates on average are almost twice as high in the South as in the Northeast.[3] When Canadians argue that theirs is a safer, gentler society, they rightly point to these homicide numbers. Americans are also more likely to be robbed, whereas Canadians are more likely to experience burglary or motor-vehicle theft. On the surface, therefore, the numbers point clearly to the United States as a more violent society in terms of serious crimes against persons. The aggregate numbers, however, are somewhat misleading. Violent crime is heavily concentrated in certain parts of U.S. inner cities. The majority of violent crimes, regrettably, are between African Americans who cluster in inner-city ghettos. The majority of homicides are black-on-black. For those living outside the ghettos, the rates for robbery and aggravated assault between Canada and the United States would be similar.

Star-Spangled Canadians quickly learn, if they did not know before arriving in the United States, where are the crime hot spots in U.S. cities. Like the overwhelming majority of their U.S. fellow citizens, they stay away from them. They buy houses in the suburbs or in small towns or upscale inner-city areas. Their places of work tend to be far removed from the hot spots. They are aware of crime and, if necessary, take precautions with their personal property, but these precautions seldom exceed what they would take were they living in Vancouver, Winnipeg, or Montreal. For them, the United States as "crime-ridden" and "dangerous" is a myth. Very few of them reported being deterred from or hesitant about emigrating because of crime, and none of those I interviewed had been the victim of a serious personal crime. The deterrent suggested by Prime Minister Chrétien did not exist for Star-Spangled Canadians, although who knows how many Canadians who ponder emigration are discouraged by the stereotype widely held in Canada about the rampant violence of U.S. society?

If U.S. crime rates are widely misunderstood in Canada, U.S. gun-control laws (or lack of them) are not. Every Canadian knows that Canadian gun-control laws are much tougher than their U.S. counterparts. If there is one issue on which Star-Spangled Canadians were unanimous, it was their reaction to the U.S. gun laws. Even the most right-wing Canadian ex-patriates—the ones most unhappy with the greater role for the state in Canada and higher tax rates—could not abide the U.S. policies towards guns. Those policies, however, do not accurately reflect attitudes of the broad U.S. public, which has consistently told pollsters that it would support tougher measures against owning guns. But U.S. gun-control policy has been thwarted by the powerful National Rifle Association (NRA) and its political allies. Gun control has also been frustrated by a skewered reading of the U.S. constitution that guarantees the "right to bear arms." That document was written in the context of a country without a standing army but in which citizens and elected officials understood that a threat to civil peace, or indeed some form of foreign incursion, could necessitate the summoning of a civilian militia. Citizens in an essentially rural country— as the United States was in the late eighteenth century—would be expected to have rifles or muskets at the ready for hunting or, if necessary, for responding to a call from the civil authorities. This constitutional clause, however, has become the rallying cry for those opposing gun-control laws, even if their interpretation of that clause is tortured to the point of absurdity.

American attitudes towards gun control, therefore, are much closer to the Canadian view than U.S. laws would suggest although guns are far more prevalent in the United States than Canada. And Canadians' attitudes towards gun possession are slightly more expansive than the country's laws would suggest, especially in rural areas, where political resistance to new federal gun-control laws in the 1990s under Conservative and Liberal governments was sustained. A majority of Americans and Canadians are actually closer together in how they view gun control than their countries' respective laws would suggest, although Canadians are somewhat more favourable to tough gun-control laws than are Americans. A thorough survey of American and Canadian attitudes towards gun control, based on analysis of public-opinion surveys throughout the 1980s, concluded that "nationwide surveys in both Canada and the United States show remarkable similarity in the public's attitudes towards firearms and gun control ... There is widespread support in both countries for 'moderate' gun-control legislation ... as well as the use of firearms for self-defence purposes under some conditions."[4]

The same observation can be made about the emotional issue of the death penalty. Canada abolished the death penalty by parliamentary votes; the U.S. Supreme Court authorized states to use the death penalty in 1977. The two countries' laws, however, differ more than the two populations' attitudes towards the death penalty.

Polls conducted between 1981 and 1995 — six U.S. polls and six Canadian — asked people on both sides of the border whether they favoured the death penalty. Support in the United States ranged from 66 per cent in 1981 to 80 per cent in 1994; in Canada, support for reinstating the death penalty ranged from 59 per cent in 1994 to 71 per cent in 1984. Americans, on balance, were only slightly more in favour of the death penalty over the period, although, by the mid-1990s, a gap of 18 per cent had emerged between the size of the American and Canadian majorities in favour, suggesting perhaps that Canadians had slowly resigned themselves to the death penalty's disappearance.[5]

General American and Canadian attitudes towards dealing with crime were remarkably similar. Asked by pollsters "Do you think the courts ... deal too harshly or not harshly enough with criminals?" solid majorities in both countries from 1972 to 1994 replied "not harshly enough." In Canada, support for "not harshly enough" ranged from 66 to 82 per cent; in the United States, from 74 to 88 per cent. In both countries, the "not harshly enough" majority was greater in the mid-1990s than in the early 1970s, suggesting a somewhat hardened attitude over time.

The United States, by statistical measurement, is a more violent society than the "peaceable kingdom" of Canada. A Canadian is more likely to be burglarized or lose a car to theft — far more common kinds of crime than murder or assault — but a Canadian is also less likely to be mugged or killed. If U.S. violent-crime rates are properly understood, however, the vast majority of Americans face only a slightly greater likelihood of being victims of violent crime than do most Canadians. And for Star-Spangled Canadians, the United States as described by Jean Chrétien is largely a country they do not recognize.

Maria, you have not the faintest idea! ... You simply cannot
imagine. Just to stroll through the big streets in the evening—not
on the little plank-walks like those of Roberval, but on the fine
broad asphalt pavements as level as a table—what with the lights,
the electric cars coming and going continually, the shops and the
crowds, you would find enough there to amaze you for weeks
together. And then all the amusements one has: theatres, circuses,
illustrated papers, and places everywhere that you can go for a
nickel, five cents, and pass two hours laughing and crying. To
think Maria, you do not even know what the moving pictures are!
... If you will marry me ... I will take you off to the country that
will open your eyes with astonishment—a fine country, unlike this,
where we can live in a decent way and be happy for the rest of our
days.—Lorenzo Suprenant, in Louis Hémon's Maria Chapdelaine

FRENCH CANADIANS

LORENZO Suprenant, having emigrated to Massachusetts, holds out the
American Dream to the woman of his dreams, Maria Chapdelaine.
Returning home, Lorenzo describes the paved streets and bright lights of
the United States, tempting Maria to leave the backwoods of Quebec.

"Lorenzo would come back from the States," Maria tells herself in
Louis Hémon's novel, "... and bear her away to the unknown delights of
the city—away from the great forest she hated—away from that cruel land
where men who go astray perish helplessly, where women endure endless
torment while ineffectual aid is sought for them over the long roads buried
in snow. Why should she stay here to toil and suffer when she might
escape to the lands of the south and a happier life?"

Maria had almost persuaded herself to "escape" when "a third Voice,
mightier than the other, lifted itself up in the silence: the Voice of Quebec—now the song of a woman, now the exhortation of a priest. It came
to her with the sound of a church bell, with the majesty of an organ's
tones, like a plaintive love song, like the long high call of the woodsman
in the forest. For verily there was in it all that makes the soul of the
Province: the loved solemnities of the ancestral faith, the lift of that old
speech guarded with jealous care, the grandeur and barbaric strength of

this new land where an ancient race has again found its youth."
In Louis Hémon's overwrought prose, the Voice speaks:

> Three hundred years ago we came, and we have remained. They who
> led us hither might return among us without knowing shame or sorrow,
> for if it be true that we have little learned, most surely nothing is for-
> gotten. We bore overseas our prayers and our songs: they are ever the
> same. We carried in our bosoms the hearts of the men of our father-
> land, brave and merry, easily moved to pity as to laughter, of all human
> hearts the most human, nor have they changed. We traced the bound-
> aries of a new continent [and] within these limits all we brought with
> us — our faith, out tongue, our virtues, our very weaknesses — are hence-
> forth hallowed things which no hand may touch, and which shall
> endure to the end … We have held fast, so that it may be, many cen-
> turies hence the world will look upon us and say: These people are of
> a race that know not how to perish. We are a testimony.

Maria Chapdelaine awakens from her dream, the Voice ringing in her
ears, and declares, "So I shall stay — shall stay here after all."

Maria Chapdelaine became a fictionalized heroine for French-Canadian
nationalists and the Catholic Church because she resisted the siren songs
of the United States. Hémon's novel, first published in book form in
Canada in 1916, with its cloying phrases and profound ethnocentrism,
slightly embarrasses today's Québécois nationalist élites, who fancy themselves cosmopolitan, some having been educated at the best U.S. universities. But *Maria Chapdelaine* was published and widely admired while
hundreds of thousands of French-speaking Quebeckers were turning their
backs on the Voice and following Lorenzo Suprenant's path to the mill
towns of New England and the prairie settlements of the Upper Midwest.
The French-Canadian émigrés tried at least as hard as, if not harder
than, other immigrant groups to the United States to keep alive their language and faith in the English-speaking and largely Protestant world they
entered. They built Catholic churches and imported Quebec priests.
They constructed homes in typical rural Quebec styles. They instructed
their children in French at home, insisted that French be the language of
instruction at school, formed communal groups such as St-Jean-Baptiste
societies, organized festivals celebrating their heritage. For two, sometimes three, and in a handful of cases for four generations, they kept
French alive in pockets of the United States, until the irresistible tides of

the English-speaking American sea sucked the life from the French language's presence in the United States, leaving only vestigial reminders of
what had once been a vast and proud migration.

All gone now are the clusters and communities of French-speaking
Canadians that dotted parts of the northern United States for a hundred
years, from the middle of the nineteenth century to the middle of the
twentieth. When French Canadians emigrate today, they lack institutions,
networks, and a critical mass of other French speakers that might enable
them to keep their language alive. Instead, they arrive as individuals or
with their immediate families in a country indifferent to French. The
speedy disappearance of their tongue is therefore inevitable.

For some francophone émigrés, the crumbling of French has already
occurred; for others, it's just a matter of time. Their French linguistic heritage will disappear, if not in this generation, then quite likely in the next.
The sense of incipient loss, the linguistic and cultural price paid by French-
speaking Canadians for pursuing the American Dream, is deeply regretted
by some, unlamented by others. The fact remains that all languages but
English face the same fate in the United States. The one exception today is
Spanish, whose speakers are spread throughout the southern tier of the
United States. (Pockets of Spanish speakers do exist in more northerly cities,
such as New York, Chicago, and Denver.) But as one generation elides into
another, the force of Spanish will likely yield to English, as has occurred
with French and all other languages of Europe and Asia. Demographic pro-
jections suggest that the Hispanic population of the United States will grow
from 9 per cent in the 1990 census to 23 per cent in 2050. Perhaps that
growth will give Spanish sufficient demographic weight in selected areas of
the country to enable it to be passed on generation after generation.

"I am losing my French more and more every day. It's very easy to lose
it, because you don't practise it, especially in Texas," said Michèle
Donato, a beautiful, brilliant, thirty-something cancer specialist raised and
educated in Montreal and now working at the M.D. Anderson Cancer
Center in Houston.

"When I call home, my mom is bilingual so we use a mixture of French
and English, but I am starting an effort this year not to lose it, so I've
bought some French books."

Reading French books, that's one way of retaining French. Michèle
Lamont, a sociology professor at Princeton University, adopted another
preventive strategy: "You have to work at keeping French … so we hired a
baby sitter from Ivory Coast who will only speak French to my daughter."

Louise Masse, assistant professor of behavioural science at the University of Texas department of public health in Houston, is married to an English-speaking Canadian with limited French. She worries about keeping French alive for her and any children she may have. "I don't know how," she said. "This is becoming more of a concern. I keep thinking that I need to read more books in French … I miss sometimes the way things are said in French … I wonder what would happen if I had kids, because I'd be the only one speaking to them in French …"

Older francophones, or those who have spent decades in the United States, find their own French sometimes failing. The chances that their children will speak the language are small; their grandchildren, next to nil.

"I don't miss it [French] at all," said Daniel Langelier, vice-president of AmSouth Bank in Tampa, who still speaks English with a mild French accent. "There are certain areas of conversation where I feel a lot more comfortable in English than in French. Even with some of my friends when I go back up there [Montreal], if we're talking about a subject like business or law, we'll switch to English."

Raymond and Carmel Ayotte, interviewed at a party to which other francophones had been invited in Minneapolis, can trace the decline in their French linguistic abilities since moving in 1965 from Winnipeg to Boston, their first U.S. destination. "I had a lot of difficulty at first," recalled Carmel. "I would tend to think in French and speak in French. For the first year or two, I was stuttering because my brain was working faster than my mouth, but it's almost the opposite now, because I feel more comfortable speaking in English." Added her husband, Raymond: "My English is better than my French, although I find that when I'm in a setting with French Canadians and am forced to speak French, I find that I pick it up rather quickly. I do think more in English than before, and I do have to think through how to speak French more than before."

The Ayottes are sorry that their children do not speak French, and probably never will. Carmel added: "They now regret it and chastise us for not having been forceful about making them speak French."

At the same gathering where I met the Ayottes, a more recent French-Canadian arrival was in the early stages of confronting the challenge of keeping the language alive. Marie Nolin-Nichols from Rimouski met her American husband standing in front of a train station in Paris. She had learned some English in Rimouski, "but when I met him my English was so poor. Even now, people sometimes don't know about my accent. Like last weekend, we went to Iowa, which is in the middle of nowhere, and in the mall, when the lady heard my accent, she was totally shocked that I was white." She tries to speak French to her children every day, but there are no French-language schools in Minneapolis–St. Paul. Marie did join the French-Canadian Society, a group in the Twin Cities whose members trace their heritage to the French fact in Canada, but she said only about a quarter of the members can speak French, "and they're the older ones, the ones over eighty."

Dr. Marc Caron, James B. Duke professor of cell biology at Duke University and the recipient of a prestigious Howard Hughes medical research fellowship, left Quebec for good in 1977. He sometimes works with French researchers, or even French-Canadian ones. He's been asked many times to lecture in Europe. These contacts have helped him maintain his French, but the family's linguistic abilities are something else. "The oldest kid is perfectly bilingual; the second is a little less so; the third one doesn't want to speak French," he said. "All of them have left home: one to postdoctoral work at Chapel Hill, one is a graduate student in South Carolina, my other son is at North Carolina State. Probably their kids, if they have kids, will speak some French because we, as grandparents, have tried to get them to speak French. But that's probably going to stop there."

John Côté, born in Quebec City and bilingual, speaks French at home with his wife and four children. He noted, however, how quickly his young children picked up English. "With the daughters it's a challenge because French in Stamford, Connecticut, isn't cool. They speak English. Our kids in kindergarten spoke no English, but within a month, they were doing fine."

Dr. Michel Gagner, a specialist in minimally invasive surgery (laparoscopy) at Mount Sinai Hospital in New York City, appreciates his family's likely linguistic fate. "We speak French at home. Many people speak French in New York. There's a French community in New York," he said. "I travel frequently in Europe, where I operate in France, Switzerland, and Belgium. We also do telemedicine in French in these countries. But I'm concerned about my children, because they do not get exposed outside the house to French. Progressively, especially the youngest has lost the ability to have really good writing in French. He can still read … It will be impossible to survive after one generation."

French Canadians, then, face a more acute identity challenge when they become Star-Spangled Canadians than do English-speaking Canadians. Unless French speakers converse in unaccented English, as Côté does, they cannot easily take the option available to English-speaking Canadians of being "hidden immigrants" in the United States. English-speaking Canadians confront identity choices, if only in their own psyches, by living in the United States, and they sometimes experience a sense of loss for elements of Canada left behind. But French Canadians confront a dual challenge of identity in the United States. They not only watch the dilution of their Canadian (or Québécois) identity, but must also acknowledge, if they are honest with themselves, the eventual but certain disappearance of their language and the cultural traditions that flow from it.

French Canadians carved their heritage on the topography of the United States. Although by far the largest concentrations of emigrating French Canadians have clustered in New England and, to a lesser extent, the Upper Midwest, French Canadians have explored and wandered far afield in the United States, leaving their language imprinted on the map of the western part of the country: Nez Perce National Historical Park, Washington; Fort Défiance and Bouse, Arizona; Des Moines and Ledoux, New Mexico; Bruneau Dunes and Malheur Lake, Oregon; Grand Teton and the Coeur d'Alene mountains in Montana; Belle Fourche, North Dakota; the Purgatoire River, Colorado; Poteau, Oklahoma; Pomme de Terre Lake, the Bon Beurre River, and the Qui Court River, Missouri — to name a few.

The novelist Roch Carrier puts in the mouth of one of his characters in *The Lament of Charlie Longsong* words that reflect on some of the French Canadians who wandered across the United States.

"A man named Ruelle discovered the gold in Sutter Mills that set off the rush to California by hundreds of thousands of adventurers," Carrier writes. "In Santa Fe, New Mexico, the first traders were French Canadians like Henri Mercure, a native of Quebec City."

French Canadians fought the Mexicans to consolidate the United States' domination of California. A wealthy French Canadian named Ménard built himself a castle in Galveston, Texas. Chabot, who'd attended school in his Quebec City village for only a brief time, became a millionaire when he invented hydraulic systems. It was also he who installed the first system to supply water to San Francisco.

Aubry set up the first commercial network between California and New Mexico. Born in Maskinongé, Quebec, he died in 1854, at the age of thirty, killed by a man with whom he'd had a heated argument about the most appropriate place to lay out the future railway that would go to Santa Fe.

Another French Canadian, named Nadeau, transported silver and lead to Arizona, Nevada and California; he owned a hundred mules and a hundred wagons with high wheels circled in steel. Would a Utah town have been named Provo if a trapper named Provost, another French Canadian, hadn't been the first to set his traps in that spot?"[1]

The transformation of "Provost" to "Provo" is but one example of the anglicization of French names. Sometimes the spelling changes; more frequently, the pronunciation.

A suburb of St. Paul, Minnesota, for example, is still today called Little Canada. The town's emblem, painted on the water tower and printed on the street signs, shows a fleur-de-lis inside a maple leaf. The first weekend of August, a modest parade winds through the streets, with people dressed in settlers' clothes, reflecting the town's French heritage.

Little Canada was founded by a group of French Canadians from the Gaspé peninsula who moved west to the Red River valley in 1812, then followed the river south to what is today St. Paul. In 1827, a group of 139 families settled beside a small lake named for the group's leader, Benjamin Gervais, who died in 1876. It is still named Gervais Lake, but the locals all pronounce the name "Jarvis." The same goes for the nearby Vadnais Heights, named after another original settler; in American mouths, the word is pronounced, not "Vadnay" but "Vadness."

At St. John's cemetery in Little Canada, a memorial has been erected to those 139 original families. A stroll through the cemetery produces a roll-call of the departed francophone settlers: LaDouceur, Nadeau, Goiffon, Demers, Bibeau, Dufresne, Ducharme, Morrisette, Vincent, Lambert. Services in St. John's Catholic Church, founded in 1857, were conducted in French until 1924.

Little Canada was but one of several dozen French-Canadian communities that in the mid- to late-nineteenth century were spread across northern and central Minnesota, often along the river valleys. Most were agricultural settlements; a few arose from the groups of lumbermen who worked the woods in north Minnesota. At the beginning of the twentieth century, Minnesota ranked second to Michigan among states outside New England and New York with the largest number of French-Canadian residents. One estimate places their number in Minnesota at almost 11,000 in 1900. Smaller clusters developed in north Illinois, where some small towns south of Chicago still bear French names, such as Bourbonnais, St. Anne, Papineau, and L'Erable.

The topographical memories of the French-Canadian diaspora, the anglicization of French names, and the Americanization of French pronunciation were replicated in the fate of dozens of other languages that splashed across the United States. French Canadians, often with consider-able resolution, sought vainly to keep their language alive. A few, however, not only gave up the struggle, but actively sought to make their French background disappear.

In Billings, Montana, stands a school—Will James High School—that to all but the supremely aware was probably named for an American settler or person of note. In fact, Will James was born Ernest Dufault, a man who spent his entire adult life hiding his French-Canadian heritage. He became in the 1920s and 1930s one of the best-loved American writers of cowboy books. Several of them were made into Hollywood movies, the most famous of which was *Smoky*. Ernest Dufault, alias Will James, is the man about whom the Canadian songwriter and singer Ian Tyson crooned that "whisky was his mistress, his true love was the West."

Indeed, James (or Dufault) always told people he had been born in Montana, whereas he was actually born in Montreal. As a kid, James was fascinated by cowboys, and at the age of fifteen he left Montreal with a sack of clothes, a bag of biscuits, and not a word of English. He went first to the Cypress Hills in the Canadian West, where he worked on ranches and sketched. He sent drawings to magazines, which usually rejected them, until he took a bunch of them to San Francisco, where they were accepted for publication. From there, James moved to Hollywood, where he worked as a stunt man. He worked on ranches, too, and even spent fourteen months in prison for cattle-rustling in Carson City, Nevada.

James's novels—he wrote twenty of them in the 1920s and 1930s—began to find a wide and appreciative audience, with their depictions of cowboy life in the U.S. West. Some of the early novels sprang not from the author's personal experience, but from a fertile imagination. When Hollywood producers bought several of them and turned them into movies, James became a kind of cowboy-celebrity, for, by this time, in the 1920s, he had married a former Miss Nevada; bought an 8,000-acre ranch in Montana, forty miles from Billings; and begun ranching himself. He was widely feted in the movie business. Hollywood celebrities visited him in Montana. Never, ever did he reveal his true past. He wrote letters to family members in Quebec, in increasingly fractured French, imploring them not to reveal his true identity. "If what you know got into the right hands, it would be in the papers," he wrote in one letter, "and I'd be described as an imposter, and after that I'd just as well go and bury myself."

James did indeed bury himself, in a manner of speaking. He began drinking heavily and his marriage fell apart. He would disappear for days on a binge. He slipped back to Canada secretly once to see his family, but he had by then largely forgotten his French. He did quietly send royalty cheques to help his family in Quebec, but he never told anyone about his past. He died on September 3, 1942, of cirrhosis of the liver in Los Angeles, Will James in name and reputation. Everything in his will, however, was left to the estate of Ernest Dufault, a French Canadian who hid his heritage until after the grave, although the students and teachers at Will James High School in Billings probably do not know that.[2]

Native French speakers not only must confront the weakening and eventual disappearance of their language, but also need to master English to survive, let alone thrive, in the United States—a fact that deters the vast majority of French-speaking Quebeckers from even thinking of leaving. The act of uprooting from one country to another is challenging enough; the act for French speakers is all the more daunting. That is one reason why the number of francophones who emigrate is small compared with that of departing English-speaking Canadians, although for the well-educated French Canadian in a field of study where English is absolutely necessary, such as medicine or science, the transition to an English-speaking environment is not difficult.

Quebec's economy is also immeasurably more diversified than in Maria Chapdelaine's day. The majority of today's francophone Quebeckers no longer live in some of the world's largest families on farms whose land cannot be subdivided again. Yesteryear's francophone émigrés who left by the hundreds of thousands because of a lack of land at home have now been replaced by the trickle who depart to partake of the American Dream of better economic opportunities and to work at the cutting edge of their fields. (No pun intended, but there are French-Canadian cutters who arrive in New York City around December 1 each year with Christmas trees from Canadian forests. The trees are sold on streets throughout the city for about three weeks, during which time the French Canadians who sell them sleep in vans beside the clusters of trees.)

They leave today, however, for the same reasons of economics and opportunities, but with a twist. The twist for some is the political situation in Quebec, which has become an irritant they could easily do without. Quebeckers, after all, must live daily with the incessant, infernal debate about Quebec's role in Canada, including two referenda thus far, interminable federal–provincial quarrels, stage-managed events, hyperventilating politicians, flag-waving nationalism, constitutional psychodramas, stilted politics, obsessed media, and stale public discourse.

A Quebecker fed up with the debate, and who thinks two No referendum votes ought to have put the issue of Quebec secession to bed, is likely to be a federalist. Not surprisingly, so are most of French-speaking Quebec's ex-patriate community I encountered. They have seen Quebec from afar and understand how insignificant an independent Quebec would be on the North American, let alone world, stage. They feel varying attachments to their native province, but they have broken free of the cloistered politics and parochial pride of their small corner of North America.

"When we left Quebec in 1969, this was a hot subject. We returned in 1975 and it was still the hot subject," Dr. Caron at Duke University said. "We go back once in a while now and it's still the same damn thing. And the economy is going down, down.

"I say stop it. I get very impatient. A lot of this is born out of a sense of inferiority. I don't feel inferior. In fact, I can run circles around many people. The politics, I find extremely fatiguing. The same damn thing for thirty years, and they're going nowhere. It's stagnant. They want to separate but they really don't want to separate. To me, Canada is fine the way it is."

Daniel Langelier, the Florida banker, agrees: "I didn't like the political climate in Canada. I didn't like it at all … The entire country, including Quebec. The bickering among provinces. The bickering between the provinces and the federal government. Constitutional questions. Everything that was related to politics had an adverse impact on the economy."

Michèle Donato, the oncologist, doesn't miss the constitutional battles and linguistic squabbles: "I notice when I go back home and I turn on the news. It drives me crazy."

John Côté emigrated for economic reasons, but politics did its part. "It's not a factor that pushed me out, but it certainly made my decision a lot easier when it was time to go," he explained. "The nonsense behind the Parti Québécois. A lot of them cling to this idea of independence because it's ideological. They haven't thought out how it's going to work."

Catherine Côté, twenty-five, worked for five years at Canadair in Montreal but sought larger challenges in aircraft design. So she applied and got a job at Boeing's main operations site in the state of Washington to learn more, experience a new environment, and improve her English.

"I know who I am now. I am a mix of Europe, Canada, and the United States, but we call that Québécoise," she said. "I am a mix of all those people. I feel European when I need my café and my newspaper and my croissant. Then I feel American when I need that rock music in English. I feel Canadian when I say I saw all those provinces and when they say down here it's peaceful up there. It's not violent like here." Speaking English with a pronounced French accent means the inevitable question from Americans about Catherine's background. "I'm single, but I need to belong to something," she explains. "I know I belong to my mom and dad. I know that Montreal will be the city that I have in my heart. But I have to answer: 'Where are you from?' They know I'm foreign. I'm an alien. I could say 'I'm from Quebec,' and they'd say 'Hmm? Quebec?' Or I could say 'I'm French Canadian,' and they'd say 'Oh, Canadian. It's that big thing up there with the red and white flag.' So I'm from that big thing in the north."

Louis-Phillippe Papin, twenty-nine, in whose Everett, Washington, townhouse our conversation unfolded, says he tries not to think of the national-unity debate. "I'm a very strong federalist ... I wear the flag on my jacket ... well, because I'm proud of Canada, more than I was before. I had to come here to realize that. Why? We're so different. We are different from Americans, their way of thinking, their mentality."

Papin, from Montreal and employed by Boeing, shares the townhouse with two English-speaking Canadians, from Thunder Bay and Winnipeg. He observes: "I don't know if it's because of the language, but most English Canadians don't like Americans. I don't know where it comes from."

Louis-Phillippe Papin and Catherine Côté may be francophones, but Boeing did not care. The company was looking for talented people, regardless of nationality. Like other American multinationals, Boeing scours the globe for talent, and in Canada, where the company hires recruiting agencies to help attract Canadians, it finds engineers, draftsmen, designers, managers. Both Louis-Phillippe and Catherine had studied at Montreal's l'École des Hautes Études Aéronautiques, then worked at Canadair—he in Toronto, she in Montreal.

"I said to myself it would be nice to work for the best company in the world," Louis-Phillippe says. "Boeing is number one. I knew they were hiring big time. The recruiters came twice for interviews. I was there for the first interviews. They made me an offer."

For Catherine, Boeing was her American Dream. "I said in the interview: 'You're Boeing. You're building a 747. It's my childhood dream.' How could I refuse to go there ... Everybody has a passion. I love airplanes. When I was a little kid ... each time I saw a plane I looked up." Money helps, too. Catherine estimates that, after taxes, she keeps twice as much as of her income as she did in Canada.

Marc Caron left Quebec in 1969 after studying at Laval University. He intended to return after graduate studies in Florida and a postdoctoral fellowship at Duke. His years in Miami were financed by Quebec government grants; his stay at Duke, by the Medical Research Council and the Quebec government. "In my mind, I was subconsciously, and for reasons of loyalty, saying that I owed it to my country to go back. And I did go back. I got a job at Laval," he said.

What he found proved a rude shock. He was earning less as an assistant professor at Laval than he had as a postdoctoral fellow at Duke. There were strikes throughout the public sector, including a four-month one at Laval. After about eighteen months, the political situation in Quebec and the low pay with little chance for speedy increments left Caron receptive to a call from a friend at Duke.

"The time I left in 1977, I knew that, if I really wanted to be successful, it's extremely hard in the Canadian system. They dole out grants a little bit at a time. They make you write grant applications constantly, so I had the thought in the back of my mind that we weren't going back, at least not for a long time."

Dr. Caron has become one of the elite medical researchers in the United States. He holds a chair in cell biology at Duke. He is one of 350 Howard Hughes investigators in the country, receiving about $800,000–$900,000 yearly for his research from the foundation. Additional money from the National Institutes of Health brings his total research budget to about $1.5 million.

"We've never looked back," he said. "We've had the chance of returning to Canada. I don't have enough fingers on my hands to count how many times." He was offered a university chair at McGill and the Université de Montréal. "it became obvious, however, that they didn't have the goods to attract me. The goods are the resources for research and simple salary." Leaving the research monies aside, the salary he might have received in Canada to match the one at Duke "was more than the [university's] rector was making."

Dr. Caron stands on the cutting edge of his field. So does Michèle Donato of the M.D. Anderson Cancer Center in Houston, a massive complex of five buildings exclusively dedicated to cancer treatment and research. She left Canada to push back the boundaries of science in her field of bone-marrow transplantation. She could have been a general oncologist doing occasional transplants in Montreal, but her dream, which she followed to the United States, was to specialize in transplants. There were neither the money nor the opportunities for such specialization in Canada. The risks to her French and the distance from family and friends could not prevent her pursuit of that dream in faraway Houston.

Michèle Lamont, a native of Hull, did her first degree at the University of Ottawa, then a graduate degree in Paris. She wrote to the celebrated sociologist Seymour Martin Lipset, a professor at Stanford University with a lifelong interest in Canada. He invited her for a postdoctoral fellowship.

Professor Lamont had job offers from the University of Ottawa but found the French-speaking world of university political science in Canada cloistered and insular. "I looked at the length of the job ladder and saw that I would quickly be tucked into a department. You're a prisoner of your colleagues and I did not welcome that possibility." She even found some resentment at her international academic pedigree. "It's like you're viewed as having done well in the bigger pond and we're not sure we want you back." Instead, she went to the University of Texas at Austin, then to Princeton, where in 1995 she received tenure, an impressive achievement won by only one young professor out of five or six at Princeton.

A better salary lured Raymond Ayotte, who emigrated in 1965. "We came to the U.S. for better job opportunities. I was in the insurance business in Winnipeg, and my future was limited. I had decided a year or two before to look for opportunities in the U.S. and found a company in Boston that was willing to hire me. The pay scales were simply higher, even at the time. The job I took in Boston was at $6,000 a year and that was fully $1,500 more a year than I was making at the time."

A higher salary and lower taxes also persuaded Daniel Langelier to continue his banking career in Florida. "I don't think taxes were a criteria when I made the decision. They became one afterwards. I remember the first year I moved down here. The year before, I remember having paid more in taxes to the Canadian and Quebec government than I made the first year I was down here."

Paul E. Papineau is five generations removed from his famous ancestor, Louis-Joseph Papineau, leader of the Lower Canadian Rebellion of 1837, the seigneur of Montebello, and inspiration for French-Canadian nationalists of every stripe. Louis-Joseph Papineau left Lower Canada after the rebellion to exile himself briefly in the United States, but some of the Papineaus emigrated permanently, and Paul is descended from them.

Retired from a career in teaching, mostly at U.S. military bases in Europe, Paul E. Papineau can still speak some French, which he displayed while escorting me around Woonsocket, Rhode Island, a city that in 1900 was called "la ville la plus française aux États-Unis" ("the most French city in the United States").

A "Bienvenue à Woonsocket" sign greets visitors to this once-thriving but now down-at-the-heel city twenty miles north of Providence, on the

Blackstone River. The first water-powered textile mill in the United States was built on the banks of the Blackstone at the turn of the nineteenth century, the first of more than 200 established along the river from Providence to Worcester, Massachusetts. The Blackstone River valley thus appropriates the description "birthplace of the American Industrial Revolution."

As the mills proliferated, so did the demand for cheap labour. The Irish came, as did smatterings of immigrants from southern Europe. But these arrivals were dwarfed, in Woonsocket and in dozens of other New England towns, by the exodus of French Canadians from the St. Lawrence River valley. Today, Canada sends some of its best brains to the United States; a century ago, it exported labourers to places such as the Blackstone Valley. Brains today, brawn yesterday — or, if you like, from the Blackstone Valley to Silicon Valley.

Nineteenth-century immigration data reflect a combination of hard numbers and guesswork. The best scholarly work suggests about 900,000 French Canadians — mostly Quebeckers, but also some Acadians — arrived in New England between 1840 and 1940.[3] A steady but small stream of French-Canadian émigrés preceded the first large wave in the 1840s. Lord Durham, in his infamous (or famous) report of 1839 about the causes of the rebellion in the Canadas, noted: "From the French portion of Lower Canada there has, for a long time, been a large annual emigration of young men to the northern states of the American Union, in which they are highly valued as laborers and gain good wages … from which they generally return to their homes in a few months or years."

French Canadians did indeed go back. Some became discouraged and disoriented in an English-speaking and Protestant land. Others worked long enough, sometimes for decades, before retiring in Quebec. Church and civic associations in Quebec, alarmed at such a mass migration, sent representatives throughout New England urging the Catholic, French-speaking faithful to stop chasing the American Dream. No reliable estimate exists, however, of how many did go home.

The French Canadians' pursuit of the American Dream, at least in the early decades of the mass migrations, was somewhat different from that of other immigrant groups. All immigrant groups try to re-create, whole or in part, some portion of the previously familiar. French Canadians were particularly determined to do just that since their homeland was nearby, unlike Poland for the immigrant Poles, or Scandinavia for the immigrants from those countries. French Canadians believed, naïvely, in retrospect, that they could re-create their society south of the border under the enveloping authority of the Catholic Church and a parochial French-only school system. They could live as French speakers and practitioners of the Catholic faith in the United States, with their own civic institutions, news-papers, festivals, and knitted communities of kin and friends, establishing a new outpost for the enduring struggle for *la survivance* of *la langue et la foi* in North America.

In Woonsocket, as Paul Papineau showed me, French-Canadian immigrants built huge stone churches with gothic spires, transplanting the architecture of rural Quebec to industrializing New England.[4] They constructed triple-decker flats, with large porches not unlike those of east-end Montreal or rural Quebec towns. They sent their children to parochial schools run by Catholic priests. The church, in Woonsocket as in Quebec, was the community's cultural anchor and a bulwark against the forces of anglicization and Protestantism. A few French Canadians moved out from the textile mills and established businesses catering especially to immigrants: A. Sylvestre and Sons shoe repair, Alphonse AuClair painters, A.J. Valois electrical supplies, Milot Broth-ers lumber, A. Bourgault movers. In time, a handful took to politics. Adam Pothier, who had emigrated at the age of sixteen, became Rhode Island's first Franco-American governor.

In the late 1990s, Woonsocket's mayor was Susan D. Menard; one of the town high school's hockey players, Brian Berard, had made it to the National Hockey League as the number-one draft selection. These all stood on the shoulders, however, of the first French Canadian from Woonsocket to make a national mark: Napoleon Lajoie.

Lajoie was working as a teamster in Woonsocket and playing baseball for two local teams when the Philadelphia Phillies discovered him. He starred for twenty-one seasons in the big leagues, from 1896 to 1916, amass-ing a .380 lifetime batting average and winning three Triple Crown bat-ting championships. Lajoie, needless to say, made it to the Hall of Fame. He also swelled plenty of French-Canadian chests in Woonsocket and throughout New England.

The trickle of migrating French Canadians noted by Lord Durham accelerated slightly after the rebellion of 1837 but began growing in the 1850s. Almost 91,000 Quebeckers emigrated in the 1870s; 147,000 in the 1880s; 121,000 in the 1890s; 46,000 from 1900 to 1910; 128,000 from 1910 to 1920; 158,000 in the 1920s. At its height, during the decade of the 1880s, the migration represented 11 per cent of Quebec's population; in the 1890s, 8 per cent; from 1910 to 1930, about 6 per cent.[5]

Such staggering population losses produced a mixture of consternation and resignation in Canada. In 1849, the legislative assembly of Lower

Canada commissioned a study that examined the departures from the dioceses of Quebec City and Montreal. Another legislative committee examined the problem in 1857. Yet another committee reported in 1893.

Repatriation committees targeted concentrations of French Canadians in New England, exhorting émigrés to return home. The Catholic clergy warned from their pulpits about the perils of leaving, speaking of rampant individualism in the United States, hostility to French and Catholicism, and the family-shredding perils of industrialization for a rural people. George-Étienne Cartier, one of the Fathers of Confederation, took a more jaundiced view. He is alleged to have said: "Laissez-les partir; c'est la canaille qui s'en va" ("Let them depart; it's the rabble who are leaving"). A few prelates dissented from the prevailing warnings. The first bishop of Burlington, Vermont, where hundreds of French Canadians worked in the textile mills along the Winooski River, thought the exodus reflected God's intentions to convert New England.[6]

Overwhelmingly, however, a sense of loss pervaded debates about the out-migration from Quebec, a natural reaction for a people already a minority within Canada. That so many francophones departed lessened the French fact in national affairs, or so it was viewed in Quebec's political and clerical circles. That English-speaking Canadians were also heading south *en masse* did not ease the sense of loss in Quebec.

The loss became a theme in nineteenth-century French-Canadian literature.[7] Essays, novels, poems, and plays all portrayed emigration negatively, with fictionalized characters experiencing hardships in the United States. Some novels, poems, and plays ended with characters giving up the false gods of the American Dream and returning to find contentment in Quebec. A few titles illustrate the preoccupation with exodus and exile: *La Voix d'un exilé*, *Le Retour de l'exilé*, *Exil et patrie*, the last a five-act play about a Quebec family that emigrates to Boston and suffers one disaster after another until, having lost everything, it returns to Quebec, settles in a newly "colonized" part of the province, and lives happily ever after. An important poem, "Colonization" by the celebrated Octave Crémazie, praised settlers in newly opened parts of Quebec and urged readers to "garder au pays le jeune Canadien" ("keep young Canadians in this country").

The French-Canadian exodus arose from the classical push–pull dynamics of mass migration that no amount of political exhortation, literary writing, or colonization could halt. New England in the nineteenth century had become the centre of U.S. textile manufacturing, the mills having sprung up along the region's many rivers and streams. The industry, despite wondrous advances in machinery, needed labour and lots of it, preferably cheap and not necessarily trained.

North of the border, French Quebec was exhausting its available farmland. French-Canadian families were large—"la revanche du berceau" ("the revenge of the cradle")—with eight, ten, twelve, or even fourteen children not unusual. Endless subdividing of land could not continue indefinitely to provide sufficient farming opportunities unless vast new acreages could be found. One answer to the exodus consisted of opening up areas of farming north of the St. Lawrence River in "colonization" drives supported by church and state. Marie Chapdelaine's fictional family near Lac St-Jean in the Saguenay River basin typified these pioneers, whose real-life equivalents were heralded as saviours of the Catholic faith and French language. But the sheer arithmetic of too many people on too little land, combined with periodic slumps in agricultural prices, sent thousands of French Canadians to places farther west in Canada, and tens of thousands of them south.[8]

The cultural wrench for departing French Canadians was necessarily painful, although most emigrated to existing French-Canadian communities in the United States, where they often found people from their former villages. Equally challenging was the switch from farm labour to industrial work. Having little or no money to buy land, the French-Canadian *habitants* could not work at what they knew best, farming, but accepted jobs in the textile mills or shoe-making factories, where the hours were long, the noise horrific, and the pay lousy. Half of Maine's textile workers at the turn of the century were French Canadians.[9]

Nearly four out of five French Canadians wound up in cities or towns, clustered in neighbourhoods nicknamed "p'tits Canadas," "Frenchville," and so on. Always strongly influenced by the Catholic Church, which viewed unions with distaste, the French Canadians were initially sceptical about the unionization drives that started in such places as Woonsocket. Union representatives organized workers to fight against poor working conditions and wages, and later to the movement of jobs from New England to the U.S. South, where companies paid even lower wages and governments were implacably hostile to unions. French Canadians eventually joined the union movement but only after the church signalled its acquiesence.[10]

The vast majority of French-Canadian immigrants were poorly educated in a formal sense, and their offspring invariably remained so. Sociologists found French Canadians, even after three or four generations in the United States, to be the poorest and least-educated group in New

England. A notable exception in French-Canadian education was L'Assomption College near Worcester, Massachusetts, which after 1904 offered an eight-year high-school and college program for elite students.

By 1920 more than 30,000 Franco-Americans—as they had become by then—resided in Woonsocket, representing 70 per cent of the city's population. Fall River, Massachusetts, and Manchester, New Hampshire, each had 30,000 to 40,000 Franco-American residents. New Bedford, Lowell, and Worcester, Massachusetts, and Lewiston, Maine, had 20,000 to 30,000. Many other places had between 10,000 and 20,000, including Fitchburg, Haverhill, and Lawrence, Massachusetts; Pawtucket and Central Falls, Rhode Island; and Nashua, New Hampshire.

Some of the descendents of the migration achieved considerable prominence in American life. Will Durant, the son of an immigrant mill operator, co-authored the massive *Story of Civilization*, a staple of Book-of-the-Month Club lists for decades. Leo Durocher, "Leo the Lip," became one of baseball's most colourful and successful managers. Rudy Vallee, christened Hubert Prior Vallee, was one of the best-known singers and orchestra leaders in the United States. John Garand, whose family emigrated from St-Rémi, Quebec, invented the rifle named after him which was used by the U.S. army in both world wars.

Jean-Louis, or Ti-Jean, Kérouac, better known as Jack Kerouac, became a cult figure as a writer for the Beat generation. He remained proud of his French-Canadian origins and snatches of French dot his work. Grace (de Repentigny) Metalious, raised in a Franco-American milieu in Manchester, New Hampshire, achieved notoriety and fame as the author of *Peyton Place*, the 1956 novel that shocked the country with steamy descriptions of sex in small-town America. *Peyton Place* shocked not only the United States; Canada Customs banned its entry into Canada under a prohibition against material "of an indecent or immoral character."[11]

Paul Papineau took me to a church basement in Woonsocket where perhaps a dozen people sat hunched over what, at first glance, seemed oddly huge books. They were registries for every Quebec parish dating back several centuries, the birth and deaths meticulously recorded by local church authorities. Any American of Quebec heritage could trace his or her family's lineage by coming here, to the headquarters of l'Union Saint-Jean-Baptiste d'Amérique, named, of course, after the patron saint of French-Canadian believers. The society boasted dozens of branches throughout New England in its heyday and established its headquarters in Woonsocket in 1920.

A handful of Woonsocket's older Franco-American residents, I was told, could still converse in French, although not many do any more. Down here, in the church basement, with the flags of Canada, Quebec, L'Union Saint-Jean-Baptiste d'Amérique, and the United States on the wall, older Franco-Americans drop by to chat, sometimes in French. But the younger generation has just about lost all contact with French, except as a subject taught in school.

Woonsocket's Catholic churches, some now used by other denominations, are still standing, as are a few of the three-storey tenements. A swath of them disappeared in an urban-renewal project a decade or so ago. Street names also speak to Woonsocket's French heritage. An excellent local museum pays homage to Franco-Americans of the Blackstone River valley and the labour movement. The buildings, the names, the museums—they all remind residents and visitors of what was once "la plus grande ville française en Amérique" that eventually yielded, however grudgingly but necessarily, to the assimilating pressures of the American Dream.

Rearguard actions were taken periodically against those pressures. In 1922, the Rhode Island legislature and Governor Sam Souci, a French-Canadian Catholic, passed a law requiring that all basic subjects in private (parochial) schools be taught in English. The law produced a predictable outcry in Woonsocket, where three out of four French-Canadian children were taught in French. A French-language newspaper, *La Sentinelle*, took up the cause to protect French instruction, and all those—clerics, teachers, parents—who opposed the law became known as "Sentinellistes." Their struggle gained support from other Franco-American communities.

The early 1920s, however, featured widespread nativist feelings in the United States, where prominent leaders and citizens worried about, or felt threatened by, the huge waves of immigration that had poured into the country before the First World War and continued after the peace treaty. The nativists, whose efforts eventually succeeded in drastically reducing immigration in 1924, feared dilution of the U.S. ethnic identity—Anglo-Saxon and Protestant—and perhaps even the national language, English. The battle over the language of instruction in Rhode Island's private schools was nothing but a tiny part of a larger national debate that pluralists lost and nativists won.

The Sentinellistes fought back. They paraded in protest. They sued their own church, whose hierarchy did not wish to pick a quarrel with the legislature. They argued publicly with more assimilated Franco-Americans who reasoned that urbanized, industrialized twentieth-century New England was not nineteenth-century Quebec. In 1928, the Vatican supported the moderates. The Pope ex-communicated sixty Sentinelliste leaders, ending the magnificently inspired, hopelessly naïve protest. The ex-communicated all signed a statement of repentance and rejoined the church.

In 1976, a detailed study of census data revealed that, in southern New England, only 18.5 per cent of people with French as their mother tongue who had been born outside the United States still used the language. Of those Franco-Americans born in the United States with a mother tongue of French—by then the vast majority of the old French-Canadian community—only 4.8 per cent used it. That study was taken a quarter of a century ago. Today's numbers would be lower still.

All that remains now of the language are meticulous parish records in French, street and family names, and the occasional chat among older Franco-Americans in places such as the church basement in Woonsocket. French speakers were once the fifth-largest ethnic group in the United States. The French Canadians of Woonsocket and the rest of New England, once Star-Spangled Canadians *à leur façon*, are now Star-Spangled Americans.

Catherine Côté's parents and friends greeted her decision to emigrate with the same mixture of admiration and fear that probably attended the departures of thousands of *habitants* decades ago. Some considered her foolish; others, brave. Some feared for her safety; others admired her courage. Unlike the *habitants*, she did not need a job. But like them, she saw larger opportunities in the United States.

"Some said, 'You're going to Boeing? You're quitting a permanent job with social benefits. In Montreal, you are with your family. So you want to quit everything and go away?'" she recalled.

"Others were very proud because I was doubling my salary. They were saying that I was a single woman going over there just to start a brand-new life. How many women will do that by themselves? They were looking at me and saying, 'We didn't know you were like that, Catherine ...'"

"After a year, I have improved my self-confidence. I know my value in the market, my workforce value. I know myself much more than when I was in Montreal. I needed that to explore myself."

Dr. Marc Caron, a bit like Lorenzo Suprenant, finds the United States a more dynamic country than Canada, and he admires his adopted country for it.

"In Canada, one of the things I find is that people are spoiled. They may have a better standard of living over there. They have grown to expect a lot. It's more socialized there. Everyone expects the government will give them something. I think it's gone overboard. It's more comfortable sitting than rolling up your sleeves," he said.

Louise Masse is perhaps most typical, appreciating the United States for the opportunities to teach and do research at the University of Texas, but ambivalent about her new environment. Professionally she made the right decision; personally she wonders.

Will she go back? Probably not. Finding work teaching in Canada for her and her husband would be too difficult. The opportunities are too limited. She will try to keep French alive with any children she might have; that is her stated ambition. Perhaps Louise Masse will succeed in this, but the struggle will be a constant one and, if the history of French-Canadian emigration to pursue the American Dream is any guide, ultimately a losing one.

Except for Hockey Night in Canada and the Bugs Bunny/Roadrunner Hour, the United States of America is where all the good TV comes from. You go over the border and then you get to Colville and things start to get a little bigger and a little brighter. A long time ago I bought a GI Joe there with a Kung Fu grip. You couldn't even get Kung Fu grip in Canada.

By the time you get to Spokane you really know you're not in Canada. Kmart is as big as a hockey arena and they've got this announcer there just as loud as the announcer guy at the Montreal Forum and he's telling you what to buy. On the street you can't even see the front end of some of the cars there. That's how long they are. We saw a car with horns on the front end. It looked like a bull. —Peter McCormack, Understanding Ken

BRAIN DRAIN

CANADIANS departing for what they assume will be greener pastures in the United States is hardly a new phenomenon. Canadians have been leaving for generations, and in much larger numbers decades ago than in recent years. And yet, the last half of the 1990s featured a sharp upsurge in public debate about the "brain drain," that is, the loss of professionally qualified people to the United States.

Scarcely a week passed without a newspaper or magazine scratching at the issue. Ideologues and think-tanks, trade associations and university professors, politicians and journalists—they all had something to say about the "brain drain." Federal government departments and agencies offered conflicting analyses. Industry Canada warned in a series of reports that Canada's productivity had slumped compared with that of the United States and that this "productivity gap" contributed to brighter economic prospects south of the border, with a consequent hemorrhaging of Canadian talent. Statistics Canada replied that, although Canada was indeed losing people to the United States, the numbers were lower than three or four decades ago, let alone at the turn of the century. Moreover, argued Statistics Canada, this "brain drain" to the United States was more than offset within most occupational groups by immigration to Canada from other countries so that, on a net basis, Canada enjoyed a "brain gain."

Politicians, never at a loss for words, read into the "brain drain" issue their own agendas. Prime Minister Jean Chrétien pooh-poohed the very notion of a "brain drain," insisting that the mere mention of the idea reflected a thinly veiled campaign by Big Business for lower taxes. "My grandfather left Quebec at the end of the last century to settle in the region of Manchester, New Hampshire. But he came back," Chrétien told a Quebec audience in the summer of 1999. Chrétien did not mention the hundreds of thousands of French-speaking Quebeckers, including a smattering of other members of the extended Chrétien clan, who had emigrated and not returned. If Canadians feel overtaxed, Chrétien argued, they are free to emigrate, but they will face more guns and violence in the United States. "If you go live in the United States," he said, "you can't go out in the park at night because crime is higher than in Canada. They have five times more murders with guns than we have in Canada." Chrétien added that the cost of private health insurance negates the difference between Canadian and American taxes. Some Americans pay $40,000 for university fees, he added.[1]

Chrétien's deeply misleading comments about what Star-Spangled Canadians actually experience in the United States were nonetheless completely in keeping with his refusal throughout a long political career to engage Canadians in serious debate about issues, an engagement that must begin with the acknowledgment of a problem. Chrétien built a political career on unbridled patriotism and "sunny ways" rhetoric, so that his dismissal of the "brain drain" as worthy of serious reflection was hardly surprising. He took the "brain drain" debate and attempted to defuse it with a personal anecdote, some cursory comments, and an appeal to Canadian patriotism. Chrétien's dismissal of the issue produced heartburn for some of his senior ministers, including those holding economic portfolios, such as Paul Martin, John Manley, Herb Dhaliwal, and Marcel Massé. Every one of them worried privately about the loss of people to the United States, but once their boss had declared that the problem did not exist, they became political mutes. Chrétien's dismissal was hardly novel. During previous spasms of national concern about emigration, Canadian prime ministers such as Sir Wilfrid Laurier and Mackenzie King had adopted the same posture of defensive denial mixed with lashings of blame towards others for even raising the issue.

The Reform Party, naturally enough, tried to make a meal of the public debate about the "brain drain" because it suited the party's campaign for lower taxes. In a paper prepared by the party's research staff in 1998, Reform argued that the "brain drain" was a serious problem "that threatens to hurt

Canadian economic prospects and competitiveness ..."[2] The party acknowledged that better opportunities often lured people south, but then focused on higher Canadian taxes as the principal culprit. "The increasing emigration of Canadian professionals, and recent moves in Congress to increase the number of Canadians that can be admitted under other types of visas, would seem to be a good sign that the brain drain will get much worse before it gets better," concluded the Reform Party paper. "The government must make radical changes to the income tax system in order to battle the negative impression most Canadians have of the current system."

Politicians and advocates on the political left, of course, heaped scorn on the "brain drain" debate. They feared, not unreasonably, that a remedy for the loss of people might just be lower taxes on those with the skills and energy to depart, especially middle- to upper-income Canadians. Canadian Supreme Court clerks, computer-science graduates, cancer specialists, financial analysts, entertainers, scientists, and many of the other mobile people who might be tempted to head south were not among the usual constituencies for the New Democratic Party or what remained of the dilapidated intellectual left. Like the other parties, the NDP read into the "brain drain" debate what suited its purposes. An agenda of tax relief for any but low- to moderate-income Canadians rubbed against the grain of income redistribution favoured by the political left whose members saw an inadequacy in the existing redistribution through the income tax system, whereby 11 per cent of higher-income Canadian earners pay 40 per cent of personal income taxes. Unions, almost by definition, did not represent many mobile cross-border migrants, so the issue was of little direct concern to them. Exceptions occurred in selected areas such as nursing, where unions used the massive migration of nurses to the United States to press their wider agenda of higher salaries, improved training, and more positions.

Political parties were not alone, however, in fitting the cloth of the "brain drain" debate to their own agendas. High-technology companies lamented Canada's less generous tax treatment of stock options and capital gains—and overall higher personal-taxation levels—in explaining their difficulties with recruiting and retaining skilled employees. A study conducted by the Ottawa-based Branham Group, commissioned by the Information Technology Association of Canada, surveyed thirty-four high-technology firms in late 1998 about their skills shortages and concluded, among other findings, that "when organizations were solicited directly for their input into what are the next steps in addressing the IT skills shortage, the issue of lowering personal income tax rates was noted a significant amount of the time."[3] Presidents at the country's leading research-intensive universities pointed to the much higher salaries and larger research budgets at U.S. universities to underscore their problems in retaining senior professors and hiring young researchers.

Big Business lobbies such as the Business Council on National Issues (BCNI) warned of the debilitating effect of high taxes on economic growth, productivity, and the ability of Canada to retain its "best and brightest." In a September 1999 letter to the Prime Minister, the BCNI wrote: "While the statistical data suggest that the absolute number of Canadians moving to the United States is relatively small, they also confirm unequivocally that Canada's 'best and brightest' are the most likely to leave." The BCNI insisted that high rates of personal taxation made recruiting difficult, and that higher rates of corporate taxation than in the United States made head-office relocation to the United States more likely.

The Canadian Medical Association and provincial medical associations pointed to the exodus of doctors and researchers in the 1990s as evidence of the underfinancing of Medicare and the underpayment of doctors. The Canadian Nurses Association commissioned research documenting the mass migration of Canadian nurses in the 1990s. Law firms in Toronto and other large Canadian cities watched New York firms recruit directly at Canadian law schools. Deans of engineering and business schools observed an increasing number of U.S. recruiters arriving on Canadian campuses. The C.D. Howe Institute, the Conference Board of Canada, the Canadian Labour Market and Productivity Centre, the Canadian Centre for the Study of Living Standards, the Bank of Montreal, and the Fraser Institute were among the organizations that commissioned research into the "brain drain," adding their analyses to those of Statistics Canada, Industry Canada, the Organisation for Economic Co-operation and Development, the House of Commons finance committee, and innumerable media reports.

Why did this spasm of concern splash across Canada's economic and political debates, when the number of Canadians emigrating was lower than, say, three decades ago, let alone a century ago? Why, too, when Canadians departing with permanent U.S.-resident status in hand had not hugely increased in the 1990s compared with the 1980s?

The "brain drain" spasm can be explained, in part, by the gnawing sense based on anecdotes and statistical evidence that the U.S. economy had pulled well ahead of Canada's in the 1990s. The "brain drain" appeared to be one manifestation of widening gaps in the two countries' economic performance. Pollsters also discovered that, in the latter half of the 1990s, Canadians finally understood clearly the importance of brain power in driving economic growth and job creation. If well-qualified people were leaving, even if similarly qualified ones were arriving from abroad, that spoke to apprehension about Canada not achieving its potential. If Canada were indeed "Number One," as Prime Minister Jean Chrétien kept insisting by reference to the United Nations Human Development Index, then why would anyone, let alone thousands of people, want out? Too many anecdotes were being told about departing Canadians, and too many media articles were being written, not to fuel at least some sense that a "brain drain" was starting again.

What, then, are the numbers? The table below illustrates the annual average number of Canadians who left for the United States over the last half of the twentieth century, most of them with permanent status in hand, compared with immigration to Canada from all countries.

Population Movements			
Annual average	Emigration to the U.S.	Immigration to Canada*	Immigrant/ emigrant ratio
1955–59	40,179	157,749	3.9
1960–64	48,007	91,229	1.9
1965–69	38,619	181,976	4.7
1970–74	19,050	158,859	8.3
1975–79	16,867	130,127	7.7
1980–84	16,612	114,056	6.9
1985–89	16,654	137,827	8.3
1990–96	21,731	230,581	10.6

Source: Statistics Canada   *From all countries

During the 1990s, yearly emigration to the United States fluctuated, but not by much: 1990, 24,642; 1991, 19,931; 1992, 21,541; 1993, 23,898; 1994, 22,243; 1995, 18,117; 1996, 21,751. The Statistics Canada data, largely compiled on the basis of U.S. figures, are unfortunately three or four years out of date when published, so it is impossible to know if, during the last four years of the 1990s, an upsurge did occur that corresponded with the burst of concern in the public domain about the "brain drain." The raw numbers from the 1990–96 period are higher than those yearly averages from 1975 to 1990—an increase of about 30 per cent, but of only about 5,000 people in absolute terms. The regrettably fragmentary statistical evidence suggests that the trend continued upward. Revenue Canada data show that the number of tax-filers who ceased to reside in Canada grew from about 22,000 in 1995 to almost 30,000 in 1997, but this is not a definitive picture of emigration. Certainly the anecdotal evidence suggested an increase was in the works, but this anecdotal evidence, reported upon extensively in the media and thrashed over in public debates, may merely have reflected heightened interest in the issue rather than being rooted in statistical reality.

Nor is every Star-Spangled Canadian a movie star, high-tech mogul, brilliant scientist or surgeon, Wall Street banker or industrialist. Plenty of them are retired, living on Canadian or U.S. public or private pensions. Others are students or individuals struggling to make ends meet. Some are out of the workforce altogether, as homemakers. According to 1996 estimates from the U.S. Bureau of the Census, Star-Spangled Canadian women outnumbered men by two to one. Only a handful were receiving welfare, food stamps, or other forms of social assistance. About 6 per cent were thought to be living below the poverty line, and only 2 per cent, or half the U.S. unemployment rate, were unemployed. The least that can be said of Star-Spangled Canadians is that they do not strain the U.S. social safety net; those in the labour force tend to earn better-than-average incomes, mostly live in owner-occupied houses, and about 85 per cent have at least some college education.[4] Bureau of the Census figures do not permit a firm analysis, but my hunch would be that the younger the Star-Spangled Canadian, the higher his or her educational qualifications, since some of those in their sixties or older would have entered the United States before the Immigration Act changes of 1968 and subsequent changes placed a greater premium on formal education and skills.

Perhaps Troy Ewanchyna's story offers another clue about why concern arose about the "brain drain," a story that in one important respect can be repeated quite literally thousands of times: Ewanchyna has been working in the United States on on a so-called temporary visa ever since university graduation.

Ewanchyna attended school in Saskatchewan and played hockey for Vernon in the British Columbia junior hockey league in his final year. There, an assistant coach for Princeton University spotted Ewanchyna and persuaded him to attend the Ivy League school. Ewanchyna's father was a letter carrier and his mother a teacher, but, like most other leading private U.S. universities, Princeton boasts a needs-blind admissions policy. If any student is good enough for Princeton and cannot afford the costs, the university provides the grants or loans to slice, or even eliminate, the burden of about $33,000 (U.S.) for tuition and lodging demanded of undergraduates.

Ewanchyna still amassed a debt of about $25,000 (U.S.) after four years at Princeton, so he considered his options after graduation.

"My first year out of school I had planned on going back and getting a law degree and my MBA. I still have that in the back of my mind. I thought I was going to work for a year and then go back," he said, sitting in his office at TravRoute, a transportation software company in Princeton, New Jersey, where he is director of marketing.

" I actually applied to a couple of American schools and the University of Toronto. I got into the U of T MBA program, but at the time it didn't seem to make a heck of a lot of sense. I didn't have a lot of business experience. I had student loans to pay off. Why incur more debt just for the sake of going back to school? So here I am living in the U.S. and making U.S. dollars and having opportunities with my current job, but also the networking that goes on, having graduated from Princeton, is phenomenal."

Ewanchyna was able to stay in the United States courtesy of a TN visa, a so-called temporary work permit that he received upon securing the job with his Princeton company. Each year, he simply renews the TN visa and keeps on working.

His friend and fellow Princeton hockey-playing graduate Craig Fiander had the same experience. A native of Fredericton, New Brunswick, Fiander received offers from four Ivy League schools. He chose Princeton and, after graduation, with loans to pay off, he decided to stay in the United States. That was in 1993. Fiander is still in Princeton, working for the same company as his friend Ewanchyna on the same kind of TN visa. Technically, these visas are supposed to be revoked if U.S. authorities believe the visa-holder intends to stay permanently in the country, but this revocation rarely occurs.

Margaret Li and her husband—she from Toronto, he from Windsor— left IBM Canada in 1996 for Microsoft's worldwide headquarters in Redmond, Washington. They had vacationed in the U.S. Pacific Northwest and liked the area. They did not have children. Both had excellent university degrees and some work experience, so they jumped at the Microsoft offer.

"If you just take salary into account, I am better off. The salary is somewhat higher and the taxes are lower, so therefore between the two I am better off. The stock options make me way better off," Li said.

And how did she get into the United States? "I'm here on a TN visa. After two years, Microsoft begins the process of applying for a green card, but that can take several years." Microsoft, like other large U.S. companies, hires people from around the world, so its staff lawyers routinely handle employees' immigration requirements, including applications for permanent status in the United States.

Luticia "Tish" Hill, originally from British Columbia and with a degree in health information from the University of Victoria, met an American and followed her heart to Seattle. She found a job within three weeks, and worked illegally for a while. "Then I realized how easy it was to put through the TN, so I did it for everybody else." "Everybody else" meant five or six other Canadians she had recruited to the successful Web-site company, Sitewerks, she and another ex-patriate Canadian founded in Seattle. Sitting around the corporate boardroom's table with six ex-patriate Canadians working at Sitewerks, I asked about their immigration status. Four of the Canadian employees had TN visas; Tish and the other co-founder had advanced to more permanent visa status. Only one of the six intended to return to Canada, and that anticipated return was the kind of affair of the heart that had originally lured Tish to Seattle.

These kind of stories were repeated over and over again in my interviews with Star-Spangled Canadians, especially younger ex-patriates. They are, in a sense, NAFTA's children, although, when Canadians plunged into the debate about Canada–U.S., and then North American, free trade, few realized the kind of human progeny the trade deals would produce.

The original Canada–U.S. free-trade deal sparked Canada's most intense economic and political debate since the Second World War. The election of 1988 hinged on the free-trade deal, and the debate sprawled over everything from social policies to economic harmonization, agricultural subsidies to control of natural resources, the export of water to the future of pensions, the effectiveness of the dispute-resolving panels to the intricacies of trade law. On many levels, from arcane detail to the transcendent question of Canadian sovereignty, Canada–U.S. free trade left many confused, but few indifferent.

Overlooked in the FTA debate, and in the later one over NAFTA, were provisions governing the mobility of labour. The trade agreements were not about immigration or emigration. These remained the exclusive prerogative of national governments. No country was asked to change the essence of its immigration policies, because these, after all, touched issues far beyond those of North American trade. But a moment's reflection clarified the logic of the provisions that assisted cross-border mobility of labour: if trade agreements were to enhance the flow of goods and services within North America, it followed that at least some of the people involved in making, marketing, and delivering these goods and services should be able to pursue business more easily in the other countries.

And so, buried in the agreements were provisions expanding the availability of "temporary" visas for those desiring to work elsewhere in North America. Visas for temporary workers, largely for business and professional people, had existed before the FTA and NAFTA, but the new trade agreements simplified the procedures for securing them. These "temporary" visas—called TCs under the FTA, and TNs under NAFTA—have provided a kind of back-door entry for Canadians wishing to emigrate. Canadians go to the United States "temporarily" on a TN visa, work there, then try to parlay that "temporary" status into something more permanent if they wish to remain. Depending on their company, job, determination, and willingness to pay the fees of an immigration lawyer, these "temporary" ex-patriate Canadians can become permanent residents of the United States.

The table below shows the number of TC and TN visas issued from 1989, the year of the entry into force of the Canada–U.S. Free Trade Agreement, to 1996 as counted by U.S. agencies and reported by Statistics Canada.[5]

Temporary Visas Issued to Canadians

	1989	1990	1991	1992	1993	1994	1995	1996
Professional workers under FTA (TC)	2,677	5,293	8,123	12,531	16,610			
Spouses and children of FTA workers	140	594	777	1,271	2,386			
Professional workers under NAFTA						24,826	23,861	26,794
Spouses and children of NAFTA workers						5,535	7,202	7,694

The number of "temporary" TC or TN visas granted to Canadians therefore increased tenfold from 1989 to 1996—from 2,677 to 26,794. To be sure, some people used more than one visa each year to do contract or other kinds of work in the United States, then returned to Canada. The number of "temporary" visas, in other words, does not equate with the number of people who left. Similarly, there had been temporary visas for business people and workers before the FTA and NAFTA. One kind of visa for business people actually dropped from 19,839 in 1989 to 11,471 in 1996. Intracompany transfers that require another kind of visa altogether almost doubled, however, from 4,138 in 1989 to 7,037 in 1996.

What then can reasonably be made of the numbers? Neither Canadian nor U.S. authorities know precisely how many Canadians have used the TC or TN visas to move *de facto* to the United States. Statistics Canada estimates—but these are educated guesses rather than precise numbers— that perhaps 6,000–10,000 of the almost 27,000 "temporary" visas issued in 1996 represent Canadians who moved to the United States. If these estimates are close to correct, then perhaps 8,000 people must be added to the numbers Statistics Canada can count of those Canadians departing with more permanent U.S. status in hand.

What would that mean? From 1985 to 1989, an average of 8,100 Canadians departed with permanent visas each year for the U.S. labour force, and from 1990 to 1996 that number increased to an average of 9,770 per year. (Of course, the total number leaving was much greater—about 21,000 per year, when you include spouses and dependants.) These are the numbers Statistics Canada has widely publicized, and no one doubts their accuracy, because those leaving Canada to work with permanent kinds of visas are easily counted by the issuing U.S. authorities. Those who diminish the significance of the "brain drain" point to these Statistics Canada numbers—8,100 on average from 1985 to 1989 and 9,770 from 1990 to 1996—to buttress their case that the loss of Canadians is of little concern because the numbers are small and are dwarfed by Canadian immigration from other countries. But if, in fact, almost the same number are departing under the TN visas—the so-called temporary ones—then the total emigration (excluding dependants) is much greater, perhaps in the range of 16,000 to 17,000 people entering the U.S. workforce.

In my interviews, I always asked Star-Spangled Canadians under what visa or other legal authorization they were living in the United States. Of course, many had become citizens or were holding a "green card," the permanent-status document for non-citizens. But among the younger expatriates, or those who had left in recent years, the most frequent answer was that they were working in the United States on a TN visa that they had obtained themselves or through their company's lawyers.

The TN visa comes with certain complications. It allows an individual to work at a certain job for a specific company and cannot be transferred if the individual changes jobs or companies. Spouses of TN visa-holders are not allowed to work in the United States, although spouses of American TN visa-holders in Canada are permitted to work. A job change requires a fresh visa, and these are not issued automatically. They also must be applied for in Canada. However, TN visas are renewable annually and for as long as the individual remains in a particular job, so that these visas can effectively confer almost permanent status on anyone who takes the trouble to renew the document each year, or ship the problem over to the company's lawyers.

Of course, for those who want to emigrate and stay permanently in the United States, the TN visa can put a crimp on job mobility. Human ingenuity being what it is, and U.S. laws being what they are, Star-Spangled Canadians determined to remain in the United States explore various options. They can marry an American, in which case they can automatically apply for U.S. citizenship. They can apply for somewhat more permanent status under the H1B visa for specialty occupations that is valid for a three-year period and renewable once. Or, they can apply for the Holy Grail for would-be migrants—the green card, which confers all the rights, privileges, and responsibilities of residing in the United States except the right to vote or the duty to serve on juries. No guarantee exists that the TN visa-holder will successfully change his or her status, but my interviewing experience suggested strongly that, for the determined Canadian living in the United States, the TN visa was a stepping-stone to more permanent status rather than some kind of "temporary" document.

TN visas are not for everyone. Carpenters, loggers, automobile assemblers, or other blue-collar workers need not apply. A university degree or another kind of specialized college training is required to get one. But the chances are excellent that the would-be Canadian emigrant with a degree or its equivalent will fall into one of the sixty-four professional or occupational groups listed under NAFTA and published by the U.S. Department of Justice.[6] These include, to mention but a few: accountants, architects, computer-systems designers, economists, foresters, land surveyors, lawyers, librarians, management consultants, urban planners, medical professionals, and scientists.

Official statistics suggest that these TN visas are seen by some of the holders as passports towards more permanent status in the United States. The B1 visas, specifically for business travellers, have been falling in popularity, while the TN visas have been gaining—in part because they are easy to obtain (they can be secured at the border) and, in part, because they can lead to a more permanent status for the visa-holder than the B1.

The following table indicates that in recent years about one in ten Canadians in the United States changes his or her "temporary" status to permanent status every year. Those transferred by companies change more frequently to permanent status.

Percentage of Non-Immigrants from Canada
Changing Status to Permanent Residents

	1993	1994	1995	1996
Intracompany transferees	31.6	27.8	22.8	37
Temporary workers	13.4	9.3	7.7	11.59

Source: United States Department of Justice, *Statistical Yearbook of Immigration and Naturalization Service*, 1993–96

The TN is also easier to obtain than pre-NAFTA "temporary" visas because it is not necessary for the Canadian to prove that he or she will displace a U.S. worker. A Statistics Canada survey of 1995 Canadian university graduates living in the United States found that 57 per cent of those who entered the country as "temporary" residents used the TN visas. For those who entered for work, rather than study, the number jumped to a staggering 80 per cent, testimony to the popularity of these visas, the ease with which they can be secured, and the potential pathway they create for more permanent status.[7]

The "temporary" visa phenomenon therefore offers one plausible reason why the late 1990s featured a spasm of concern about the "brain drain," although we should bear in mind that the precise number of people using these visas to remain in the United States is unknown. It is certainly not close to the number of nearly 27,000 visas issued, but it may be in the range of 6,000 to 10,000.

An example of the way the picture is incomplete can be gleaned from statistics for health professionals leaving Canada. Statistics Canada has reported an annual emigration of 360 physicians "and other health diagnosing professionals," and of 816 nurses, for the 1990–96 period. These are presumably individuals with permanent-resident status in hand upon arrival in the United States. However, the Canadian Institute for Health Information reports that the average annual departure of physicians between 1990 and 1997 was 640, with higher numbers leaving in the 1992–97 period. Physicians entering the United States on "temporary" visas that are then converted to permanent status largely account for the difference. The same gap between Statistics Canada data and other information exists for nurses. Whereas Statistics Canada says the average annual emigration of nurses was 816, the Canadian Nurses Association reports between 2,000 and 5,000 nurses leaving annually since 1992; the bulk of the nurses used "temporary" visas.

Precise figures are also impossible to secure when calculating the number of Canadians living and working illegally in the United States. By definition, Canadians without authorization who live in the United States are unlikely to pop up and so declare themselves, although thousands did when, in recent decades, amnesty was granted to U.S. illegal immigrants, encouraging them to legalize their status.

In the 1990s, Congress and the Clinton administration increased by more than 100 per cent the budget of the Immigration and Naturalization Service (INS), in part so that better estimates could be made of illegal immigration in the United States. The INS estimates illegal immigration by counting people who have been in the United States for more than twelve months. On that basis, the INS believed that 5 million people were living there illegally in 1996. Of these, more than half (2.9 million) were thought to be Mexicans. The next largest numbers of illegal immigrants were from El Salvador (335,000), Guatemala (165,000), and Canada (120,000). Canadians, then, were the fourth most numerous group of illegal immigrants in the United States. The INS estimated that the number of illegal Canadians had grown to 120,000 from 85,000 in 1992, an increase of 41 per cent, compared with an overall nationwide increase in illegal immigration of 29 per cent. The INS further estimated that 6,000 to 12,000 Canadians illegally emigrate to the United States each year, so that, at least nominally, these Canadians should be counted in the total number who leave each year, although determining their precise number is difficult.[8]

How many Canadians, then, are living in the United States? The best estimate, based on the U.S. Census Current Population Survey of March 1999, is 661,000. The numbers have been declining for decades. Figures for recent years include: 1980, 843,000; 1990, 772,000; 1994, 679,000; 1995, 677,000; 1996, 660,000; 1997, 542,000; 1998, 661,000. (The 1996–97 drop is believed to be a sampling-variation error.) This means that the share of Canadians living in the United States in relation to Canada's own population is now about 2 per cent, compared with 3.4 per cent in 1980, 5 per cent in 1960, 7 per cent in 1930, 16 per cent in 1910, and 20 per cent in 1900.

Any discussion of the "brain drain," therefore, should acknowledge three facts. First, the number of Canadians emigrating today—even including those emigrating with "temporary" visas—is smaller than in the 1960s and before. Second, the portion of Canada's population living in the United States is a fraction of what it was a century or fifty years ago. Third, no discussion of the "brain drain" should be conducted in isolation because, by attracting more than 200,000 immigrants per year, Canada is obviously importing many more people than it is losing to the United States. However, developments in recent years suggest that, after three decades of decline, emigration has started to rise slowly again, courtesy of temporary visas and widening economic opportunities for highly skilled and mobile people in the United States vis-à-vis Canada.

That Canada attracts immigrants—more in relation to its population than any other advanced industrialized country, incidentally—contributes to the country's pool of human talent. Rather than using this immigration to discount the "brain drain," the proper Canadian response should be to keep those immigrants coming, especially those of the highly skilled variety, while adopting policies at home that will encourage fewer talented Canadian to leave the country. The risk of comparing today's emigration with that of thirty, fifty, or a hundred years ago, or with immigration flows, is that comparisons can breed a shoulder-shrugging complacency about those who leave and the reasons why.

John Helliwell of the University of British Columbia, one of Canada's finest economists, stood the "brain drain" fears on their head in 1999.[9] The raw number of Canadians departing for the United States, he correctly observed, is but a fraction of those of fifty or a hundred years ago. He endorsed Statistics Canada's argument that the "brain gain" from other countries dwarfs whatever losses to the United States Canada suffers, even in some categories of professionals and skilled workers. Helliwell then asked a pertinent question: Why did even more Canadians not emigrate in the 1990s, given the large discrepancy between U.S. and Canadian unemployment rates? Canadian and U.S. unemployment rates were roughly similar in the 1970s. In the 1980s, however, the gap widened to two or three percentage points; and, in the 1990s, to three or four percentage points. In the last half of the 1990s, the U.S. rate ranged from 4 to 5 per cent, whereas the Canadian rate was 6.9 to 9.0 per cent. The two countries measure unemployment differently. If Canada used the U.S. method of measurement, Canadian rates would have shown 0.7 per cent less unemployment per year, but, even after accounting for the different methodologies, Canada's structural unemployment rate was higher, and the unemployment gap widened from the late 1970s to the turn of the century.

Helliwell estimated that the stronger job-creation performance of the United States, and the correspondingly lower unemployment rates, should have pulled an additional 10,000 Canadians south per year. "This estimate is based on migration behavior in previous decades, and is therefore subject to a large margin of error, but it does signal that migration from Canada to the U.S. has been surprisingly small in the 1990s, when seen in the light of the widening gap between job opportunities in Canada and the United States," Helliwell wrote. If one assumes, as I do but Helliwell does not, that a significant increase did occur—of Canadians *de facto* emigrating courtesy of "temporary visas"—then very close to what Helliwell states ought to have happened did occur. Neither the United States nor Canada knows precisely how many people used these visas to move to the United States, as opposed to going there several or more times per year for short-term assignments, but a reasonable estimate suggests 6,000 to 10,000 people. The overwhelming number of young Canadians I interviewed had entered the United States on these "temporary visas," and many of them aspired to parlay these into more permanent status. In other words, something approximating 10,000 additional Canadians emigrated—an estimate subject to a "large margin of error"—which is what one might have expected, given the two countries' respective unemployment rates.

Unemployment tends to be skewed regionally in Canada, with rates much higher in the East than in the West. It also tends to be especially prevalent in seasonal industries, among lower-skilled and -educated workers, and among aboriginal Canadians. Decades ago, when the border was relatively porous, these kinds of Canadians could and did emigrate in large numbers to the United States. If an almost free Canada–U.S. labour market existed today, as it did a century ago, then the unemployment gap would have pulled many more Canadians south. That is why comparisons between today's emigration and that of a century ago are interesting but irrelevant, because today's immigration rules are much tighter. If, suddenly, the United States and Canada eliminated immigration restrictions—as the Europeans have done within their Union—Canadians would be flocking south in much larger numbers. U.S. immigration lotteries suggest how strong the pull of the United States is. Twice in recent decades, U.S. authorities have organized lotteries for those wishing to emigrate. Both times, the authorities were swamped with requests from Canada.

A more relevant comparison is with emigration patterns in the recent decades of the 1970s and 1980s, and these do show that, when "temporary visas" are included, an upswing in emigration has occurred, especially among skilled, educated, motivated, and therefore potentially mobile, Canadians. If the economic performance of Canada continues to lag behind that of the United States, both in the aggregate and in growing sectors of the knowledge-based economy, there is little reason to suggest emigration will diminish. If anything, it may continue to rise.

Between 1989 and 1997, according to Statistics Canada, employment rose by 10.4 per cent in the United States, compared with only 6.5 per cent in Canada.[10] Canadians apprised of stronger job growth in the United States sometimes reacted defensively by insisting the U.S. economy was churning out hamburger-flipping, low-paying service jobs. Not so. Seventy per cent of the new U.S. jobs in this period came from full-time paid employment, and the majority of the new jobs were in industries and occupational groups that pay high wages. Only 10 per cent of new U.S. jobs arose from self-employment, compared with 80 per cent of Canada's overall jobs increase. The U.S. unemployment rate in 1997 for those with less than a high school diploma was about 50 per cent lower than the Canadian rate—8.1 per cent compared with 12.6 per cent. For those with university degrees, the U.S. unemployment rate was 2 per cent compared with 4.6 per cent in Canada.

The more robust job-creation record of the United States in the 1980s and 1990s can be measured regionally. After examining unemployment rates on a state and province basis from 1980 to 1997, Statistics Canada concluded: "With a few exceptions, the American states had lower unemployment rates in 1997 than in 1980, while all Canadian provinces had higher unemployment rates in 1997 than in 1980. Between 1980 and 1997 the state rates experienced an average decline of 30 per cent, while the provincial rates increased by 30 per cent." The provinces with the least unemployment (Alberta and Saskatchewan) had rates roughly the same as those of the ten U.S. states with the highest unemployment rates.

During the 1990s, public agencies in Canada such as hospitals and universities were eliminating positions, just as U.S. hospitals and universities were adding them. Research budgets declined in Canada but expanded in the United States for most of the 1990s. Canada poured money into programs such as regional equalization, social welfare, agricultural assistance, regional development, and pensions, all ostensibly humanitarian programs that reflected Canada's desire to be a "kinder, gentler" society. These programs assisted those people least likely to cross the Canada–U.S. border. And all the while the gap in the average per-capita income between Canada and the United States grew, as did the gap in personal disposable income. Canadians, in aggregate, grew poorer for most of the 1990s while Americans, again on aggregate, grew richer. No wonder, then, that higher incomes could lure the potentially mobile south. Average after-tax income in Canada—adjusted for inflation—fell 7.2 per cent from the first quarter of 1990 to the second quarter of 1998, before recovering in the last half of 1998 and in 1999, whereas average after-tax income grew 9.5 per cent in the United States during the same period.[11] Just how poorly after-tax income had fared in Canada was made clear in late 1999 when newspapers headlined a Statistics Canada report revealing that incomes were back to where they had been in 1989!

    Low- to modest-income Americans missed the 1990s boom. Their wages stagnated, and income differentials in the United States widened as the rich enjoyed a phenomenal decade. Inequality between the richest and the poorest remained higher in the United States than in Canada.[12] A study by the Center on Budget and Policy Priorities, a liberal think-tank, found that in 1999 the wealthiest 20 per cent of Americans had 50.4 per cent of all personal income, compared with 44.2 per cent in 1977, whereas the share for the poorest fifth during that period had fallen from 5.7 to 4.2 per cent. In the 1990s, the incomes of all groups rose, although the richest Americans benefited the most from the robust economic times. Thus, the poor did not get poorer in absolute terms; indeed, the number of Americans deemed to be living in poverty fell. But the top 40 per cent of American earners did especially well from the boom, and within that group the very wealthy did best of all. Almost by definition, Canadians leaving for the United States have education and skills. They are therefore likely to be earning better-than-average incomes, which makes the United States much more attractive financially for some of them.

    Across the board, Canadians' disposable incomes in the 1990s fell 25 per cent in relation to those of Americans. A presentation from Industry Canada to other government departments stated, "In 1998, based on the range of estimates of purchasing power parity (83 to 85 cents), real per capita income was 25% to 30% higher in the U.S. than in Canada (or about $7,500 to $8,700 per capita)."[13] Industry Canada observed that, in the 1990s, U.S. real income had increased at double the pace of that in Canada. Standard and Poor's, the bond-rating agency, reported that the 1990s were Canada's second-worst decade this century for economic growth.[14]

    The vast majority of the Star-Spangled Canadians I interviewed earned at least as much, and frequently much more, in the United States than they had in Canada. If they were earning much more and lived in a low-tax jurisdiction, their disposable income would have been far greater than in Canada; earning the same salary and living in a high-cost city such as New York or Los Angeles might shave or even eliminate the difference. (The effect of lower incomes and higher taxes sometimes makes recruiting difficult for Canadian firms who must pay Americans more money to work in Canada.) They did not like to dwell on how much they were earning, but the gap surfaced periodically. Don Carty, president of American Airlines, commented that his company has pilots who make more than Kevin Benson, president of Canadian Airlines. Medical doctors, especially specialists in private practice, earn three or four times what their Canadian counterparts do. High-technology workers with successful U.S. companies have made a bundle when their stock options matured. Movie and television stars, of course, are in a league by themselves.

Nurses and assistant professors, on the other hand, earn about the same in Canada and the United States. Schoolteachers make considerably more in Canada, so few Canadian elementary- and secondary-school teachers leave. Government employees generally are less well paid in the United States than in Canada, although obviously numerous exceptions exist. Unemployment-insurance benefits are also better in Canada, although pension payments are not. Those earning minimum wage are also paid less in the United States, another reflection of how it's never good to be poor, but better to be poor in Canada than in the United States. The poor, however, do not migrate today to the United States as they did a century ago.

Superior aggregate economic performance in the United States pulls some Canadians south, just as weaker aggregate Canadian performance pushes them south. Aggregate explanations, however, mask the complexity of the emigration. In the "push–pull" dynamics of emigration, specific Canadian "pushes" have sent trickles of Canadians south at certain times. Seated in a private dining room of the Houston Petroleum Club on the top floor of the Exxon Building, with the city sprawling below in all directions, a cluster of Canadian oilmen told me their tales. They had all worked in Western Canada, mostly Alberta, in the 1970s and 1980s. Government policies, they insisted, had driven them south.

In the early 1970s, recalled Bert Dunn, Alberta premier Peter Lougheed raised royalties on old and new property leases, and the federal government imposed limits on natural-gas exports. Dunn was working then for an independent drilling company. "A whole bunch of people with the company decided that, if the Liberals won the 1974 election, we were out of there," Dunn said. "We moved our rigs down here. We took them from northern Alberta to Laredo and opened an office in Denver. When I think of it now, it was somewhat of a scary move. But we got a little emotional about it, and we had a leader who was very emotional about it. We were going to get out of that socialist environment and try to make a good living."

Glenn Brant, a self-described "farm boy" from north of Edmonton, graduated from the University of Alberta with a degree in petroleum engineering. He was working for a U.S. energy company when "we ran afoul of the National Energy Policy, Pierre Elliott Trudeau, and the Eastern Establishment." Brant recalled: "We took this wholly owned U.S. company. We converted it into a 50 per cent Canadian one. We went public with it, and we still got slaughtered. I didn't feel it was in me to start again in Canada and to buck that system because the confidence of investors in Canadian oil was in the pits. The U.S. had a better system for the entrepreneurial spirit, so I came down here."

Peter Duncan, the youngest of the group and a geophysicist, left Canada a few years after the National Energy Policy of the early 1980s.

"I had to come down here to find out what it was like to play in the big leagues. I told my wife we'd come down here for three or four years, but Texas has treated me so well, business has treated me so well. I started my own company that I haven't left, and I don't see a vehicle whereby I will return."

Alberta is a bastion of free enterprise within Canada, yet Duncan feels entrepreneurs such as himself can flourish even better in Texas.

"I like the business climate. When I was in Calgary working as a geophysicist for a large oil company, or even as a contractor, there was very little opportunity for me as an individual to step out and be an entrepreneur," he said.

"I could work for a big company, the way Pierre Berton describes the two societies: Canada being a top-down society and the United States being a bottom-up society. I found I was in a top-down society and I wanted to do better by myself. It struck me that there was more opportunity down here, and when I got down here I found that this was true. Everybody was working to be in business for themselves. Even the guys who were working for big oil would have deals on the side. I liked that sense of being responsible for yourself, and that was not a sense I got in Calgary."

Energy policies drove some oilmen to the United States; Canada's unity troubles drove others to distraction, then to other parts of Canada and, in the case of a few of them, south.

Phil Migicovsky, a Montrealer with degrees from McGill and the Harvard Business School, was living in Quebec in the mid-1970s. He is now a consultant in Dallas.

"In November 1976, [René] Lévesque was elected. His whole campaign was on honest government," Migicovsky recalled. "But at the Paul Sauvé Arena, where he had his election night, it was one of those 'Vive le Québec libre' speeches. I said to myself, 'I'm out of here.' That night I decided I'm gone. Not necessarily from Canada, but from Quebec. I felt like a second-class citizen in the place of my birth ... I totally resented Bill 100 or 89 or whatever it was. [Bill 101 actually.] I used to ski a lot in

Vermont. I remember so clearly that they had a sign at the border saying 'Ceintures de sécurité sont obligatoires / Seatbelts are mandatory.' Then one day someone had spent the money to erase the English. And I thought to myself, 'They're mooning the Americans. They're sticking their asses at the Americans and saying you had better speak French here.' I resented that so much."

Sean Murphy graduated from Concordia and had worked in the Internet business in Montreal until he visited a Canadian friend who had established a successful Web-site company in Seattle. She offered him a job, and he jumped at it, despite earlier intentions to remain in Montreal.

"I was really all for it. I was going to stick it out. I was going to stay there," Murphy said. "I was one of those depressed anglos. The conversations at the bars were all about how 'sucky' it was. I come out here, and there's no time for that. When I went back at Christmas, it was sad to see four pages of the *Montreal Gazette* were all about politics. I'm so glad to be out of that."

Caroline Birks grew up in Montreal, but despairs when she returns.

"I don't miss it [Montreal]. In fact, when I go back, I get this funny, weird, lonely feeling. Where is everyone? Everyone's gone and the stores are for rent."

Bryan Chadwick, a relative in whose New York loft Birks was staying when we spoke, immediately agreed. "You go back and pick up the newspaper. It's the same story for the past five years—separation. I'm so bored with that. Let them go or do something."

Asked about the national-unity debate in Canada, French-speaking Star-Spangled Canadians invariably said they were fed up with it. Typical was the reaction of Catherine Côté from Boeing in Everett, Washington: "I hate it. Even in Quebec, I was kind of sad that there were thinking about another referendum. Come on, guys. Get a life. Do something else with the money."

Mike Seeley, a manager with the People's First Bank in Altamonte Springs, Florida, took a voluntary buy-out package from the Royal Bank, for which he had worked throughout Ontario. He came to Florida for more after-tax income, new opportunities, and a hedge against the possible separation of Quebec.

"Every time they had a referendum it was getting closer and closer," Seeley said. "[Quebec Premier Lucien] Bouchard obviously wants to keep bringing it up. I think at some point there's going to be a Yes vote. We thought that, if Quebec separates, our seventy-five-cent dollar is going to be [worth] fifty cents. We won't be able to afford to get out. We'll be the laughing stock of the Western world. We've got everything, yet we're intent on blowing ourselves apart. It would sever Canada in two. If the States walked in and offered dollar-for-dollar parity, they could probably buy Canada."

Neil Druker, a principal at Pangaea, a Boston-based hedge fund specializing in investment in high-technology-company stocks, came to the United States to attend business school, then have access to better economic opportunities. He likes his home town, Montreal, but regrets that little has changed in the province's politics.

"We'd joke whenever we'd drive up to Montreal, when we got to the border and turned on the radio we heard the same news we heard five years ago, which is somebody talking about the language law and somebody else is highly insulted," Druker said. "I said I could have sworn I heard that debate five years ago."

Witold Rybczynski, author of *The Most Beautiful House in the World*, among other titles, is one of North America's best-known writers on architecture and urban planning. He had practised architecture and taught at McGill University for two decades but gradually became disllusioned with Quebec. He inquired about working at the University of Toronto, the University of British Columbia, and the University of Victoria, only to be told they were not interested, a classic case of missed opportunity. The University of Pennsylvania was, however. Penn offered him a chair. "I wasn't sympathetic to separatism," Rybczynski said. "I speak French. In fact, my wife is half-French. It seemed to me that either the province would separate eventually or, at least in my lifetime, it would keep going back and forth. I had already seen Montreal significantly worsen as a city, and I could only see this continuing. It was an irritation at this constant inability to resolve the issue ... and the sense that there wasn't really a future for me there."

Opportunity. My dictionary defines "opportunity" as a "favourable occasion" or a "good chance." In the real world, opportunity can mean almost anything. It can be defined protectively, as in U.S. president Franklin Roosevelt's "freedom from want" and "freedom from fear." It can be defined derisively as laissez-faire gone wild, as in novelist Anatole France's suggestion that opportunity can allow people to sleep under the bridges of Paris. It can be defined as the exploration of life's chances, and, if that definition suits, as it does me, then a successful country is the one that enhances the life chances of the largest number of its citizens.

Canada, by that definition and in comparison with other countries in the world, has been and remains a success. The country's attractiveness to immigrants suggests that ongoing success. The United Nations Human Development Index (HDI) ranking, much trumpeted by federal politicians, puts Canada as number one in the world. (The HDI is a very limited measure, however, because it excessively discounts the factor of per-capita income.) Canada's excellent international reputation suggests that the rest of the world considers Canada a successful country, even if Canadians are wont sometimes to minimize their own country's accomplishments. The Scots have a good word for an element of the Canadian spirit—"minginess," which means a crabbed and cramped attitude. Wallace Weylie, a cheerful and successful ex-patriate lawyer in Indian Rocks Beach, Florida, captured it best, if a little harshly: "Americans are upbeat and Canadians are downbeat. Canadians are pessimistic. They don't have the enthusiasm or drive, the fun ... Things are upbeat here, and it's go, go. It's positive and Canadians don't have that." "Pessimism" may overstate this element of the Canadian spirit, but there is a strong sense from the Star-Spangled Canadians I interviewed that Americans recognize, honour and thrive on success, whereas Canadians are more likely to think that a successful person, economically speaking, got there by mysterious means, might have a skeleton or two lurking in the closet, or somehow doesn't quite deserve to be there.

Canadians get "pushed" from their country or "pulled" to the United States for lots of reasons. Some hate the snow and prefer the heat. Some fall in love, and love respects no political boundaries. Some are taken there at a young age with their families and never return. Some grow up dreaming of palm trees, or Hollywood movie stars, or the bright lights of Manhattan, and they will never rest until they live among them. The United States, after all, can dazzle Canadians with its exuberance and repel them with its excesses. The United States leaves few Canadians indifferent.

Just as the word "opportunity," therefore, can mean different things to different people, the motivations for Canadians heading south are varied and always have been. But asked by pollsters, and recently by me, why they left Canada, Star-Spangled Canadians overwhelmingly mentioned "opportunity." Opportunity to earn more income. Opportunity to pursue more expansively their dreams. Opportunity to provide more financial security for their families. Opportunity to test themselves in a bigger market and against tougher competition. Opportunity to work with more resources and clusters of highly trained people. Opportunity to work at the "cutting edge," be it making films, doing research, driving innovation, negotiating deals, or practising their art. Opportunity to play on a bigger stage, before larger audiences, under brighter lights. 'Twas ever thus. In

1927, at the height of a previous spasm of national concern about the "brain drain," *MacLean's* magazine published findings of a questionnaire submitted to 1,000 Canadian university graduates living in the United States. Of the 203 who responded, 77 per cent said that they had left home for greater opportunity in the United States.

Not every Star-Spangled Canadian attracted by "opportunity" in the United States realizes his or her ambitions; indeed, some get disgusted or discouraged and return home. Hollywood and New York are littered with Canadian actors who sought the big part or tried to sell the dynamic script, only to wind up living illegally, waiting on tables or driving a cab. Canadian real-estate developers have lost fortunes in volatile U.S. markets. Some Canadian-trained doctors could not abide the inequities of U.S. medicine; some lawyers could not hack the relentless hours demanded by Wall Street firms; Canadian would-be high-tech millionaires have been burned in failed initial public offerings. The United States, as some chastened Star-Spangled Canadians have learned, is not for everyone. The American Dream can be an illusion, an oasis on the horizon that, once entered, offers only a dry well.

The sheer size of the United States, however, offers a range and scale of opportunities that a smaller country such as Canada struggles in some areas to match. Canada is not alone in that struggle, because the United States sucks up human talent from around the world. If sectors of the U.S. economy need more personnel than the country can provide, American authorities will ease entry. The U.S. Congress, for example, doubled the quota for visas available to workers in high-technology fields for two years after U.S. technology companies complained of skill shortages. Americans may tell pollsters they think there are too many immigrants entering their country—exactly as Canadians respond when asked similar questions by their pollsters—but, when the United States needs talent from abroad, little stands in the way of the pursuit of economic self-interest.

A country with a richer, more powerful neighbour usually faces this challenge of larger opportunities and scale elsewhere, especially if language is not a barrier. New Zealand, for example, has always lost people to Australia. In June 1999 an estimated 405,000 New Zealanders were living in Australia, compared with New Zealand's own population of 3.6 million. Put another way, about 11 per cent of New Zealand's population was living in Australia. The migration pattern of New Zealanders and Australians is similar to that of Canadians and Americans. New Zealanders and Canadians migrate to their more populous neighbour country in ratios of 2:1 to 3:1. In every year from 1982 to 1998, but one (1984), New

Zealanders headed for Australia in larger numbers than Australians to New Zealand.

In one important sense, however, the New Zealanders-to-Australia and Canadians-to-the-United States comparison is skewed. Since 1973, New Zealanders and Australians have been allowed to work and live in either country without visas. A free labour market—not restricted by immigration or visa policies—has therefore existed in the Antipodean countries, whereas, although NAFTA has made access by Canadians and Americans to each other's country somewhat easier, significant restrictions still apply.[15] Under this free market in labour, it would appear that economic conditions in New Zealand had a marked effect on emigration. Emigration soared in the 1980s—30,000–40,000 per year—as the heavily regulated New Zealand economy stagnated. Sweeping, even Draconian, moves to liberalize the New Zealand economy towards the end of that decade and the early 1990s encouraged domestic economic growth and slashed emigration by more than half, although, by the end of the 1990s, annual emigration to Australia had crept up again, into the 20,000–25,000 range.

The lure of "making it" in the United States, or finding more opportunity, has always attracted some Canadians. The bigger stage is sometimes hard to resist, and not always in high-profile, highly remunerative occupations. Movie stars and producers can earn millions in Hollywood and reach a worldwide audience. The United States has the world's largest space program. Wall Street cuts the biggest deals. M.D. Anderson Cancer Centre does the most cancer research. Microsoft designs the most software. Boeing manufactures the most planes (in North America). Universities such as Harvard, Stanford, and Princeton offer arguably the best PhDs—and so on. These leading institutions scour the world for talent because their vision is international, as is their clientele. What you can do is more important than where you are from. These pinnacle institutions have always attracted bright, determined Canadians, and they always will. What has changed in recent years—at least at the margin—is that more and more of these U.S. institutions and companies have "discovered" Canadian talent and now scan Canada as well as the rest of the United States. If Canada does not try, with whatever means it can, to compete even selectively in these elite areas, the flow south towards these pinnacle institutions will intensify.

The "opportunity" offered by the United States is sometimes financial—higher salaries, lower taxes, more disposable incomes. But opportunity also means bigger challenges, a chance to stretch intellectually.

Gordon Leighton grew up in Dundas, Ontario, studied at McMaster and Western Ontario, and was transferred by Honeywell, the company he worked for, from Canada to Minneapolis–St. Paul. When Honeywell sold its computer business, Leighton could have returned to Canada or stayed with the new owners. He stayed. "In my line of work, public relations and communications, the state of the art is more advanced here. One of the reasons I came to the U.S in the first place was because there was more opportunity in my line of work than north of the border," he said.

Chuck Scullion, a twenty-seven-year-old fresh from the Harvard Business School, was enjoying Dallas when we met. Scullion mentioned that he occasionally thought about returning to Canada, but paused after reflecting on the more limited opportunities. "There was a very brief time when I was very homesick for things like the cottage," he said. "There's nothing like that around here. The whole idea of going to a cottage is ridiculous because almost every lake here is man-made and goes down by twenty feet in the summer, so it's all shale and clay. "The hockey game when the river freezes over. Watching the kids play. I used to coach my niece's hockey team — those are things that pull at me. But, by the same token, there are business opportunities that will have to be there too, and the opportunities in the United States are much bigger than they are in Canada."

John Keiser, touring director for the San Francisco Symphony, previously worked for the National Arts Centre Orchestra in Ottawa. Frustrated by management's "conservatism and unwillingness to take risks," Keiser began looking south. "I didn't plan to stay here for fifteen years, but it's proven very challenging," Keiser said over lunch. "Once I came to the U.S. and got a foothold here, I knew that unless some wonderful opportunity presented itself, I probably wasn't going back to Canada."

Keiser picked up a refrain echoed repeatedly by Star-Spangled Canadians: the apparent satisfaction of Canadians with being second best.

"I realized after a while there that there wasn't much opportunity for me to join or to be part of an ensemble that had the same sort of push I had … to be a world-class group," he said. "Now that sounds pretty harsh, but if you look at Canada right now, which are the orchestras that are known internationally? Montreal and Toronto. Montreal is still a far better-known ensemble because of the high profile of Charles Dutoit. They still have a certain number of recordings in the catalogue. Toronto less so. There seems to be — and I felt like I ran into this a number of times — a reticence to try to excel, or to say to hell with it, 'We're going to be the best there is out there'."

Dimitri Pantazopoulos moved from Ottawa to Washington, D.C., to work in a market-strategies firm. He found more opportunity by virtue of the larger size of the U.S. market. "One of the things the U.S. achieves is a better critical mass than Canada. I don't think I would have had the opportunity in Canada to try the diversity of things that I could here," he said. "If you work for the Electrical Institute, they have a million-dollar budget … The budgets are much larger, so you get a chance to do more research than you would in Canada." Pantazopoulous did return subsequently to Ottawa for family reasons.

David Frum, also living in Washington, D.C., writes from a conservative perspective in Canada and the United States. Locating in the United States opened up more opportunities for his writing.

"The sheer fact of having so many other places to publish," he said of his decision to write from the United States. "For Canadian journalists, career management is an overwhelming preoccupation. There are so few people who control whether what you want to say can get into print. If you offend one of them, you probably destroy one-third, or maybe one-half, of your opportunities."

What about taxes? How important are tax rates and overall tax burdens to luring Canadians to the United States? No aspect of the "brain drain" debate is more emotive. Canadians who lobby for lower taxes, especially for better-off Canadians, point to the "brain drain" as proof positive that higher Canadian taxes are driving away some of the "best and the brightest." When they depart, so do the innovators, creators, and entrepreneurs, who generate wealth, tax revenues, employment. Defenders of Canada's social programs see in this campaign a thinly disguised effort to emasculate these programs, thereby turning Canada into a clone of the United States. The "brain drain," runs this argument, is not numerically significant and is easily compensated for by immigration. If Canada pumped more money into its public sector for health care, higher education, and other public services, the emigration from Canada of nurses, doctors, professors, and researchers would diminish, the loss of Canadians to the United States would shrivel, and Canada's superior "quality of life" would be maintained, perhaps even enhanced. And "quality of life," not lower taxes, is ultimately what will keep Canadians at home.

The facts about comparative tax rates are slightly muddled, because they vary from state to state and province to province. They can also vary considerably according to family size, personal circumstance, nature of income (salary or investment), home ownership or rental accommodation. For every baldly stated rule, there will be an exception. Tax rates also are adjusted in almost every budget—federal, provincial, or state—so that comparisons today may have to be altered tomorrow. Tax rates say nothing about an individual's subjective impression of "quality of life." New York State has one of the highest tax rates in the United States and some of its most blighted urban areas; Colorado has one of the lowest tax rates, yet an outstanding urban and rural environment. Atlantic Canadians face Canada's highest provincial tax rates, and Albertans and Ontarians the lowest, yet plenty of Atlantic Canadians would say that they prefer their "quality of life" while paying higher taxes. A focus on tax rates alone ignores costs Americans must bear for services Canada provides through the state, such as health care and somewhat higher fees for public universities.

That said, Americans on aggregate do pay significantly lower taxes, and the tax gap between the countries has widened in the last quarter of a century. In 1965, when Canada began expanding its social programs, especially health, taxes represented slightly less than 27 per cent of the gross domestic product, whereas today they take about 37 per cent. This compares to a U.S. rate of about 24 per cent in 1965 and 28 per cent today. In the last three and a half decades, therefore, the tax-to-GDP gap has risen from about 3 to 9 per cent.[16] Canada's taxes stand at about 37 per cent of GNP, midway between those of the United States and the European Union. The U.S. comparison is the only relevant one, given the interdependence between the two countries' economies, the similarities in language and culture, and the potential mobility of citizens. Canadians are more likely to emigrate to the United States than to Finland, Germany, Britain, or Spain. Nor are lower taxes alone the only magnet, because, if they were, Canadians would be fleeing to tax havens such as the Cayman Islands or the Channel Islands or to low-tax states such as Korea, Turkey, or Mexico.[17]

Canada depends more on personal income taxes than does the United States—indeed more than any other advanced industrialized country. Income-tax rates are also steeply progressive in Canada: 10 per cent of taxpayers earned 28 per cent of national income and paid 40 per cent of the federal taxes and 44 per cent of the provincial ones.[18] Anyone who therefore claims Canada's tax system "favours the rich" obviously does not know what he or she is talking about, although ignorance has never been a barrier to public intervention in democratic societies. Canada's personal-income-tax burden as a share of GDP is about 14 per cent, compared with about 10.7 per cent for the United States.

Canada is a more decentralized political federation than the United States, so Canadian provinces both spend and tax more than do U.S. states. U.S. federal marginal tax rates are actually higher than Canadian ones—except among low-income people, where the U.S. rate is 15 per cent, and the Canadian 17 per cent. But Canadian provincial rates are higher, and sometimes staggeringly higher, than those imposed by U.S. states. Some U.S. states levy no state income tax (Florida, for example); rates in states with higher taxes range from 7 to 9 per cent (New York and California, for example). Canadian provincial tax rates, often calculated as a percentage of federal tax (Quebec excepted), range from 40 to 59 per cent of federal taxes. If those provincial taxes are recalculated to reflect taxes on income, they range from about 17 per cent in Ontario to upwards of 25 per cent in Atlantic Canada. That's the fair Canada–U.S. comparison: state income taxes range from 0 to 9 per cent, provincial ones from 17 to 25 per cent. Combining federal and provincial/state taxes, therefore, produces higher aggregate personal income taxes in Canada.

Americans, however, contribute more in payroll taxes for Social Security (and receive higher pensions when they qualify) than Canadians do for Canada (and Quebec) Pension Plan contributions and Employment Insurance (EI) deductions. CPP contributions, however, are rising to ensure the solvency of the plan for the baby boomers' retirements; EI premiums are declining. The United States has not figured out how to make Social Security solvent, so perhaps in due course U.S. payroll taxes will rise. In any event, any fair Canada–U.S. comparison of tax rates must include both personal income taxes and payroll taxes, the former being higher in Canada, the latter higher in the United States. Taking both together, however, still produces the same result: Canadians, in the aggregate, keep less of their paycheques and investment income than do Americans.

How much less, as we said, depends on geography and personal circumstances. As a rule of thumb, from a tax point of view it's better to be poor in Canada and rich in the United States. A single person earning $20,000 in a high-tax U.S. state such as New York will pay about $4,100 in combined taxes; that same person in a low-tax Canadian province such as Ontario will pay about $3,500. If that same $20,000-earner lived in Florida, a state without an income tax, the tax bite would be about the same as Ontario's.[19] Low-income families with children are significantly better off in Canada, because refundable credits and the Child Tax Benefit in Canada are more generous than earned-income tax credits in the United States at either the federal or the state level.

A study of income differentials in the 1990s showed that Canada's social programs did produce lower poverty rates, especially for low-income families, although this progress was produced by Canadian transfers that exceeded U.S. transfers on a per-capita basis by a factor of two to three. In other words, Canadians paid a lot to achieve those lower poverty rates. Union membership also helped, it being twice as high in Canada (33 per cent of the workforce in 1990, compared with 16 per cent in the United States), since unionized wages are often higher than non-unionized ones.[20] Canada's social safety net weakened in the 1990s under the exigencies of deficit-reduction, but the Canadian transfers still kept inequality from reaching U.S. proportions.

Further up the income chain, tax gaps widen in favour of U.S. taxpayers. The gap is small but noticeable in the $50,000–$60,000 range (again, differing slightly among provinces and states), but becomes large above $100,000. The top U.S. federal tax rate is 39.6 per cent. Adding the state income taxes, where they exist, rarely drives the total rate above 46 per cent. The critical difference, however, lies in the income thresholds at which these highest rates apply. In Canada, a taxpayer faces the highest marginal tax rate at $62,500. This will rise to $70,000 in 2004. In the United States, a taxpayer strikes the highest marginal tax rate at $283,500, or about $440,000 Canadian, roughly seven times the income on a currency-adjusted basis. Since average family incomes in Canada are about $42,000, it means that once taxpayers earn about 50 per cent above the average, they start paying Canada's highest marginal tax rate. A young professional could reasonably expect, depending on his or her career, to be earning an income of 50 per cent above the family average not too long after arriving on the job market. This would be especially true in business fields. At the very time in their lives when young professionals are thinking of forming a family or buying a home or experiencing childcare expenses, Canada's taxman hits them with the highest marginal tax rate, a rate often considerably higher than that faced by an American in equivalent circumstances.

The Chrétien government's February, 2000 budget did very little about taxes on those earning $70,000 or more, the people most likely to emigrate. The government re-indexed the tax system, but that was of no consequence for those already in the highest tax bracket. The threshold at which the highest rate is paid only increased to $70,000, hardly a king's ransom of a salary. The government announced the removal of the 5 per cent personal income surtax for those earning up to $85,000, but kept it in place at declining levels for everyone else until 2004. In other words, a tax first imposed to fight the deficit in 1986 would not be removed until 2004, eighteen years later and eight years after the deficit had disappeared. The 2000 budget, in short, did next to nothing for the Canadians most likely to move south, a recipe for continuing losses of talented people.

Canadian taxpayers also face sharply higher sales taxes (although U.S. property taxes tend to be higher). The average state sales tax in the United States is 6 per cent; in Canada, the combined average provincial sales tax and Goods and Services Tax is 15 per cent. (Albertans and residents of a few U.S. states pay no local sales tax.) Consumption taxes account for about 25 per cent of total government revenues in Canada, compared with 15 per cent in the United States.[21] Provided there are significant offsets for low-income people, it can be argued that consumption taxes are a better form of revenue-raising than income taxes because they tax consumption rather than earnings, which are the basis for savings and investment. Whatever the merits of consumption versus income taxes, the combined effect in Canada and the United States of consumption and income taxes means a significantly smaller U.S. tax burden on individuals and families, except at the very bottom of the income scale.

People at or near the bottom of the income scale are the least likely to have the skills and educational qualifications to become Star-Spangled Canadians, even if they wanted to emigrate. Those in the middle- to upper-income scales are the ones with the skills and qualifications to leave if they so desire, so that, for some of them, the tax differential can be a contributing, if not a determining, factor. Put crudely, those who cannot move to the United States are taxed more lightly than their opposite numbers south of the border, whereas those who are potentially mobile are taxed more heavily, and sometimes appreciably so, than their equivalents in the United States.

For the potentially mobile, there are the extra costs of securing medical insurance in the United States and, depending on their locations in Canada, possibly higher housing costs. Silicon Valley housing is much more expensive than Ottawa's. An apartment in New York costs more per square foot than one in Toronto or Calgary. There are cruel and dangerous swaths of U.S. cities where crime, drugs, and prostitution, to say nothing of bombed-out streets, graffiti, broken sidewalks, and boarded-up stores, would scare away all but the helpless, destitute, or trapped. U.S. property taxes are often higher than in Canada, although, as with everything else, this depends upon location. American homeowners can, however, deduct their property taxes and mortgage payments from income tax—the most significant middle-class tax entitlement in the United States. Star-Spangled Canadians do not hesitate to take advantage of this plum; the U.S. Bureau of Census estimates that almost 500,000 of the 660,000 Canadians in the United States live in homes they own.[22]

Mortgage and property-tax deductibility is, on balance, bad public policy.

Canadians were wisely hostile when the Progressive Conservative party pledged a variation on the U.S. scheme in the 1979 election campaign. The U.S. policy favours homeowners over renters, thereby setting up two categories of taxpayers. The policy is socially regressive since homeowners tend to be more affluent than renters. It artificially inflates housing costs by encouraging Americans to refinance larger houses, and it drains potential revenues from the treasury. Canadians may correctly chastise the policy, but, like it or not, mortgage and property-tax deductibility is firmly established within U.S. policy; it is there for keeps. Comparisons of marginal tax rates, and the overall tax burden faced by Canadians and Americans, must include this policy as a factor because it will lower still further the tax burden on some of those who emigrate and buy homes in the United States.

The greatest scare for Canadians about U.S. society is arguably the costs of private health care, and these can, under certain circumstances, be scary indeed. It would not be unusual for an individual in business for himself who needed health care for his family to pay $8,000 to $10,000 a year for comprehensive coverage, and coverage might be difficult to find if a family member had a serious, ongoing health problem, a so-called pre-existing condition. About 44 million Americans are without any health-care insurance, and they must rely on policies for "indigent" care at public hospitals or the *pro bono* services of local doctors. The majority of those without coverage are not the very poor or the elderly; government programs cover these people. The most vulnerable are those with low to moderate incomes who do not qualify for government programs.

By virtue of being skilled and educated, Star-Spangled Canadians seldom fall into the pit of having no insurance. They are covered, like most Americans, by company or collective plans providing reasonable or excellent medical care. Their costs depend upon the plans, the number of family members, and how much coverage they are willing to buy. My interviews suggested that many are paying $1,500 to $3,000 a year for comprehensive coverage through plans organized by their places of employment. For Star-Spangled Canadians, this additional cost eats into, but usually does not eliminate, the larger after-tax income they enjoy.

Consider a few cross-border tax calculations. The table below presents information compiled in 1999 by the KPMG consulting firm. It contrasts personal income-tax rates and taxes payable in Canadian dollars for a one-earner family with one child.

Canadian / United States Tax Comparison

	British Columbia	Alberta	Ontario	Washington	Oregon
$50,000					
Income tax	11,905	11,717	11,188	4,080	6,732
Social Security	1,069	1,069	1,069	3,101	3,101
Medical Care	864	816	—	725	725
	13,838	13,602	12,257	7,906	10,558
Effective tax rate	27.68%	27.20%	24.51%	15.81%	21.12%
Marginal tax rate*	38.87%	38.86%	36.53%	22.65%	31.65%
$100,000					
Income tax	36,467	34,102	34,859	13,359	20,473
Social Security	1,069	1,069	1,069	6,200	6,200
Medical care	864	816	—	1,451	1,451
	38,400	35,987	35,928	21,010	28,124
Effective tax rate	38.40%	35.99%	35.93%	21.01%	28.12%
Marginal tax rate*	52.70%	45.60%	49.60%	35.65%	44.65%

Rate on last dollar of income earned

Any cross-border comparison can be poked full of exceptions and anomalies. If a person living in Oregon or Washington were not covered by a company health plan, he or she might be paying well in excess of the amounts shown here for "medical care." Similarly the yearly contributions for Canada Pension Plan premiums (shown under Social Security) are rising in Canada. No accounting is shown for child-tax-benefits programs, mortgage and property-tax deductibility, sales taxes, user fees, or money taxpayers might need to save for university education. On the other hand, Americans get to deduct a portion of their health-care premiums and payroll taxes from net federal tax paid. The fairest comparison would be between two "high tax" jurisdictions (Oregon and British Columbia) and two "low tax" ones (Alberta, or Ontario, and Washington). Accepting all that, the table clearly shows that the U.S. taxpayer at middle- and upper-income levels is left with more disposable income after tax. At $100,000, the U.S. resident is $10,000–$15,000 better off after taxes; at $50,000, he or she is $1,700 to $6,000 better off.

These tax gaps can be illustrated in another way suggested in a table prepared by CIBC–Wood Gundy, based on Canadian Department of Finance figures. The table reinforces how hard middle-income Canadians get hit by personal income taxes when they start earning $50,000 to $70,000 per year: the governments tax 40 to 50 per cent of every additional dollar they earn. For more affluent people, those earning $95,000 to

$250,000, the marginal tax gap is as high as nineteen points. These middle to upper-income Canadians tend to be the most potentially mobile because they have the most education and skills. They are the ones, therefore, most susceptible to entreaties from U.S. companies or institutions.

Comparison of Canada–U.S. Marginal Tax Rates (Fed. & Prov./State)			
Income	Marginal Tax Rates		Difference
($000 Can)	Canada	United States	(% points)
7–30	25	17	8
30–60	40	26	14
60–95	51	32	19
95–200	51	35	16
200–430	51	40	11
over 430	51	45	6

Kevyn Nightingale, a Toronto tax expert specializing in cross-border tax comparisons, kindly sent me a computer program that allows anyone to make comparisons of tax loads, including payroll taxes, in the two countries for any income level and family size.

One of the disks he sent contained comparisons for 1999 between Ontario, a low-tax Canadian province, and California, a high-tax U.S. state. For a single person without a mortgage, the total tax paid in these jurisdictions is about the same for incomes from $40,000 to $125,000, Below $40,000, the Canadian taxpayer is slightly better off, paying 7–9% less than an equivalent American; above $125,000, the American is better off by 4–5%. A California couple with two children and a mortgage is better off at every income level above $15,000, paying $1,165 less in income and payroll taxes at $45,000, $5,798 less at $90,000, and $15,733 less at $150,000.

Nightingale's other disk offered comparisons for 1998 between Ontario and states with no income tax, such as Florida. Obviously, the tax gap was much larger than between Ontario and California. For example, a couple with two children earning $45,000 keeps $1,472 more in one of these states than in Ontario; at $90,000 of family income, the gap is $9,155 and, at $150,000, the gap is $25,527. Single earners pay less tax in these states at every income level above $30,000; below that figure, the Canadian tax regime is slightly more favourable.

An old saw in Canada–U.S. tax comparisons had it that it was better to earn money in the United States but to die in Canada. Or, to flip the phrase around, Canada would tax you more heavily in life, the United

States in death. Canada abolished estate (or death) taxes decades ago, believing them to be administratively cumbersome and easy to avoid. The United States kept its estate taxes. Theoretically, therefore, the U.S. authorities will capture in death what they allowed a taxpayer to enjoy during life. That is the theory. Why, therefore, does an observer of U.S. life see so much accumulated wealth? Why are fortunes apparently passed down from generation to generation? Aren't estate taxes supposed to prevent, or at least mitigate, this kind of inherited wealth?

One effect of estate taxes is to encourage philanthropy. Wealthy families confronting estate taxes often prefer to create some sort of foundation and give their money away than wait for the taxman to arrive. Foundations run by grandchildren are an effective tax dodge used by wealthy families. Philanthropy alone, however, does not explain the apparent ineffectiveness of estate taxes. So I asked ex-patriate Canadians what happens to U.S. estate taxes.

Wallace Weylie, an ex-patriate practising law in Indian Rock Beach, Florida, patiently explained some of the dodges. The U.S. Congress has raised the exemptions for estate taxes from $600,000 to more than $1 million, "so you have to have a lot of money for it to be relevant," Weylie explained. "Parents create trusts for children or grandchildren, sock money into those trusts so that upon death their own net worth is below the estate-tax threshold. The U.S. taxman may come knocking upon death but he will find little or nothing to tax. People even put their expensive houses into the trust, so they avoid having to pay capital-gains taxes on their houses. A whole industry of lawyers and accountants exists across the United States to arrange matters for Americans so that they avoid or certainly minimize estate taxes."

David Roberts, an Albertan practising cross-border tax law in San Francisco and at his home near Yosemite National Park, explained that "there are so many funny little vehicles with funny little evaluation principles that you can use." He continued: "However artificial Revenue Canada rules might be in some income-tax areas, U.S. estate-tax rules make no sense in any planet. They're quite comfortable with the idea that you can magically give away value. It will just go 'poof.' Which is the name of the game: getting value out of the older generation and into a younger generation through transactions that in my mind are so patently transparent. But that's accepted. They're artificial and everyone accepts that. Maybe because estate taxes are so high, people accept that you can't practically impose a tax of 55 per cent of gross value, so the price is you accept the artificial means to reduce the tax exposure.

There's this theory in criminal law that if you have unduly harsh penalties, judges and juries won't convict. Maybe it's the same principle being applied." Roberts underscored his point by referring to a congressional study into estate taxes that concluded their administration rendered them "essentially voluntary."

All kinds of clever dodges therefore allow Americans to avoid altogether, or minimize, estate taxes, from deeding money to children each year to creating trusts for grandchildren, to putting fixed assets in grandchildren's names. Thousands of grandchildren of affluent Americans are attending university, including private schools with their hefty fees, on money placed in trusts by their grandparents.

Another difference in Canadian–U.S. taxation involves the basic family home. In Canada, no capital gains taxes are paid on primary residences. What you earn in appreciation you keep upon sale, and for many Canadians this capital-gains exemption is life's largest nest egg. In the United States, in theory, capital gains are paid on sale. But wait for the exceptions. Capital gains are tax-exempt below a certain sale price, and the U.S. Congress in recent years has been racheting up that price, to more than $600,000. The vast majority of Americans do not live in houses that cost more than $600,000, so they are effectively exempt from capital-gains tax.

Raw after-tax comparisons still do not adequately capture cross-border differences in income. People must spend some of what money they have on life's necessities, so a fairer method of calculating the economic standard of living is to consider purchasing power. Star-Spangled Canadians who move from Toronto to New York are often shocked at New York's high prices for food, lodging, entertainment. For those lucky enough to earn some of the city's high salaries, the higher costs can be offset; for those earning the same in dollar terms as they did in Toronto, purchasing power goes down. Conversely, someone who moves from Toronto to, say, Dallas or Raleigh–Durham enjoys a sharp rise in after-tax income and finds that housing, food, gasoline, and entertainment are cheaper. And no winter heating bills are required.

Assertions that lower Canadian taxes will stop the "brain drain" completely are wrong. Canadians move to the United States for a multiplicity of reasons, only some of which involve lower tax rates. Canada could drop its tax rate overnight to U.S. levels and people would still emigrate. If you want to make the world's most expensive film, as ex-patriate James Cameron did with *Titanic*, you do it in Hollywood but not for tax reasons. If you want a job in nursing, you might have to move to the United States, not for lower taxes per se, but to find a full-time job. If you want to perform cutting-edge research, you may have to move to areas where the libraries and laboratories are better financed and bigger clusters of experts are found, not because taxes are lower. And so on.

Taxes, however, do drive some Canadians to the United States, especially in the business and entrepreneurial groups, where economic calculations influence many personal and company decisions. Among those I interviewed, they were the ones who complained loudest and longest about Canadian taxes. And taxes do figure in that generic word "opportunity." Talking only about money and economic factors does strike people as somewhat grubby: when I asked Star-Spangled Canadians how much they earned, they often hesitated or refused to answer, the question being as impolite and intrusive in the United States as it would be in Canada. I sensed, however, that, for some of my interlocutors, lower taxes, which contributed to more personal disposable income, were subsumed in their explanation that greater "opportunities" brought them to the United States. Taxes were a contributing factor, but not necessarily a defining one, in their decision to take advantages of "opportunities" in the United States.

Taxes, however, did climb almost to the top of the mind when I asked Star-Spangled Canadians if they would consider returning home. Having lived in the United States, and having filled out tax forms and compared them mentally with what they remembered of Canadian taxes, did dampen Star-Spangled Canadians' interest in returning home. In almost every case, they would be making an economic sacrifice in income and tax terms by returning. Emotionally attached as they might still be to Canada, the economic sacrifices of returning tended to overwhelm those emotions. A few sample reactions, culled from many on the same subject, illustrate the point.

Stephen Elop, senior vice-president of Macromedia, a high-technology firm in San Francisco, who emigrated from Toronto, offered a typical kind of response. "I'm a Canadian. I always will be ... I'd love to contemplate going back, but as you think of it with the tax structure, it's very difficult to contemplate," he told me. "Part of the big attraction of moving down is the tax situation, and one of the big barriers for going back is the tax situation."

Gary Dupuy, who moved to Seattle from Calgary, is an environmental engineer who has made a successful career. He said: "My roots are still firmly in Canada. If I were economically comfortable I would move back. I think one thing that keeps me down here is the taxation situation in the U.S. I probably gained 40 per cent in income without taking a raise by moving to the U.S. It [taxes] would probably be higher now because my income is much higher."

Wallace Weylie, working as a lawyer in Florida, said lower taxes did not originally lure him south from his home in Kitchener. But he added: "Taxes are definitely cheaper, especially here in Florida, because we don't have state income tax. Now, that makes a tremendous difference. I figured out my tax last year on a gross income, and it worked out to about 12 per cent. We do have a sales tax that is 7 per cent. So I'm just way ahead of the game. Here, we can deduct interest on all the taxes we pay. We can deduct all our mortgage interest."

The motivations for moving from one place to another, let alone from one country to another country, can often be complex. Taxes do contribute to the migration of Canadians to the United States, but they are not the only reason and in some instances not a factor at all. Once established in the United States, however, ex-patriate Canadians are often deterred from returning home having experienced first-hand the lower taxes and greater post-tax incomes offered south of the border. If Canadians dismiss the widened tax gap between their country and the United States, they are being as foolish as those who believe the "brain drain" would disappear if tomorrow Canada and U.S. tax rates were even.

"This lazy fellow, Pugnose," continued the Clockmaker, "that keeps this inn, is going to sell off and go the States; he says he has to work too hard here; that the markets are dull; and the winters are too long; and he guesses he can live easier there. I guess he'll find his mistake afore he has been there long ... How on airth could we, if we were all like old Pugnose, as lazy, as ugly, make that cold, thin soil of New England produce what it does. Why, sir, the land between Boston and Salem would starve a flock of geese: and yet look at Salem; it has more cash than would buy Nova Scotia from the King. We rise early, live frugally, and work late; what we get we take care of. To all this we add enterprise and intelligence; a feller who finds work too hard here had better not go to the States." — Thomas Haliburton, The Clockmaker

HEALTH

IN the early morning of October 15, 1999, Shari Seymour and Michael Szymanski arrived at the U.S. border near Ogdensburg, New York. They had packed their personal possessions in a rented U-Haul truck, and three days after leaving Canada, Shari and Michael intended to arrive in St. Joseph, Missouri, to begin a new life. At the border, authorities handed them "temporary" visas to work for one year in the United States, a visa renewable every six months for Michael, a nurse, and every year for Shari, a laboratory technologist. As soon as possible, they would apply for "green cards" giving them permanent status in the United States. Some day, Shari and Michael thought, they would return to Canada, perhaps for retirement. But for as long as Shari and Michael could see themselves working, the United States would be their home.

Shari and Michael had been thinking for some time about emigrating. Shari had graduated in 1985 and worked in a hospital in Muskoka, but then cut-backs hit the local hospitals and "I was basically out of work in my field." In 1994, she moved back to Ottawa but could not find work in a laboratory. She fell back on her talent as an artist, illustrating children's books, and her interest in animals, working as a therapist for those recovering from injuries or surgery. But lab work was her first love. "I did some investigating in the Ottawa area since I heard the health-care area was getting a boost, but people said I would be looking at two years or so before it opened up. That was what prompted me to check things out in the States and Western Canada."

Michael had heard about the difficulties of securing steady employment as a nurse in Ontario while completing his nursing education. His parents had been urging him to head south, where they felt greater opportunities lay. In June, Michael and Shari attended a job fair at St. Lawrence College in Brockville, then, a few weeks later, a much larger one for health-care professionals in Toronto. Each came supplied with thirty résumés to hand to prospective U.S. employers, including those from St. Joseph, Missouri. The representatives from the hospital in that city of 75,000 people north of Kansas City liked Michael and Shari, and they in turn liked what they heard.

"The people in Missouri flew us down in July. We loved the hospital. The staff was tremendous. Both of us are outdoors people and the area was beautiful," Shari said over breakfast three days before the U-Haul crossed the U.S. border. "We checked the cost of living. We couldn't believe our good fortune. It was too good to be true. Great people. Low crime rate. On and on and on. We came back and we were ready to move."

Michael could have worked in Toronto or Ottawa, where a few nursing positions had opened up. But the St. Joseph hospital was paying the couple's relocation expenses and a signing bonus, in equal installments when he started, after year one and after year two. The Missouri hospital offered him a starting salary of $14.66 an hour, slightly lower than what he would have earned as a first-time nurse in Ontario, and he and Shari needed to make only small monthly payments to be covered by the hospital's private health plan. They would not be earning more at first in gross income, but after taxes Missouri looked much better than Ontario.

"We're being taxed to death here. It's very hard to get ahead living in Ontario," Shari explained. If they could have earned and kept comparable amounts in Canada, Shari and Michael said they would have remained. He was thirty and she forty years of age, and they saw limited opportunities to save for their future in Canada.

"The way the government has things set up—without looking at the cost of goods and services here—once you're making above a certain level then you're basically working for them. There's a big joke up here about Tax Freedom Day on or about July 1 after which you start working for yourself. My God, that's scary," Shari said.

"If I'm going to be working twelve-hour shifts for as many days as I can so that I can get ahead and have a little nest egg and provide for my family,

I'll do that. But when the government is taking a third or a half on top of what I have to survive, that's frustrating as all get-out.

"A lot of our friends unfortunately are unable to move to the States because they're not on the NAFTA list of approved professions, so they're going to be stuck here. We have friends who are making anywhere from $40,000 to $50,000 each and they are struggling just to make ends meet. They don't have fancy aspirations. They just want to have a comfortable life and provide for themselves and their kids, and they are barely making it. And that's where we would be if we had stayed here."

Michael chimed in: "The hospital we're going to has two MRIs [magnetic resonance imaging machines]. There are no waiting lists. The nurses I have worked with have told me, 'Go to the States. If we had the chance, we'd go. You're crazy if you stay here.' Nurses who have been working for twenty years said, 'We wish we had the same opportunity you have.'"

Shari's two brothers had already relocated to the United States, one to Maryland, the other to Raleigh–Durham, North Carolina. She would have preferred, everything else being equal, to remain in Canada. But things were not equal for Shari and Michael, so they became two more statistics—Canadians heading south, full of hope for the future mixed with regrets for what they were leaving behind.

"We love Canada. It isn't that we don't like the country, because we intend to come back. We aren't leaving Canada because we're fed up. We love it here. We'd rather stay here. If we had a choice. If things were equal, we'd stay here," Shari said.

Monica Green, who grew up in Tillsonburg, Ontario, graduated from the University of Western Ontario's nursing program in 1993, eager to practise her profession as a pediatric nurse. Just in case, however, Monica and a group of friends drove across the border to Michigan to write that state's nursing examinations. As she was uncertain about job prospects at home, those Michigan credentials would stand her in good stead throughout the United States, where not every state recognizes Canadian nursing credentials. It turned out to be a wise trip.

When Green graduated, a bunch of her classmates headed south immediately, but she wanted to remain in Canada. Green emerged from Western, however, to find an evaporating job market. She could not find any work at first, then she found some casual employment, on call whenever someone was needed.

"I worked like that for two and a half years, with no prebooked hours. That's okay for someone not married like me, but after two and a half years

I got tired of it. It was hard on the bills. There was nothing I could depend upon, and I just got tired of it. My only option was to look in the United States," she recalled one morning at the Duke University Medical Center cafeteria.

Green took a week off and, with her sister, began driving through the eastern part of the United States: Syracuse, Boston, Providence, Baltimore, New York City. "I just copied a whole bunch of résumés, brought some nice clothes and basically showed up saying 'Can I speak to your nursing manager' or whoever was doing the recruiting. Some places said they weren't hiring; others said they were and interviewed me on the spot.

"That's what happened at Duke. It worked out really well. It just seemed to click ... That week, they just happened to have two positions in the pediatric intensive care unit ... I started less than a month later."

Green started working at Duke for a little more than $16 (U.S.) an hour, an hourly wage that rises with shift differentials, about what she would have earned as a young nurse in Ontario. But, she added, Duke pays 80 per cent of her tuition while she studies for a Master of Nursing degree, a subsidy Canadian hospitals would not match. After taxes, she's much better off financially in Raleigh–Durham, North Carolina, than in southern Ontario. And Green won't be returning to Canada. Pierre, whom she will likely marry, is a young surgeon in training at Duke—an Acadian by descent whose father, a family doctor, moved for financial reasons to Pennsylvania from Caraquet, New Brunswick, when Pierre was eleven.

Scott Holmes, a twenty-five-year-old from Brantford, Ontario, did not want to leave Canada either, but, like Monica Green, he discovered the same parched job market for nurses. He, too, attended a nurses' recruiting fair in Toronto, learned about the Duke Medical Center, and signed on with a one-year "temporary visa" that can be renewed or used as a springboard for more permanent status.

When we spoke, Holmes had been only nine months in the United States. "Dollar-wise," he said, "the salary is about the same, but the cost of living is cheaper." He'd like to return to Canada some day, "but I don't know when. When I came down here, I gave myself a year, and if I didn't like it I'd go home. Right now, I'm ready to stay for several years, but I do eventually want to go home." A lot of Canadians who go the United States share Holmes's hope or intention to return. Many of them do not, as Holmes discovered: "A guy I chum around with has been here fourteen years, and he always said he was going to go home."

Vicki and Jim Jack headed south from Oshawa, Ontario, about the same time Monica Green graduated from Western. Vicki was a nurse, Jim a paramedic. They are the kind of salt-of-the-earth people communities depend upon: dedicated parents of three children, hard-working, involved in a range of local activities. But they had a bad break. They invested with other family members in a furniture business in the early 1990s, when the recession and the introduction of the Goods and Services Tax drove down consumer demand for durable goods. The combination swallowed up the furniture company and the Jacks' savings. They declared bankruptcy, then wondered how to stitch together their finances. Canada, to which they were fiercely attached, seemed nonetheless the wrong place to begin again.

Vicki had practised nursing for sixteen years in Canada. Looking for work, she attended a recruiting fair in Toronto, returned home to Oshawa and asked her husband, "What do you think about North Carolina?" Two months later, they visited the state. Vicki found a job at a Chapel Hill hospital that arranged her work visa. The Jacks' extended family in Oshawa organized a going-away party, collecting $700 as a going-away gift.

Vicki's visa only allowed her to work. Jim could not, so they approached an immigration lawyer who applied for green cards for both of them. The legal fees cost $1,500, but the magic green cards arrived within three months. Jim could therefore join Vicki in the workforce, and he found a paramedic's job at Durham Regional Hospital, an eye-opening and disturbing position even for an experienced Canadian paramedic.

"The first thing they issued was a bullet-proof vest. In six months I did more shootings than in eight years in Oshawa. I don't think a paramedic has been killed in this state, but there have definitely been paramedics and ambulances shot at. That's what caused them to make bullet-proof vests standard equipment in Durham," Jim recalled.

Deciding the paramedic's life was not for him in Durham, Jim enrolled in nursing school while continuing to work part-time. When I spoke to the couple, they were both employed at Rex Hospital in Cary, a suburb of Raleigh. They had bought a house. Jim earns $16.50 an hour, Vicki a basic rate of $23.46 an hour that goes up for a night shift. Their three children have done splendidly in school. All are in a program for gifted students. Their oldest received early acceptance to the University of North Carolina at Chapel Hill, an excellent state university. Vicki and Jack calculate his education will cost about $7,000 a year, including $3,200 for tuition—roughly comparable to, or perhaps even less than, the cost to a Canadian family for a son or daughter studying at a university near home.

With North Carolina's low state taxes and the deductibility of mortgage interest and property taxes, the Jacks are financially much further ahead than in Oshawa. North Carolina has been good to them. Vicki has eleven siblings in Canada; Jim has eight. They consider Canada "home," but they have no intention of returning.

While in Canada, Jim was always the one most interested in heading south. He groused about high Canadian taxes and excessive government spending, and considered himself on the conservative side of the political spectrum. As we chatted in the Rex hospital cafeteria, however, Jim-the-conservative made a rather unexpected admission.

"I'm actually opposed to this health-care system ... In Canada, we sorted out the priority patients by need. Down here, there is sorting out according to economic power," he said. "Although no one is denied care, I have seen instances where there is a difference between people with and without insurance. I have seen legitimate tests that should be performed turned down because the insurance company says no. At least in Canada it's the health-care professionals who decide who gets treated and how."

Vicki offered a more divided opinion based on extensive experience in Canada and the United States.

"They both have their advantages. You go to the cardiology floor, and you see people who've had a heart attack and the next day they're having their bypass. Back home, you wait months unless you're an emergency. But then I went to bone-marrow transplant, and they're not accepting people because their insurance won't pay for it," she said.

Monica Green, Scott Holmes, and the Jacks were among the 314 Canadian-trained nurses working in North Carolina in 1998 (according to the state's Board of Nursing), exiles from the shrivelled Canadian job market for nurses of the 1990s. Their experiences represent a classic example of people being "pushed" out of Canada by lack of opportunities in addition to being "pulled" by certain U.S. attractions. Even sceptics of the "brain drain," such as Statistics Canada, admit that during the 1990s the country did suffer significant losses among health professionals not compensated for by imported talent. No "brain drain–brain gain" equilibrium existed in the health professions, just a net drain.

Fiscal restraint and restructuring of health-care delivery became orders of the day in the 1990s as Canadian governments wrestled with the soaring costs of Medicare and grappled with their budgetary deficits. Hospitals closed, in whole or in part, and the lost full-time nursing jobs in hospitals were not offset by new positions in home care or clinics.

Nursing positions were either eliminated altogether or became part-time, contributing to the so-called casualization of the nursing profession Monica Green experienced. In the mid-1980s, two nurses were employed full-time in Canada for every part-time nurse; by the late 1990s, one nurse was working full-time for every part-timer. In theory, as governments sought to deliver lower-cost health care, hospital closings ought to have been accompanied by new clinics and home care. Not surprisingly, reduced enrolments at nursing schools reflected declining interest in pursuing a nursing career.

The United States had always lured Canadian nurses, and that attraction intensified as the tax gap widened between the two countries. U.S. nurses are not necessarily better paid than their Canadian counterparts, but their after-tax income is certainly greater. Not just the wealthy and mobile have more disposable income in the United States; middle-class people such as nurses do too. Núrses are invariably enrolled in excellent and inexpensive health-care plans at their place of employment. Still, the ever-present "pull" of the United States could not have alone accounted for the sharp increase in Canadian nurses departing in the 1990s. Rather, the "push" factors of "casualization," hospital cut-backs, and a shrinking job market in Canada forced thousands of Canadian nurses to look south, where they found eager employers and often pleasant communities.

Canada's publicly funded health-care system had suffered previous exoduses of nurses, but not on the scale of the 1990s. The following table illustrates the extent of the movement to the United States, although an explanatory note is required.

Before nurses apply for positions in the United States (or elsewhere outside Canada), their nursing credentials must be verified by the Canadian Nurses Association, which forwards the verification to the appropriate U.S. state licensing body. Not every nurse who asks for verification of credentials will leave, but the vast majority will depart, since the only purpose of asking for verification is to prepare for work outside Canada.

	RNs requesting verification of credentials			
Year	To USA	To other countries	Total	Number of graduates of Canadian nursing schools
1988	930	102	1,032	8,381
1989	1,218	137	1,355	8,964
1990	1,466	173	1,639	8,659
1991	1,788	143	1,931	8,758
1992	4,653	180	4,833	8,493
1993	2,005	119	2,124	8,391
1994	3,912	185	4,097	7,960
1995	3,922	338	4,260	8,180
1996	5,040	393	5,433	7,262
1997	4,336	453	4,789	6,750

Outflow of Registered Nurses from Canada, 1988 to 1997

Source: Canadian Nurses Association[1]

Compare the third and fourth columns. In 1988, verification requests were made by the equivalent of 12.3 per cent of graduates; by 1994, 51.5 per cent of graduates; and, by 1997, 71 per cent. In other words, by the late 1990s, for every ten graduates from Canadian nursing schools, seven nurses either working, unemployed, or starting in the profession were requesting credentials verification as a necessary requirement for working abroad, overwhelmingly departing for the United States. The inflow of nurses from other countries to Canada was very small, so that the "brain gain" from other countries did not compensate for the "brain drain" from Canada to the United States. In 1996, for example, 5,433 Canadian nurses requested verification, but only 628 nurses registered in Canada from other countries.

To put the exodus in another context, Statistics Canada conducted a study of Canadian university and college graduates from the class of 1995 who had moved to the United States between graduation and the summer of 1997.[2] The study found that nearly one in five of the 4,600 Canadians who emigrated were nurses.

Twelve U.S. states (as of 1998) did not recognize Canadian nursing credentials, and some states require Canadian nurses to pass nursing examinations or English-language proficiency tests. These exams hardly deter Canadian nurses, whose education is as good as, and in some cases superior to, that offered in the United States. So minor obstacles to emigration do exist, but, as the numbers in the table suggest, these have scarcely deterred thousands of Canadian nurses from becoming Star-Spangled Canadians in the last decade.

Several doors open for every obstacle. U.S. recruiting firms for nurses have been active for years in Canada. They place advertisements in Canadian newspapers such as one entitled "GRADUATE RNs! Get out of the snow and head for the coast. Thirty new grad positions are now available in Los Angeles, California." Or: "Texas is looking for you!!!! RNs are needed now in Med Surg/GYN, Telemetry, OB, Nursery, Critical Care." Web sites abound from U.S. recruiters, hospitals, and clinics enticing Canadian nurses—further evidence that when the United States needs talented, trained workers, the private sector will aggressively seek that talent outside the country, and public authorities will support those private-sector efforts.

Each year, the Canadian-owned Marskell Group organizes a two-day recruiting fair at Toronto's Royal York Hotel that attracts hundreds of nurses checking out employment opportunities across North America. U.S. institutions pay up to $2,750 (Can.) for booths to pitch their hospitals or clinics as desirable places for Canadians. In 1998 and 1999, for example, 125 U.S. institutions or recruiting agencies participated in the fair, dwarfing the number of Canadian institutions searching in this talent pool.

These fairs speak to the one factor above all others that lures Canadian nurses south—opportunity. While the market for their services stagnated or contracted in Canada, it boomed in parts of the United States. Wages did not drive Canadian nurses south. Nurses in North Carolina, for example, launch their careers earning about $16 an hour. That wage compared to these 1997 starting salaries across Canada: Quebec, $15.97; Ontario, $17.66; Saskatchewan, $17.89; Manitoba, $18.36; Alberta, $19.38; British Columbia, $19.61. Taxes are much lower in North Carolina than in any Canadian province, so that nurses working in North Carolina may pocket more in after-tax income, but the opportunity to work, rather than wages drove many of the Canadian nurses south.

Optimists might hope that, when governments recharge health-care spending, some ex-patriate Canadian nurses will return. Wages are not wildly dissimilar. Some ex-patriates might wish to return home to friends and family. My experience, however, suggests such optimism would be misplaced. Nurses are no different from other Star-Spangled Canadians. Once they have been gone for four or five years, they tend to forge new friendships and connections, start moving upwards in their careers, enjoy lower U.S. taxes and warmer weather (depending on the state), and change their "temporary" visa status to something more permanent. A trickle of nurses might return, but the vast majority will remain.

Maureen Hession and Nancy Barham are nurses whom optimists might have expected to return. They roomed together as nursing students two decades ago at Sheridan College, west of Toronto. They decided upon graduation that they would move somewhere together. Nancy was keen on Nova Scotia, but nursing in the province had entered a lean employment cycle. Instead, they went to a nursing recruitment fair.

"Everybody came up from the States recruiting," Barham recalled, a southern lilt now inflecting her speech. "California, New Orleans, Florida, North Carolina. Raleigh? Like who ever heard of Raleigh? So we chose Raleigh. We had a cute recruiter.

"Our plan was to come down here for one year and get our experience, which we thought would make us more marketable in Canada. Then we decided we'd stay for another year, then after two years we knew we could get our permanent visa after three years, then basically go anywhere in the States. Then it was another year, then another ... So here we are twenty years later."

Going home is out of the question. Hession is married, and both Hession and Barham like Raleigh-Durham. A return would entail too great a financial sacrifice. They're settled, employed, happy, and yet, like so many Canadian nurses who work on the front lines of U.S. medicine, and therefore witness the system up close, they are of two minds about it.

"I feel health care is a right for all," states Hession. "Here, they don't offer health care for all ... I think there's got to be a balance between socialized medicine and the kind we have here. There's such abuse that we see: a CAT [computer axial tomography] scan on every corner, an MRI [magnetic resonance imaging machine] on every corner. You could present yourself at the emergency room with a headache today and before you leave you'll have every test and you'll know what you have. On the other hand, Nancy's father [in Canada] needed a hip replacement and had to wait months."

Alison Casey grew up and trained as a nurse in Winnipeg. Her family came to Raleigh–Durham on her father's sabbatical in 1979. She met a "guy," kept in touch, and kept thinking of Winnipeg's winters. "After we lived here that one year," she said, "I saw that there were other places than Winnipeg that I liked. I had a hard time adjusting to Winnipeg. I didn't like the climate at all. That was a big part of it."

A bigger part of it was the "guy," who became her husband. Now, when Casey visits her family in Winnipeg, she finds that "most of my friends from nursing school have left, either to go south or west. When I go back to Winnipeg now, I have very few people to call on. I think there's a general sense that I'm going to get my education, then I'm leaving ... I don't feel it's home any more. This is home, but that's where I'm from. When I go back, I can't wait to get back here. I talk differently now."

The nurses I interviewed—of whom I have quoted only a few—may have had mixed feelings about the U.S. health-care system in which they work, but very few contemplated returning to Canada. If Canada somehow fills its looming shortage of nurses, to which the exodus of nurses to the United States has contributed, the country will not succeed by luring back very many of those who left.

The aging of the nursing profession presents one of Canada's most severe health-care challenges. In 2011, without a large new infusion of young nurses, the average age of a Canadian nurse will be forty-eight, according to a study for the Canadian Nurses Association. That will mean as many sixty-year-old nurses as thirty-year-olds.[3] In Ontario, to take one example, the average age of nurses in 1997 was forty-three, and 62 per cent of the nursing workforce was more than forty years old. Forty-one per cent of the province's nurses were under twenty-nine in 1975, compared with only 11.6 per cent in 1995.[4] Government studies predict thousands of additional nurses—a study for the Canadian Nurses Association says 10,000—will be needed in the next decade, and Canada's nursing schools will be unable to graduate nurses in sufficient numbers to fill the gap. Nurses who left the profession for lack of opportunity will have to be enticed back, or those "casualized" will have to be offered full-time employment. An obvious place to recruit would be among the almost 29,000 nurses who left Canada from 1990 to 1997, but, if my interviews are any indication, very few of these will want to return.

This worrisome greying of the nursing profession also applies to physicians. According to the Canadian Institute for Health Information, 29 per cent of Canadian doctors were under forty years of age in 1998, down from 37 per cent in 1993. Part of the reason that fewer young physicians are practising today is that medical-school enrolments have been reduced since 1992, when provinces agreed to shrink medical-school enrolments by 10 per cent in an effort to slow spiralling medical costs. That was the kind of top-down decision inevitable in the command-and-control Canadian system, in which doctors are seen by governments as cost centres. The logic, appealing to bureaucrats and "rational" planners in a command-and-control system, suggested that fewer doctors would mean lower costs. Another reason for the greying—and for selected shortages of physicians' services— was one governments and "rational" planners neither foresaw nor could bring themselves to acknowledge easily because it highlighted problems with publicly financed health care: the migration of an unprecedented number of Canadian doctors to the United States throughout the 1990s. That 1990s wave built on smaller ones during the previous three decades.

An earlier wave carried Richard Townsend to Texas. He grew up in Oshawa, studied at the University of Toronto medical school, and opened a family practice in Newmarket. "I'd been there for about four years, and under the OHIP system your practice was practically 'maxed' out after four years," he said while taking a break from patients at his Spring Valley clinic in suburban Dallas. "We were working many, many hours a week, working in the emergency room, delivering babies. We had a very successful practice, but it was very frustrating. We were having OHIP problems. There were cut-backs. Those were the days of negotiating fee schedules with the Ontario government."

So, Townsend attended a meeting organized by U.S. medical recruiters in Toronto. They were offering to pay doctors' relocation expenses, find office space, secure a visa, and provide income guarantees at the rapidly expanding hospitals in Texas.

"I came down here and my eyes just opened up," he said. "There was this tremendous opportunity to restart my practice in a little more limited scope, which would be better for my young family. And yet economically the horizons were limitless ... In Canada, I was seeing sixty to seventy patients a day. I was being paid by OHIP. It was very frustrating. I had some quality-control worries about practising like that. If you didn't see more and more patients, it was a bit of an economic squeeze."

Townsend moved in 1978 and found "that within six months I was doing better economically than in my five years in Canada. I felt I had been on a treadmill. Here I was at thirty years of age, practising for four years, working seventy-hour weeks, and seeing more and more constraints. The doctor-bashing had started. I felt this was a bit more of a free-enterprise system, and I could practise medicine in my way, more like my father had done in the early years, and my grandfather in the days before him."

Richard Townsend was more the exception than the rule in the 1970s for southbound Canadian doctors because he was—and remains—a family practitioner. Specialists and researchers represented the majority of Canadian doctors then emigrating. The U.S. health-care system, based largely on private enterprise, demanded more specialists than general practitioners in those years. Doctors intending to maximize their incomes headed towards specialties, so that the U.S. system had more specialists than generalists, the reverse of the Canadian pattern.

That ratio poorly served U.S. health care following its restructuring through "managed care" of the 1990s, especially upon the arrival of health maintenance organizations (HMOs). These HMOs flowed from the free-market belief that the price of medical care could and should be set by bargaining. Individual patients, or even individual companies, had little bargaining clout with hospitals or doctors. But if companies (and their employees) could be grouped together into much larger bargaining units, HMOs, these could then secure lower prices from health-care providers and institutions, especially drug companies, doctors, and hospitals. HMOs with vast numbers of subscribers could then sign up doctors to deliver services, but if the price was not to the HMO's liking, it could either force a lower fee schedule or move the patients elsewhere.

"Managed care" represented an economic response to the soaring costs of U.S. medicine. HMOs, as profit-making enterprises, would try to secure services and products for the lowest prices possible and encourage patients to seek medical care in the least costly fashion. Cost-containment could hardly be achieved if patients' first call was to a specialist. There needed to be a system of funnelling patients to lower-cost physicians—family practitioners—who would then decide if the patient required the attention of a specialist. The economic logic of lower-cost access points for patients drove up demand for general practitioners in the United States.

The Canadian system uses this funnelling process for the majority of patients—generalists first, specialists later—because it makes organizational and financial sense. The Canadian system already had more generalists than specialists, whereas before the HMOs became widespread the incentives for physicians in the United States steered more of them to specialization than to general practice. With the arrival of HMOs, the demand within the United States for general practitioners rose and the country's supply could not adequately meet the demand. Increased attention began to focus on Canadian family practitioners at precisely the moment when physicians' incomes were being constrained in Canada, and many physicians were grumbling about their working conditions. To the specialists and researchers who had always been lured south was then added a wave of family practitioners, recruited by companies, HMOs, clinics, hospitals, and communities in the early and mid-1990s. A 1997 National Family Physician Survey found that 5 per cent of the doctors surveyed were planning to leave Canada within the next two years.

Every year, of course, some Canadian physicians who have moved abroad return to Canada. In the early 1980s, shortly after Richard

Townsend headed for Dallas, Canada's yearly net loss of physicians to other countries (overwhelmingly the United States) stood between 105 and 165. In the late 1980s, the net losses were tiny—37 in 1986, 51 in 1987, 17 in 1988. But the effects of budgetary constraints in Canada and health-care restructuring in the United States began to be felt in the early 1990s and pinched hard towards the decade's end. The table below illustrates the movement.

Annual Net Losses of Civilian Physicians from Canada to Other Countries

Year	Moved abroad	Returned to Canada	Net losses
1989	384	249	135
1990	478	263	215
1991	479	256	223
1992	689	259	430
1993	635	278	357
1994	777	296	481
1995	674	256	418
1996	731	218	513
1997	659	227	432

Source: Canadian Institute for Health Information; excludes doctors who moved abroad immediately after earning an MD or during post-MD training (prior to being licensed in Canada)

The net departures in the mid-1990s were about ten times higher than in the mid-1980s. Of some significance, too, was the statistical fact that 1996 and 1997 saw the smallest number of returning Canadian physicians in more than a decade. Apparently, the United States provided an increasingly powerful lure for Canadian physicians—the "pull factor" in emigration—while incentives to return weakened.

Put the outflow in another context. Every year, Canada graduates medical doctors who enter the labour force. How does the number of these graduates compare to the number of physicians departing? The following table shows the comparison, although in this table "physicians who moved" includes those who departed before being licensed in Canada because, for example, they were doing post-MD training (hence the higher numbers in the first column of this table than in the one above). Remember, not everyone who left headed south, but the overwhelming majority did. Remember, too, that the table should not be read as meaning that those who moved were necessarily those graduating.

Annual Ratio of Graduating and Departing Physicians

Year	Physicians who moved	Number of MDs awarded	Graduates as % of those leaving
1991	586	1,704	34%
1992	806	1,749	46%
1993	766	1,702	45%
1994	896	1,686	53%
1995	775	1,739	45%
1996	845	1,685	50%
1997	758	1,582	48%

Source: Eva Ryten, former director of research, Association of Canadian Medical Colleges, Ottawa

The stark, alarming, inescapable fact is that the outflow of physicians in recent years has been so great that it represents *almost half the number of new physicians entering the Canadian labour market from the nation's medical schools*. When doctors and policy analysts now criticize governments for having negotiated a 10 per cent reduction in medical-school entrants in 1992, and blame that decision for shortages of physicians, their argument has only limited validity. Even if that reduction had not occurred—and another 150 or so doctors had begun practising in the late 1990s—the record of recent years suggests they would have replaced only about one-third of the net losses of Canadian physicians to other countries, overwhelmingly to the United States. Counting only active doctors—not the ones who left before receiving their licences—Canada suffered a net loss of 3,069 physicians from 1990 to 1997 from a total pool of about 55,000 doctors, or about 6 per cent of the total. If that kind of net loss continues, Canadian medicine will experience increasing shortages of physicians, with attendant pressures on service delivery and waiting lists.

At the other end of the doctors' pecking order from family practitioners are specialists such as Canadian ex-patriate Peter Shedden, who did his medical training at Queen's, his surgical and neurosurgical training in Toronto, and now practises happily and lucratively in Houston. Shedden thinks that in the year he wrote his neurosurgical examinations in Canada, nine of ten students emigrated to the United States. Upon graduation, Shedden sent his résumé and an application to the American Association of Neurosurgeons and received three or four feelers. He originally worked in Houston hospitals, but now runs a private practice in the city and his income eclipses anything he could have made in Canada. Shedden insists that for the kind of medicine he practises, the

U.S. system is superior to the Canadian, financially for practitioners and functionally for patients.

"My perception in general is that people here get much better care regardless of whether they have insurance or not," he said over lunch. "For high-acuity things, there's absolutely no doubt in my mind that people can get care here that is far superior to anything I saw in Canada."

Even HMOs, so reviled by many doctors for their cost-cutting, intrusive policies, do not bother Shedden: "There's a good side to everything, and let me tell you that, whether we admit it or not, the HMOs have taught us to be more efficient."

Highly specialized doctors, especially surgeons in private practice, can gross more than a million dollars a year in the United States. As a neurosurgeon, however, Shedden must pay about $30,000 a year in medical-malpractice insurance, a staggering sum by Canadian standards. But hefty insurance premiums are an absolute necessity in the United States, the world's most litigious society. They add greatly to the cost of doing "business," and U.S. doctors must organize their private practices as a "business." Shedden docs receive a rebate of about $10,000 at the end of any year in which he has not been involved in a suit, and he has not been sued yet.

Eugene Kovalic grew up in Montreal, studied at McGill, then decided to do postgraduate studies in North Carolina. "After my first year or so here, I kept wanting to go back," he said. "But in the third year I was really enjoying it down here, so I decided to stay for a fellowship, then to stay permanently. It's a great institution [Duke Medical Center] and economically it's in a booming area. Then, I looked at what my friends were making back home versus what I was going to make in the U.S., considering the tax rates."

Kovalic, who runs a dialysis unit and conducts research in addition to his clinical practice, earns about $150,000 per year, about what he might have made doing similar work in Quebec. But North Carolina taxes are much lower and he has to process fewer patients to earn that income. He pays only about $2,000 a year for medical insurance for himself and his family through the Duke Medical Center plan. He scoffs at Canadian criticisms of the U.S. health-care system.

"The impression that Canadians get about the U.S. health-care system is that it's very expensive," he said. "They're going broke. You can get denied care. Everyone gets the best care possible. The poorest people here in Durham on Medicare and Medicaid [government programs for seniors and the poor] get better care sometimes than HMO patients, and as quickly as we can give it. There's no waiting around for six months."

Kovalic came to the United States without student debts, courtesy of Canadian taxpayers' generous subsidization of medical training. Many young U.S. physicians emerge from medical schools, where yearly fees can run as high as $50,000, with large debt loads. They have to repay those debts, which is another incentive to charge high rates in private practice. Kovalic doesn't sound remorseful or embarrassed, as some Canadian expatriate doctors do, about having had his medical training heavily subsidized before he headed south.

"I paid my tuition," he said. "Whatever I had to pay, I paid out of my own pocket. The time I spent working in the hospital I did a lot of work that they would have had to pay someone else more to do. I did a lot of work as a resident, and that was one less doctor that they had to pay."

Kovalic, without probably realizing it, is representative of Canadian physicians in the United States, by virtue of having stayed in the country after pursuing postgraduate work. According to one study, about two-thirds of Canadian specialists practising in the United States studied in the country.[5] He is also typical for another reason: he's a contented Star-Spangled Canadian physician.

A comprehensive study of the two groups—Canadians physicians practising in the United States and Canadians practising at home—revealed that Star-Spangled Canadian physicians were professionally happier. The survey, conducted among 4,000 physicians in each group, about half of whom responded, was reported in a 1996 edition of the *Canadian Medical Association Journal*. As the study noted, "the three least attractive features of working in Canada or the United States ... differed between the two groups. Canadian respondents most often chose levels of taxation, government control and level of remuneration; U.S. respondents most often chose incidence of malpractice suits, managed care and multiple insurers." Here are the survey results.

Comparison of physicians' satisfaction

	Very/somewhat dissatisfied	Neutral	Very/somewhat satisfied
Professional/clinical autonomy			
Canada	31.9	8.7	59.4
United States	11.9	8.7	79.4
Availability of adequate medical facilities/services			
Canada	28.4	9.8	61.9
United States	1.9	4.9	93.2
Volume of patients in specialty			
Canada	7.4	16.6	76.0
United States	6.1	11.6	82.3
Availability of professional backup			
Canada	11.6	10.7	77.7
United States	2.8	10.6	86.6
Level of remuneration			
Canada	38.2	17.3	44.5
United States	6.3	9.5	84.5
Availability of academic/research Opportunities			
Canada	15.9	50.6	33.5
United States	5.1	35.9	59.5
Government involvement			
Canada	74.5	16.4	9.1
United States	45.4	32.0	22.6

Source: *Canadian Medical Association Journal*, January 15, 1996, p. 17.

Shedden and Kovalic left Canada recently for what they believe are the greener pastures—medically and financially—of the United States. Huntley Chapman got out in the late 1970s. He's a respected, financially well-to-do orthopedic surgeon in one of the oldest practices in Dallas, specializing in lower-back operations. Operations on or near the spinal cord can be risky, so Chapman carries insurance to cover him for up to $1 million for any one suit, or $3 million for the entire year. It's part of the cost of doing "business" in medical U.S.A.

After graduation, Chapman phoned a couple of physician friends in San Antonio, who referred him to Baylor University hospital, where they needed orthopedic surgeons, or, as he puts it, "someone who could fix backs." He has never returned to Canada to practise, but, when he returns, he says his medical friends tell him, "Boy, are you lucky that you got out."

The waiting lists that plague the Canadian system indict it, says Chapman.

"I have a father who waited eighteen months after being diagnosed with an arthritic knee," he recalled one night at his home after dinner. "He needed a total knee job. He thought he'd be a good guy and wait until the last day. He refused to come down here to get it done, although I could have arranged for him to get it done quickly. He got to the stage where he strapped two boards to his leg to be able to walk straight. I have a brother-in-law who was diagnosed with prostate cancer and waited four months for a prostatectomy in Halifax. That doesn't happen here."

Chapman has done well in the U.S. system. But, during a conversation, a measured response emerged about the merits and problems of the two countries' systems. When asked for a preference between the two, Chapman offered an alternative.

"I'd do it on the Swiss or British model. I'd have a public system that was a good, equality system like the Canadian system, then a Swiss system of private clinics, or the British one with the Harley Street clinics ...," he said. "Of course, in Canada it's become unreasonable for a doctor to receive money from a patient. In any other walk of life, a lawyer's time is worth money, an accountant's time is worth money, an engineer's time is worth money. A physician is like a lawyer, an accountant, or an engineer. Is his time not worth money? If it happens to be holding an old lady's hand in a private clinic, fine."

Chapman on balance prefers the U.S. system to the Canadian one, but the U.S. system is changing, and, in Chapman's opinion, for the worse. Like so many U.S. doctors, Chapman fulminates against the restraints placed upon him by the HMOs. Peter Shedden may think the HMOs have introduced needed efficiencies to U.S. medicine; Chapman believes they are weakening patient care.

Richard North agrees with Shedden and Chapman that the U.S. system delivers speedier care than the Canadian for those with proper insurance, but that even those without insurance—some 44 million Americans—can still get good care at county hospitals, which by law must treat them. The waiting lists in Canada reveal the system's fundamental weakness, and even unfairness. "Here, if I have a patient that I thought had multiple sclerosis and needed an MRI, I could have it done within a couple of days," he said in his office. "There, I might have to wait six or eight weeks, which doesn't make any sense to me at all. I've had relatives who were sick, and the care they were getting seemed to take an awfully long time. Maybe the end results are just as good, but I don't think people have to be sick for that length of time when they could be sick for a shorter period."

North, now in his sixties and looking a bit like Marcus Welby, came to

Texas in 1960 for postgraduate study intending to return to Canada. At one point, he received a good job offer from the University of Western Ontario but at the last minute decided to remain in Texas to practise neurology at the sprawling Parkland Medical Center in Dallas. He has had a fine career practising medicine, teaching, and doing research, and he has been well paid for it. As a neurologist, North pays less in medical-insurance premiums than, say, a surgeon—about $4,000–$5,000 a year. They cover him for $200,000 per incident and $600,000 a year in total. The medical world North knew and liked, however, is changing for the worse.

"Managed care is changing how you take care of patients dramatically. I'm not sure I'd be able to say if things keep going the way they are that it would be easier or better here [than in Canada]. It may even be worse here," he said, warming to his criticism of the HMOs.

"I have to get on the phone and yell at people that the reason I'm ordering this test is because it's needed. Usually, you start by talking to someone who maybe has a high-school education who's been told to stall. You demand to talk to their supervisor. You get the supervisor, who will not approve anything. You demand to talk to the medical director, and eventually you get him. It may take a day or two, and almost always the medical director will agree with me ...

"The business side of medicine is just a mess. We're having to hire more people to do all the things that we have to do now to satisfy the HMOs. Each year, they ratchet down, pass you a little bit less for the service you provide."

North deals with the sometimes cruel underside of U.S. medicine as a specialist in epilepsy, a so-called pre-existing condition in U.S. medical-insurance parlance. "If you work for a large company, they have to cover you. If you're working for a small company, you can be excluded and you're on your own," said North. Faced with precisely this situation, what are his options? North replied that he could treat the patient for free, which he sometimes does; ask the hospital to admit the patient for free, which it sometimes does; or refer the patient to the county hospital. His daughter has a "pre-existing condition" that no company will insure. "When she requires treatment, she goes to Emergency and I pay for it. She can't afford it.

"All my classmates back in Canada are griping about how they're mistreated as doctors, but then we're all doing that down here too," said North. "If you go into the doctors' dining room and listen to the conversations, it's mostly about how they've had this hard time dealing with this HMO today. We're not talking about how we saw this interesting problem, as it used to be. It's all about how bad things have gotten … I won't be surprised if doctors here start asking for a Canadian system rather than the HMOs. They may rather have the government be the third-party payer and allow patients to go where they want."

Some U.S. doctors are so angry at the HMOs that they're conspiring against them.

"Doctors almost never took out disability insurance, so the insurance companies loved to sell us disability insurance," North said. "Today, they don't want to touch a doctor's disability, because doctors are bailing out. They say, 'I've had it. I'm disabled.' You can get another doctor to write that you have a bad neck and are disabled. They've now changed disability insurance for doctors because doctors were retiring right, left, and centre, whereas before doctors died in office."

Don Clark, like Richard North, has been practising medicine in the United States for a long time. Originally from Pictou, Nova Scotia, he studied medicine at Dalhousie and McGill before heading to Denver, Colorado, in the mid-1960s. He spent his career in pathology at the Denver General Hospital and was for a time a forensic pathologist for the City of Denver. He echoes Richard North's description of the evolution of U.S. medicine, and the role of physicians within it.

"Health care in this country is in a mess, despite what everybody will tell you," he said, sitting in the living room of his comfortable suburban home, decorated with memorabilia from Nova Scotia, where he still has a summer home. "I worked in a university and in a public-health type situation all my life and they [my American friends] would say, 'You've got a socialistic approach to medicine up there.'

"When I look at the health-care system up there—we hear all kinds of horror stories down here about the Canadian system—but people I know in Nova Scotia seem to get all the care they need when they need it. The problem I see with the health system there is that it's a total give-away. There's an overutilization over small things. I don't know how you regulate that. It's almost too available, and as a result people get put off when they need care.

"But can I say they've been brainwashed here? Organized medicine in this country has fought too hard. When I first got down here, they fought so hard against being taken over by the government. Now they've been taken over by the private world. I think some of them would like to see the government move back in again. Having said that, most American physicians would say they're glad they're not up there, even though they've made the jump from a totally independent practice to a corporate practice."

David Low, son of the former Social Credit national leader and Alberta treasurer Solon Low, landed in the United States in 1989 with a mission. He had been at the University of British Columbia from 1967 to 1989 as a professor, associate dean of medicine, and co-ordinator of health sciences, the equivalent of a university vice-president. In that capacity, Low frequently attended conferences of the Association of Academic Health Centers, where he got to know leading U.S. academic health administrators with whom he often discussed the differences between the Canadian and U.S. health-care systems. In 1989, having acquired a reputation in these U.S. circles, Low received a call from a headhunter inquiring about his interest in becoming president of the massive University of Texas Medical Center in Houston, essentially a stand-alone medical university that forms part of the University of Texas system. Years earlier, Low had studied and worked at Baylor University in Houston, so he knew the city well. He also believed he understood the weaknesses of the U.S. health-care system and could contribute to its becoming closer to a Canadian-style, single-payer system. How wrong he was.

"At that time, in 1989, I was very, very, very interested in the fight over health-care reform in the U.S., and I thought I could get into the fight and do something useful ... I was going to bring these heathen to the faith," he told me at breakfast.

"A year after I got here, my boss at the university administration in Austin took me aside and said, 'David, you're going to have to stop talking so much about the Canadian health-care system, because I'm starting to get questions and complaints from practising doctors in the Houston area who are afraid that you are a socialist and are going to socialize American medicine.' I said, 'Oh really, Charlie, that's what I'm here to do.'"

Low met with legislative committees studying health-care reform in various states, including Texas. He discussed Canadian health care with Hillary Clinton at the White House after the President gave his wife responsibility for drafting a blueprint for reform. She acknowledged the strengths of the Canadian-style approach, Low recalled, but she believed such a system would never be politically acceptable, so her task force did not examine it. Her proposals died under a thunderous assault from Republicans, the American Medical Association, and the insurance lobby, although some of the ideas advanced by Clinton's task force later emerged in the thrust for "managed care."

"Reform got killed by misinformation and by one statement: 'That's socialism'," Low recalled. "That's the ultimate stopper to any argument about anything. I can't tell you how often I stood in front of audiences—

there was always some doctor or insurance-company person because the doctors and insurance industry made this kind of hellish pact that they were going to kill anything resembling a Canadian system and they did it very effectively—and in most cases all they had to do was stand up and say that what I was talking about was socialism. And most people in the audience said, 'Oh, my God. Socialism equals Communism equals evil equals death of rights and freedoms of the American people.' So it was all over."

Having squelched a national debate about a Canadian single-payer system and even the much more modest reforms proposed by President Clinton, the medical profession found itself coping with managed care and HMOs.

"Doctors hate managed care more than they professed their fear of a Canadian-style system," Low said. "The reality of managed care is worse than anything they ever dreamed of. American doctors are frantically angry with managed care. You can't deal with it rationally. They're afraid, mad, depressed. I've got a whole bunch of them because we have the biggest multispecialist practice in the city."

Having worked in both systems, and having directed large health-care institutions in both, Low believes neither country's health-care system can survive without fundamental changes, although politicians in both countries are reluctant to broach the subject.

In the United States, Low says, "there are going to be a series of small or medium train wrecks, and after each one of them there's going to be a lot of fuss and eventually, in five to ten years, there's going to be a major rethink about where it's going because it can't continue the way it is. In spite of the apparent initial success of managed care in controlling the rate of increase of health-care costs, they're out of the box again." Soon after we spoke, some HMOs began responding to the torrent of criticism about their practices. Some eliminated company representatives who had to approve treatments recommended by doctors or dispensed with prior approvals for diagnostic tests or hospital admissions. These changes were welcomed by doctors and patients, although they may send medical costs skyrocketing again.[6]

According to Low, the Canadian system, too, will have to change fundamentally.

"I'm absolutely convinced that the Canadian model is missing at least two things, maybe three," Low said. "As long as the Canadian economy was expanding, as it did in the 1970s, it was easy to afford the Canadian system. As soon as the Canadian economy began to contract, as economies did all over the world, the system became unaffordable in its original form. The mistake that the federal government and the provinces made was to pretend that they could continue to afford this system as it had been affordable when the economy was expanding faster than they could spend the earnings. And they keep pretending to this day that they can afford it.

"I have argued passionately for the principles and values behind the Canada Health Act. Canadians, bless their hearts, have seriously tried to do the right thing in health. Medicare is the shining jewel of an example of how a country can do the right thing with the right intentions, but they forget something. You've got to be able to pay for it.

"While you can argue endlessly about the merit of co-pays—ask a patient for $5 every visit or $10 for every day they're in the hospital—I think that is salutary. It draws attention to the fact that the service being provided does cost somebody money. There's no question that Canadians have gotten used to the idea that health care is free. Rarely do they ever think that they're paying for this in their income taxes. The notion that health care is free is a wrong notion, because somebody's got to pay for it. I predict that Canada, in order to save Medicare, will have to introduce some form of co-pay.

"Canada is alone in the world in not having a private option. Nobody is for a two-tier system, but the way Canada tries to pretend that everybody gets the same care borders on hypocrisy. So it's far better to say, 'It's been wonderful, but until our economy starts to expand as it did in the 1970s, one alternative is to let the private sector, within certain bounds set by the government, take part of the burden'."

A few blocks from David Low's Houston office, Gordon Mills, formerly of Toronto, picks up some of Low's criticisms of U.S. medicine. "I will tell you medically that there are things that bother me enormously," Mills said. "To have to worry whether a patient can pay for care rather than whether a patient needs care … I swore I would never leave Canada because of that. To have to sit with a patient and say, 'Can you afford the proper care?' is something I find incredibly difficult … Right here in Houston, as an example, we see a significant number of patients with cancer of the cervix where the cancer is late and heavily developed because these women were unable to access pap smears and early care. So we see patients with late-stage disease that would have been picked up in a system where access to medicine was not a limiting factor. The working poor are probably in the worst situation in terms of access to medicine. No matter how good the care is, if you can't get access to it, you're getting Third World care."

Yet Gordon Mills practises medicine in Houston, and not for the million-dollar incomes available to specialists in the city's private practices. "I'm here," he said, "for the research."

"Here" is the M.D. Anderson Cancer Center, the largest, busiest, and wealthiest cancer-treatment and -research hospital in North America. M.D. Anderson epitomizes the old saying that everything is bigger in Texas. Twenty-two jumbo jets could park in the cancer-research space. It contains sixteen buildings stretched over six city blocks, and is still expanding. It anchors a square mile of hospitals that form the Texas Medical Center, the enormous institution run by David Low. Seven per cent of the centre's patients come "here" for treatment from around the world, their fees subsidizing the hospital's care for poor U.S. patients and extensive research.

"The positives for me are that, if we are going to do something in the long run for cancer patients, it is more likely to arise out of the system here than it is from the Canadian system," Mills explained. "Let me be fair. It's more likely to arise from M.D. Anderson than it is from anywhere else in the United States. This is the biggest, most aggressive concentration of [cancer] researchers pretty much anywhere in the world. This was for me a 'pull me.' It was not a 'push me' out of the system. I was actually quite happy where I was. Well taken care of. But the opportunities and potentials of this place were just unbelievable."

Mills had been head of cancer research for seven years at Toronto General Hospital. His academic pedigree was long and impressive: a PhD in biochemistry, training in obstetrics and gynecology at the University of Alberta, postdoctorate in immunology and oncology from Toronto's Hospital for Sick Children. He is the kind of researcher no country wants to lose and any country would be delighted to attract. As one of Canada's leading cancer researchers, he left because "the opportunities to do something for patients under this system are by orders of magnitude better than they are in the Canadian system."

M.D. Anderson's research budget equals, Mills claimed, the combined budgets of the Medical Research Council of Canada and the National Cancer Institute of Canada. He is one of 15 Canadian physicians on the M.D. Anderson staff of about 700 doctors. All of them see patients, and some of them enlist those patients in experimental treatments that form the backbone of the scientific work that keeps M.D. Anderson on the cutting edge of international cancer research.

Medical researchers such as Gordon Mills have access in the United States to public and private funds that eclipse greatly what Canadian researchers can secure. Republicans and Democrats in Washington fight over the budget of the National Institutes of Health (NIH), the federally funded medical-research agency, to see which party can appropriate more money than the other for the Institutes. Medical research is so well funded, so politically popular, and deemed so commercially vital that the U.S. government spent $1 (U.S.) in 1998 for every $0.20 (Can.) spent by public authorities in Canada for medical research. The $500-million (Can.) infusion of funds for medical research through a newly created program announced in the 1999 Canadian federal budget, plus increases to the Medical Research Council budget, will slightly but temporarily close that gap. Since the NIH remains a political favourite in Washington, its budget will almost certainly continue to enjoy increases well in excess of inflation. Canada's recently renewed commitment to medical research, therefore, will assist some Canadian researchers, and encourage some of them to remain in Canada, but it will not prevent a stream of them heading south to tap into the vastly larger U.S. resources.

The U.S. government's commitment to medical research is buttressed by huge U.S. pharmaceutical companies' determination to push back the boundaries of science and increase profits for their products. Every company searches for the breakthrough drug that, once established in the market, will be a proven money-spinner. Medical research is therefore deemed to benefit not just patients, but the entire U.S. economy. It's part of a model for economic growth that also provides much greater per-capita public funding for university research at U.S. universities than at Canadian ones.

Medical research also illustrates the U.S. determination to be first and best in as many fields of endeavour as possible, especially in science. That determination elicits massive philanthropic donations by wealthy citizens and institutions, contributions that are encouraged by the U.S. tax system. M.D. Anderson, for example, was founded with a gift in 1941 from Monroe Dunaway Anderson, a banker–turned–cotton broker.

David Low, who presides over one of the largest medical complexes in the United States, believes the commitment to research is rooted in deeper American imperatives.

"Americans do a lot of what they do because they really love competing," he said. "If many of them would be honest with themselves, the doctors would not say it's the altruism or because they want to help people or to do research, but because they love to compete and win. The medical game right now is a huge competition, much more than ever before, and infinitely more competitive than anything we see in Canada. It's a real battle out there—for business and for market share."

Scientific research appeals to elements of the widespread "can-do" American spirit, the rooted belief that, if problems exist, so must solutions.

"Americans think that death is a problem to be solved," Low observes. "It's avoidable if you can only figure out the right approach. There are millions of people in this state who believe that we are just one medical miracle away from eternal life, and we at the Texas Medical Center are going to find it."

Tim Evans, a member of one of Toronto's most distinguished families, has an MD degree from McMaster and a PhD in health economics from Harvard. He runs the Rockefeller Foundation's international health program from the foundation's office in New York City. He has observed how Americans have responded to medical research.

"There was a huge lobby by the biomedical research community in the early 1980s, because at that point public opinion was highly unfavourable towards biomedical research. Only 7 per cent of people thought research was useful. Now, that same question gets 77 per cent of people saying biomedical research is valuable. There's been a huge sea change.

"I was listening to the new dean of the School of Public Health a couple of nights ago. He was talking to a bunch of gentrified, monied New Yorkers ... What he was saying was that we were the best, and not just in the U.S. The knowledge, he said, that we're generating here is absolutely, unquestionably cutting edge in every way, and there isn't a place in the world that's better

"There was no humility. There was an incredible sense of pride, and of a dream, a commitment to be the best. It goes back to the American competitiveness, to be the best. I think that drives all the big institutions, and they can do it because they're not waiting for the cue from governments, wondering what the budget has for us this year. They know they have high-powered alumnae and they'll milk them for all they can, with the understanding that they will deliver.

"It's seen as much purer than making a social investment and something that is going to benefit society. Related to that, this is big business. The genomics [cracking the DNA code] revolution is upon us. This has untold potential for diagnostics and pharmaceutical companies. So America's competitive edge is probably going to be strengthened."

Gordon Mills placed his finger on Canada's dilemma of living beside this U.S. drive to be first and best in every field of medical research, including his own, of breast and ovarian cancer.

"The question we have to ask is whether a smaller country with smaller budget and a different social system—a kinder, gentler society with a social safety net that costs but is well justified—should we simply say 'Let's let all the research and all of the new advances happen in the United States, and once they've happened import them into Canada'?" he wondered.

"As a public-policy matter, I would not even pretend to answer that one. The alternative is 'Should we be attempting to compete on a level playing field with equivalents?' Should we be putting a similar amount of our gross national product into research? Remember that Canada ranks at the bottom among the top twenty industrialized nations in the world in terms of money spent on medical research. So if you're going to keep your best on a level playing field, you're going to have to ante up. The other approach is to pick a few areas where we have advantages because perhaps the Canadian system is different."

Mills poses questions that defy simple answers. Canada lags so far behind the United States in per-capita spending on medical research that billions of additional dollars would be required to catch up. When Canadian governments imagine spending billions on health, they think first of feeding the voraciously costly health-delivery system, with medical research as an afterthought. Some U.S. Institutions—M.D. Anderson being just one example—are so rich and are possessed of such a prestigious international reputation that Canada could not build an equivalent. Such U.S. institutions possess the key ingredients for success—a huge critical mass of skilled people and money. They build on that critical mass of talent, and the success it engenders, to attract talent globally. Canada, next door and with well-trained researchers, represents an easy target. A "brain drain" of medical researchers is therefore inevitable.

Canada, until recently, barely put up a fight in the area of medical research. It could always point to a handful of medical-research pioneers—Frederick Banting, Wilder Penfield, Sir William Osler (who emigrated to the United States), and others—but Canada has not ascribed the same importance to medical research as has the United States. The link between research and economic development, although mouthed by Canadian politicians, is not as acutely understood in Canada as in the United States. The pigmy Canadian biotechnology and pharmaceutical companies, many of which are foreign-owned branch plants, are less aggressive in forging links with researchers. The desire to be number one that permeates the highly competitive U.S. society does not resonate in Canada, a country that too often satisfies itself with sitting in the first row of the second tier while proclaiming its superior moral virtue.

Exhibit A of the Canadian dilemma works in Gordon Mills's unit at M.D. Anderson. Michèle Donato is an outstanding thirty-year-old graduate of

McGill who desperately wanted to specialize in bone-marrow transplants rather than practise general oncology. Only a few such specialists practised in Montreal, so Donato would have had to wait her turn there. Her research is also very costly. If Canada's state-run health system had made a financial commitment to her work, it would have kept a wonderful young medical researcher and physician in Canada, who perhaps some day would have put Canada at the leading edge of a medical subspeciality, but the ongoing costs would have been high. The United States can try for cutting-edge science in every field; Canada can target only a few speciality efforts, and even those are usually underfunded in comparison to U.S ones.

"If you're a transplanter and they offer you a job here, how can you turn it down?" Dr. Donato said. " I'm doing 550 transplants a year. I have the opportunity to learn and be exposed to great research. I have the opportunity to set up a new program for ovarian-cancer transplants. We were doing that at home, but we did four ovarian transplants in a year and a half. Here we did thirty last year, so this was an opportunity I couldn't pass up."

Dr. Donato is one of a handful of people in the United States specializing in bone-marrow transplants for ovarian cancer. She would return to Canada if asked to establish a bone-marrow transplant centre, but chances of such an offer are slim. "I agree that transplants benefit a small portion of the population. That's not the mentality in Canada where you want to benefit as many people as you can. But it's not by doing that that you advance medicine.

"Quebec's publicly funded health system is not geared towards super-specialized medicine. I would have been a general oncologist … The amount of research that this institution is funding, if you compare it even to any other place in the U.S., you'd have a hard time finding a place where I could do this."

Donato also reflects ruefully, even bitterly, on aspects of health care in her native province.

"This attitude towards patients is very different," she said. "We're very much geared here towards patient satisfaction, and this is a state institution. Patient satisfaction back home in Montreal was just dreadful. We made patients wait. It took months to get an appointment, to get a CAT scan done, whereas here we like patients to be happy and pleased with the treatment they are getting. And maybe we feel that way, and patients feel they deserve that, because they are more directly paying for it. The whole thing of waiting forever to get anything done, which was so difficult to deal with back home, we don't have to deal with that here.

"If you have insurance, we're better off down here. My mother has had a few health problems back home, and it takes forever for her to get an appointment with a physician. It takes forever to get a test done. I remember how it was, and it's very frustrating. My family can't reach their doctor as easily as patients here can reach us. They can't get tests done in a prompt fashion ... But if you have bad insurance, then you're in trouble."

Even when Canada does impressively finance a medical researcher, it may not be enough. Andrea Joyner had been eight years at Toronto's Mount Sinai Hospital. She had received funding from the Medical Research Council and Bristol-Meyers. She was married and happy in Toronto when New York came knocking, specifically the Skirball Institute of Biomolecular Medicine at the New York University Medical Center. Joyner's new position provides her with more money and scope to pursue her research in the development of the brain between six months and two years of age. As a Howard Hughes investigator, supported by a fellowship that runs off the $10-billion endowment of the Howard Hughes Foundation, she has her salary paid plus receives a generous research budget.

"I was offered this position here that was very exciting, and a position for my husband that was very exciting, so the offers were too good to refuse," she said in her New York City office. "This research building was brand new five years ago, [and] has four floors, each with a different research program. Each has eight to ten research scientists and labs. I was to be coordinator and set up one of these programs," Joyner said. "I would have an environment that would be potentially richer than what I had in Toronto because there'd be eight development biologists on this floor and on the floor above ... In Toronto, there just isn't a large neuroscience group doing developmental neuroscience."

Months after meeting Joyner, I caught up with Emma Patterson on another trip to New York. Patterson was on the cusp of a decision: to practise her speciality in British Columbia, where she was born, or in Portland, Oregon. "I'm struggling with it, but deep down I think I'll wind up in Portland," she said.

Patterson had begun her medical training fifteen years before. She was completing her fellowship in laparoscopic surgery, or minimally invasive surgery, at Mount Sinai Hospital in New York, one of that city's great teaching hospitals. In laparoscopy, a new field of surgery, a patient's initial incision is small; the surgeon's work inside the patient's body is guided by cameras and executed with precision tools. Patients recover more quickly than they do after traditional surgery, but costs in equipment and staff are high. When doctors refer to "cutting edge" medicine, they mean fields such as laparoscopic surgery. Emma Patterson was being trained at Mount

202] Star-Spangled Canadians

Sinai by two ex-patriate Canadian laparoscopic surgeons who had left Quebec—Michel Gagner and Alfons Pomp, and had intended to take her expertise back to Vancouver. Until Portland called.

"It's a big dilemma for me that I'm trying to decide on. I'm leaning towards the States, Portland … It's really a matter of having the tools of my trade available, just being able to do the job, the best job I can do," Patterson said. "So resources [are important] in terms of operating equipment, operating-room time, infrastructure, support staff, researchers. All the things that I wouldn't have in Vancouver … My old bosses back there are frantically working on it right now to try to scrape up a little bit of money here and there to buy a couple of little things to bring the equipment even remotely up to date. But it won't come close." Patterson thought British Columbia would need about $500,000 in equipment to support her work but had scrounged up less than $100,000. Would she go to B.C. if that half-a-million dollars materialized? "Probably," Patterson replied.

Patterson and I spoke during a kidney-transplant operation conducted by her laparoscopic mentor, Dr. Michel Gagner. For ninety minutes, with nerves of steel and an array of tiny scissors, hooks, and clips affixed to long, pencil-width instruments, Dr. Gagner cut away the tissue affixing the kidney to a patient's abdomen, sliced and clamped the artery and vein, then slowly removed with his left hand the precious kidney that would subsequently be implanted in the body of the patient's son. No complications. A good kidney. The patient should be home within two days, Dr. Gagner pronounced. To an onlooker, the whole procedure had been awe-inspiring.

Dr. Gagner worked previously at Hôtel-Dieu and the Université de Montréal. "After struggling and trying to get resources to do laparoscopic surgery, the institution or the university[in Montreal] did not have the resources to develop teaching in a minimally invasive surgery centre," Dr. Gagner said after the operation at Mount Sinai. "We did not have enough operating time to take care of all these patients. We did not have any team to take care of patients after surgery or organize their pre-operative care. So we decided it was time to move.

"I have thirty to thirty-five years of career, and I'm not going to spend it wasting it and fighting on the phone to get a patient on my operative list. I had a two-year waiting list, if you can believe that. Every day, patients were calling me and saying, 'When, when, when?' I couldn't take the pressure any more."

When Dr. Gagner decided to leave Quebec, he had four American offers and one from Toronto. He chose a clinic in Cleveland, where he spent four years before arriving at Mount Sinai.

"I visited all these centres and interviewed. We discussed plans to develop a minimally invasive surgery centre. This is what I wanted to do. I chose the institution that was best prepared for that," Dr. Gagner said. "It came close between Toronto and the Cleveland clinic, but in the end I decided to go to the Cleveland clinic.

"The problems were not as acute in Toronto as in Montreal, but it was very similar. I thought that it was just a matter of a year or two before it became the same. Already there was one surgeon there doing minimally invasive surgery and he was complaining that he did not have enough time or equipment."

Dr. Gagner trained at the University of Sherbrooke and McGill and spent his two fellowship years in Paris and Boston, thirteen years to become a surgeon, then a laparoscopic surgeon. He will make more money, much more money, in New York City than in Montreal, although living costs are considerably higher in New York. Money, he said, was not the reason he left: "When you look at doctors, and particularly surgeons, they're still in the wealthiest 1 per cent of the members of the population in Canada. What are you going to do with more money? You're still going to live a good life."

But not operating under conditions imposed by the Quebec government under the Canadian system. Hôtel-Dieu had seven surgeons and six operating rooms. Each surgeon got to operate only one day a week and each had an extensive waiting list. More operating-room time would have meant more costs to the public system. Quebec, in other words, was rationing availability of care.

Alfons Pomp, Dr. Gagner's partner in Montreal, waited five additional years before leaving to practise at Mount Sinai.

"Dr. Gagner had been talking to me for about two or three years about how much better it was in the States for the procedures we do. I'd been resisting it because I thought there was potential in Montreal to continue to do laparoscopic surgery," Dr. Pomp said. "I had a good clientele. My family was established there. My wife is French Canadian. We were very happy in Montreal.

"But things progressively deteriorated, especially in the university-hospital setting. There were administrative fusions. There was cost-containment. Everybody was entrenching and trying to keep what they had, so there was no capacity to introduce something new into the system."

Dr. Pomp, like Dr. Gagner, grew frustrated with the limited availability of operating rooms. "There is no comparison because the basic difference is that in medical care in the United States, the more patients you operate on the better you are. You bring money in. The patient is a source of revenue," Dr. Pomp said. "Whereas in Canada, the patient is a source of expense. So, it's to the hospitals' benefit to reduce costs to do the least operations possible [in Canada], as paradoxical as that may seem."

Dr. Pomp continued: "The basic surgeon in Quebec, he's lucky if he operates one day a week. If you're going to do a laparoscopic case, and it takes five or six hours to do a case, especially early on in the learning curve, your whole O.R. [operating room] day is going to be one case. When you have a waiting list and you're doing only one patient in every week, and you add three or four patients … to the waiting list and you only do one a week, it's obvious it's an untenable situation."

Doctors Gagner, Pomp, and Patterson are numbers to Statistics Canada. Three more doctors who left, to be replaced by doctors from abroad. "Brain drain; brain gain," although Statistics Canada does admit there has been an outflow of doctors from Canada in recent years. How does Canada replace these kind of surgeons with their twelve, thirteen, fourteen years of training? Certainly not by importing people from other countries, because those who practise laparoscopic surgery elsewhere tend to stay put, their potential for saving money and helping patients recognized. The cash-strapped Canadian system, organized by bureaucrats and hospital administrators, cannot afford to invest the large sums required to establish centres of laparoscopic excellence, even though this kind of investment would later be repaid just for kidney transplants alone, since patients return to work more quickly, and are more likely to donate organs and thereby reduce demands on dialysis machines.

Dr. Gagner's solution to what ails Canadian medicine and forces doctors such as him south is, of course, anathema to Canadian politicians frightened of opening a debate on the Canada Health Act. "Canada has done well, but it does not have a pressure valve where when the system does not go well—the emergency room is packed, you have waiting lists for operations for certain technology that has not been able to be developed in public hospitals—I think the system should allow a certain private sector," he said. "These valves are available in France, England, Switzerland, Germany. It's not possible in Canada. If it would be permitted in Canada, you would have a very small system that would be able to decompress all these problems. This is what is missing."

Dr. Pomp might agree that a small private system would decompress pressures on the public system, but, he argues, so would more spending.

"I am personally dismayed that the public system, that was better ten years ago, has fallen into the state that it is now. I think there is some serious reorganization that has to be done, but I still believe public health care should continue. It sounds strange because I'm now here in the private system," he said. "For the overall patient or population, I truly believe that a public medical system is a better system. It's universal and gives quality care to everyone.

"What the public system cannot do at the present level is do a high academic, cutting-edge technology because that was not its purpose. It was never designed for that. It was designed to treat the most patients for the most common good. The way things are now, you try to do cutting-edge technology but it's always on your own time. You're always fighting administration. You're fighting to get patients in. You're fighting to do these procedures."

Canadian physicians who emigrate to the United States invariably wind up earning more money, especially in private practice. Their higher gross incomes, and their greater after-tax incomes, usually compensate for the larger administrative costs of U.S. medicine.

Dr. Andrew Reid, an eye, ear, nose, and throat surgeon, left North York General Hospital in 1996 for Findlay, Ohio, about forty-five miles south of Toledo. He became fed up with the lack of technology and the cap on his income in Canada.

"It's a technologically based surgery. You're operating around the eyes and ears, so you need a CAT scan before you do a lot of surgery. You need a lot of equipment in the operating room," he said. "It turned out that I couldn't do what I was trained to do. Medicine had moved on in the fifteen years since I finished my surgery training … We had a CAT-scanner at the North York General. Somebody would come in with a problem and I'd say 'You need a CAT scan, so we'll see you in a month.' In an operating room, we had the first generation of sinus equipment, but the second generation coming along is more expensive, and I could see it was going to be harder to get that second generation. We had one-third of an MRI, which we shared with Sunnybrook Hospital, so the waits could be six months."

Like so many other doctors, Reid entered the United States and has remained there on a "temporary" or TN visa. Financially, he's miles ahead.

"I was hitting the cap in Ontario—$385,000 for your practice. So that's the maximum billing for your practice," he said. His personal net income was therefore in the $190,000–$200,000 range on which he paid the highest marginal income tax rate, put aside money for retirement, and paid disability insurance. In Ohio, his joint practice of eleven persons—doctors, a hearing-aid specialist, nurses, and secretaries—grosses $1.7 million, and his net income before taxes is about $325,000 (U.S.) "My take-home in Canadian dollars is three times more, and in U.S. dollars twice as much," he said.

For those who desire a mixture of practice and research, however, the lure of research budgets and advanced research often outweigh the financial advantages. A case in point is Kevin Landolfo, a heart-transplant surgeon at the Duke Medical Center. He studied at the Universities of Winnipeg and Manitoba before going to Duke for specialized training in cardiac surgery under one of the world's leaders in the field. Had Landolfo returned to Canada, the country would have gained enormously from his U.S. training; instead, he stayed.

"I had come here with every intention of going back ... As time went by and I realized the professional opportunities here, there was no question that, for me to blossom and to go as far as I could in an academic sense, I needed to stay here." When Landolfo left Canada for specialized study, "I would have signed a contract to go back to Manitoba," but no one in the province's medical world seemed interested in tracking his progress or enticing him back. He wonders why, and extends that question more widely to ask why Canadian institutions don't keep track of talented people who leave, then try hard to get them to return.

"I was certainly not the first person to have left my geographic location in Canada with skills that are not commonplace ... It's quite easy to recruit people to a place like Duke. Quite frankly, it's hard to recruit people to the University of Manitoba. You really need to grow that talent. If you are born and grow up there, that's home and that has a substantial pull for you," Landolfo said. "One of the things that bothers me when I pick up a paper and read about physician exodus from Canada is that they say, 'Well, only a small list of 1 per cent of physicians leave,' but my question always is 'Yes, but which 1 per cent?' If it's people like me, it's hard to train people like me or replace someone like me, and I mean that in an unpretentious way. We lost people in many specialties when I was training in Manitoba, people whom I viewed as irreplaceable."

Doctors at the Duke Medical Center are big revenue-earners. They conform in that sense to the Canadian stereotype about rich U.S. doctors. But the stereotype for doctors at research-intensive and teaching hospitals is misleading. Doctors divide their gross income among their own pockets, the hospital's research and teaching responsibilities, and the hospital's budget for patients without insurance, or those Americans call "indigents." A look at Dr. Landolfo's gross billings would produce an eye-popping reaction from a Canadian, but what Landolfo gets to keep at

Duke is a fraction—he estimates one-third—of what he could earn as a cardiac surgeon in private practice.

"For cardiac surgeons in Canada, because of the way health care is funded, you are looked at as a cost-centre, someone who costs the provincial government a lot of money because what I do is expensive, technology-driven, a lot of cost per life saved," he said. "In the United States, it's seen as the exact opposite. We make a tremendous amount of money for the hospital, for the division of thoracic surgery, and for the university ... In this setting, we're paid a salary, and the income we generate goes into supporting the infrastructure of the other things that are important to me. The real reason I'm here is the ability to be a scientist and an educator, the ability to be an innovator in the world of surgery, to move my particular speciality forward. "

Landolfo insists he has always operated on patients regardless of income or insurance policy, but even the Duke Medical Center feels the pinch as cost-containment pressures are felt within U.S. medicine.

"One of the things that inherently bothered me about the U.S. system was this two-tier idea," he said. "That's why I didn't want to practise medicine in a private hospital. Here, we probably operate on as many cardiac-surgery patients who have no insurance as those who do, but increasingly as this system changes, we are being forced to evaluate that."

Could Landolfo find a similar kind of practice—research-intensive work, cutting-edge heart transplants, same income—in Canada? "Not even close. I went to medical school first to be a healer, and there's no question I could do that in Manitoba," he said. "Then I went to be a surgeon, and I could have been a surgeon. But I could not have been a scientist and an educator to the degree that I am able to do that here, not only in a local sense, but in a national and international sense."

He adds: "I would love to have socialized medicine in this country, but it isn't going to happen. When there's 280 million people in a country, there's a critical mass for anything. There's a critical mass for technology ... that you don't have when there's a tenth of the population. But public-health policy alone in this country would bankrupt socialized medicine. Many of my colleagues don't realize that because they're clamouring for it because they're so fed up with insurance forms and calls ...

"We have one of the worst illiteracy rates in the country here, along with one of the highest PhD rates. We have the best medical care, and the worst medical care, right in this state, and the irony is lost on many people who live here. You and I, as Canadians, view health care as a right. They really view it as a privilege here, and that in a word sums up the fundamental difference."

Basic philosophical differences separate the Canadian and U.S. health-care systems, differences so fundamental that they place the two systems at polar opposites on the spectrum of health care in industrialized countries. Roughly speaking, two-thirds of all health-care spending in Canada is publicly financed versus one-third in the United States, although Canadians might be surprised to learn that Canada and the United States spend about the same share of their GNP on the public cost of medicine. No other industrialized country has followed Canada's insistence on the public provision of all essential medical services, and no country has adopted the U.S. model of relying so heavily on private enterprise. Canada is much closer to the philosophy of the rest of the industrialized world in defining health care as an essential public service, a deemed public good and a right of citizenship, yet even countries with the same definitional philosophy allow some essential health care to be delivered privately or require patients to pay user fees.

Health-care-spending pressures will intensify in both Canada and the United States as populations age and medical technology explodes. These will combine with existing inefficiencies in both systems to worsen the fiscal burden on each country of their respective systems, and that burden, over time, will produce further strains, and eventually fundamental changes. The severe upwards pressures on health-care spending will force reforms to each country's system so that in health care, as in so many other ways, the two countries will come, over time, to resemble each other even more than now. Starting as they do at polar opposites on the international health-care spectrum, the two countries' systems will not become carbon copies. Important differences will remain, based on the fundamentally different assumptions about health care as right and public good, versus health care as service to be purchased.

Neither country acknowledges rationing health care, yet each does just that. Canada rations health care through central budgeting, government-directed purchasing, and allocation of scarce resources; restrictions on medical school enrolments; limitations on doctors' incomes; and so on. Since no financial deterrents exist preventing citizens from using the system, and few financial rewards are offered within the system to those effecting savings or earning greater revenues, limits and priorities are often externally imposed by governments or their agencies. Externally imposed limits inevitably create supply shortages, because the supply of services is not tied tightly to demand. Government planners and hospital boards attempt to anticipate demand; they may even channel it by forcing hospitals to specialize or dictating the location of critical pieces of equipment. But planners cannot hope to dampen demand for medical services, except by periodic campaigns exhorting people to stop smoking, get fit, or eat more nutritious foods, and they are often frustrated on the supply side by the uneven distribution of doctors across specialties or regions, a distributional problem worsened when doctors pull up stakes and head for the United States. When demand exceeds supply—as it does in certain geographic areas or for certain treatments—waiting lists develop. No one in official circles describes waiting lists as rationing, and Canadians, quick to point to weaknesses in the U.S. system, will insist that delay is still better than no treatment at all, but waiting lists are indeed a form of rationing. They may make sense to medical planners, but they are distinctly unpleasant for patients-cum-taxpayers.

The United States rations health care by allowing about 44 million residents to be without any health insurance and an estimated 30 million others to have much less than full private coverage for essential medical services. The lack of insurance falls hardest on the working poor and the self-employed—public plans cover seniors and the very poor—and on employees of small companies that do not provide adequate company plans. Lack of coverage may deter some Americans from seeking proper medical care; it can deter others from routine but necessary check-ups and tests, so that illnesses may go undetected until they have reached a more critical stage, at which point they become more expensive to treat.

The U.S. system is also a mixture of admirable efficiencies and expensive inefficiencies. At its best, the system delivers top-quality care—and fast—to those who can pay for it from their own pockets or through private insurance. Despite the habitual Canadian criticism of U.S. health care, the majority of Americans are properly insured. Polls taken by Gallup, ABC News/*Washington Post*, and Princeton Survey Research Associates revealed that a solid majority of Americans are satisfied with their health-care system and their coverage within it.[7] American medical research is the best in the world. U.S. medicine employs the best technology and makes that technology widely available, even if sometimes the technology is almost too widely available because hospitals within a concentrated geographic area all purchase the same expensive equipment.

Yet the United States spends 14 per cent of its gross national product on health care, compared with 9.2 per cent for Canada, and 6.5 to 10 per cent for other industrialized countries.[8] It is fair to ask, therefore, whether in the aggregate Americans are receiving fifty per cent better health care than Canadians, because the United States is spending about 50 per cent more of its GNP on health. (The comparison is somewhat skewed since U.S.

spending includes health expenditures for the U.S. military.) By almost any aggregate measurement—life expectancy, infant mortality, incidence of disease, overall patient care—the answer is no.

A vast and costly layer of U.S. health care consists of administration. Almost every doctor or health-care administrator I interviewed complained of the administrative complexities and burdens of U.S. medicine: multiple insurance companies, a blizzard of different forms, widely divergent insurance plans, debt-collection agencies for patients behind in their payments, HMO bureaucracies and regulations. Doctor after doctor recounted having had to increase administrative staff or set aside extra time to cope with the administrative side of a practice. More U.S. doctors are coming to realize the enduring irony of the U.S. free-enterprise approach to medicine: the system is more administratively cumbersome and costly than the so-called socialized, single-payer system.

Most U.S. doctors overwhelmingly oppose anything that smacks of Canadian-style medicine, in part because they fear that it would restrict the freedom of patients to establish relations with doctors of their choosing and curb doctors' incomes. Under the new HMO regime, however, those patients covered by an HMO plan receive a list of doctors whom they are required to use or risk loss of payment. They must request permission or negotiate to consult a doctor outside that particular HMO. U.S. doctors and patients are in some cases now more restricted in their freedom than their Canadian counterparts.

Like Canada, the United States has struggled to contain soaring costs for its programs of publicly funded medicine for seniors and the poor. Few disincentives exist within these programs against frivolous demands on the public system (Canada's problem). The numbers within the affected groups are rising as the population ages and income disparities widen in the United States.

U.S. politicians, refusing to challenge the essence of the free-market system for health, are constantly scurrying to patch up its inefficiencies and inequities. They have toyed with or introduced everything from "patients' bills of rights" to laws preventing HMOs from dropping coverage for people with long-standing health problems, to juggling government fee schedules for payments to HMOs under Medicare and Medicaid. The HMOs, for their part, managed to squeeze some efficiencies from the health-care-delivery system in the early years of "managed care," but higher costs and resulting lower or non-existent profits set off a round of HMO mergers, so that a small handful of huge conglomerates now controls the majority of privately insured patient plans. The fear of size, so deeply rooted in the

U.S. psyche, now haunts U.S. medicine, with the largest HMOs covering patients whose numbers are greater than the entire population of Canada.

Since the driving purpose of so-called managed care was to contain cost increases, and since these costs after a temporary pause are rising sharply again, "managed care" must be deemed a failure. The United States is the world's wealthiest society, but if costs continue to rise as they have in recent decades, the United States could be spending close to 20 per cent of its GNP on health within a decade. And almost 15 per cent of its population would still be without medical insurance, a damning indictment for the world's superpower.

Nothing happens easily or quickly in the U.S. political process, where the checks-and-balances system, the federal structure of the country, and lobby-group pressure tactics all contribute to make sweeping reform exceptionally difficult. But the already apparent costs and inefficiencies of the health-care system will eventually force a series of steps to curb those cost increases. The United States may introduce elements of a single-payer model to reduce the system's administrative burden; without ever adopting a Canadian model, the U.S. health-care system may borrow from the Canadian example in the years ahead.

As for Canada, Medicare remains the most popular government program. Thomas Courchene, the Queen's University economist with an eye for the clever phrase, has described the health-care system's national cement as the twentieth-century equivalent of the nineteenth-century transcontinental railway. Every public-opinion survey shows massive support for the system. When pollsters ask Canadians what distinguishes their country positively from the United States, respondents always point to health care and gun control. Politicians do not dare to call the system into question. They blame each other for administering it poorly or providing insufficient resources. They claim the other is responsible for policy mistakes. They fall over themselves to promise more spending than their political adversaries. But not one of them will question the underlying philosophy of Canadian health care, including the requirement that all essential services be financed publicly, even though in private conversations some will admit that the system cannot last. Despite this political consensus, it is hard to imagine the Canadian system not changing profoundly in the next decade by incorporating at least some elements of the private-enterprise system to ease the relentlessly increasing burden on the public purse.

Canada and the United States are in certain respects each other's worst enemy in health care. Major changes to the U.S. system are usually deplored by critics as leading to Canadian, or "socialized," medicine;

serious reforms to the Canadian system are often debunked by critics as leading to American, or "two-tier," medicine. Each system is the other's critics' worst nightmare, a leitmotif of what not to do. Neither country, fixated on the other's health-care system, cares to cast a glance at European or Asian countries. Every country in Europe and Asia organizes health care somewhat differently, but the standard model in those areas offers a complete, public-financed system with either a parallel but smaller private-sector system or some private-sector add-ons to the basic public system.

In 2000, Canada spent about $90 billion on health care, of which about $62 billion came from the public purse. Total health-care spending accounted for 9.2 per cent of gross national product, down from a record high of 10 per cent in 1992, but far above the 6.9 per cent in 1979.[9] From 1976 to 1991, annual increases in health-care spending ranged from 7.8 to 17.9 per cent, well above the national inflation rate. In each of those years, the federal government also operated with escalating deficits and amassed the second-highest per-capita national debt in the G-7. Provinces, too, often ran deficits, so that combined federal and provincial debts totalled 95 per cent of gross national product in 1995.

Critics blasted the Mulroney government for its attempts to curtail government spending, the Opposition Liberals being among the most vocal. Yet during the Mulroney years, increases in overall health expenditures ranged from 5.3 per cent (1992) to 10.2 per cent (1989). In dollar terms, health-care spending in Canada almost doubled: from $36 billion in 1984 to $72 billion in 1993, of which the public share went from $29 billion to $52 billion, hardly a record of fiscal parsimony.

As part of an assault on the deficit, federal and provincial governments in the mid- and late 1990s slowed their rates of spending increases or rolled spending back. Health was not spared; indeed, the federal government sliced $6.5 billion from provincial transfers for health. The result was a sharp decline in yearly increases for health care to a range of 1.2 to 2.7 per cent from 1993 to 1997. No sooner had the nation's fiscal health improved, however, than politicians began to pour money back into the voracious health-care system. Poll after poll showed that concern about the future of health care topped voters' concerns, and politicians responded. The federal government announced in its 1999 budget an injection of $11.5 billion for health over five years, and provinces quickly followed suit with promises of their own. The $11.5-billion federal commitment in the 1999 budget did nothing, however, to quell the anxieties about the future of Canada's health system. Within months of the 1999 budget, cries were heard again that the system needed even more money, and those cries became a cacophony in the winter of 1999–2000. Premiers demanded billions of dollars more from Ottawa; citizens grew alarmed at media stories of over-croweded emergency rooms. More in panic at the political situation than anything else, the federal government "found" another $2.5-billion in the 1999–2000 fiscal year and included that sum in the 2000–2001 budget for the provinces to draw upon over the next four years. This sum was immediately denounced as inadequate, and so the clamour resumed for ever greater sums to be poured into a system that in private most policy-makers admitted could not last in its existing form but that no politician dared to admit had become the fiscal equivalent of a bottomless pit.

The sums promised by politicians were impressive but would still be inadequate. Health-care costs rise faster than the Consumer Price Index, so that 3 or 4 per cent yearly increases for health would not necessarily represent real increases in spending. The new spending would therefore patch holes and perhaps prevent the system from deteriorating; but the money would not fundamentally improve it. Quite apart from continuing demands from patients, internal cost pressures will not easily be resisted. If they are resisted, then the sharp upsurge in numbers of nurses and doctors who headed to the United States in the 1990s will continue, worsening strains on the system.

Nurses across Canada, having watched positions disappear and incomes stagnate, began, in the late 1990s, demanding real increases in their wages as soon as government spending on health care resumed its upwards spiral after five years of restraint. The pent-up demand for nurses within the system, coupled with the gap between supply and demand for nurses that will likely appear in the next decade, will force governments to spend at least some of the allocated billions on nursing positions and salaries.

Physicians' remuneration has dropped in real terms in recent years. Physicians' incomes rose annually by 7.2 to 16.3 per cent each year from 1975 to 1991. Since then, they have risen by 0.5 to 3.9 per cent, except in 1995, when they declined by 1.4 per cent. With figures like that, no wonder doctors departed for the United States, creating shortages in selected occupational and geographic areas. If doctors' remuneration continues to be squeezed, the exodus will continue and Canada will be the loser.

At about 2010, the share of Canada's population over sixty-five years of age will start to grow rapidly; an older population will put tremendous additional strains on health-care spending as baby boomers begin to retire in large numbers. They have driven public policy throughout their lives. They have been, in some respects, a quite selfish lot, demanding government services for which they were unwilling to pay during the years of deficits and debt. Their insistent demands for self-satisfaction will undoubtedly continue in their older years. This is not a generation accustomed to sacrifice or delay, so that whatever public irritation exists today over waiting lists and insufficient equipment will intensify when they retire in large numbers. Then, there is medical technology. It can sometimes save money—drugs are cheaper than hospital stays—but it can drive up costs, as in knee or hip replacements, expensive equipment, transplant techniques.

The cost pressures, therefore, on the Canadian system—from pent-up demand, the lack of disincentives for patients, demographics, medical technology, and the fierce attachment of Canadians to health care as a right of citizenship—will be relentless and growing. Only by pouring very large real increases in spending into the system can it be maintained. Very large real increases in spending on health will, by definition, make spending increases in other areas and lower taxes more difficult. Health care, to put it metaphorically, is like an elephant in a tent with a voracious appetite—when fed, the beast keeps growing, squeezing out every other occupant of the tent.

Since Medicare became fully operational in 1972, Canadians have never confronted the health-care system in the context of public choices. Canada spent hugely on it from 1972 to 1993, despite the country's deteriorating fiscal circumstances. Then, from 1993 to 1997, all government spending was curtailed; health care took a hit along with other government activities. Now health-care spending has resumed in real terms, but it will take a while for Canadians to realize that this new spending will not fundamentally improve the system, just prevent it from deteriorating. When that recognition dawns—that tens of billions of additional dollars have not markedly improved the system—and when governments are forced to curtail spending increases elsewhere to pay for those in health care, the public may come to understand that the Canadian system cannot continue as an exception in the world, denying a role for any private-sector provision of essential services to relieve at least some of the pressure on the public purse. The problem at the moment is that the merest hint of change to the Canadian system is immediately equated with the dreaded "two-tier" U.S. system.

When, as is likely, Canadians eventually come to realize that their beloved health-care system cannot become significantly better despite billions of additional dollars, the system will be reformed to bring it closer to models in Asia and Europe. One major obstacle to those reforms will be Canadians' obsessive preoccupation with everything American, which causes them to see only the U.S. model as an alternative to the Canadian. There will be political casualties among the first leaders brave enough to point the way towards a more blended public–private model, just as there will be casualties in the United States among those who inch American medicine towards the single-payer model for reasons of economic efficiency. Without Canada and the United States adopting each other's system—now each other's blueprint of what not to do—Canada's health-care system will feature more private delivery of essential services a decade or so from now and that of the United States will borrow some ideas from the single-payer model. Without being at all the same, the two systems will look somewhat more alike a decade from now, and Canadians and Americans will become even more alike too.

Sometimes I realize I may never go back. About a year ago I was
standing on a corner waiting for the light to turn, and in a mood
of sick alarm started to count: one year in Salem, two years in
Brooklyn, one year in Manhattan. We came intending to stay two
years; we still have no plans to leave. — Elizabeth Hay, Captivity Tales

ACADEMICS

RICHARD Taylor beckoned me towards a laptop computer on a counter separating the kitchen and living room of his home in Palo Alto, California. The laptop took a minute or two to fire up before Taylor began pointing to icons. "Taube, Taylor, Marcus, Altman ...," he repeated in a *basso-profundo* voice until he reached the end of the list of Canadians who had earned a Nobel Prize while working in the United States. Depending on how you count them, Taylor explained, there were eight or nine Star-Spangled Canadian Nobel winners in sciences and economics compared with four who won the prize in Canada. (He had not included Frederick Banting.) Six months after we spoke, another Star-Spangled Canadian, Robert Mundell at Columbia University, received the Nobel Prize for economics. Three other U.S. Nobel winners had studied extensively in Canada but returned to the United States.

"I don't subscribe to the usual view that it's the salary," Taylor explained. "There is some salary effect, but the reason isn't that all the smart ones are going to the States but that the climate for winning Nobel Prizes is much better here. There's more support. It's easier to start something. Most of these people start things when they're quite young. And when you're quite young in Canada, it's very hard to do something really big."

Taylor, a professor of physics at Stanford University, won his Nobel

Prize in 1990 for discoveries in particle physics that grew out of his work on the university's linear accelerator that snakes its way through the hills behind the campus.

"After I was established as a high-energy physicist, it would have been very hard to go back," Taylor said. "From the time I was a graduate student until now, I had more money for research than the whole high-energy-physics community in Canada. In the beginning, it was not very much money, but in the end it was a lot. In most of those years, I could essentially say I wanted to do this and have enough money to do it, whereas that much money would not have existed in Canada."

Taylor, born in 1929 in Medicine Hat, Alberta, was among the top students in his high-school class. Selected by fellow students to deliver the valedictory address, Taylor recalled telling them he hoped they would not move to the United States, the path he eventually followed. The detonation of the atomic bomb sparked his interest in explosives, if not physics, an interest that led to an accident in which he lost several fingers. At the University of Alberta, Taylor completed his bachelor's and master's degrees in physics, then looked around for a place to do his doctorate.

Canadian universities in the 1950s were pale shadows of today's institutions. Taylor's southward migration for an advanced degree—in his case, to Stanford—was an altogether common tale in those years. Only Toronto and McGill offered doctorates in physics.

"I had intended to go back to Canada," Taylor recalled. "As I got near the end of my studies, I wrote to McGill and Toronto. One of them wrote back a fairly nasty letter; the other wrote back to say they didn't have any money at the moment. A few days later a letter came from Paris asking me to work there." And he did, for three years, before accepting a post at Stanford, where he remains to this day. Many young Star-Spangled Canadian academics repeated to me variations of Taylor's story: they could not find a job in Canada, or they sent résumés that went unanswered, so they wound up teaching in the United States. Canadian universities apparently do not track gifted graduates who head south, and make few systematic attempts to bring them back to Canada. Some academics remain in the United States by default rather than design.

"There are several reasons for it," Taylor surmised. "The Canadians would be pessimistic about the outcome. Therefore, why bother? Second, they are a little bit jealous about what's available in the United States."

Star-Spangled Canadian Nobel Prize winners generally followed Taylor's academic path: undergraduate studies in Canada or the United States, graduate work in the United States, then bye-bye Canada. Henry

Taube (chemistry, 1983) went from Saskatchewan to the University of California at Berkeley; Sidney Altman (chemistry, 1989) from a boyhood in Montreal to the Massachusetts Institute of Technology; William Vickrey (economics, 1996) from Victoria to Yale and Columbia; Myron Scholes (economics, 1997) from McMaster to Chicago; David Hubel (medicine, 1981) from McGill to Johns Hopkins; Rudolph Marcus (chemistry, 1992) from McGill (PhD) to the California Institute of Technology; Charles Huggins (medicine, 1966) from Acadia to Harvard; Robert Mundell (economics, 1999) from UBC to Chicago, and later Columbia, with brief stops at McGill and Waterloo; and, of course, Richard Taylor (physics, 1990) from Alberta to Stanford.

These Canadian-born Nobel laureates represent the tip of the iceberg of the "brain drain" to the United States, but any reasoned discussion of the "drain" must include Canada's brain "gain" from elsewhere. Three of Canada's five Nobel Prizes in science and medicine were won by immigrants: Michael Smith (University of British Columbia) from Britain; John Polyani (University of Toronto) and Gerhard Herzberg (National Research Council) from Germany. Bertram Brockhouse was born in Lethbridge, educated at the Universities of British Columbia and Toronto, and employed by Atomic Energy of Canada at Chalk River. He won the Nobel Prize in 1994. And, of course, Frederick Banting shared the Nobel Prize in medicine in 1923 for the discovery of insulin.

Despite Taylor's forty-plus years in the United States, he retains strong ties to Canada, unlike the other Star-Spangled Canadian laureates for whom Canada has meant little more than a place of birth and adolescence. Taylor remains a distinguished university professor at his first alma mater, the University of Alberta, although the position is more honorary than anything. He and his wife bought a summer home in Blairmore, an Alberta town in the Crow's Nest Pass. He still carries a Canadian passport and, during our conversation, kept using "we" when referring to Canadians. He travels occasionally on academic business to Canada. He even once lectured Prime Minister Jean Chrétien at breakfast about the lack of university research monies in Canada. In a newspaper interview after receiving an honorary degree at Carleton University in Ottawa, he elaborated on what he had told me during our conversation. "The climate for growing Nobel Prizes is better in the United States than it is in Canada," he said. "I don't believe that we're shipping all the people who might win Nobel Prizes to the States. I just think there's much more chance for any individual to end up with the prize if he's in the States compared to Canada because of the support … I think that many people in Canada now have enough opportunity. I'm not arguing that we won't lose people. There's still too much equality in Canada. Research is a highly elitist business. Your colleagues won't be happy if you start to get too successful at universities here … It's the politics of jealousy. That doesn't exist much in the States, where you're supposed to get out there and kill."

Not every university boasts a particle accelerator, and only a handful around the world have one the size of Stanford's on which Taylor worked. Then again, only a handful of universities anywhere—and certainly none in Canada—benefit from the kind of multibillion-dollar endowment Stanford enjoys. Quite apart from salaries, which are much higher at Stanford than at any Canadian university, Stanford scholars can attract research monies, from private and public sources, that would make any Canadian academic salivate. What Taylor told me about the field of high-energy physics could be repeated in dozens of fields: "It's always tough in Canada to get enough resources to fight on the same level."

Taylor left Canada in the early 1950s when opportunities for graduate and postgraduate work in physics were extremely limited. Today's Canadian universities are much better equipped, yet they struggle against the lure of research-intensive U.S. universities such as Stanford. The night before I visited Taylor, a group of Canadian graduate students at Stanford sat in a semicircle at the Tressider student union building and recounted their hopes. A few definitely wanted to return to Canada; most were unsure.

"The funny thing is that the longer I'm here, the longer I can see myself staying in the States before I go back to Canada," said Matthew Lawrence, a doctoral student in physics. "For what I want to do in applied physics, it's a lot easier getting jobs. Through my adviser—he's started three or four companies in the area—getting a job here is going to be no problem, as opposed to going back to Canada, doing all the networking, trying to find a job. Plus the work that I do here is a lot more interesting than the work I could do back in Canada. But eventually, yes, I'm going to go back to Canada."

Lawrence's reference to the job market "here" was to the entire Silicon Valley area that stretches from San Francisco to San Jose, with Stanford sitting literally and figuratively in the middle of the valley. Stanford has produced many of the ideas, inventions, and people that have fuelled the valley's phenomenal economic growth. Stanford and the valley offer a classic case of synergy between universities and the private sector, brain power and economic growth, research and industrial innovation that form part of the U.S. model for success. That synergy exists in pockets throughout the United States, from the suburbs of Boston, which feed off the

region's colleges and university, to the "Research Triangle" in Raleigh–
Durham with its links to Duke and the University of North Carolina, to
the high-technology and engineering firms of Dallas, which are tied into
research at the University of Texas. Dozens of smaller, yet still powerful,
examples are scattered across the country.

Not only is Stanford, as a private university, unbelievably rich by world
standards, let alone by Canadian ones, but it is also estimated that one-quarter to one-third of the individually held venture-capital pools in the United
States are controlled by people who live on or near Sand Hill Road, a half a
mile from the Stanford campus. Almost every leading high-technology firm
in the United States—Microsoft excepted—has a huge presence in the valley. Once "there," it's hard for Canadians to think of going home. They
might insist that they want to return, and some clearly will, but the intellectual vitality and economic wealth of the valley entice many to remain.

"I came down here saying I was going to go to graduate school, then go
back to Canada," said Myles Snider, a Queen's graduate who recently
embarked on his PhD in physics. "It's still my view six months later, and I
hope I can hold to that in five years. But there are lots of opportunities
down here, in this area especially. It would certainly take a concerted effort
after five or six years to say 'Okay, I'm going to give this up and go back'."

The research opportunities available at Stanford bowled Snider over:
"The resources here are like night and day. Some of the labs at Queen's
are well stocked but there's two or three graduate students per lab. Here,
some professors have twelve students and five labs. If you went to Kentucky State, mind you, it might be different."

Matthew Lawrence chimed in with his impression of the differences in
resources: "Here, they say they've been going through a downshift because
defence spending has gone way down because the Cold War is over. Here
people complain about how little money they have. But if you compare it
with the research group we had at Queen's, we got excited if somebody got
to buy a computer in a year. When I first got here, we just signed a contract for a $3-million government program. They were throwing money
around for experiments that we hadn't even designed yet. They were saying 'Got this money. Here's a catalogue. Buy something.'"

Adrian Butcher spent six years studying for his PhD in mathematics at
Stanford and would like some day to return to Canada. Just when, however, remains in doubt. "I always have wanted to go back to Canada, and
I think I still do, but I feel my horizons are much wider and broader than
they ever were. I could perhaps go to Germany or New York, but eventually I do definitely want to go back to Canada."

Henry Vanderkwake was attending Stanford as a postdoctoral fellow, having completed his PhD at Waterloo. He was looking for a job, but saw none necessarily forthcoming in Canada for someone with his expertise in soil engineering. Vanderkwake hoped nonetheless to return: "I would like to go back to Canada. We want to start a family, so you get—what is it?—six or nine months off as opposed to six weeks here. So there's some advantage in terms of the social safety net."

The conversation, a typically lively one among Star-Spangled Canadians asked to compare their lives in the United States with their experiences, dreams or frustrations in Canada, swirled on for another hour. Two of the group of eight were definitely staying in the United States; only one was sure he would return to Canada. The others were suspended between a nominal desire to return and an awareness of the greater opportunities in the United States. If half of those gathered that night eventually returned to Canada, I would be surprised.

I had a similar, although less focused, discussion with a dozen Canadian students at Princeton. At the end of what had been an informal seminar, I asked how many were returning to Canada. Three of twelve hands went up.

At Harvard, nine Canadian graduate students were good enough to spend time with me. Unlike in the Stanford group, scientists did not dominate this discussion. The general theme was one I often heard: a general wish to return to Canada coupled with uncertainty about job prospects there and a consequent willingness to pursue their careers in the United States.

"I'm targeting top-ten schools," said Michael Raynor, who grew up in Wasaga Beach, Ontario, attended the University of Toronto and the University of Western Ontario School of Business, and was completing his doctorate in business at Harvard. "This really is a global market for what I do. When I look at the list of schools with the resources and contacts that I would want to go to, it's a pretty short list: ten or twelve schools. Eleven and twelve would probably be the U of T and Western." Raynor was in the job market when we spoke. "U of T and Western have said, 'Gee, you smell right. You've done all the things you're supposed to do. The problem is that we're not hiring entry-level positions until next year. Well, that's fine, except that I'm not available next year. I'm available this year. The other schools tend to be in the market every year for people they think meet their profile." His business-school colleague, David Ager, from Ottawa, shared the same perspective. "I'll go wherever there's an opportunity. The market is robust for my degree. I'm just looking for a school with a lot of resources."

Angela Pearson completed her undergraduate degree at McGill and her PhD at the U of T. At Harvard, she was completing a postdoctoral fellowship in medical research courtesy of a grant from the U.S. National Institutes of Health. "In science in the 1990s, it was really sad. You saw professors around you applying for funding and getting it cut," she said. "There was the mantra that when all these professors retire all these jobs are going to open up, but it wasn't true, because when one of the tenured faculty retired they closed down the position. In the last couple of years, it's gotten much better.

"I want to wind up back home. I grew up in Montreal. I'd love to go back to McGill, but McGill has had money problems for a long time. I'm probably going to wind up in a major centre because, in biomedical research, it really makes a difference if you have around you people doing high-level research, and there are more centres like that in the United States than in Canada. But Canada has some and I'd like to go back to Canada."

Laeka Reza would like to return to her home town of Toronto after her Harvard MA in regional studies with special emphasis on the Middle East. "But, as I'm doing my job applications, I see that there are more opportunities for me in the States. Trying to get my foot in the door in Canada has been really hard … They say, 'We're not hiring, or we're hiring consultants so you can send in your résumé. I looked at the Ontario Ministry of Education. CIDA [Canadian International Development Agency]. Whereas in the States, I took one trip to D.C. and came back with a whole bunch of opportunities."

Sandra Badin, a Torontonian completing her PhD in political theory, has designs on studying law at Harvard. When she returns to Toronto, "I remember how much I loved the city and how much I loved particular neighbourhoods, but I also find that it's not enough for me any more, and that's why I left. I wanted new, broadening experiences." Canada, she said, "is too small a country right now, but I love it."

Stanford's Robert Tibshirani is precisely the kind of professor Canada risks losing, to the best U.S. universities. Tibshirani enjoyed living in Toronto and teaching statistics at the University of Toronto. When Stanford came knocking in 1997, he joined a university with Star-Spangled Canadians scattered through the faculty, including Richard Taylor; Paul Sniderman, one of the leading analysts of public opinion in the United States; Michael Spence, the former dean of the university's business school; and a number of professors in the medical school.

"In my field, this is the best department in the world. That's the main attraction," Tibshirani said over lunch at the Stanford Faculty Club. "Toronto has a good department, maybe ranked twentieth or twenty-fifth in the world, and that's a hard gap to make up from twentieth to first. You have to attract the very best people, and that's hard to do in Canada.

"I was happy at the U of T but I'm happier in a professional sense here. The very best students at the U of T and Stanford are comparable, but the average student is better here. This place has the pick of the United States. Here the graduate students are excellent. Some in Toronto were, but others I wondered if they should have been in the program."

Tibshirani, who received considerable publicity while in Toronto for his study linking cell-phone use and car accidents, specializes in analysing health and medical statistics. In particular, he's done a lot of work on gene studies—genomics—arguably the hottest intellectual field in science. The United States, always desirous of being first, is determined to lead the world in mapping DNA, a process involving a series of discoveries that will unlock a world of medical secrets. It is predicted that this advance will produce numerous pharmaceutical breakthroughs, and the U.S. Congress, the pharmaceutical companies, and wealthy U.S. universities are pouring billions of dollars into the effort. Stanford has not one but two genome research centres. Harvard is putting $200 million (U.S.) into genome research. The California Institute of Technology is building a $100-million centre. Princeton is raising $60 million for its Institute for Genomic Analysis. Its first head—Dr. Shirley Tilghman, a Canadian scientist. By contrast, the federal government invested $160 million (Can.) in genome research in the 2000 budget.

Stanford, like other top U.S. universities, will pay for the best. These institutions will compete furiously with one another for the academics they consider the best in their fields, including scholars from other countries such as Canada. Leading U.S. professors will often "shop" themselves around for the best offer. Tibshirani reckons he earns about one-fifth more at Stanford than at the U of T but for only nine months of work per year. That's a standard method of paying U.S. faculty members. They receive nine months' salary, which they can then augment by research grants or private-sector work. "Getting the grants is critical," Tibshirani said, "but not everybody gets them." What the search for grants does encourage is competition, something that helps define the American character and the structure of U.S. institutions; professors are offered a series of rewards for getting those grants. Successful access to research contracts can bring academic prestige, advancements, and much higher incomes; failure means lower incomes and academic stagnation. The same dynamics, to be fair, apply at Canadian universities, but the system of rewards is much less lucrative. This weaker system has been compounded in recent years by the reduction of university budgets, and research-granting agencies have also seen their budgets cut. The result has been fewer incentives available to reward excellent performers.

As always, comparisons between U.S. and Canadian standards of living depend in part on what is being compared. Aggregate cross-border comparisons are valid to a point, but tax rates and living costs obviously vary within both countries. Tibshirani is earning more money, but housing costs in Palo Alto are stratospheric. He sold his house in North Toronto for $250,000 (Can.) and bought a modest four-bedroom house in Palo Alto for $800,000 (U.S.) "It's scary quite honestly to see the price tags, but it's a good investment, I'm told," he said. "It's a good investment because housing prices just keep rising throughout the valley and because mortgage-interest and property-tax deductibility makes it easier carrying a large mortgage." Stanford understands the valley's expensive housing market—the university has lost top-flight professors who do not want to bear the housing burden. So the university subsidizes the housing costs of professors such as Tibshirani, a policy only a university as rich as Stanford could afford.

Tim Colton left the University of Toronto nine years before Tibshurani. Colton was a key member of the U of T's International Affairs team, specializing in Russian studies. The U of T tried hard to keep Colton when Harvard came knocking, offering him a raise and a reduction in teaching load.

"Financially I did come out considerably ahead, but I don't think I thought of that in the late 1980s. I got a somewhat higher salary and a housing subsidy. It really wasn't something I did for financial reasons. However, over the years the gap has grown," Colton said.

"The [research opportunities] are greater here, although this isn't black and white. This university is not systematically underfunded. Harvard doesn't have a lot of loose cash for research purposes, but you use it to get money from wider circles. I don't think there's any doubt that I've been able to do things here that I would have had no hope of doing in Canada." Colton's research has included extensive surveying of public opinion in Russia, an expensive undertaking.

When Harold Shapiro left Montreal in the early 1960s to study economics at Princeton, after a degree at McGill, he firmly intended to return to Canada, perhaps to work for the Bank of Canada. His father had owned the then-famous Ruby Foo's restaurant in Montreal.

"I came down here without any intentions whatsoever of staying here. I was sure that I was going back to Canada," he said, seated at his desk as president of Princeton University. "My whole family was there ... I was headed back to Canada."

Walking across the campus one day, Shapiro recalled, his thesis supervisor mentioned that someone from the University of Michigan was on campus interviewing prospective recruits. "I said, 'Sorry, I don't want to go there because we're going back to Canada.' And he said, 'There's a problem because I already said you would interview.' I said, 'If you told him, then all right.'

"What the man from Michigan State said to me was 'We are looking for people with new ideas who want to try things. All we are looking for is new ideas. We'll take care of the rest. If you've got ideas, we'll provide you with the things you need to work on.' No one had ever given me any answer like that. No one had said it's your ideas we want.

"So, I went home and talked to my wife and said, 'Look, there's someone who wants me to try out these ideas I've been working on.' I'd never been to Ann Arbor. The University of Michigan was just a name to me ... I said to my wife we'd do it for two or three years, and then we'd go back."

Shapiro never did return, except for occasional summers. Things went well at Michigan, their children were happy in school, and Shapiro began to climb in the Michigan hierarchy. Within five years, Shapiro was a full professor, then became the economics department's youngest-ever head, then provost, and finally president of the university in 1980.

Shapiro has therefore seen both sides of the U.S. university system: as president of the state-funded University of Michigan and president of Princeton, one of the leading private U.S. universities, an Ivy League school where tuition and lodging cost about $31,000 (U.S.) per year. He can compare his U.S. experiences with those in Canada in part because he still considers himself a Canadian (despite having taken out U.S. citizenship) and because his brother, Bernard, is president of McGill.

Canadian university presidents will tell any listener how many strings are wrapped around the money their institutions receive from provincial governments. Harold Shapiro has heard those laments in spades from his brother at McGill, and contrasts such complaints with his experience at Michigan.

"The funding of higher education in Michigan was much less intrusive," he said. "At Michigan, we got a cheque every year and we didn't hear from them until the next time you had to appear before the legislature to determine what the size of the next cheque would be."

On a per-student basis, Michigan and most of the other better-off American states supply more money—and often much more money—to their publicly funded institutions of higher learning than does any Canadian province. Not every state is as generous as Michigan, and indeed some of the poorer American states have underfunded their universities for decades. But the big states, and now almost every state, have got religion about the importance of higher education.

"The American states view themselves as playing a role that is not well articulated in Canada," Shapiro explained. "For example, at the University of Michigan and other state universities I know well, they all think of themselves as purchasing a very high-level research capacity. They view this as an economic investment, and that's what makes the per-capita money so high, because you're supporting these very expensive graduate programs and the research program that swirls around them ...

"Many state legislatures—not all by any means—look at it as an economic issue. They think that, not only are they going to provide their citizens with opportunities, which is important, but they are going to attract funds from the central government that are larger by far by a significant factor than any investments they make."

As Harold Shapiro explained, the vast expansion of U.S. publicly financed, widely accessible, research-intensive universities began after the Second World War. The GI bill encouraged returning fighting men to enroll in higher education. The U.S. federal government made a commitment to actively promote research. What President Dwight D. Eisenhower called in 1959 the "military–industrial complex" would underwrite some of that research, especially in sciences and engineering.

A crucial report recommending active government involvement in promoting university research was written by Vannevar Bush, at the behest of President Franklin D. Roosevelt. It seems hard to imagine today, given the superpower economic strength of the United States, but U.S. policy-makers were quite unsure what the postwar world would mean for the U.S. economy. The war had pulled the U.S. economy from the Great Depression that had begun in 1929 with the stock-market crash and continued with only periodic and slight improvements until Pearl Harbor. The Depression's attendant misery was not some distant memory for Americans as they emerged from a war. The war's staggering demand for weapons and material had unleashed the industrial potential of the U.S. economy, but what would happen after that demand evaporated? Just as after the First World War, the United States anticipated a rapid demobilization of men and a massive scaling-back of military procurement. Few in the immediate postwar period could envision the length and cost of the Cold War, the brutal war in Korea, and the demands that would be made by the "military–industrial complex" on the nation's treasury. The United States had devoted massive resources during the war to military research (the atomic bomb being the most spectacular example), but it remained an open question whether that kind of research would continue after the war, and, if it did, whether research would be directed by military or by civilian institutions.

"Americans started this research in World War Two," Shapiro explained. "Americans, rightly or wrongly, interpreted that investment as having played a big role in World War Two. In the postwar years, as Americans began to think about the future of the economy, they talked themselves into the argument that education and research were the keys. They said that the universities are the vehicles for this.

"The Bush report ... suggested that this was the best vehicle the country had. You invest in universities. You invest the best research. It ought to be peer-reviewed. It ought not to be allocated by numbers of people. And this would have an enormous multiplier for the whole economy. That was very much reinforced a decade later with the Sputnik [the first Soviet satellite to orbit the earth] and that just redoubled the effort."

Private U.S. universities such as Princeton enjoy endowments that run into the many billions of dollars. They attract a vast amount of research monies from private and public sources. Students may pay more than $30,000 (U.S.) to attend these schools, although almost all leading private-sector universities and colleges boast a "needs-based" student-assistance policy whereby anyone who qualifies academically receives financial assistance (loans, part-time work, grants) to offset the staggeringly high tuition and residence fees. The very rich and the comparatively poor, however, are best able to defray these costs: the rich, because they can afford them; the poor, because the universities will underwrite their costs. Middle- and upper-middle-class parents are often the least able to finance their children's education at elite universities because, even with the combination of their own means and some financial assistance, the burden is extremely heavy.

Canada, with only publicly financed universities, can scarcely compete with private U.S. universities whose per-capita funding levels can reach $40,000 (Can.). The only Canadian alternative would be to create privately financed universities—an idea espoused in a report to the Ontario government by former Queen's University president David Smith and now taken up by the Ontario government—but formidable obstacles would arise, and not just the likely political reaction against "two-tier" higher education. No Canadian private university that started from scratch could count on the huge endowment funds that contribute to making U.S. private universities what they are. Better yardsticks for measuring Canadian universities are the publicly funded U.S. universities, and by those yardsticks Canada has not measured up.

In 1996, per-student funding at U.S. public universities stood at about $22,500 (Can.), compared with $15,000 in Canada—a gap of about 50 per cent. From 1976 to 1996, per-student funding in the United States rose, but it fell in Canada.[1] Overall government investments in U.S. universities rose by almost 20 per cent (in inflation-adjusted terms) from 1980 to 1996, while they dropped 30 per cent in Canada. The private and public funds available for research in the United States outstrip on a per-capita basis those available in Canada, so that the lure for Canadian scholars to head south extends beyond the U.S. private universities to the better public ones as well.

As Canadian governments' support for universities declined in the 1990s, governments allowed fees to rise far faster than inflation in most provinces (Quebec and British Columbia excepted). The result narrowed the gap substantially between fees paid by students at U.S. and Canadian public universities, shattering the prevalent, erroneous, but nevertheless self-comforting belief among Canadians that somehow their universities are more accessible than equivalent U.S. ones. Canadian fees (outside Quebec and B.C.) are now approaching $4,000 (Can.) whereas those in the United States range from about $3,000 to $7,000 (U.S.). The average tuition and fees among Ontario universities in 1998–99 was $3,736 (Can.), whereas the average for public universities in the eight U.S. Great Lakes states was $4,415 (U.S.). Since average personal incomes are higher in the United States, the portion of income eaten up by tuition and other fees in Ontario was about the same as in the eight Great Lakes states. Elsewhere, fees were $3,300 at Memorial University in Newfoundland, $3,290 at the University of New Brunswick, $3,840 at Dalhousie, $2,683 at the University of Manitoba, and $2,813 at the University of Saskatchewan. Fees at Quebec universities were below $2,000, and were $2,295 at the University of British Columbia. The partial or complete deregulation of fees for professional-graduate-school programs in a few Canadian jurisdictions means that these schools are now almost as expensive as U.S. public equivalents. The gap in tuition fees is therefore narrowing, but the gap between research and government support for universities is widening in favour of the United States. That gap, more than taxes or after-tax income, explains the loss to the United States of some of the best-established or rising Canadian scholars, and the difficulty universities sometimes experience in luring them back home.

It is hard to explain a contradictory report prepared by the Canadian Association of University Teachers (CAUT) in 1999.[2] The first part of the report insisted that the "brain drain" from Canada to the United States is more myth than reality. It then switched gears to argue that the number of faculty had plummeted at most Canadian universities and underlined the significant salary gaps that exist between Canadian and U.S. university teachers. The salary gap, according to CAUT, was about 25 per cent for full professors, 14 per cent for associates, and 22 per cent for assistants, gaps adjusted for purchasing-power parity. Having argued the brain drain was largely a myth, CAUT's report then concluded: "Given that a significant number of current university teachers will retire in the next decade, Canada's universities, without a significant increase in core government funding, will increasingly face serious difficulties in competition with their better-funded and better-paying American counterparts." An essay with such inherent contradictions would have flunked any examination set by a competent CAUT professor.

Quite apart from whether faculty from abroad can replace those who head south, there is the question of quality, an admittedly slippery judgment. Harold Sharpiro, who knows both sides of the border and both private and public U.S. universities, commented on the issue.

"I know some Canadian universities where their biggest concern is that they're finding it very difficult not to fill positions on the faculty but to replace distinguished faculty who are retiring," he said. "Their problem is they can fill those positions without any problem at all, but they can't fill them with people of distinction. That's a very bad sign for any institution … Is that true for Canada as a whole? I actually have no idea at all. But if it is, then that would be very worrisome because I believe that the best people produce enormous social dividends for a country."

Canada's university presidents are divided about the imperatives of the academic "brain drain" from Canada. The concern is greatest among leading research-intensive universities such as the University of Toronto, where former president Robert Prichard spoke often and urgently about the challenge his university faced to hold and compete for top professors and new researchers in a continental labour market for academics. When I interviewed Prichard, he gathered around him the deans of law and business and the university's vice-president for research, who echoed his concerns. "It's the number-one challenge I have as president," Prichard declared.

Other presidents who preside over more regional and less prestigious universities than the University of Toronto worry a good deal less than Robert Prichard. Their universities do not pretend to compete on a continental scale. Their research budgets are small; their faculty members are not extensively recruited in the United States. They worry more about losing professors to other Canadian universities than to U.S. ones. Indeed, a survey for the Association of Universities and Colleges of Canada by the ARA Consulting Group in 1997 showed that, of all faculty members who switched jobs over a two-year period, 190 moved elsewhere in Canada, 100 went to the United States and 70 moved to other countries. (The numbers in the study did not add up, by the way.)[3] Those who left the country were replaced in the aggregate by professors coming to Canada from abroad, so that on balance it was hard to prove a "brain drain" to the United States.

But as Shapiro signalled and Prichard insisted, averages and aggregates do not adequately capture the effect on Canada, since those academics who are tempted to go south tend to be teachers or researchers of particular or potential renown, otherwise their names would never have come to the attention of U.S. universities. As in other fields, when competition for talent extends beyond a country's borders, the mobile are often among the most motivated, best trained, and highest regarded. They are not automatically replaced by faculty of similar quality. Aggregate numbers do not lie, but they can mislead.

The year 1967 was the last one for mandatory, provincewide final examinations in Ontario secondary schools, a practice buried by avant-garde "progressive" ideas of "child-centred" educational "reformers" whose philosophy was advanced by the Hall–Dennis Commission on education and implemented by Ontario and provincial governments across Canada. In that year, 1967, one of my classmates at the University of Toronto Schools finished first in the provincewide examinations. That achievement was made the more remarkable by Gordon Legge's blindness.

Today, Gordon Legge is Distinguished University Professor (a title held by only a small number of faculty members) in the psychology department of the University of Minnesota and director of the Minnesota Laboratory for Low-Vision Research. When he graduated from UTS, Legge never thought he would spend the rest of his life in the United States, where he has married and become a citizen.[4]

"What I knew was that I wanted to do some kind of science or engineering, and I made inquiries at several universities in Canada and the U.S. I was accepted at MIT [the Massachusetts Institute of Technology].

In addition to being a prestigious school in the sciences, they were also very forthcoming and welcoming with respect to my vision disability. I felt good about going there," he told me in his university office.

"Not only the Canadian universities but some of the U.S. universities were apprehensive or negative. Some basically said, 'Congratulations on your record but it's not reasonable to pursue a career in science or engineering.' Some others said, 'We really don't know how you'll do this and the other' ... I remember one Canadian university [McGill] saying 'Yes, you could perhaps do theoretical mathematics, but we really don't want you to come here expecting to major in any of the experimental sciences.' When all was said and done, I think I was surprised that I wound up in the States. I had no particular predisposition to go to the United States.

"I thought for many years I would to back to Canada. While I was an undergraduate I thought I'd probably go back. When I was a grad student I thought I'd likely get an appointment in Canada."

Upon graduation from Harvard, where Legge did his PhD, a job opening appeared at the Erindale campus of the University of Toronto. He went for an interview, but did not receive an offer and "I'm not sure I would have gone if they had."

Instead, after postdoctoral work at Cambridge University, Legge accepted a position at the University of Minnesota, an exceptionally strong and well-financed public university in the United States. At the time, Legge said, "Canada was definitely on my agenda, but there either weren't appropriate positions or they weren't at the best Canadian universities."

Legge's laboratory, which he proudly showed me around, conducts pure research, but optical and other companies are interested in its application to commercial products. Could he have done similar research in Canada? "In a general way, yes. There are people doing broadly similar work, very good people at Canadian universities," he replied. "But whether the particulars of it would have worked out as well, I don't know. I've been successful in finding money for biomedical research. Would the same level of funding have been available?"

Legge didn't put the question rhetorically, but the answer is almost certainly no. His work is financed by two $200,000 (U.S.) grants from the National Institutes of Health, and such sums would very likely not have been available in Canada from government granting agencies.

David Card is similar to Gordon Legge in three respects: he is intellectually outstanding; he left Canada assuming he would return; and he teaches at a public university. Card grew up in Fergus, Ontario, attended Queen's, then went to Princeton for a PhD in economics. His Queen's undergraduate education prepared him wonderfully for Princeton, Card said at his office at the University of California in Berkeley.

"I probably intended to go back to Canada, even in the first few years when I had a job in the United States," Card recounted. "But the very best jobs for economists are in the United States, and I think the gap between jobs in the United States and Canada has widened a lot: the quality of colleagues, the support for research, benefits, salary.

"Right now, the differences in salary are enormous. It's a very serious problem. Canadian universities are just being raided, especially in Ontario, where they just seem to be letting their universities go down the tubes. Looking at it externally, it looks pretty bad."

When Card graduated from Princeton, he talked to Canadian universities such as Toronto, Queen's, and Western Ontario, but the very best Canadian PhD graduates from U.S. universities were then, as now, being recruited by top U.S. universities. Card headed to the University of Chicago, home of one of the world's leading departments of economics. At Chicago and Princeton, to which he later returned, Card's accomplishments earned him the John Bates Clark Medal for the top U.S. economist under the age of forty, the award first given to Paul Samuelson, a Nobel Prize winner. Another Canadian has also won the Clark award: Michael Spence, who left UTS, and did his undergraduate degree at Princeton and his doctorate at Harvard, where he subsequently served as dean of arts before becoming dean of the business school at Stanford. Spence, like Card, never returned to work in Canada.

Card specializes in labour economics at Berkeley, part of one of the finest public university systems in the world. The California state system is divided into research-intensive campuses such as Berkeley, UCLA, and UC San Diego and UC Irvine, and state colleges such as San Jose State. California, unlike many other U.S. states, has let funding slide for its university system and for other public institutions. Card deplores the consequences.

"We're in a high-tax state and we have the shittiest school system in the country. California is doing a Canada. We're not sustainable. We're kind of like Canada in the 1980s. We're not investing in the infrastructure," he asserted. "I don't think governments should have structural deficits, because that just passes along problems. That's probably the only public-policy pronouncement I believe in.

"Although it doesn't show up in the books, in California we're running a huge deficit. The level of infrastructure per person is falling like a rock — schools, highways, hospitals. Population is growing and everybody is happy but we're really not investing enough, and that irks me." That may be so, but nonetheless Card is not planning to return to Canada.

Munroe Eagles was happy teaching at St. Mary's University in Halifax. He's a political scientist with a special interest in political geography, for which only a small academic niche exists in Canada. So when the State University of New York at Buffalo expressed interest in his expertise, Eagles came for an interview.

"I couldn't turn it down. They had just been awarded ... a $6-million grant from the National Science Foundation to become a National Center for Geographical Information," one of just three such centres in the country, he told me over lunch.

"The salary was slightly higher, but after tax it's considerably better. It's therefore a better standard of living. I think that explains why it's going to be difficult if I ever wanted to go back to Canada. It wasn't a big draw to come down, but once you're into the system, I look to what it would take to reproduce the lifestyle were I to come back. It's prohibitive in dollar terms. It would take 30 to 35 per cent more than I'm earning here."

Downtown Buffalo is an ugly, even scary place, with boarded-up storefronts and gap-toothed urban decay. Bits of attractive inner-city redevelopment are being attempted, but businesses and the affluent long since departed for the suburbs. Canadians, especially politicians, who trumpet the superiority of Canada over the United States invariably point to places such as downtown Buffalo. Three or four decades ago, southern Ontarians flocked to Buffalo for shopping and entertainment; now the flow has reversed, so that Toronto vastly eclipses Buffalo in attractiveness, vitality, and safety. But Munroe Eagles doesn't live anywhere near downtown Buffalo. The university campus is well north of the city, near Delaware Park, designed by Frederick Law Olmsted in the last century in an area to rival the swankiest suburban parts of Toronto. Like thousands of other Star-Spangled Canadians, and most middle- and upper-middle-class Americans, he lives in a safe, attractive neighbourhood with a reasonable quality of life. U.S. inner cities have monumental problems compared with their Canadian equivalents, but apart from serving as rhetorical fodder for Canadian politicians, these troubled areas do not touch the daily lives of most transplanted Canadians.

Eagles, professionally attracted to the State University of New York by better research opportunities, acknowledged the trade-offs between services and taxes. Society might be better off if people paid more taxes; he would not necessarily be.

"I would gladly pay higher taxes to eliminate the one-third of children in Buffalo who are living below the poverty line. Is that [poverty] good for the country? I don't think so. I was kind of raised as a Canadian to believe that the measure of civility of society is how it treats its least fortunate," he said. "But going back to Canada to pay those higher taxes? That's where the rubber hits the road. I'd have a hard time doing it."

Michael Rose spends part of his time with fruit flies in the California public university system, at the University of California at Irvine (where Munroe Eagles did his PhD), a ninety-minute drive south of Los Angeles. Rose, who graduated in 1976 from Queen's, has become one of the most brilliant, talked-about, and controversial evolutionary biologists in the United States, perhaps even the world. He is among the pioneers in the science of aging; his discoveries are probing the possibility that human life can be greatly extended, perhaps by dozens of years, as well as all the ethical, moral, financial, and political consequences such an extension would entail.[5] In a country obsessed with the imperatives of youthfulness, and working in an economy where biotechnology is spawning huge investments and new commercial applications, Rose's work and theories have become widely known. His research has been covered and debated in scientific journals, of course, but also in such mainstream media as *The New Yorker* (where his findings were assessed in an article by another Star-Spangled Canadian, Malcolm Gladwell), *The New York Times, The Economist, Time,* and *Newsweek.*

Rose was not your usual kid at high school in Ottawa. He started reading books about astronomy at age eight, devoured everything he could find about science, caught out his teachers on mistakes they made, skipped grades, and landed at Queen's at age sixteen.

"A lot of people came from small towns and cities, or were elite kids, and I didn't relate to either one of those groups," he related in his university office stuffed with leaning towers of papers and books. "When I went there, I had shoulder-length hair. Most of the kids were fairly conservative, but then they grew their hair, so I cut mine. I was always out of step ... I really had intellectual interests. I had no interest in getting drunk, which was the number-one or -two interest of my fellow students. I will confess an interest in the other thing they were interested in."

Like so many other Canadian ex-patriate professors who studied as undergraduates in Canada, Rose lauds his Canadian education.

"Queen's is an outstanding undergraduate university. I think it's one of the very best in the world. I say this as an educator. I'm a professional university person," he said. "For example, this university [UC Irvine] is ranked number eight in public universities in the United States, and Queen's is far superior in terms of its undergraduate education. It's not even close. They have high standards and they maintain them."

After his PhD at the University of Sussex, where he began his research into the evolution of aging, and a postdoctoral fellowship at the University of Wisconsin, Rose returned to Canada, accepting a post at Dalhousie University in Halifax. He enjoyed Dalhousie, received adequate funding from federal granting agencies, and acquired tenure, but in 1984 UC Irvine beat a path to his door. Three years later, he left.

"I was largely working on my own at Dalhousie. The prospect of coming here was to be part of a research group doing similar things. I set up a large research group that is so productive it's embarrassing. Last year, I published fourteen or fifteen publications, and that's because I'm in a group that is so productive, whereas in Canada it would have been hard for me to get out four or five ...

"Dalhousie did what it could, but its resources were so limited then, and I think they're worse now ... Everything in Canada might compete in evolutionary biology with everything that's in this department and this building ... You're looking at a classic small country/big country problem. In all of Canada, they can't compete with this."

The combination of money and people produces a critical mass of research that feeds on itself by attracting more resources, financial and human. The United States, with its size, wealth, and commitment to leading-edge research, encourages these clusters in every field.

"It's institutionally harder for Canadians to achieve world-leadership positions because there are no institutions in Canada that can compete with U.S. or British institutions, so the people who are involved in those institutions have huge competitive advantages. Like the National Institutes of Health here. I had a grant from the NIH that was worth several millions of dollars. You don't get grants of that size in Canada."

The temptation for a smaller country such as Canada is for governments, recognizing that they cannot compete across the board with the United States, to focus research monies in particular areas. Theoretically, that approach makes sense for the smaller country, but Rose disagrees with it in practice.

"Picking winners from the top is not really a great way to go," he said. "I know that process fairly well and it's really lame. What you're looking for in science and mathematics, and other high-tech niche areas, is the critical little burst of insight and inspiration that is the product of a few people who are in the right place at the right time.

"It's not just IQ. There's nothing predictable or measurable. You're the lucky person who sees something that no one else has seen and, bang, you're off. Usually, those are young people, people in their twenties. Having middle-age goofballs—my glory days were twenty years ago—picking where they think something like that will happen is totally stupid."

A U.S. professor such as Rose can make a great deal of money, depending on his field, usually more than an equivalent Canadian professor. Pay scales for university professors in the two countries will often begin at about the same level, but then the U.S. salary scale marches upwards much faster than the Canadian. And since professors are often engaged on salary for just nine months of the year, many academics are free to earn what they can for the other three months; earnings can come from research projects or private-sector consulting, which can be lucrative in a field such as evolutionary biology. Young professors starting out don't talk as much about earning more money than in Canada as they do about their larger "start-up" research money for labs, experiments, travel. It's that "start-up" money for young researchers that keeps many of them in the United States after they've finished their graduate or postgraduate work.

Consider Tom Long, a young assistant professor of microbiology at the University of California at Irvine. His office is down the hall from Michael Rose's. Originally from Barrie, Long began his PhD at McMaster University and completed it at the University of California at Davis. "Down here, you have a critical mass of colleagues, which you're not going to have at most Canadian universities. So that's comforting because you can get to feel intellectually isolated," he told me. "Then, the other issue is funding. In the U.S., the funding has this boom-or-bust flavour to it. Right now, I'm very fortunate because I received my first grant, and this grant as an assistant professor nine months into my job is probably larger than I would get at the peak of my career in Canada and certainly not what I would get as an assistant professor ... When you start a job here, there's a sense of urgency that you've really got to go. You can't rest. If your work seems hot and it looks like you're there, they'll give you the resources."

Long receives a starting salary of about $45,000 (U.S.) for nine months, then his research budget supports him the other three months, bringing his total income to the $60,000–$65,000 range. (At that income in Canada, he would be hit with the highest marginal tax rate for his first year in the workforce.) "Plus," he said, "at UC you continue to get grants and produce, you accelerate, and wham, off you go. Every year, I could get a 7 or 8 per cent pay raise. They give you $200,000 to set up your lab. They give you a big pot of money to get your lab rolling. When they brought me and another person, they bought some major pieces of equipment."

Canada's undergraduate education system trained Long well for graduate work; Canada's smaller job market kept him in the United States.

"I was actually surprised. I thought American students would be better," he said. "The undergrads at McMaster are intellectually superior to the ones for whom I have been a teacher's assistant here. Students when they come out of high school in Canada are far better prepared, and the ones who work hard in university are often better students as well. That's why a lot of us end up coming here. A lot of us are academically well equipped to come to American graduate schools ...

"But you realize that Canada is just so much smaller than America. The fields of science are so small. If you're a really qualified person coming out of your postdoc, the chance of you hitting up your particular position at the school you want to be at is very low. There were jobs that would have been just perfect for me in Canada, but you saw them coming three years before you were ready, or three years from now. It's hard to find matches."

Take James Reynolds. He's a researcher in the department of anesthesiology at Duke, having studied at Queen's and the University of Iowa. He grew up on Vancouver Island and told me that in perhaps five or ten years he might like to return to British Columbia. "I guess it's the money that brought me to the state [North Carolina]," he said. "It's the opportunity to do research. The levels of NIH [National Institutes of Health] funding compared to the Medical Research Council [in Canada] are exponentially greater, and the NIH budget is going to double in the next four years." As for returning some day to Canada: "I keep looking at the University of British Columbia for occasional jobs, so maybe in five or ten years. It's not that I want to stay in the United States; it's just that the opportunities are here." As we parted, Reynolds used a lovely phrase. He was so well treated as a researcher at Duke that it was like being held there by "golden handcuffs."

Or Louise Masse, assistant professor or behavioural science at the University of Texas school of public health in Houston. She had degrees from McGill, the University of Ottawa, and the University of Montreal. "At the university, assistant professors are paid more than assistants in Canada. And there is more research money," she said. "It would be hard to do better from a professional point of view."

Or Kathryn Stoner-Weiss, an assistant professor of politics specializing in Russian studies at Princeton. She completed her PhD at Harvard, and then turned down several positions in the United States because she wanted to return to Canada. She had been at McGill for a month and a half when Princeton called.

"To be honest, Princeton has overwhelming resources," she said. "McGill asked me what my salary would be here [at Princeton], and the chair of the department said that it would be almost twice what a tenured professor at McGill makes.

"At McGill, once I left, that position was never replaced. It disappeared. There were no resources to replace it. The physical plant of the university is in terrible, terrible shape. The students are great. The best students there are easily as good as the best students here. But I had to do all my own photocopying for my courses at McGill—thousands of sheets of paper—and some of them I had to pay for myself. The library, they just don't have the resources. I feel badly for them. I admire what they do with how little they have.

"In the library, I brought a flashlight because not only is every second row of lights out—standard practice in libraries to save energy—but every second light bulb was out. It was incredibly dim. The books you want aren't there.

"So when a big American university walks up and says I'm going to pay you a heck of a lot more than you're getting and you get a huge research budget and you won't have to teach half as much, it's pretty hard to resist."

Or Ray Truant, a postdoctoral fellow at Duke doing research in HIV microbiology. "There's no way a Canadian university can compete with a U.S. university in terms of salaries and start-ups," he said. "A starting professor in Canada will be making between $55,000 and $60,000 (Canadian) as an assistant professor in a department of biology or biochemistry. The numbers down here will be the same but in U.S. dollars. The big difference, though, is in start-up money: the money that they will give me to purchase things to put in my space to do research."

Truant spent five years in the United States. He loved his work and the intellectual opportunities. He did not like U.S. society, so he decided to return to teach at McMaster University in Hamilton, Ontario, as a repatriated Star-Spangled Canadian.

"The medical system here is insane ... It's a very violent society. There's racism down here that I've never seen," he said. "There's always racism here and there, but I don't think I've seen anything quite like what I've seen down here. In terms of the complaint about higher taxes in Canada, you get what you pay for, and although taxes are less down here, you get a lot less down here ... I lived thirty years in Canada and I never knew anyone who was a victim of violent crime. In the three years I've been down

here, I know by degrees of separation seven people who have been murdered. I know of people whose relatives have been shot or robbed ... I
have been introduced to fear."

These scattered reflections from a handful of the many young Canadian
academics I interviewed in the United States are in line with a more comprehensive survey of Canadian postdoctoral fellows studying in Canada
and the United States. The 1996 survey of 1,568 postdocs—79 per cent of
whom were in Canada and 17 per cent in the United States—found those
Canadians in the Uunited States better-positioned in their research pur-
suits and more optimistic about finding a job.[6] Canadian postdocs in the
United States reported higher levels of satisfaction with library services
and research monies, and were "generally more optimistic about future
employment that postdoctoral fellows currently in Canada." What brings
them back are families, roots, or distaste for aspects of U.S. society; what
keeps them there are opportunities for research and income. It's comforting for Canadians to hear emphasis being placed on the negative aspects
of U.S. society that distress people such as Ray Truant and cause them to
return, but unless Canada can provide more opportunities for research,
the Ray Truants will remain too few.

The number of university-educated Canadians who emigrate to the
United States after graduation is small, but those who leave tend to be
among the "best and the brightest." That was the major conclusion of a
Statistics Canada survey of Canadian graduates from the class of 1995 who
left for the United States between graduation and the summer of 1997.[7]
Only 4,600 of 300,000 graduates relocated to the United States within two
years after graduation—or 1.5 per cent. But that raw number does not adequately convey the seriousness of the loss. The higher up the academic
ladder, the more likely graduates were to leave. Only 1.4 per cent of com-
munity-college graduates remained in the United States and 1.7 per cent
of holders of university bachelor's degrees. But 3.2 per cent of master's
degree-holders remained, as did 12 per cent of those with PhDs.

Forty-four per cent of those who left reported themselves as having
ranked in the top 10 per cent of their graduating classes, and another 36
per cent below the top 10 per cent but in the top 25 per cent. That meant
that four out of five of those departing stood in the top quarter of their
class. At every level of study, those who left Canada were more likely to
have received a scholarship than those who stayed behind. Statistics
Canada concluded: "These results indicate that those who moved did
tend to be above-average graduates from the class of '95."

Why did they leave? asked Statistics Canada. Forty-four per cent cited "jobs in a particular field"; 39 per cent, higher salaries; 35 per cent, jobs "in general." Who can blame some of them for departing when salaries were so much higher. Bachelor's graduates working in applied- and natural-science jobs earned $47,400 upon arrival in the United States, considerably higher than the $38,400 earned by their counterparts in Canada (that calculation includes inflation and purchasing-power parity). The median salary for all bachelor's graduates who emigrated was $43,400, compared with $30,500 for those who remained in Canada. Nearly two-thirds (63 per cent) of those who left Canada earned more than $40,000 upon arriving in the United States, compared with just 15 per cent who stayed. Starting salaries for college graduates in the workforce, in other words, were on average one-third higher in the United States than in Canada, although it should be remembered that these were among the brightest graduates. Had they stayed in Canada, their incomes at home might well have been higher than the Canadian average income for people with equivalent academic training.

Statistics Canada also wanted to know how the Canadian graduates got into the United States. The vast majority took the initiative themselves by responding to advertisements, contacting friends, or sending out applications and résumés. Only 12 per cent were recruited on Canadian campuses or after being contacted by a recruiter or headhunter.

Two-thirds of these graduates entered the Uunited States on "temporary" visas, most on the so-called TN visa provided for under NAFTA. Leaving out those departing for graduate work in the United States on student visas, four of five who entered the U.S labour force right away did so on "temporary" visas. The TN visa, once again, allows well-educated people to work "temporarily" in the United States, but the visas are renewable each year and they provide a relatively easy passport for Canadians wanting to get a toehold in the U.S. labour market.

Two years after graduation, about four of five (82 per cent) of the Canadians who had departed were still in the United States. Of these, more said they intended to remain (44 per cent) than return (38 per cent). Evidence suggests, though, that the longer a Canadian stays in the United States, the more likely he or she is to remain. Many Canadians, as suggested by this survey, say to themselves, family, and friends in Canada that they will return. But as their years in the United States stretch on, and new friends are made, roots are put down in a community, job prospects continue to be good, and the fact of higher salaries and lower taxes becomes part of a person or family's lifestyle, the likelihood of a return diminishes. Of the 38 per cent who said they would return, chances are most of them will not.

A less scientific survey by the Association of Colleges and Universities of Canada asked deans, alumni officers, and heads of departments about the whereabouts of 1993 and 1994 graduates. The survey, not as reliable as the Statistics Canada study of the 1995 graduating class, found almost 16 per cent of physical-sciences graduates were living outside Canada, 18 per cent of biological-science graduates, 16 per cent of computer science graduates, 14 per cent of engineering graduates, and about 10 per cent of business-school graduates.[8]

The Harvard Business School (HBS) may not be representative, because of its ranking as the continent's leading business school, but that ranking makes it important. People who study there are incontestably among the "best and the brightest" from across the United States and around the world. The HBS has always attracted some of the best business students in Canada, and until recent years the vast majority of Canadians who attended HBS returned to Canada after finishing their degrees. That was the finding of a survey of Canadian graduates of HBS conducted by the school under the supervision of its former dean, ex-patriate Canadian John McArthur. In a foreword to the study, McArthur wrote that he and the school were gratified that so many Canadians had taken their HBS training back to Canada.

The McArthur study surveyed all Canadians who had attended HBS over many decades, but a different analysis of more recent graduates revealed another trend: increasing numbers of Canadians at HBS were staying in the United States This study, conducted by Toronto management consultant and HBS graduate Noel Desautels, looked at 331 Canadian graduates from 1986 to 1998. He found that in those thirteen graduating classes, only 41 per cent were working in Canada, but that aggregate figure masked a more significant trend. Of the 1986-to-1989 graduates, 58 per cent were in Canada, whereas only 33 per cent of the 1990-to-1998 graduates had returned home. In the 1993-to-1998 period, only 30 per cent came back to Canada. "In short," Desautels suggested, "the numbers are poor and getting worse." Desautels, who kindly shared his paper with me, also concluded that Canadians who had attended an American university prior to HBS were more likely to stay in the United States than those who had gone to a Canadian university.

According to data from the Institute of International Education, 22,984 Canadians were studying at U.S. institutions of higher education in 1996–97, compared with 2,647 Americans studying at Canadian institutions. The Department of Foreign Affairs crunched those numbers by factoring in tuition and living costs in both countries and concluded that

Canadians were spending $504 million (Can.) at U.S. institutions, whereas Americans were spending $42 million in Canada. The department described this spending mismatch as a "Canadian deficit," but at least some of that "deficit" could also be regarded as U.S. subsidy. Some Canadians receive scholarships at U.S. institutions, especially scholar/athletes and graduate students. U.S. universities are extremely generous to foreign students. At public universities, foreigners are charged the same fees as students from other American states. The costs of education in the United States are usually subsidized in some way, through either government grants or endowment funds, so that Canadians studying at U.S. universities without scholarships are usually being helped by U.S. taxpayers or private interests. It can be argued that a Canadian who returns to Canada after studying in the United States, especially at the graduate level, has received a subsidy that amounts to a "gain" financially for Canada. To speak of a "deficit" of nearly $500 million, therefore, distorts at least somewhat the financial picture of Canadians studying in the United States. Of course, if the Canadian student goes to the United States and remains there, then the only "gain" is for the United States.

If what Desautels found in his limited sample of Canadian HBS graduates—that those who attend U.S. universities as undergraduates are more likely to remain in the country than those who study first in Canada—what does that lesson, if more widely applied, suggest about the Canadians who head south for U.S. athletic scholarships? The short answer is that no one has tracked how many of these Canadian scholar/athletes remain in the United States after graduation, and no one has compared their return rate against that of the broader mass of Canadians who do undergraduate work in the United States.

With the exception of Simon Fraser University in British Columbia, Canadian universities do not offer full athletic scholarships. These are, however, the bread and butter of U.S. university athletic programs, which are big business, a major recruiting device, a source of alumni attachment and, for about 1,800 Canadians a year, a reason to go south.

It used to be that Canadian athletes were recruited by U.S. universities with strong hockey programs—to elite schools such as Cornell and Princeton; to state universities such as Michigan, Michigan State, and Vermont; to private colleges such as St. Lawrence and Colgate; to state colleges such as Lake Superior State. Today there are Junior B leagues in Ontario and Western Canada—a level below Ontario Junior A or the Western Canadian Junior League—where Canadian student athletes deliberately play because these are widely scouted by U.S. universities willing to offer athletic scholarships.

In recent decades, however, the number of sports attracting Canadians south has exploded to include everything from track and field to gymnastics, swimming, wrestling, volleyball, basketball, and a host of other sports. New athletic scholarships have opened up for women since court rulings in the United States, based on provisions of the Civil Rights Act, require universities to offer the same number of scholarships to male and female athletes. Since almost every U.S. university fields a football team, and that's a sport played only by men, a large number of the scholarships offered for all other sports go to women, and Canadian female scholar/athletes are now as eagerly recruited as Canadian men. If U.S. athletic programs don't find the determined Canadian student/athletes, some of the Canadians will try to find suitable programs themselves, paying Canadian recruiters up to $2,000 (Can.) to shop their résumés around the United States.

Alarmed by the loss of young scholar/athletes to the United States, some Canadian universities have demanded a revision of Canadian policy stating that athletic scholarships are not permitted for first-year students, and a cap of $1,500 a year applies to all other athletic awards. The scholarships were valued at about $2 million (Can.) in 1998. These questions have sorely divided Canadian university athletic administrators.

Mike Wadsworth, a former Canadian Football League player, Ontario lawyer, and Canadian ambassador to Ireland, runs Notre Dame's huge athletics program. When we met before a Notre Dame–Michigan State football game, Wadsworth, himself a Notre Dame student, explained that athletics create tremendous alumni loyalty, provide a little less than 10 per cent of Notre Dame's revenues (courtesy largely of television revenues from football), and build character and create opportunities among students. But Wadsworth advised that Canadians thinking about the need for athletic scholarships should be clear why they might be necessary.

"I don't think Canadian universities should enact athletic scholarships simply to prevent young Canadian men and women from going to school in the United States," he said. "If they are going to introduce scholarships to subsidize the cost of university education, they want to think positively about why they are doing that. If you do things for defensive reasons, they don't tend to work out. I don't think there's a right or wrong answer. You have to ask what you want to do with your university system."

The dilemmas—what universities are for and whether or not Canada should try to retain more of its scholar/athletes through athletic scholarships—split Canada's universities down the middle. At a 1998 meeting of the Canadian Interuniversity Athletic Union, every Ontario university voted against first-year scholarships and a higher cap, but every Atlantic Canadian, every Western Canadian, and all but one Quebec university (Concordia) voted in favour. The result was a 23–23 tie, but a two-thirds majority was required to change the policy. The tie suggested, however, that the issue will not go away, and universities unhappy with the status quo policy are rumbling about restructuring leagues in order to provide those scholarships.

Wadsworth's advice is sound — in fact, it should guide all discussions about the "brain drain." Adopting policies specifically to stop the "brain drain" would be futile and lead to a skewed allocation of resources. If Canadian universities were to offer athletic scholarships to match those in the United Staes, they would badly tilt their student-assistance programs, robbing them to pay for a minority of students at the expense of others. Even if they tried, Canadian universities could not compete with the mega-scholarships offered to a handful of athletes to play in the United States, where collegiate athletics in some sports are huge revenue-earners for the universities. In other words, Canadians might think, instead, about what policies are good for Canada. If those policies have the ancillary benefit of keeping more Canadian at home or luring more of them back, especially highly motivated and educated ones whose contributions are so beneficial to society, then fine. The case for athletic scholarships therefore rests, if one exists at all, on what athletics at a high level can do in shaping character and expanding horizons for students, not on how it may stop Canadians from leaving for the United States.

Canada should never adopt an approach because it is Made-in-America and therefore considered by some to be better, but neither should Canada fear to take a U.S. approach and adapt it for Canadian purposes because it is Made-in-America and therefore considered by others to be inferior. Canada should make policies because they are sensible for Canada, and if they happen to derive inspiration from a U.S. example, so be it.

An emphasis on research, pure and applied, has been a hallmark of the postwar United States, felt throughout the country's universities and, by extension, the entire society. True, the demands of the U.S. military and space program, and the links between military spending and academic research, find no counterpart in Canada. The military and space-program imperatives that expanded American research efforts in certain years, however, do not completely explain that country's determination to spend public money in the pursuit of the economic advantages and "public goods" associated with research and universities. Americans, it is asserted wrongly but pervasively in Canada, will not spend tax dollars on "public goods" as will Canadians, and therefore the conclusion is drawn that U.S. society is somehow less worthy, caring, and fair. That assertion is correct in some important areas, but it is demonstrably false in the case of funding for higher education, which provides both opportunities to individuals and "public goods" in the sense of the discovery and dissemination of knowledge, economic innovation and growth, and a better-educated citizenry.

Canadian universities, to their credit, have geared up efforts to raise money from private individuals, companies, and unions, and the success some of them have enjoyed suggests the "by extension" argument is being more widely appreciated in Canada. These efforts have been driven, let it be said, by reductions in government funding that left many universities scrambling to find additional sources of revenue just to maintain themselves or slow down their decline. Not only did per-student appropriations from governments stagnate during the 1990s, but the major federal research-granting agencies suffered actual dollar declines in their budgets—at least until the trend was reversed in the late 1990s. Encouragingly, in 1999 the federal government created an $800-million Canadian Foundation for Innovation(CFI), later augmented by another $200 million, that, when married to additional provincial government and private monies, might produce up to $2 billion in new research monies. The 2000 budget provided another $900 million for the CFI. The government also created a new fund for health research that might pump an extra $500 million into that critically important area. Also recently launched was a $900-million program over five years to fund 2,000 research chairs at Canadian universities, one of the single best programs ever undertaken to assist university research. The impact of the Canada Research Chairs program will be enormous at the country's leading research-intensive universities and will definitely help them compete for top scholars and keep some of Canada's best at home. It will take many years before the full impact of that program is felt but the impact will surely be positive.

These measures are excellent first steps towards helping Canadian universities, and "by extension" Canadian society, better equip itself for the demands of the twenty-first century. Americans, however, are already funding their public universities better than Canadians are theirs, and every sign suggests that U.S. funding will continue to rise in real terms. Democrats and Republicans may squabble over everything else, but a bipartisan, national consensus exists on the model of strong financing for research and universities. When Canadians congratulate themselves on recent improvements in university funding, they must temper those congratulations with the knowledge that Americans are accelerating their efforts too.

Star-Spangled Canadians repeatedly told me they had gone to or remained in the United States for "opportunity." That meant for some of them more money, both in absolute and in after-tax-dollar terms. If Canadian universities do not have the financial resources to compete to retain or hire at least some of these scholars of renown or considerable potential, the institutions will suffer and "by extension" so will students, fellow scholars, and society as a whole. But "opportunity" means more than salary and after-tax income to at least some Star-Spangled Canadians; it means a chance to work with more money for research: better equipment and laboratories, experiments and conferences, graduate students and postdoctoral fellows. It is illusory to believe that even-better-financed universities will hold all scholars and students in Canada, but the country could hold more of them. The United States, by virtue of size, wealth, and power will always be better able to cover the scholarly waterfront more fully and to create more of those "critical masses" of people and money that Michael Rose described. Only a handful of universities in the world can afford the kind of linear accelerator on which Richard Taylor worked to earn his Nobel Prize. Very few Canadian universities will specialize in the kind of political geography that excites Munroe Eagles or the low-vision research that attracted Gordon Legge.

A less powerful country such as Canada, therefore, has to be realistic. It cannot compete in every field with the United States, and it should not adopt policies specifically designed to stop the "brain drain." It should, however, recognize that giving university funding and research a much higher priority makes good sense for Canada whatever its long-term effect on the emigration of some of its "best and brightest" students and faculty. Even a cursory glance at provincial government budgets over the last quarter-century reveals that universities have lost, and lost badly, in the race for public funds against Medicare, social assistance, and preuniversity education. Canadian governments, like Gulliver, are tied down by a thousand threads of past spending commitments, too many of which flow from the obligations of yesterday rather than the demands of tomorrow. If the experiences of Star-Spangled Canadians, and the relative weaker performance of the Canadian economy vis-à-vis that of the United States over the last quarter-century, are telling Canadians anything, it is that, in the fields of research and university funding, U.S. determination is worth emulating.

As the train went south along the Hudson River, I realized that I
was travelling through the setting of many of the books I had read.
I was not just city-bound, but world-bound, it seemed, where the
books I read were published, where the papers I read were written.
… Doubts that would never be wholly laid to rest started up in me
on that journey south through the Boston states. I passed a land
border for the first time in my life, the one between Massachusetts
and Connecticut, an arbitrary border on either side of which the
landscape was identical, as I had no doubt it was on either side of
the border between New Brunswick and Maine, Canada and
America. —Wayne Johnston, The Colony of Unrequited Dreams

ENTREPRENEURSHIP, BUSINESS

CANADA could ill afford to lose Kevin O'Leary. But lose him Canada did when O'Leary moved from Toronto to Boston in 1993, taking about thirty employees with him. O'Leary, a graduate of the University of Waterloo and the University of Western Ontario School of Business, had started a software company in the basement of his Toronto home. His business was growing fast in the early 1990s. By merging with or acquiring other firms, O'Leary turned his original company into Learning Co., which then became the second-largest producer of consumer software in North America (after Microsoft), but by then O'Leary was in Boston. O'Leary sold Learning Co. to Mattel, the toy-company giant, for a staggering $3.5 billion (U.S.) in the spring of 1999, a bloated sum that shocked Wall Street analysts. (A year later, Mattel put parts of Learning Co. up for sale.)

O'Leary, married to a woman from Orillia and currently building a summer home on Lake Joseph in Muskoka, explained why he left Canada.

"We got to a point where we had to crack into the U.S. market and we were having a really tough time. There was some kind of invisible wall," he told me during a conversation at his luxurious home in Belmont, a Boston suburb. "I look at growing business from two points of view. One is revenue, which is selling to customers. The other is access to capital.

"Capital doesn't adhere to any borders. It just flows all around the world to the point of lowest resistance: the highest returns with the lowest taxes. Period. That's how it works. What we were running into was that there were many American companies that didn't want to do business with a Canadian company because there were risks associated with it; risks associated with supply, the difference in accounting systems … The whole idea of trying to raise capital when you're trying to grow your business became very problematic.

"To their credit, Americans believe in the big vision. They get it when you say you're going to start from scratch, that it's going to create millions of dollars, and, more important, they are willing to invest in it. It's harder to do that in Canada."

The Canadian corporate tax system, he explained, makes merging companies more difficult than under the U.S. system, which impedes the ability of Canadian companies to grow. Corporate income taxes on services were higher in Canada than in the United States, and higher, too, than taxes on manufacturing. The Chrétien government's 2000 budget tried to address some of the factors that drove O'Leary from Canada. The budget lowered the inclusion rate for capital gains from three-quarters to two-thirds. It allowed the rolling over of capital gains of up to $500,000 upon reinvestment in another company, the issue that so roiled O'Leary. It changed the system for taxing stock options up to $100,000 by imposing the tax at disposition rather than receipt. Finally, it gradually lowered the corporate tax rate on services, which had been more heavily taxed than manufacturing and resource-extraction industries. It cannot be known if these changes might have kept entrepreneurs such as O'Leary in Canada, although they might have helped. Canada has to realize, however, that in addition to a more favourable tax regime, the United States had other advantages such as market size and access to capital so that to be really competitive Canada has to do even more than the measures introduced in the 2000 budget.

Then there are personal income taxes.

"The taxes! What's the deal with taxes? Why tax your industries into oblivion when they can just walk over the border. What's the point? When I was there, it was outrageous," O'Leary said. "In the early 1990s I was trying to hire a head of sales, who was in New York at the time. I flew his wife up to Toronto. We sent her down to the Eaton Centre to show how civilized we were. She bought something and they hit her with the GST and PST, and she said, 'What's this?' That killed the deal … I couldn't hire people out of the U.S. to compete when they looked at Canadian dollars and they said they didn't want to live in that kind of tax environment."

What's the solution, I asked O'Leary, to keeping people like him and companies like his in Canada?

"In Canada, we don't have to reduce our taxes below those of the U.S. There's enough bright ideas in Canada. There's terrific research going on, great brains coming out of Waterloo, Queen's, etc.," he replied. "Step one would be: normalize the tax rate. Don't discount it. Make the levy level for that industry … The quality of life in Canada surpasses most standards in the U.S. … Living in Canada for most people is a better lifestyle … But you have to make it attractive for this pool of capital to put this money in Canada. Make the general accounting principles the same … Forget about the border. Just make it look the same."

O'Leary, entrepreneur and deal-maker extraordinaire, intended to return to Canada after a few years in the United States.

"We were chasing a dream, thinking we could build this into something really big and, when that was over, it would be over and we could all come back and do whatever we liked," he said. "It turned out to be a much longer process than we thought and it became very, very big. But it would be very hard for me to move back to Canada because, while I'm doing what I'm doing here, I need this market. It's very, very active. It's growing very quickly and the players who do the deals are in this market, and once you get involved, you don't want to extract yourself out of it."

O'Leary, then, will remain in the United States: "Access to market is number one. Access to capital is number two. Taxes are number three. All these things push you to the U.S. I'd argue that five engineers coming out of Waterloo in the right group with the right idea will create more wealth twenty years from now than the entire forestry industry. Unfortunately, they're on their way to work in the United States."

Dennis Andersen had spent fifteen years at Microsoft's vast headquarters in Redmond, east of Seattle, when I caught up with him and half a dozen other University of Waterloo graduates.

Andersen was one of the first Waterloo graduates hired by Microsoft, which was a fraction of its current size when he joined the company in 1983. Andersen estimated that he was the longest-serving Canadian employee of Microsoft. The company had about 300 employees when he joined; now the Microsoft "campus," as it's called, stretches over twenty-eight buildings and more were under construction when I visited. Andersen, a thirty-eight-year-old soft-spoken man, admitted to being a millionaire courtesy of stock options, a staple in the software business. (Microsoft's stock price pops up daily on employees' computer screens.)

"One year, when the stock price was $29, I said, 'Okay, I've always wanted a new car.' That stock that I sold to buy the car would probably today be worth three or four million dollars. But life goes on. Those options are gone forever, but I've gotten other ones since. I'm doing okay," Andersen said.

Andersen joined Microsoft following one of the company's first recruiting trips to the University of Waterloo, then building its outstanding reputation in computer science, electrical engineering, and mathematics. Andersen's reasons for joining Microsoft seem ironic today. "When I left Waterloo, I was looking for a smallish company, and Microsoft fit the bill. They were doing interesting things, so I came here ... I said, 'Why not? If I don't like it, I can leave.' Plus, at the time there was a recession in the Canadian economy and a lot of people weren't getting jobs."

Waterloo graduates such as Dennis Andersen paved the way for others. As Microsoft expanded, so did its appetite for human talent. Microsoft kept finding talent at Waterloo, so that, in the 1990s, Waterloo became one of Microsoft's preferred universities for North American recruitment, alongside the Massachusetts Institute of Technology and the California Institute of Technology. When I first visited Microsoft's Redmond headquarters in January 1998, the University of Waterloo alumni office reported that 110 of its graduates were working there. Presumably, that number has since risen.

Brian Arbogast, a Montrealer, joined Microsoft three years after Andersen. "In 1986, Microsoft wasn't that big a company. It had about 1,200 people when I started. The first year I was here it doubled. I had been here just a year and I was already in the senior half of the employees," he said.

Arbogast later helped Andersen to form Watpub, a Friday-night gathering for University of Waterloo graduates at Microsoft. Watpub eventually petered out, like so many Canadian networks in the United States. Canadians are too busy integrating into U.S. society to need formalized contacts with other Canadians. As Andersen observed, "Canadians are good assimilators everywhere. The ones I know down here all seem to fit in anywhere."

James and Jennifer Hamilton completed their undergraduate education at the University of Victoria and their master's degrees in computer science at the University of Waterloo. They had joined IBM in Toronto when a headhunter called about working for Microsoft. The competition for people with the Hamiltons' skills is so intense, said James, that "recruitment was pretty much a day-to-day thing. You would always be getting calls. For me to have gotten less than a call every month or so would have been surprising." Canada lags far behind the United States in designing systems software and building programming languages, Hamilton reported. Their careers therefore took them south, to Microsoft.

"When you look at the intellectual capital that's available in Canada, it's as good as any in the world," James said. "There's a lot of technical talent in Canada [and] an excellent educational system, with schools such as Waterloo, Queen's, Toronto, so the country is strong from a human-resources perspective.

"I suppose it's not a crime, but it's unfortunate when you see these human resources hatched in the country and nurtured, and yet, when they come to be valued in industry, having to head south or somewhere else to earn their living.

"What's attracting people down south is a couple of things. First, the capital markets down here are infinitely more friendly to start-ups. A friend of mine has recently been working on a start-up. For him to get money in Canada versus in the U.S. is fundamentally different. It's very easy to get money down here. Second, taxation is considerably lower down here on a personal level. They're taxing at 32, 33 per cent versus 54, 55 per cent. That difference is a fairly substantial one."

James added: "It's unfair to generalize ever, but Canadian managers as a whole tend to be less aggressive in pay issues and in things like that. So as the industry goes through a change and becomes more competitive, people start heading south in a heck of a hurry. Canada's just not adapting quick enough. I've seen businesses going years losing people you cannot afford to lose. It's absolutely backbreaking for the business. People know it's a catastrophe, but it takes two years to respond. That's a crime. It's slitting the competitive throat of business. They absolutely have to compete. If you think your competitors are in Toronto, you are really wrong. If you think your competitors are in Ontario, you're wrong. Competitors are everywhere."

To be clear and fair: the majority of University of Waterloo graduates do not become Star-Spangled Canadians. They stay at home, or, like Laurie Lithwick, a Waterloo electrical engineering graduate, they work in the United States but intend to return to Canada. She holds a green card (many Waterloo grads spend two years at Microsoft on "temporary" visas, after which the company applies for their green cards) but when I spoke with her she was thinking about returning to her home city, Montreal.

"I have one child now and I intend to have another one, and I want them to learn French. So I'll live there for a while so they can be near the grandparents, learn French, and get to know Montreal," Lithwick said. Her husband, an American, is prepared to give Montreal a try "as long as it isn't forever." Unlike so many other Star-Spangled Canadians from Montreal, Lithwick doesn't worry about the national-unity issue: "Montreal is a very cool place to live, so I'm not worried about the constitutional wars."

Microsoft's discovery of the University of Waterloo provides a classic case—perhaps *the* classic case—of Canadian success being fed upon by U.S. institutions or companies. Once a Canadian program appears on the radar screen of a U.S. institution, the graduates from that program enter a continental labour pool. Canadian companies then must compete not just with each other, but with U.S. firms, to attract Canadian talent.

Of course, Canada does, in turn, recruit talent from other countries both to replace those who depart and to fill its own labour-market needs. And yet senior people in Canada's high-technology industry have recently decried labour shortages, just as U.S. companies have for their market, so that a sort of worldwide competition has developed for talented people in high-technology industries. Not only does Canada compete with the United States for Canadians, it competes in other markets for labour. A 1999 survey by the Branham Group for the Information Technology Association of Canada revealed that the top priority for high-technology firms was an "adequate supply of qualified individuals with experience. The number-three priority was the "ability to offer competitive compensation packages."[1]

The Canadian high-tech sector therefore both absorbs from abroad and loses to the United States (a few U.S. citizens come to Canada), but the sector illustrates the weakness of Statistics Canada's "brain drain/brain gain" analysis. In an October 1998 document, Statistics Canada produced a chart entitled "Immigrant computer scientists vastly outnumber emigrant computer scientists to the U.S." The chart purported to show that, whereas Canadian imports of computer scientists, mathematicians, and statisticians had increased more than sixfold from 1990 to 1996—from about 1,000 to about 6,500—emigration "to the U.S. from Canada [has] not increased much since 1986," that is, about 120 people per year. What this chart—and indeed Statistics Canada's entire approach to the brain drain—missed were those who emigrated on "temporary" visas as a stepping stone to more permanent status in the United States. Statistics Canada's findings took into account only those who left and arrived in Canada with "permanent" status in hand, whereas the vast majority of technology workers who left Canada for the United States in this period did so with some form of less-than-permanent status. The notion that Canada lost only about 120 people a year in high-technology occupations to the United States throughout the 1990s was completely absurd, based on faulty presentation of visa data and manifestly unhelpful in creating an informed public debate, as anyone in Canada's own high-technology industries would attest.

"Temporary" visas eased entry for Canadians into the United States, as underscored by my discussions with Waterloo grads at Microsoft and Star-Spangled Canadians at small and large U.S. high-technology companies in Seattle, Silicon Valley, and Boston. The vast majority had not entered the United States with permanent status of the kind that would have been captured by Statistics Canada, except for the entrepreneurs who came with money. Companies such as Microsoft that recruit internationally routinely smoothed the way for green cards, ensuring permanent status in the United States. And not just for Canadians. The U.S. Congress, under prodding from the U.S. high-technology industries, doubled its quotas for high-technology workers from around the world, including for Canadians. Indeed, shuttle buses were ferrying potential recruits all over the Microsoft "campus" the day I visited. In casual conversations with some of these potential recruits I learned that they had come from countries in Asia, Europe, and even Latin America.

Canada always hopes that giant foreign companies will establish branch plants in Canada and give them "world product mandates," that is, responsibility for generating one or more products for the company's worldwide operations. Canada's research-and-development tax incentives are said to be among the most enticing in the world. In the high-technology field, companies such as IBM have had a long-standing research presence in Canada. But the Canadian presence of giants such as Lucent Technologies, Sun Microsystems and Cisco Systems is limited, a fraction of the presence Canadian-based Nortel Networks maintains in the United States. In Microsoft's case, Canada supplies human talent but is treated merely as a consumer market. The company concentrates all its research and development in Redmond, except for tiny research operations in Cambridge, England, and Israel. If Canadians want to work designing software or systems for the world's largest software company, they must move to Redmond.

Star-Spangled Canadian "techies" in such areas as software design or systems engineering are scattered throughout Seattle, California's Silicon Valley south of San Francisco, Raleigh–Durham's "research triangle," Dallas's high-end suburb of Plano, and Boston's network of companies along Route 128. Then there are the high-tech entrepreneurs building their own companies south of the border rather than in Canada.

I sat around a table in a converted Seattle warehouse with five young

Star-Spangled Canadians, two of whom—Graham Hill and his cousin Luticia "Tish" Hill—founded Sitewerks, a Web-site company, in 1995. Sitewerks began with four people, including the two Hills, but now employed forty-three. The company had been doubling its gross earnings every year. Just before I arrived, Sitewerks had been sold to a giant U.S. company.

"Tish had moved down here to be with a man she had met. She urged me to come down," Graham Hill recalled. "I got a job where she was ... Then we started our own company. We did a whole bunch of pitches to companies. None of them turned out that well, but we got a contract with Microsoft. It sort of went from there."

Graham is a child of the NAFTA agreement. With a Carleton University degree in architecture and a diploma in industrial design from Emily Carr College in Vancouver, Graham entered the United States on a "temporary" visa, which was subsequently upgraded to more permanent status.

Tish Hill, a graduate of the University of Victoria, followed her man to Seattle and began "working illegally as a starter. Then I realized how easy it was to put through the TN. Then I did it for everybody else. I've brought six or seven Canadians to the company."

The Canadians she attracted to Seattle had something in common. "There is a theme that ties them together," she said. "They were really smart. They needed a break. All of us were doing stupid things back home. We couldn't find a job. We didn't find that there was the backing that we needed, the financial or mentoring help. The best hires were the ones who felt they were being held back."

Sean Murphy was working in the Internet business in Montreal when he and Tish, who had known each other when they were children, met again, and she invited him to work for Sitewerks. He agreed after getting discouraged about the prospects of finding venture capital in Canada.

"The conclusion I came to was that, in Canada, they're willing to invest after you're successful, whereas in the States ... there are people out here who have so much money they don't know what to do with it. They're just interested in people with great ideas," Murphy said. He estimates he is 40 to 50 per cent better off in after-tax-income terms in Seattle than in Montreal. "I've got friends who are in high-tech back home, and I try to tell them to come out here. I tell them what they could make here and they just freak," he said.

Some of those gathered around the table, especially the more recently arrived, still missed "Hockey Night in Canada," the Canadian Broadcasting Corporation, and, of course, family. Graham Hill, the son of an airline pilot, said, however, that being a Canadian meant nothing to him, there being few differences in his mind between Seattle and Vancouver. Except one.

"This place allows us to think big. Is it the States? Is it high-tech? I'm not sure," he said. "When I think back to my peer group, nobody's got real jobs. They have jobs but they don't have careers. They're like a nine-year-old. You could coach them into this fantastic era, but they don't realize it's there. I feel like I should go back and say, 'Come on. Look at all this stuff. Quit complaining. Get those shackles off, shackles like government ...' It seems to be a perception. It just seems to be the case that they don't have the courage to take the big bites."

Seattle has its share of "angels"; Silicon Valley has even more. "Angels" are venture capitalists, some of them phenomenally wealthy, who constantly seek out exciting, intriguing, and, they hope, exceedingly profitable investments in small technology companies. "Angels" and those with new ideas are constantly searching for each other: at "angel" parties, through word of mouth, industry contacts, or direct pitches by would-be high-technology entrepreneurs. This kind of venture capital fuels countless "start-ups" in the technology business. Many of these fail for various reasons; indeed, more fail than succeed. But in the intensely competitive high-technology clusters of Silicon Valley or Seattle, "angels" and product innovators are always dreaming of stunning profits that can come with the right product, proper marketing, and good fortune. The dream that drives all before it in the world of "angels" and "start-ups" is taking a company public, the initial public offering (IPO), then watching the stock soar. A handful of billionaires and a plethora of millionaires have been made from such successful IPOs. A few losses by an "angel" can be easily redeemed by one stunning success. It is this world, this kind of enterprise, this access to capital, this dream of riches unknown, that lures Canadians south and attracts would-be capitalists from other parts of the world.

Neil Druker grew up in Montreal, attended McGill, worked for two years in Toronto, then attended the Harvard Business School. He started an investment fund in Boston with two other principals, concentrating exclusively on high-technology companies. Locating the new firm in Montreal or Toronto would have meant "being out of the loop," that is, being too far from capital markets, people in the industries, the networks, hourly information. By way of illustration, Druker mentioned a Montreal friend with a high-technology project. "I sent him down to Florida to deal with a specialized law firm who'll put him in touch with angels and capital in the States, and he'll take it public here," Druker said. Capital, networking, and market size, rather than marginal tax rates, bring people south. I heard variations on Druker's comments everywhere: capital is more abundant in the United States, IPOs are best done in the States, Canada is just not on the radar screens of U.S. high-technology investors.[2]

"To my mind, there is a very different dynamic in the brain drain even from when I was on my way to business school and now," said Druker in his office overlooking Boston harbour. "We are in a very unique period. We are in a gold rush, at least in the Internet and technology world … Everybody has a pick and a shovel now and is trying to get their hands on these easy riches.

"There is a palpable sense among people my age that there is a very short window here—five, maybe ten years—where, if you've got the right idea and access to capital, you can be wealthier than you ever possibly dreamed, and that's only happened in the last three or four years. There are countless business-school colleagues of mine who are deca-million-aires by now. They've done it only in the last eight to thirty-six months, and in my mind it's causing a brain drain from everywhere to the U.S.

"There are so many examples of people rushing here to try to get in on this gold rush, access to capital, and interaction with people in order to get noticed. Doing it anywhere else is becoming harder, and yet the rewards for doing it properly are getting greater. That's just driving tremendous amounts of brain power here that we hadn't thought about. Access to capital and very sophisticated financial markets tend to drive people, and right now they're all here.

"[The brain drain] is so painfully obvious that even debating it isn't warranted in my mind. It's just so clear … There's an infrastructure here that just doesn't exist, in Canada or anywhere else, of capital seeking its best possible return. It's so incredibly sophisticated and works on so many levels—mezzanine financing, pre-IPO, seed—so much more vastly developed than what exists in Canada."

John McArthur left Burnaby, British Columbia, to attend the Harvard Business School (HBS) in 1957. He taught there from 1959 to 1980, when he was made dean, a position he relinquished in 1995. He's seen Canadians—indeed, people from all over the world—pass through HBS. For him, the current high-technology lure of the United States pulls people from everywhere—at least for the moment.

"People tend to see the centre of the universe as where they are," McArthur said. "The same kids are coming from all over the world to the U.S., and from Canada. So I suppose one might wonder if there's anything special about the Canadian case, which is minuscule in comparison to the people coming from other parts of the world … They don't have Canada's tax problems in China … or Bangladesh. I don't think the answers are to be found in Canada. It's a problem, but you can't study or deal with it by looking just at Canada."

Perhaps McArthur is correct in saying, based on his years of experience, that "where students go is a fashion business. They go in waves like schools of fish, so where they are fifteen years later is what's important." Certainly Canadians graduating from HBS are flocking to all parts of the technology industry. That a majority of them will return to Canada seems unlikely as long as the U.S. dominance in high-technology is maintained, especially venture capital, software and systems design, Internet development, Website creation.

Some may return because certain costs are lower in Toronto or Ottawa than Silicon Valley, the epicentre of the high-technology universe. Some Canadian entrepreneurs, having established their headquarters in Silicon Valley, have opened Canadian offices where employees write code.[3]

This is the high-technology equivalent of hewing wood and drawing water; the raw material, the code, is then shipped south where others add value, then market and sell the product. All the important strategic decisions are made in the United States. Commands are issued there; orders are followed in Canada. It's better than being shut out of the action completely, but it's a decidedly second-best solution. If Canada, which already trails so badly in the e-commerce and Internet world, does not wake up and close the gap quickly, the country risks becoming what it has always been for the U.S. entertainment industry: a feeder of talent into the U.S. maw, content with domestic bit productions, with being costume designers to the industry, and dressing up somebody's else's actors, with playing somebody else's scripts for somebody else's audiences.

Jamie Millar, who grew up in Ottawa, attended the University of Toronto and the Harvard Business School, then served for seven years in the admissions department of the HBS. He agreed with Noel Desautels's finding that a majority of Canadian HBS grads were now orienting themselves towards the United States. But he echoed McArthur in saying "It's not just Canadians. For us to look at it as a uniquely Canadian problem — even if we think it is a problem — is probably short-sighted. You could say the same thing about the French or the Chinese. It's worse for some of the Asian countries where virtually everybody stays in the U.S."

Tania Zouikin, a Montrealer who attended the Massachusetts Institute of Technology after heading Alcan's pension fund, has been analysing developments in the U.S. economy as president of Batterymarch Financial Management, a Boston-based pension-fund-management firm. She stayed after graduation from MIT in the United States for the usual reasons, that "finance and investments were invented here, and it's where all the research is conducted. That's just a fact of life, so you have to come here at some point. You have to experience life in U.S. markets." She did return to Canada from 1985 to 1991 to run her own pension-management company, a Canadian franchise of Batterymarch, until the company's head office pulled her back to run the company's U.S. operations. Zouikin has therefore seen business on both sides of the border. She keeps a little Canadian flag in her office, but she'll spend the rest of her career in the States.

"We have a skilled-labour shortage in that area of high technology, and will for years to come. So that makes it difficult for countries like Canada because the packages are huge here ... The social infrastructure and benefits may loom large when you're sixty, but when you're twenty-five the present value isn't very big, especially if you think that the system is going to be bankrupt anyway," she said.

"So that's Canada's biggest problem: being on the border with the big capitalist country when it's successful here. Canada has a very hard time competing; other than family roots, there's not much to keep young people there. The opportunities, the pay, the research, the challenges, the resources, the institutions—they're here. There are some very competent investment managers in Canada, but the stars will want to be here because the marketplace is just so much more challenging. The Canadian market is very limited in terms of opportunities to invest in. To be an expert in U.S. securities from Canada is difficult. People don't come to you. The players aren't big enough. So if you want to play in the market, you've got to be here."

To offer one small example of this drive "to be here," the Edmonton-based biotechnology company AltaRex transferred fifteen people in 1999 to Waltham, a suburb of Boston. AltaRex is researching a drug that might help those with ovarian cancer. Clinical trials are being conducted at sixteen hospitals across North America, but AltaRex felt its executives and marketing people should be in the United States. "The perception was that there was a little more access to potential partners here," explained Trudy Chimko, who was among those who decamped from Edmonton to Waltham. "There's more clout, if that's the word, in dealing with clinical sites and the Food and Drug Administration."

Rob Burgess moved from Toronto to San Francisco for opportunities in the high-technology industries, which for him included running a multimedia company, Macromedia. Burgess has been impressed by, among other things, how the Clinton–Gore administration understood the importance of high-technology for the U.S. economy. "They're sponges for what's happening in the new economy. They're all over us in terms of involvement," he said. "I think Canada at the moment runs a strong risk of being marginalized from an economic standpoint because they're not with the new economy.

"What Canada has are the students who can compete with anybody— the math and computer students, the engineering ones, the animation students. But it's a combination of the government starting to get it and focus on the new economy as they focused on the French problem ... Down here, the venture capitalists run the place; in Canada, the venture-capital industry is a joke ... High-technology companies have got to be favoured somehow, because all the other regions are going for it. Lower real-estate costs in Canada? Yes, Canada has that going for it, but so do Austin, Boulder, Ireland, Scotland."

High-technology is perhaps today's most purely capitalist field. Unions are totally absent. Private capital drives the industries. Stock-market speculation abounds. Companies that have never earned a penny have experienced a quadrupling or quintupling of their stock prices. Government regulation of the Internet and e-commerce is almost non-existent. Huge companies such as Microsoft, Lucent Technologies, and Sun Microsystems coexist with hundreds of smaller players. Fortunes are made or lost in a week. The financial rewards are staggering for those who have profited. The sense of being in tomorrow's economy today drives the excitement palpably felt by those who dream of technology's possibilities. A messianic fervour defines the belief of those who work in the world of fibre optics and the Internet and e-commerce that the world is irrevocably changing and that they are prophets destined to open the eyes (and pocketbooks) of their fellow citizens (and consumers). In this world of pure capitalism of creation and innovation, destruction and renewal, profits and losses, the quintessential American myth of striking it rich through luck and chance finds classic expression. Horatio Alger, the fictional up-by-the-bootstraps millionaire, does not live in South Dallas or on the assembly lines of Detroit or among the bank tellers of Manhattan, the family farmers of Iowa, or the street cleaners of Miami, but his spirit does thrive among the financiers and creators of high-technology.

The Star-Spangled Canadians of U.S. high-technology are not immune to this secular messianism. Of all the Canadians in the United States, they are the most critical of the Canadian preference for collective action through government, supported by higher taxes. They work in pure capitalism's maw, thriving or hoping to thrive, excited by the energy and money around them. Canadian taxes, in their unanimous view, are a serious impediment to economic growth, an article of faith that arises from their immersion in these industries and their own previous ideological convictions. They left Canada feeling it to be yesterday's country, a place peripheral to their sense of tomorrow's high-technology possibilities, run by bureaucracies and governments that fetter innovation, creativity, and the entrepreneurial spirit. The future for them is now, and it must be located in the United States.

Canada offers among the most generous tax credits for research and development in the world. This is the traditional Canadian way of luring industries and creating employment. It's not the American way; Silicon Valley, the centre of the U.S. high-technology industry, grew up for reasons unrelated to government.

Andrew Daniel, a Montrealer who has been in Silicon Valley for twenty-two years working as a consultant and entrepreneur, told me that "Silicon Valley, for all intents and purposes, created itself. It wasn't like the government of the U.S. or California said 'it shall be here and we're going to give these incentives'."

No, explained Daniel, the "valley" began with Bill Hewlett and Dave Packard, who "happened to start it here. It could have happened anywhere. That being done, this is an area that is very attractive to people because of its climate. Thereby it became very expensive. Therefore, this area will attract industries that can offer very high salaries.

"The reason that high-tech can offer such high salaries is that, comparatively speaking, you don't need a lot of employees to produce an awful lot of goods. A lot of the chip companies don't have fabrication facilities. All they need is a number of very bright people. When you're hiring 50 or 100 people you can afford to pay the $100,000 salaries, more so than if you are General Motors, which needs 20,000 people to build cars, and tons of land …

"Another disadvantage [for Canada] is that there is still a feeling in many parts of the world that America is the place you want to go, the land of opportunity and freedom. The streets are paved with gold. In my opinion, I will tell you that Canada's streets are just about as paved with gold and a lot cleaner … but what this means is that the majority of the people I work with are not American-born.

"If, for the sake of argument, there was a right-wing coup in America and a dictator came in and said, 'America for Americans only. All foreigners go home,' every single Silicon Valley company would basically shut down for lack of people."

The high-technology industry in the United States has entered its third phase of innovation and wealth-creation. The first phrase was that of hardware, the second software, the third the Internet.[4] From this third phrase sprang e-commerce, the notion that buyer and seller can be hooked through cyberspace. If e-commerce is your business, then the United States is definitely the place to be. And why not? From mid-1998 to mid-1999, 160 Internet or e-commerce companies made the transition from start-up to public company in the United States, compared with just 2 in Canada.

Terry Drayton had just raised another $100 million (U.S.), to supplement a similar amount previously secured, when we met at the brand-new headquarters of HomeGrocer.com, the company he and two other Canadians founded in Renton, just south of Seattle. Driving around Seattle, HomeGrocer.com's pale orange trucks with the logo of a large piece of fruit on both sides—"billboards on wheels," Drayton calls them—could be seen on streets and Interstates. HomeGrocer.com opened for business, delivering groceries ordered on the Internet, in May 1998 with 60 staff and 100 customers. By the end of 1999, Home-Grocer's staff had grown to 850, and its group of customers to more than 50,000. Click on HomeGrocer.com's Web site, place a $75 or greater order from a huge selection of food and beverages, and one of those arresting HomeGrocer.com trucks will deliver your order to your home, or even to where your car is parked, at a fixed time the next day. From Seattle, Drayton expanded HomeGrocer.com into Portland, Oregon, and Los Angeles, and was eyeing other markets across the United States. Drayton, the most cheerful of men, talked with the conviction of a prophet.

"A lot of historians would point to this period as something akin to the Industrial Revolution. Things are changing dramatically," he said. "You only have to look at the market evaluation of some new e-commerce players that are eclipsing huge established businesses ... Here in Seattle, you can do pretty much everything on the Internet. You can get your groceries delivered, your prescriptions from a pharmacy, flowers, dry cleaning, gardening supplies, pet food. It's a very different world."

Drayton had been successful in the bottled-water business in Canada before deciding e-commerce was retailing's future wave. He scratched together some capital in Toronto and Vancouver but, he recalled, "e-commerce was pretty new, and I wouldn't say the venture-capital community in Canada has got a lot of venture in it. It was even hard to explain to them what it was all about."

He and his partners attended a conference of venture capitalists in California.

"We were just overwhelmed by how receptive they were, how much they understood about it and how much money there was available for ideas like this," he said. "It became difficult to say that we were going to start up in Vancouver because we lived there. That wasn't one of the five top responses that the venture capitalists wanted to hear. There was no reason to go to Vancouver or any of the Canadian cities. They didn't crack the top twenty [in North America] so what we really wanted to do was to get a logical roll-out to markets where it made sense."

And that meant starting in Seattle, where other Canadians have flocked to the high-technology sector.

"E-commerce [in Canada] is trailing here by a huge margin," Drayton said. "Part of that probably is the capital issue. [Canadians] have to dramatically revise the tax system really quickly. We're just stunned by how many Canadians are pouring across the border. Technology workers are probably the most mobile workforce there's ever been. They're in huge demand. Every company here—our company being no exception—has dozens of openings for unfilled technical positions.

"The differences in taxes is dramatic. If I compare operating in the province of British Columbia, where I came down from before here, and Seattle, across-the-board taxes are roughly half. And half is a big difference … People can ignore it and hope it goes away, but it's a reality. If you want to stem the tide and build the kind of infrastructure that keeps those folks back in Canada, you're going to have to address it in a serious way. Nothing I've seen indicates that anyone is ready to do that."

Taxes. Taxes. Drayton and the other Star-Spangled Canadians in high-technology industries and in many other businesses return constantly to the theme. "It's a wonderful country, Canada, if we just got the tax system sorted out. If you miss out on the next industrial revolution, you're really going to put a whole generation behind," Drayton insisted. "That's just stupid politics. I'm stunned at some of the articles my mother and mother-in-law send down. I read the quotes from current politicians. They just don't get it at all. It's like, 'If you don't like it, then go.' Well, that's a really enlightened attitude. The world's changing and you need to look at the fundamentals."

Glenn Ballman did $1 million of business in 1997 at Onvia.com and $25 million in 1998. Ballman, a native of Wilcox, Saskatchewan, took the company from Vancouver to Seattle, where it employed 160 people in late

1999. Ballman said he relocated because of lower taxes and the need to capture the American market for his on-line business serving the needs of small companies.

"One of the things I learned when travelling is that a lot of the outside world thinks that America is the economic powerhouse. It was difficult when I was travelling even to explain which university I was from," Ballman said. "The brand-name recognition of American universities, American companies, is much higher abroad.

"I realized even when I was working for a publicly traded company in Canada that, if you are going to dominate and control the space in any marketplace, you have to be able to conquer America. When I started this company, it was designed to be big. It would never work if it was small just by its very nature. For it to be big, you have to do it in the U.S. You have to own this marketplace."

In March 2000 Ballman took Onvia.com public. In one day, the stock price tripled. Ballman's 13.5 per cent share instantly was worth $944 million (Can.). There is simply no way Ballman could have done that in Canada where venture capital markets are so small, the high-technology industry so modest, the e-commerce world still so limited. A few weeks after the IPO, however, the stock price plunged, evidence of the roller-coaster nature of the e-commerce economy.

Having a shot at "owning this marketplace," especially in high-technology, means branding your company as American, sticking close to the hot spots of U.S. venture capital, thrusting your product at U.S. consumers and businesses, trying to stay one step ahead of the competition. Canada may be a nice country to be from, but it does not appear on the radar screen of venture capitalists.

"We're going global from here ... We're going to be expanding globally into other countries," Ballman said. "Canada has roughly the same population as California, and you would never limit an Internet company to operating just in the State of California. So could I do this from Canada? There's no staffing reason, but there's a market reason. If you're a market-driven company you have to realize ... that we have to own this market. We couldn't do that from Canada. We have to do it from the U.S."

And then, again, there are those Canadian taxes: "When you run the math on your ability to achieve your personal goals and to save and grow and achieve whatever financial goals you may have, it makes it difficult with the burdensome tax rates we have in Canada, in particular in British Columbia. I found it prohibitive. When you compare the marginal tax rate in the U.S., not only is it easier to hire talented people down here, it's easy to hire talented people out of Canada ... because you can show them that you can save so much." Indeed, according to a survey by the B.C. Technology Industries Association, 22 per cent of employees who leave British Columbian companies head for the United States. Fifty-two per cent remain with other B.C. companies; 22 per cent relocate to companies elsewhere in Canada.

Pierre Gallant, president of Oralis.com, an Internet company that sells products and services to dentists and employs thirty people in Seattle, said taxes drove him out of Canada.

"I left Canada because of the taxes. No ifs, ands or buts. It's a great clean place, but my last year in 1994 my tax rate was something like 59 per cent ... adding in the 15 per cent GST [sic] on everything I bought," Gallant said. "Down here, the big dream is to own your own home and to get ahead ... To be an entrepreneur, they tolerate failure a lot better here. You can fail once or twice or three times and your value actually goes up. People will want to invest in you because they assumed you learned something, whereas up there you've got five big banks and a nasty old government that's into everybody's pocket. If you screw up once or twice you probably don't have any friends."

Gallant knows whereof he speaks: a company he founded failed, as many small Internet start-ups do. "It was so devastating for me to lose people's principal, but within the first day I had eight job offers." Some of those who lost money in that previous failed venture have nonetheless invested in Oralis.com, including "a couple of Canadians who want to leave Canada."

Gallant, a native of Edmonton, just does not believe he could build Oralis.com from Canada.

"Canada in my world is a bit like North Dakota. It's not a bad place to be from. In fact, it's nice and clean and beautiful," Gallant said. "But there's a reason to move out of there, to get talent [and] access to capital. It doesn't do you any good to be in the wrong place, and if you are, you move.

"There's an absolute war for talent. Worldwide, there really are only three centres of excellence. There's San Francisco, Seattle, and Boston. That's where you find the more experienced people who know how to market on the Internet ... We started this business in a basement [but] you have to raise so much money so quickly that you can't stay there very long. You have to get a lot of money to go get market share. You have to throw a lot of technology at it. Therefore, you have to be in a place where there are pools of capital that you can access."

Contrast Seattle and Vancouver as locations for these pools of capital. The cities are of roughly comparable size and they share the same Pacific

Northwest geography and weather. Almost every Star-Spangled Canadian I interviewed in Seattle remarked upon the similarities between the two cities. And yet in the first nine months of 1999, venture-capital firms made 200 investments worth $1.8 billion (U.S.) in Washington State, according to the National Venture Capital Association. During the same period, ninety-five venture-capital investments worth $97 million (Can.) were made in British Columbia. B.C.'s top ten technology companies had a market cap of about $20 billion in Canadian funds (about $13.5 billion U.S.). Microsoft's market cap in late 1999 was $465 billion (U.S.).[5]

By world standards, Canada's high-technology sector is no shrinking violet. Clusters of impressive companies, small and large, are found in many parts of Canada. Canadians are hardly technologically illiterate. The proliferation of computers and the Internet is among the most impressive in the world. In 2000, half of Canadian homes had a computer. The country is not operating on abacuses and typewriters. By the standards of Europe and Asia, Canada is a front-runner, not a laggard, in high-technology. It's just that the United States, always the Canadian yardstick in things economic, experienced a surge in high-technology innovation and financing in the 1990s that left the rest of the world behind.

John Roth, chief executive officer of Nortel Networks, ignited a firestorm of debate in 1999 when he charged that high Canadian taxes were driving his company to relocate senior personnel in the United States. Of Nortel's top 400 executives, Roth said, only 28 remained in Canada "and that number will probably continue to shrink."[6] The stronger U.S. dollar, a much higher threshold for the maximum income tax rate, better treatment of capital gains, and the "huge excitement level in the United States" were luring senior executives to the United States. "My project leaders run teams that have 75 to 150 people. If the leader is in Boston or Silicon Valley, those 75 to 150 people won't be in Canada," Roth said. "And you can't find these leaders in the brain-drain statistics. They're such a small percentage. Small in numbers but large in impact and multiplier effect. Large in their ability to create high-value jobs and career opportunities with a future ... When I talk about the brain drain, I'm not talking about commodity engineers. I'm not talking about the average software programmer. I'm talking about the achievers who are going to lead projects ... That's the real brain drain—the real threat to Canada's future in the Internet economy. We need these people to lead Canada in the Internet economy, but we're losing them. Canada loses."

Nortel Networks has the highest capitalized value of any company on the Toronto Stock Exchange, so, when its chief executive officer speaks, his remarks about losing talented Canadians to the United States should be considered. The Chrétien government, predictably, responded to Roth's remarks in its favoured denial mode. High taxes were not a problem. Roth was exaggerating. Canada is the greatest country in the world. End of discussion.

Roth's comments ought to be deeply disturbing. Nortel Networks in the United States is, for all intents and purposes, an American company. It even changed its name from Northern Telecom to appear less foreign. Now, Nortel maintains a shell of a head office in Canada (in Mississauga) while nearly all of the senior executives work in the United States. Any young up-and-coming Canadian within Nortel must say to herself or himself: the United States is the place to be if I want to get near the top of this company. This is the nightmare scenario for Canada: head offices of Canadian companies remain at home but only as shells. The same phenomenon has struck Quebec over the last quarter of a century. Montreal is littered with head offices where few executives of consequence work, the rest having quietly departed for Toronto. For appearance's sake, or by incorporation statute, the plaque on the door says head office; the reality says otherwise. Nortel has now done to Canada what companies have been doing to Quebec: kept the plaque on the Canadian door but moved most of the key personnel to the United States.

Taxes alone do not dictate where head offices and senior personnel are located. If they did, then the Cayman Islands or the Bahamas would be head-office heaven. Taxes are one factor among others in determining where people want to live and work. Roger Martin, dean of the Rotman School of Management at the University of Toronto, took exception to Roth's explanation that taxes were driving personnel from Canada.[7] Martin argued that Nortel's own salary structure caused the movement because employees in the United States were being paid more than Canadian employees for identical work. A starting engineer at Nortel earned $49,000 in Canada but $53,000 in the United States. Martin compared tax rates in Ontario and California, the most favourable possible comparison from Canada's point of view: namely, that between a high-tax state and a low-tax province. Had Martin compared the Ontario employees with those in Texas or North Carolina, where Nortel has tens of thousands of employees, the results would have been quite different. Within Nortel, the salary gap is more consequential than taxes in influencing where employees might wish to work, and that was Nortel's problem, not the government's.

Yes and no. Salary differentials do influence decisions, but what if Nortel equalized the salaries? The Canadian would still be behind, owing to higher average and marginal taxes, so for the Canadian and U.S. employees to be in the same position in terms of after-tax income, the Canadian would have to be paid more. That higher payment, multiplied over many employees, would drive up the company's cost structure in Canada, making diversion to the United States more profitable.

Higher costs in Canada might be offset if corporate taxes were lower; here again, Canadian corporate taxes average about three to four points higher than U.S. corporate taxes. Within Canada itself, corporate taxes are higher in the service sector, which includes high-technology, than in the natural-resource or manufacturing sectors, a dangerous anachronism for an economy because more jobs now and in the future will come in the service sector than in any other. The Chrétien government's 2000 budget attempted to provide some relief on corporate taxes for the service sector. Canada, then, expects its high-technology sector to compete with the red-hot United States although it taxes personnel more heavily, taxes companies more, and arranges its own internal corporate tax system to favour rocks and oil over e-commerce and the Internet. Canadian companies, facing North American competition for labour, will have to adjust salaries and benefits upwards but unless governments assist by lowering tax rates, the companies will still face a competitive squeeze.

A study of five different locations in each of the United States and Canada by Personnel Systems revealed that on average high-technology workers in the United States would have $18 to $20 more their pockets than in Canada after taxes and living expenses (including health care) for every $100 earned. The study looked only at salaries. It ignored stock options and treatment of capital gains, both of which tend to be more generous in the United States than in Canada. This survey followed another by Personnel Systems of high-technology graduates that revealed 80 per cent of them would happily emigrate if they received a call from a U.S. firm.[8] Canadians can count on their superior health-care system and other civic virtues, but these alone will not help close the wide gaps that have developed between Canada and the United States in innovation, unemployment, personal disposable income, taxes, and growth.

Canada's economy picked up steam in the last half of the 1990s, but for the decade taken as a whole its progress was eclipsed by the growth in the U.S. economy in almost every dimension. The Paris-based Organisation for Economic Co-operation and Development (OECD) issued a gloomy report in 1998 on Canada's productivity, insisting that unless Canada's productivity improved dramatically, the country's standard of living would decline. The OECD analysis offered an immediate incentive for newspaper editorialists and politicians to trot out their favourite remedies for what ailed the Canadian economy. Statistics Canada and policy analysts poked holes in the OECD's analysis, and it became clear that Canada's productivity—measured either by "total factor production" or "labour productivity"—had actually matched that of the United States except in two areas: electronics and manufacturing equipment. Electronics, however, included high-technology industries. The United States had stolen a march on Canada in that absolutely critical sector.[9]

The U.S. economy has often shown an astonishing ability to adapt to new opportunities; a constellation of factors provided the environment for high-technology industries to flourish in recent years. The U.S. internal market is vast and rich. Enormous pools of capital exist, and some of those pools became much larger through the stock-market gains of technology industries in the 1990s. The tax system treats favourably high-income earners and has been structured to favour capital-gains earnings. Highly educated and motivated people abound, and where more are needed the United States imports them. Great universities, some public and others private, provide the impetus for the development of innovative ideas: Stanford and the University of California at Berkeley, Harvard and MIT, University of Texas, Duke, to name a few. In a society that admires, even worships, material success, the instant millionaires, multimillionaires, and even billionaires of high-technology have become role models for others who believe they, too, can cash in on the gold rush. In a country that does not doubt it is the best in the world, the drive to lead economically seems utterly natural. And in the U.S. capitalist system, with a premium on individual initiative, industries such as high-technology flourish on ideas and innovation, with a minimum of government interference, unions, or regulation.

The performance of the high-technology sector distends analysis of recent aggregate economic performance in the United States. Without this sector, the United States would have enjoyed solid aggregate economic growth, but, with it, the aggregate numbers look impressive indeed. A growing body of economic thought in the United States now maintains that high-technology has indeed produced a wave of sustained productivity growth that will keep U.S. living standards rising in real terms. Companies will undoubtedly fail; some stock-market gains will be wiped out for e-commerce companies. But the "new economy" is spreading across the United States, suggesting that, for the foreseeable future, Canadians will have to reckon with the challenge of their largest trading partner and find new ways to grow and offer opportunities.

This drive "to be here," in Tania Zouikin's phrase, is a powerful lure for Canadian business people, both entrepreneurs and managers. Head offices, not branch plants, are where the action is, where the biggest decisions are made, the largest challenges found, the grandest remuneration and stock options granted. Canadians, it is sometimes said by Canada's forelock-tugging crowd, are just not as entrepreneurial as Americans. Public-opinion data show nothing of the kind. Canadians are just as respectful of the values of the free-enterprise system as Americans, the only difference being Canadians' willingness to give the state a somewhat larger role in the economy. The size and wealth of the U.S. market, coupled with a less onerous tax regime, provides opportunities for wealth-accumulation and business challenges that turn some Canadians into the Star-Spangled variety. U.S. business is littered with Canadians at or near the top. They are sprinkled throughout Wall Street, the entertainment industry, Silicon Valley. In recent years, there have been Canadian chief executives at companies as significant and powerful as 3M, Pfizer Pharmaceutical, Avon, MCI WorldCom, and Young and Rubicam.

Perhaps the most powerful of them all was Bernard Ebbers, president of MCI WorldCom, who struck a $115-billion (U.S.) deal in 1999 to purchase Sprint Corp. A native of Edmonton, Ebbers emigrated to Mississippi to play basketball after flunking out of the University of Alberta and a small religious college in Michigan. He never returned to Canada, except in a manner of speaking. In the summer of 1998, Ebbers bought the Douglas Lake Ranch, 200 kilometres northeast of Vancouver, from the Woodward family.[10] The 65,000-hectare ranch had 20,000 herd of cattle and significant timber reserves. The property had been listed on the market for two years at $67 million (U.S.) before Ebbers purchased it.

Twenty years ago, Star-Spangled Canadians ran such giants as Xerox, Standard Oil, and U.S. News and World Report. In the 1960s, Canadian ex-patriates were presidents of such companies as Otis Elevator, Harper and Row, Elizabeth Arden, Tidewater Oil, Continental Life Insurance, and ABC Television. In professional sports today, Pat Bohlen from Edmonton owns the Denver Broncos of the National Football League, and Paul Beeston, formerly president of the Toronto Blue Jays, is based in New York City as the chief operating officer of Major League Baseball.

Robert Schlegel had a dream from childhood: to be an entrepreneur. He grew up in a Mennonite family near New Hamburg, Ontario, and after getting his degree from Wilfrid Laurier University (then Waterloo Lutheran) in 1972 and his CA degree, Schlegel started in the retirement-home business. But when he wanted to expand, Schelgel was frustrated by the Ontario government's regulation of retirement homes. Growing the business would take a long time in Ontario, so he began to look south. He settled on Dallas.

"We had a small motor van. We put the dog, the nanny, the kids, grandma into it. Every other week we drove back and forth—22 ½ hours. We had the thing down to a science," Schlegel recalled in his Dallas office crammed with Canadian memorabilia. "In 1984, when our girl was in Grade 4 she missed eighty-four days of school. So we decided we had to live here or there. We moved here and have no regrets. The business grew. By 1992, we had thirteen facilities. We were expanding by about a home a year."

In the early 1980s, Schlegel also started a concrete paving company, and when he sold his retirement-home business in 1994 he devoted all his energies to Pavestone Co., one of the largest companies of its kind in the United States.

"Friends of mine in Ontario are in the same business. They probably started at the same time and at the same level," he said. "We'll do $100 million this year servicing 25–30 states, with ten plants across the country, whereas my buddies find it harder to expand and grow. There's much more incentive here."

Schlegel has prospered hugely in the United States, but he is not a starry-eyed observer of U.S. life. Public schools, he feels, are much better in Ontario than Texas. Canadians are "more wholesome, more honest. I think there are more con artists in America." He adds, "In America, in general, there's a wider range of choices. You can live in a cardboard box under a bridge or you can live in a mansion, depending on how hard you want to work or how lucky you are." Schlegel and his family live in a 25,000 square foot mansion.

Schlegel may be a Star-Spangled Canadian now but he remembers his roots. In 1998, he donated $2 million to Wilfrid Laurier University to help build a centre for the study of entrepreneurship and technology at the university.

Mel Goodes, the former chairman and chief executive officer of Warner-Lambert (he retired in 1999), gave $2.1 million to his alma mater, Queen's University. Then he donated another $10 million to the university's business school. Goodes, born in Hamilton and a Queen's graduate, was the first non-American to head Warner-Lambert, the giant U.S. pharmaceutical company. He was also the first member on either side of his family to go to high school. When I caught up to Goodes at the company's New Jersey head offices, he had only a few weeks of work remaining after almost eight years as CEO.

"Warner-Lambert has grown by 500 per cent, and we were very heavily rewarded with options, so what I wanted to do was to provide educational opportunities in Canada, to give back," he said.

Queen's had helped him win a Ford Foundation grant to study at the University of Chicago. "Where would I have been if I had not won this kind of fellowship? And isn't it wonderful to have a chance to give back? And the need is greater in Canada than in Chicago," he said.

Goodes left for Chicago intending to return to Canada, and he did. He worked for Ford and O'Keefe Breweries in Canada before joining Warner-Lambert in Toronto in 1965. By 1969, however, he was in the multinational's international operations, and by the early 1980s, at its head office in Morris Plains, New Jersey. Goodes never did get back to Canada, because he was on the multinational's fast track, and Canada in Warner-Lambert's world is a small market appended to that of the United States. In the late 1980s, when he was chief operating officer, the company put pressure on Goodes to become a dual citizen. He had held out against becoming an American for ten years.

"Canada is home. It's where your parents are, where your relatives are. It's always been home. It will always be home," he said. "Every Christmas I get misty-eyed because I start thinking about being over at Westdale United Church walking back on a night that looked like something out of Currier and Ives with the white snow, walking with my mother and father and singing Christmas carols."

Misty-eyed maybe. But he's an American now, with his children all intent upon staying in the United States. Goodes got to the top in U.S. business. Once he left Canada, only the top or something close to it would do. "I'd been offered opportunities to go back to Canada, but every time it involved such a financial sacrifice that I said, 'Why should I do it?'"

Don Carty faced the same trade-off when Air Canada wanted him as president. He had already left American Airlines once to run Canadian Airlines for two years, and was forced at one point to decide whether to stay at American and hope for the top job eventually, or head back to his home town of Montreal to run Air Canada. He and all his brothers and sisters had left Montreal, part of the anglophone exodus from that city.

"At that point in my career, I decided I'd like to be a CEO. I had aspired to that in my career, and I was looking for the right opportunity," Carty said late one afternoon at American Airlines' corporate headquarters in Dallas. "Given that I had a fairly good probability of success here and that this was a bigger airline, one of the trade-offs was financial certainty. I finally decided that I would consider the job in Canada but it had to be suitably rewarding. I was obviously going to take a financial hit taking the Air Canada job, but the hit I was willing to take was only so big. That was the stumbling block."

Carty's own decision highlights the difficulty for Canadian companies in offering sufficient salaries and bonuses to keep the very best business executives at home. "I look at what we — I say 'we' in the sense of American [Airlines] being a shareholder — pay Kevin Benson, president of Canadian [Airlines]. I've got a lot of people, including a lot of pilots in our company, who earn more."

Carty ruminated about the pressures on Canada from U. S. competition.

"It's a real dilemma. There's a lot more transparency [about what people are earning] in Canada, and I think there will be more in the next five to ten years about what the economic differences are, and I'm not just talking about CEO jobs, but for everyone," he said.

"The cost of Canadianism as we currently have it formulated is going to become clearer to more and more Canadians, and while not everyone will choose economics obviously, and not everyone will have the opportunity because it's not all that easy to cross the border, I think more and more people will be looking at those opportunities.

"This gradual globalization in the economy, which to some extent is regional and focuses Canada to see more of the United States market in particular, is likely to accelerate the time frame in which these pressures are going to build in Canada. People are going to want to cross the border for economic opportunity ... My own view is that at some point there's going to be more pressure for tax harmonization between the two countries.

"The dilemma of tax harmonization for Canadians is that you don't raise as many revenues and you can't pay for the infrastructure that Canadians have decided that they want. Therein lies the economic trade-off ... In the 1960s we all wanted everything and the government did it and it was fine and no one paid any attention to who was paying for it. Then we had the deficit, so we had a common understanding that we had a problem and therefore somebody was paying for it and that's why taxes were going on ... We said that we wanted it. Now that we know the price, do we really want it? And I don't know the answer. But I know that for a lot of Canadians it's not the decision that they thought they were making, and those represent the potential for brain drain."

A dual citizen, Carty thinks of himself on balance as a Canadian.

"I probably feel more comfortable among Canadians. I think I do. But there's been twenty years between me living there full-time. I'm probably not as comfortable with it as I once was," he said. "I'm increasingly frustrated by some of the inhibitions that Canada puts in place towards greater economic progress, the rationale being that we've got to take care of everybody in society. That's sometimes misplaced. They argue this trade-off, but it isn't a real trade-off. Can you have it both ways? I don't know."

Don Carty may still think of himself as a Canadian, and Mel Goodes may get misty-eyed thinking of his childhood church at Christmas, but Peter Vegso's Canadian roots have shrivelled. Apart from a few old friends, no one in Canada would know Vegso, but thousands of Canadian bookshelves feature his products.

The "Chicken Soup for the Soul" series of books has been a publishing phenomenon. In 1998, Vegso's publishing company grossed $95 million (U.S.) and 80 per cent of the revenues came from "Chicken Soup" books. The first in the series hit the market in 1993 and took everybody by surprise, including Vegso, with its huge appeal. A compilation of uplifting, motivational stories, the first "Chicken Soup" book begat another and another and another. Twenty-seven books have been spun off the original one, and the number grows each year. By late 1999, when Vegso and I spoke, the "Chicken Soup" series had sold almost 50 million copies.

Thirty-three New York publishers rejected the "Chicken Soup" project before the authors turned it over to Vegso.

"I took it with me and I was sitting in an airport somewhere with a delayed flight. So I sat down and started reading one story after the next, and after about five stories I had been reduced to tears," Vegso recalled. "I thought to myself, 'I can't read another or people in the airport are going to think there is something wrong with me'."

Vegso was already a principal of Health Communications, a publishing company he had founded with another Canadian in Deerfield Beach, Florida. They had been doing well specializing in drug- and alcohol-treatment books until, in the early 1990s, Health Maintenance Organizations became all the rage in U.S. medicine and budgets were slashed for treatment programs. In one year, the company's business was halved. They were looking for new publishing ventures in the fields of spirituality, inspiration, and self-help, when along came the first "Chicken Soup for the Soul" manuscript. Since the authors were motivational speakers on the self-help lecture circuit, Vegso reckoned the book might sell 20,000 copies a year. He never dreamed of 27 titles and 50 million copies.

Vegso, fifty-five, grew up in Montreal, and attended McGill and St. Francis Xavier before completing a degree in business administration at

McMaster University. He was working at Toronto's Addiction Research Foundation, publishing a tabloid newspaper for those in the addiction and treatment fields. They were allowed only 30 per cent U.S. news, but found U.S. professionals appreciated their publication. Only by emigrating, Vegso and two colleagues felt, could they expand their horizons, intellectually and financially.

They settled in 1976 near Washington, D.C., then later moved to Florida. They had green cards within three years. ("We had to advertise our own jobs and interview people for them and then turn down the people who had applied.") Vegso said he had no burning desire to work and live in the United States, but the opportunities seemed larger there. The streets, however, were not immediately paved with gold.

"We got to the end of the first year and we're going, 'Boy, this is tough, running your own business in terms of cash flow and managing your money, generating revenue and trying to keep your expenses down,'" he said. "We managed to accomplish that often by not paying ourselves for periods of time, having to wait for cash to build up before we could withdraw some. The first year was pretty much an eye-opener. Then it was hunker down and start living and working with realities."

Vegso never despaired, even in the lean times. "I was never that discouraged. There was always the feeling that we would figure this thing out, and that if we stuck to it, it would be okay." Going to the United States was for him a new beginning; he never thought of returning. And today, although he has not bothered to fill out application forms for U.S. citizenship, being a Canadian hardly matters. "I wasn't one into making these great distinctions," he said. "We're on the same continent. There isn't that much difference among us as human beings, and I never saw myself as a Canadian island in a sea of Americans. To me, you are where you live and whom you're with. I'm just not that nationalistic."

Canada was barely emerging in the late 1990s from the staggering burden of national indebtedness it had imposed on itself through continuous federal deficits from 1973 to 1997. Those decades of fiscal profligacy had cost the country dearly. Interest payments on the debt flowed overseas; domestic interest rates remained too high to attract foreign capital to finance the debts. Taxes had to rise in an effort to restore fiscal equilibrium, and valued government programs were cut.

When we speak of government budgets being encumbered by the commitments of yesterday rather than being attuned to the demands of tomorrow, the most obvious example is the federal debt that still gobbles up about one-third of all government revenues. Money that could be spent planning for the future, or used to reduce taxes, is still flowing into servicing yesterday's debt.

There was nothing inherently Canadian about massive peacetime debts, just a string of irresponsible governments and a population that came to believe that deficits did not matter. Looking at the national accounts dating back to 1867 reveals that peacetime surpluses have outnumbered deficits. From 1947 to 1974, fifteen federal budgets were in the red (but none of them seriously), eleven were in the black, and one was balanced. The large deficits the country assumed to finance the Second World War were followed by nine budgets in eleven years in surplus, as governments paid down the wartime debt. It's hard to recall in these years of $500- to $600-billion federal debts that, in 1960, the federal debt stood at a paltry $19 billion.

Higher taxes follow larger debts almost as certainly as night follows day, or, to put matters another way, today's accumulating debts are tomorrow's higher taxes. One reason among many why Canada's economic potential was not realized in the 1990s, while the United States flourished, was a tax load that grew much heavier in Canada than in the United States. Whether or not these higher taxes drove Canadians south, the impact was felt most onerously on the Canadian economy itself. Closing the tax and income gaps is among Canada's most urgent tasks for the early years of the twenty-first century if the country's economy is to perform better. Otherwise, the buzz that Star-Spangled Canadians have already felt in the booming United States will lure more Canadians south and, more significantly, handicap the Canadian economy's ability to create more entrepreneurial activities, jobs, and ultimately buoyant tax revenues from strong, sustained economic growth.

Kathleen is truly and utterly and completely Kathleen in New York. That's what the city does for you if it's meant for you. She's got plenty of personality and no history, and she has never breathed so much air in her life. She comes from an Atlantic island surrounded by nothing but sea air, yet in the man-made outdoor corridors of this fantastic city, she can finally breathe. This air is what the gods live upon. The gods who get things done. Not the gods who mope on ancient promontories and exhale fossil vapours, waiting for someone to fill in the fragments of forgotten sagas that have come unraveled with age. Those gods have sagged so long on their rocks, they are well on the way to turning to stone themselves.

But the new gods. The bright baritone chorus. They inhabit every steel support, every suspension bridge, every gleaming silver train, all things vertical and horizontal, all glass, gravel and sand. They take big breaths and they make big sounds and with every breath and sound they open up more sky … It's clear: the whole world comes to New York City. —Anne-Marie MacDonald, Fall on Your Knees

NEW YORK

EVERY morning, Audrey Regan awakes to the thrill of New York City.

"New York is Frank Sinatra. It's Ava Gardner. It's Kim Novak. I know where they lived. It's like a total charge. I wake up every day and think I'm on vacation," she explained at lunch in SoHo. "It's like a drug. Even after eighteen years, I wake up and say, 'My God. I can do the East Side, the West Side, the South Side, the East Village,' and I know that when I get there everything is going to be brand new again. I've met the most fascinating people."

More fascinating, in all probability, than the ones she met in Hornpayne, Blind River, and Algoma Mills, the Northern Ontario communities where Regan grew up. At eighteen, desperate to leave the Northern Ontario bush, she took a bus, with $84 in her pocket, and headed to Toronto. "I got a job as a secretary making $63 a week, started taking courses at the Ontario College of Art, gave up the Catholic Church, and got a really cute boyfriend, all in one year."

Toronto, however, was but a way station *en route* to the American Dream, specifically the New York Dream.

"I knew all about Yonkers and the Bronx and Queen's and SoHo through movies and magazines. My parents had a store in Algoma Mills that sold magazines. So I had every magazine available to me as an adolescent, and I read every one of them. I knew all about New York. I knew I would live here one day, one way or another. I figured if I could get to Toronto, I could get to New York. I used to draw yellow cabs and Ava Gardner in a yellow cab."

Audrey Regan got her wish after she moved with her husband to New York in 1981. They separated, but she stayed in New York, as did her daughters. Regan has run an art gallery on Wall Street and moved in the city's thriving arts scene. She also wrote a novel that she went to Montreal to complete, thinking perhaps she might return permanently to Canada. "But one day I was walking along Maisonneuve, and I thought, you know, my novel is pretty well finished. I don't want to live in a city that has a fucking language police. I'm going back to New York."

The allure of New York that touched Audrey Regan as a girl in Northern Ontario also reached across the border and attracted Graydon Carter, today the editor of *Vanity Fair* magazine. Carter grew up in Ottawa, edited the University of Ottawa magazine, started another called *The Canadian Review* ("It wasn't an embarrassment. I've seen worse, but it lost vast amounts of money") and itched all the time to get to New York.

"I knew from about the age of ten that I wanted to live in New York City. It was probably a combination of magazines, movies, and books. Reading *Life* magazine. Reading John O'Hara. Reading John Cheever. Reading Theodore Dreiser. I read everything about New York. I had great affinity for New York movies. It was a black-and-white city, and I wanted to live here," Carter recalled one day in his *Vanity Fair* offices.

Carter came to New York on an editing program at Sarah Lawrence College and through a serendipitous break met someone who introduced him to Henry Grunwald, the legendary editor of *Time* magazine. It was the last day of Carter's program, after which he would have had to return to Canada, but Grunwald offered him a job. "I went home, picked up some worldly goods, came back down, and never looked back," he said, chuckling.

If Carter had stayed in Canada, "I'd probably be miserable because I'd be thinking about being in New York every day ... My parents couldn't understand it. For the first ten years, they always thought I'd move back." As editor of *Vanity Fair* (he had previously been the first editor of *Spy* magazine), Carter is where he dreamed of being as a kid: close to the epicentre of North America's most vibrant, exciting, chaotic city rather than in what he considered to be dull, parochial Canada. "It was like being in the non-smoking room in a restaurant, and the smokers are having so much fun, drinking and listening to music, dancing, and having a great time," he said.

"And you're sitting listening to the radio in the non-smoking room. That's what it felt like. Everyone here was having more fun. I know Canadians don't want to hear that, but it's true."

Carter's parents were not the only ones who expected their offspring to return. Sparkle Hayter, an author of mystery novels, got a taste of New York on her first trip from Edmonton and resolved to return. "My friends just knew what I was going to do, what I wanted to do. My father would put out tabloid stories about anything bad that was happening in New York so I'd see it in the morning," she said.

We spoke in the lobby of the Chelsea Hotel, where for five years Hayter has rented an apartment. A New York landmark, the Chelsea was the city's tallest building a century ago. It later became one of New York's first co-operative apartments and has long been a haunt for artists, some of whose works adorn the walls or hang from the lobby ceiling. Jimi Hendrix, Joni Mitchell, Jack Kerouac, Arthur Clarke ... the list of famous writers, painters, sculptors, and musicians who frequented the hotel runs on and on. The list includes Canadian poet and songwriter Leonard Cohen, who wrote about his sexual encounter with Janis Joplin there in the song "Chelsea Hotel."

Hayter, a long way from her birthplace of Pouce Coupe, British Columbia, and Edmonton, where she grew up, loves the ambiance of the Chelsea and the pulsating energy of New York. She visited New York with a friend during a study break while at the University of Alberta and resolved to move. "I fell in love with New York, which I don't think of as a city of America but as a city of the world, " she said. "There was just something about the city. I got here and I felt, 'Ah, home!' The energy. I'm a very hyper person and the energy attracted me. The openness of people. The grandeur. The surprises. You can just wander and find something surprising down any street. There's such a spirit of freedom here."

Fabio Savoldelli believes that from that freedom springs the kind of creativity that drives his world of finance. He's been out of Canada since 1986 and now wheels and deals for Merrill Lynch, one of Wall Street's and the world's largest financial-services companies.

"We operate on a different scale," he said in his World Financial Center office. "One of the fundamental differences in the mindset of American regulators is that unless they say it's illegal, it's legal, whereas in Europe and to some extent in Canada unless they say it's legal, it's illegal. Look at the financial products that have been developed. The options market. The hedge-fund market. The swap market. None of those has been developed outside the U.S. They were developed right here, and yet if you think about it the market for cross-currency swaps should just as easily have occurred somewhere else."

Savoldelli, whose parents emigrated to Toronto from Italy, is now in his late thirties but has responsibilities that exceed what he believes people his age would be allowed to assume in Canada's financial industries. He worked in London, England, for the Bank of Toyko until the Chase Manhattan Bank offered him the job of chief investment officer. Savoldelli's theme is a recurring one among Star-Spangled Canadians: that the United States is somehow a less hierarchical society than Canada and therefore cares less about someone's age in apportioning responsibility within companies and institutions.

"I wouldn't have this job in Canada. Stroll around the chief investment officers of any Canadian bank—and Chase is bigger than any of them—and see how many [employees] had reached forty before they got offered this kind of job," he said. "You'd be surprised at the number of bright young guys, at my age and earlier, who thought about moving or did move to the States. What you're seeing in terms of who moves is not someone who is reliant on government. You're seeing people in the prime of their career or the bright young sparks. A lot of those guys want to leave or do a stint in New York." The scale of New York—another recurring theme of Star-Spangled Canadians in the Big Apple—provides a bigger and brighter stage on which to perform. Salvoldelli concludes: "It's easier to be a star in one of Ed Mirvish's theatres in Toronto than his theatre in London. There is a sense that if you can make it here, you can make it anywhere."

Cliché though it has become, the old line from Frank Sinatra's "New York, New York" nonetheless explains some of what lures Canadians to New York: testing yourself against the city's challenges.

"It's the major leagues. When you work in New York as compared to Toronto, it seems to me not just that the sums are bigger and people are more aggressive, it's also that this is New York," said Douglas Smee, a long-time officer of the Bank of Canada and the federal Department of Finance, now a senior vice-president with Citibank. "Everybody is looking at you. You're dealing in the U.S. dollar. I'm working for an institution that has more than $700 billion in assets, and that's bigger than the Canadian economy. There's a certain personal satisfaction. You're dealing with other people like yourself who are very competent and experienced and qualified. Plus we're [Citibank] just so huge both in New York and in the world that you tend to be involved in some of the most exciting things going on in the world and not as a bit player."

The city calls itself the Big Apple, but for thousands of Canadians in a dizzying variety of walks of life, New York is the Big Sponge, soaking up their energies, talents, ambitions, and dreams. The Statue of Liberty symbolizes the dream of freedom that lured millions of immigrants to and through New York; today, thousands of immigrants still arrive yearly in New York, many of them at or near the bottom of the socio-economic ladder. But not the Canadian immigrants. They usually arrive at least in the middle of the socio-economic ladder, with impressive academic credentials and marketable sets of skills. New Yorkers think of them as apple-pie Americans until they are identified as Canadians, after which they may be thought of as wayward Minnesotans. They melt into the city, as they do into the broader United States, hidden immigrants seeking the New York version of the American Dream. No one knows how many Canadians live in New York. Many of them such as real estate tycoon and owner of *U.S. News and World Report* Mortimer Zuckerman have long since abandoned any links with Canada. They seldom, if ever, think of Canada any more, except as a place where they were born and raised. As Zuckerman told an interviewer from *Maclean's* in 1972: "What's to come back to? What's to leave? I mean, I created my own life here. I love the dynamism of the country. I love the politics. The rewards have been beyond my own expectations."

Malcolm Gladwell, essayist at *The New Yorker*, believes New York's image of itself assists Canadians.

"There's this incredible attitude here, this incredible acceptance," he said. "In many ways you have an advantage if you're an outsider. This country is so attuned to outsiders that they prefer them to their own. In New York society, if you run into someone who's European or from somewhere else, the assumption is always, 'Wow, if they're here, they must be brilliant.' New Yorkers pat themselves on the back. So the notion that someone would come from a foreign country and make it here means that they are special. If someone reaches your level, you think they must be a genius."

Tens of thousands. That's about the only guess anyone can offer about the number of Canadians in New York City, but how many tens? A scattering of yearly events brings a few hundred Canadians together in New York: the Canadian Club, the annual hockey dinner, events sponsored by the Canadian consulate. Even the organizers of these events acknowledge, however, that they attract only a handful of the Canadian community in New York. Very few Canadians grow up or become educated dreaming of Topeka or Tallahassee, but the sheer size of New York, its vaulting ambitions, kinetic energy, kaleidoscopic variety, and immense wealth, give the city a magnetic force for Americans and foreigners alike, from Wall Street to the lofts of Brooklyn.

Marcus Leatherdale, forty-six, sits in a converted loft that doubles as apartment and studio, and explains to me why he has to be in New York City. "Where is the centre of photographic arts?" he asks, repeating my question. "You're sitting in it. It's here. There are a lot of art and photo fairs, and for that moment that's [the place to be]. But for an ongoing, 365-day-a-year thing, nothing beats New York. There's no vital dealer that works internationally that doesn't have a foot somehow in New York. I need to show in New York so I can continue to sell so that I can continue my work."

New York is a city of broad avenues and quaint (or dilapidated and dangerous) communities. It's a mosaic of neighbourhoods, ethnicities, and occupational niches, such as photographic art, into which Canadian expatriates slide for experience, fame, personal satisfaction, and money. For Leatherdale, the niche is photography, but for others it could be fashion, magazines, cooking, finance, law, architecture, painting, sculpture, music, costume designing, business of every kind, retail merchandising, television, freelance writing, medical research ... the list of niches runs on and on.

Leatherdale takes his arresting photographs in India, where he spends four months every year. He has owned a house in the Hindu holy city of Benares, and was moving to one in West Bengal when we spoke. He specializes in portraits of Indian people, and his latest ambition is to photograph the aboriginals of India. New York provides his income; India, his photographic inspiration; Canada, an international identity and a respite.

"I have a log cabin on the edge of Algonquin Park where I spend two or three months. All my creative work is done in India, all my marketing work in New York, all my battery-charging is done in Canada. Canada is what stabilizes me. It's what keeps me clear. It's home base. I'm world-weary when I go to Canada, and I get all charged up again and I'm fine." A green-card holder in the United States and a resident of New York, Leatherdale says Canada remains important to his sense of identity, in the United States and when travelling. "When I travel to Third World countries such as India, it's much better to have a Canadian passport than an American one. They love Canadians and hate Americans in the Middle East and India because Americans are always sticking their nose in other people's business. The Canadians are neutral. We don't bother anyone. In India, I say I live in New York but I'm a Canadian. That whole thing about putting a Canadian flag on your backpack is true."

From photographic art to cuisine. One midwinter Saturday night, I made my way to the James Beard House, former home of the famous American chef and food writer. A group purchased the brownstone after his death, created a foundation to run it, and now almost every night of the week offer meals prepared by the finest chefs from around the United States and sometimes from abroad. It's there that I found Ellen Greaves and Andrew Hewson, two of seven Canadian chefs preparing a multicourse evening of Canadian cuisine for more than a hundred guests. Two other Canadian chefs that night were part-time New York residents. Normand Laprise owns Toqué restaurant in Montreal but has made his name in New York as executive chef of Cena restaurant. Robert Feenie owns Lumière in Vancouver but is *chef de cuisine* at Le Régence in the Hotel Plaza Athénée on East 64th Street. Laprise and Feenie are super-chefs of the kind New York boasts in abundance: culinary stars from elsewhere with a foot in the New York restaurant scene because it's the biggest on the continent. Greaves and Hewson are, so to speak, further down the food chain.

"I loved cooking here professionally, but I like living in Canada," said Greaves, the top chef at the Tea Box restaurant in the Takashimaya Department Store on Fifth Avenue. "I think the quality of life is better, especially if you have children. I like the social support, but in terms of professional life, it's better for me here ... I like cooking for New Yorkers. They're very easy to cook for. It's a city where everybody is living in tiny spaces. They don't have large kitchens," she said. "So everyone eats out. They're fairly jaded. If you show them something fresh and new, they'll really like it."

With so many restaurants operating in a highly competitive environment, chefs have to look for an edge. "New York is a media centre, and all the chefs here have to be sort of media savvy. They have to be aware of the restaurant as a business as well as a passion. Doing publicity. Having a television program or a book. That's very important in this city. It's part of being considered a well-rounded chef here," Greaves said. She's lived her credo, having co-authored in 1998 a cookbook, *Typical Menus for the Bento Box*.

Cooking is an international business. Chefs and staff move constantly. Greaves worked in Stratford, Ontario; New York; California; and Toronto before settling in New York in 1985. Like so many Canadians in New York, she loves the city but admires certain Canadian traits. "I identify myself as Canadian. It's where I grew up," she states, but when she returns to Canada she finds Canadians are often "hostile" and "covetous" because "there does seem to be a sense that there's more money here, there's more something, which is a pity. I see Toronto looking to New York and trying to be like New York, and that makes me sad because Toronto is special and it should stay that way."

Andrew Hewson was brought to New York from Vancouver by Robert Feenie to be executive chef at Le Régence. His wife had just graduated with a doctorate from the University of British Columbia, and she was anxious to take a break between studies and work.

"I love it. It's a huge difference from the West Coast, but there's so much going on. There's so much stuff to see and do. There are opportunities everywhere," he said. "Professionally, there are so many great chefs in this city, and just to be exposed to that … On the West Coast, the restaurants are well known, but here the chefs are big stars."

New York City is hardly an automatic-teller machine. Hewson reckoned his gross income is higher than in Vancouver, but his net income is lower after paying $1,500 a month on the East Side for a one-bedroom apartment. Hewson also had to acclimatize himself to union power in New York City.

"The biggest difference down here is the very strong unions," he said. "In Vancouver, the only hotel I knew that was unionized was the Hotel Vancouver. It's an attitude down here. They work nine-to-five. They put in their seven hours and that's it. I hadn't worked in a unionized kitchen before, so it's a big change for me: all the rules and regulations, and even how to talk to people, disciplining them, telling them to do something that isn't in their job description."

From the niche of cooking to the niche of architecture. Melda Bur, a Torontonian who graduated from Columbia, found her niche working for a small architectural firm that designs upscale retail stores especially for Armani. She hooked into a network of other young Canadians, mostly from Toronto. Her descriptions of the group demonstrate a mixture of excitement about being in New York and certain ambivalent attitudes towards home, as well as an underlying sense of Canadian identity that somehow survives the attractions of the United States.

"We jokingly call ourselves the 'Toronto posse.' It's silly. There's a whole gang of us and we're often together. All the people I work with are Americans and I have great relationships with Americans and I've actually only dated Americans since I've been here, but my closest friends are all Canadians," she said.

"Often people meet at my apartment. We reminisce about Toronto all the time. Our American friends who get swept up in our web, they'll be sitting with us and say 'Guys, stop talking about Toronto.' Friends look back on Toronto and, although they have good feelings about it, the thing they remember the most is that they were either bored or depressed or frustrated, and that would stop them from going back.

"However, all of us, when we go back … there's this feeling, 'Oh, it's good to be back in Toronto,' this feeling that we could always go back. We all have very good friends there. It's that you feel safe in the sense of being home. Everybody in the back of their minds thinks they might go back. But making plans? No."

As Bur continues, the ambivalence deepens between her love of New York and the frustrations and pride of being Canadian.

"I love the energy and I've always been attracted to the kind of chaos of New York. You meet an amazing number of interesting people. I've met a lot of young Americans who have so much energy, so much drive. Really, really young people doing incredible things. Not just big talkers, but talented people who don't seem to think there's a limit or a ceiling," she said, recounting that her first job with the firm involved designing Armani's store on Toronto's Bloor Street. Since then, she's designed stores in Hawaii, Phoenix, and Montreal.

"The people I know in New York who are Canadian—I don't know if it's moving to New York or they always had it—but they have an amazing energy as well. They come to New York because they want more. They know it's not an easy place to live, but you come here because you feel there's more than where you are and you can somehow get a little closer to it." And yet, she adds: "I'm so proud of Canada. There's still something about being Canadian: the mentality and attitude and history … I miss the Canadian perspective on the world. We have an ability to be objective and step outside ourselves as Canadians, whereas Americans tend to see things through their vision … I don't think I appreciated being Canadian until I was outside of Canada, and then I became much, much more patriotic. You become overwhelmed here by the American perspective … American culture is dominant."

Like architect Melda Bur, Johnathan Hausman completed graduate work at Columbia. Upon graduation, Hausman had job offers from two Toronto firms and an interview from a New York investment firm. After many interviews, the New York firm hired him. At thirty-one years of age, he deals in "sovereign risk management," advising clients about political conditions and investment opportunities in twenty-five countries, including Canada. Hausman is ambitious, obviously smart, a Type-A personality, a young man who loves his work, adores public policy ("There's more public policy done in my office in Wall Street than there is in Ottawa"), cherishes the opportunities afforded by his firm, yet remains ambivalent, even worried, about what living in New York is doing to him.

Hausman was scarred by what he calls a "horrific experience" moving apartments in New York. "I was screwed by every single person this way to Sunday. You begin to realize that everyone is out to get you, because it's just built into the culture. You get exposed to it. It just opened my mind to how everything is a hassle," he said. "How if you don't have tons of money, service is terrible. How everything is shoddy, how everybody is essentially trying to cheat you. That is something I never experienced in Canada, maybe because I was so young I never had to experience it ...

"There are differences between the two places. It's absolutely clear to me that there is—it's not something you can put your finger on, per se, which is, of course, the whole Canadian condition—and it's not just the sense of not being American. I think there's a sensibility that I know I'll never lose, and that sensibility is that not everything can be reduced to transactions, because this is a transactional society.

"Do I feel that I'm changing? Yes. Do I feel I've been made hard? Yes. Do I feel that, when I go home, I'm constantly honking at people who don't deserve to be honked at? Yes. I walk too fast. Essentially, I was like that anyway, but you hit a wall and you realize that you are essentially different. I will never be American, and that's why I will never be a citizen here ... In Canada, there's a combination of the Family Compact and Fabianism. Things get done because they need to be done for others, whereas here, things need to be done for yourself. It's the essential difference."

Will Hausman be returning to Canada? He jokes: "I'd like to be one of Ontario's first elected senators." Until then—and Canadians have been debating Senate reform for more than 130 years—New York City's financial and intellectual challenges will hold him.

The most casual stroller through the fanciest sections of Manhattan cannot help but notice the number of poor people, including homeless and beggars. Leave the glittering parts of the Big Apple and wander up to Harlem or out to the black ghetto of Corona in Queen's, or drive through drug-ridden South Bronx or central Brooklyn. These are not scenes from tourism brochures, but they are inescapably part of New York City. If the United States offers extremes of wealth and poverty, excellence and misery, hope and despair, New York City, as one might expect of the country's largest metropolis, offers extreme extremes. Some Star-Spangled Canadians scale the heights of New York's ambitions and wealth far from infested neighbourhoods of deserted tenements, endemic criminality, scarred streets, and pain. The ex-patriates may be aware of these neighbourhoods. They may deplore the existence of such extremes that contribute to the sense of moral superiority that Canadians sometimes feel towards the United States, but these neighbourhoods are off beyond the mental horizons of Star-Spangled Canadians.

Central New York City, where most Star-Spangled Canadians who have not fled to the suburbs of Connecticut or Westchester live, has undergone a renaissance in the 1990s. The central city is cleaner, safer, and more vibrant than a decade ago. Violent crime has fallen for seven consecutive years in the United States, and New York City has enjoyed a similar decline. As the U.S. economy roared ahead in the 1990s, New York City's more than kept pace, especially in bastions of capitalism such as banking, stocks-and-bond trading, and law. The soaring values of the New York Stock Exchange and the increasingly global nature of business allowed New York to reassert its supremacy as the world's leader in corporate finance and international legal transactions. New York bestrides North America in these fields, considering rivals to be on some other continent: Tokyo, London, and, to a lesser extent, Hong Kong and Frankfurt. The implications for Canada are obvious: Toronto is more than ever a second-tier player in a continental economy, a kind of Chicago North. Those who recruit talent for the New York firms that command the heights of the global cconomy are scanning the world. Next-door Canada is an easy and obvious place to look, but only recently has the country been "discovered" by recruiters. The numbers attracted to New York remain small as a share of the total Canadian talent pool, but the talents of the departing Canadians are considerable.

"When I started working at the firm, there were maybe two or three people from Canada. We now have maybe fourteen or fifteen," said Jay Dubiner of the law firm Paul, Weiss, Rifkind, Wharton and Garrison. "The quality of the recruits was really, really good, so that people used to come up to me and pat me on the back, saying 'These Canadians are very good.'"

Dubiner has done the recruiting rounds for his firm in Canada. He has witnessed how U.S. firms are casting a wider net for talent: "Last year, there were seventeen American firms, of which fourteen were from New York, recruiting at the University of Toronto and McGill, whereas five years ago there were just a few."

The states of New York and Massachusetts allow students who have studied elsewhere to write the bar exams. Canadians who arrive in New York City can sit for the state bar, an examination few of them find taxing. "When I came down, I was a bit intimidated by the Harvard and Yale grads. But University of Toronto law school is a terrific law school, every bit as good," Dubiner said. "One of the reasons we went to Canada (and to other places) was to find pools of talent that were untapped. Canada was essentially a bit of an untapped resource with tremendous talent."

David Sharpe, thirty-five, stood at the top of his University of Toronto law-school class. He clerked at the Supreme Court of Canada, and when we spoke he was working for Debevoise and Plimpton, a New York City law firm. He had debts to pay off after completing his legal studies, and the $100,000-plus starting salary offered by the New York firm helped turn him south.

"I could have gone back to Toronto. But I went to New York for the following reasons: pay off debts, get experience, enjoy the city," he said. "Now that I'm living in Manhattan—the city, the culture—the more I can think of being here several years, beyond just paying off my debts."

Sharpe, the son of a Canadian diplomat, spent part of his childhood abroad, including periods in London and Paris. He developed early on, then, an international perspective. Like other well-educated and well-travelled young Canadians, he views Canada as a nice-enough country, but unless Canada can offer the opportunities, intellectual challenges, and, yes, financial rewards, then he is gone and Canada will have lost another internationally minded person with superior training and skills. Graduates are not leaving Canada's top law schools in floods—the vast majority remain in Canada after graduation—just some of the very best and brightest. In 1998, for example, 8 of 180 graduates of the University of Toronto law school went to the United States, although that number would be slightly higher if it included graduates such as Sharpe who had clerked first. The number also ignores those who by-passed the U of T altogether for top U.S. law schools. As U of T law dean Ron Daniels told *The Globe and Mail*: "The statistic that really captures the changing nature of our recruitment practices is that last year we lost more students to Harvard than to any single Canadian law faculty." The best law school in Canada, then, now finds itself competing not with other Canadian law schools to attract talented students, but with the top U.S. schools. In 1998, more than half of the law clerks at the Supreme Court of Canada went south. Upon graduation, New York City holds a special allure for these intellectual astronauts.

"One way to see this whole question of why do certain Canadians come down," Sharpe said, "is a willingness to take risks, a willingness to throw yourself into a larger community of people who are better than you are, who are working harder, moving faster. You arrive and you know that you're either going to succeed or fail, but at least you've taken the risk.

"There are people who stay back. They stay in an environment they are familiar with, and they know what the ranking system is, and they know where they are in that ranking system. If you come here, you're willing to admit in advance that maybe you're not good enough, that maybe you'll fail.

"My sense was that in Toronto, there are a lot of people from small towns in Ontario and across Canada for whom Toronto is the be-all and end-all. They think that when they arrive in Toronto and get a job, they pay for an apartment and go to College Street and hang out at Bar Italia, they've made it. They really think that."

Sharpe, however, found that although he loved New York, working for a big law firm did not suit him. "After a stellar academic career and some very challenging work experience in my past, I found myself doing largely clerical work: document review, document sorting, indexing, preparing summaries of interviews, doing minor legal-research jobs that ended in brief oral reports," he told me. So Sharpe left the firm, took a pay cut, moved to less expensive digs in Brooklyn, and became an assistant attorney-general in the Health Care Bureau of the New York State Attorney-General's Office.

New York City law firms are a churning mass of lawyers working killing hours below the level of partner, for more money than would be available in Toronto, Montreal, or Calgary. It's quite common for young lawyers to work five years at New York firms, then move into business or away from New York, because only about 10 per cent will some day become a partner in a blue-chip firm.

Amyn Hassanally grew up in Vancouver, the son of Pakistani immigrants. He attended Brandeis, began his law studies at Osgoode Hall in Toronto, but became dissatisfied and transferred to Duke. "At Osgoode, the level of facilities, and even to some extent the instruction, was pretty weak. The calibre of the students went from really good to really bad, so there was a huge chasm, between the good and the bad," he said. "The best two professors at Osgoode are better than any of the professors at Duke, but there are no bad professors at Duke whereas there are at Osgoode. And then there are the facilities, computers, Internet access. You're paying for it, believe me, but the facilities are amazing. The biggest difference is the calibre of the students, the kind of self-starter who goes to Duke."

As Hassanally said, "you pay for it" at a U.S. law school such as Duke: $12,000 per semester. He left Duke with about $80,000 (U.S.) in debts. That debt load made New York attractive, because his starting salary at the

Manhattan firm of Dewey, Ballantine was $103,000. The law firm will take care of his visa.

"The market realities were very apparent to me. Bay Street is a bigger market than Vancouver, but even Bay Street was very limited in terms of how many grads they could hire," he said. "I was considering transactional work, more corporate stuff, and the heart of that stuff takes place in New York. My brother left KPMG in Vancouver to go to Chase Manhattan in New York, and I kind of caught the buzz from him that, if you want to do transactional work, New York is the centre of that."

Hassanally tells himself, as he embarks on his New York City legal career, that the city will be a way station to another U.S. city or perhaps Vancouver. When Hassanally speculates on his future, however, Vancouver's chances of luring him back seem slim.

Charles Morse seems more determined to return to his native Calgary. After studying at the University of Alberta, Morse attended Harvard Law School, where he was executive editor of the prestigious law review, then clerked at the Supreme Court of Canada. The result: the familiar refrain of debt, and the lure of New York salaries. His firm, Debevoise and Plimpton, bumped up his salary in recognition of his clerkships with courts in Ottawa and Alberta. As a result, in his first year in New York, Morse earned $151,000, far above what he might have made in Toronto. And yet he says, "I feel what you could call a simple patriotism. I feel that Canada has treated me very well. I received a top-notch education at the University of Alberta, so that, when I arrived at Harvard, I was very well prepared." As for higher Canadian taxes, Morse says they are a "decent bargain" for what they produce.

Some of the best Canadian law students pass through Harvard Law School *en route* to New York. Paul Weiler, once a Harvard student and since the early 1980s a Canadian ex-patriate law professor at Harvard, has noticed a shift in the aspirations of Canadians and Harvard Law School.

"My sense is that, in post-NAFTA, there is a growing degree of across-the-border lawyering," he told me during a long interview in his living room in Cambridge, Massachusetts. "Far more of them now ... are interested in staying in the U.S. It was just unheard of in the 1980s, let alone the 1960s. That was one of the little features [of NAFTA], free trade in services. That has created this market.

"One key reason is the difference in money. The disparity is incredible. So if you get a law degree from Harvard, that's the biggest asset for a top firm in New York or L.A., and they just offer so much more than a top firm in Toronto, let alone what they offer in Vancouver or Montreal. They only look at you here if you are a star student from U of T or Osgoode, then you have no problem getting interviews …. Some—and I think a growing number—are being attracted by the money, and this [New York] is the base for the world now in terms of practising law."

Top-flight Canadian law firms took a while to understand that they no longer could pick at random from the best of Canada's law-school graduates. This drain of young legal talent to New York forced at least some of them to respond. They were competing against New York firms that in 1998 were paying first-year associates $100,000 (U.S.), third-year associates $130,000, fifth-year associates $182,000. Of course, the cost of living in New York is often higher than in Toronto, and by U.S. standards New York taxes are high, roughly comparable to those in Ontario. Still, the gap between New York and Toronto salaries had grown too wide and demand for the best Canadian law-school graduates extended increasingly to New York City. The wealthiest Toronto firms responded by increasing base salaries to first- and second-year lawyers by $10,000–$15,000 (Can.) and by establishing enriching bonuses, a response referred to in Bay Street legal circles as the "please-don't-go-to-New-York bonus." Firms began to offer guaranteed summer employment to the best students in first-year U of T law, and guaranteed articling positions for those who worked in the summer. Firms even offered financial assistance with the students' tuition.

The market response by leading Toronto firms underscores two points about a continental search for talent. Once Canadian firms find themselves competing with U.S. ones for the best of Canadian talent, it's not enough for the Canadian firms to bemoan higher Canadian taxes. If U.S. salaries, or overall compensation packages, are substantially higher in selected industries, Canadian companies have to make adjustments in compensation or run the risk of failing to retain or hire some of the best and brightest, on whom the companies' future may depend. These upward adjustments, in turn, may widen income gaps at home.

Canadian multinational companies have faced this competitive environment for years, but this environment is new for leading firms in the field of law. The law used to be thought of as highly rooted in place. Lawyers studied in one Canadian jurisdiction, articled, and wrote their bar-admission exams there, then practised. Or, they took the bar exam in another Canadian province prior to setting up shop in that province. The success of young Canadian lawyers in New York may feed on itself; indeed, the feeding process has already begun. Once a firm hires and becomes impressed by a few well-educated Canadian law graduates, the firm forms a generically favourable image of certain law schools in Canada. It then keeps that school within its recruiting pool and wonders if perhaps other Canadian schools might be producing graduates of similar quality.

Once a Canadian institution gets "discovered" by a part of the U.S. economy, the company or industry begins to include that institution on its list of preferred places for hiring, and the job market for graduates ceases to be confined to Canada and becomes North American. That inclusion of Canadian institutions long ago touched such industries as computer animation, software design, high-technology, real estate, and entertainment, but now the prospect of becoming a Star-Spangled Canadian is available for some of the best graduates of Canadian law and business schools. The numbers who leave, compared with the total number of graduates, remains small, although numbers are higher than a decade ago. The talent, however, is almost universally excellent, since only the best are hired into the demanding and stressful world of New York City law and finance.

In 1988, when Graydon Carter edited *Spy* magazine, the ex-patriate Canadian editor commissioned a story entitled "The Canadians Among Us" that mockingly warned Americans about the Canadian take-over of their country, and especially New York City.

"This take-over is not a lightning *coup d'état*," the article read. "It is maple-syrup slow, altogether tedious, the way Canadians do everything. They will sap strength through interminable conversations about distances between cities, undermine our aggressiveness through relentless courtesy, lull us into somnambulism with endless re-runs of Lorne Green raising one eloquent salt-and-pepper eyebrow. Their mission: to show us what *nice* really means." The article continued: "The sluggish sleeping giant is rousing. The Great White North is becoming ... the Great White Menace. Canadians have had enough. For too long they have played Jimmy Olsen to our Superman, the Mertzes to our Ricardos, Augie Doggie to our Doggie Daddie. We imported Saul Bellow and gave them *Three's Company*. They marinated themselves in American culture but felt excluded from it. No one ever asked them to dance. No one ever noticed them." (Superman, unbeknownst to the author, was not "our" Superman, but a comic-strip character invented by a Canadian.)

Carter remembers the response to the *Spy* article: "It got more hate mail than anything in my journalistic career. There were concentrated letter-writing campaigns from high schools." Canadians may have been upset; New Yorkers were indifferent or mildly amused.

"The sad thing is that Canada never comes up in conversation. I know Canadians think Canada should be on everyone's lips, but ... New Yorkers are so inward-thinking. Only things in New York come up," he said. "If you opened *The New York Times* in the morning and there's a story that said 'Canada Destroyed in an Avalanche' up in the right-hand corner, and down in the right-hand corner it said 'Squeegee-Washers Wage Revolt on FDR Drive,' what story do you think New Yorkers are going to read first?"

Being "Canadian" in New York does not resonate. Nobody fundamentally cares. The Big Apple is too busy to notice who is worming inside. Limp stereotypes abound: Canadians are polite, live in a cold place ... and that's about it. Carter himself claims authorship—a contested authorship, I might add—of the clever line that Canadians are so polite that they say thank-you to automatic-teller machines. In a slightly more aggressive description, *The New Yorker* once quipped that Canadians are the people who go around on skates without any teeth. More typical was the mock contest run by *The New Republic* in which the magazine asked readers to submit the world's most boring headline and selected as the winner: "New Canadian Initiative Unveiled."

Carter sees a certain difference between Canadians and New Yorkers. "Forget about Americans," he said. "I don't know much about Americans; they're pretty much the same as Canadians. But New Yorkers are tough on the outside and soft on the inside; Canadians are soft on the outside but hard on the inside. It means Canadians are pretty tough, long-term. When I got here, a lot of people mistook politeness and niceness for softness, and they tried to run roughshod over me. I called them in and said, 'Don't ever fucking confuse the two, because I'm a hundred times tougher than you are.' And eventually I got rid of them. Canadians are hard inside perhaps because of 300 years of bad winters. They're not push-overs, but they have this polite exterior that people mistake, and that serves them very well."

Just don't play on the "Canadian" bit in New York, because it will not wash. "I tell Canadians, come down here and get into the melting pot and melt," said Carter. "Nobody really gives a fuck. They don't care if you're from India or Pakistan or South Africa or Canada. Canadians have this advantage in that we kind of look like them [Americans], and if you're smart you can talk like them. I immediately stopped using the word 'serviette' for 'napkin.' Canadians were very thick on having family crests on blazers; I cut those out."

Bruce McCall, humourist and illustrator at *The New Yorker*, agrees: "Americans are so used to assimilation that everyone comes from somewhere else here in New York. There's no great difference if you're Canadian because they are so much like Americans compared to Senegalese or Australians or Brazilians. They're very blasé about it. They're an immigrant society."

McCall wrote a mordantly funny book describing the cloistered, smug Canada he experienced in his youth during the 1950s in Simcoe, Ontario, and Toronto. *Thin Ice: Coming of Age in Canada* outraged various Canadian reviewers, who apparently could not abide his withering portrait of their country. (The book was also a searing portrait of McCall's dysfunctional family.) Graydon Carter, who reviewed *Thin Ice* for *The Globe and Mail*, loved the book, and Carter was right. How could any literate person, with a sense of humour and an understanding of Toronto's history, not appreciate McCall's description of the postwar "Queen City":

> Toronto the Good it was, if "'good" was narrowly defined as a million middle-class white Protestants of Anglo-Saxon descent marching in lockstep along the path of moral righteousness. Something about the place suggested, even to an irreligious thirteen-year-old, that it had decided around the time of Queen Victoria's diamond jubilee just to stop and freeze everything, then and there. Had Victoria herself appeared downtown one typical pewter-gray Sunday in 1948, just to check up, she should have found a gratifyingly stone-dead Sabbath being observed, as 100 per cent joy-free as she could have hoped. Toronto's moral tone was set and assiduously monitored for the slightest signs of slippage by the Lord's Day Alliance, a self-appointed star chamber of churchly hard-liners, whose dour vision of the Christian life had a way of getting transmuted into law. No Sunday sports. No Sunday drinking. No Sunday shopping. This accorded with the views and values of Toronto's barely postcolonial ruling class of Anglo-Saxon politicians, divines, lawyers, business leaders, and the odd Colonel Jingo. Their devout Anglophilia, Anglicanism, temperance, and solemnity set the model for the municipality and much of the nation—backward Papist French Quebec, of course, excepted.

McCall escaped Toronto, only to land in Windsor doing stultifying work designing automobile advertisements for the Canadian car market. His dreams about the United States were then, quite literally, across the river. Detroit, he thought, represented the "New Jerusalem." And he left.

> I had been a failure as a Canadian. I had never, ever responded to the tone of the place. The patience, the mildness, the taste for conformity that seemed prerequisites for a tolerable life were beyond me. Canadians

294]   Star-Spangled Canadians

so flinched from giving offence, much less seizing the initiative, that it had seeped into the way they talked. For half the population, every utterance ended in a ... question? And the famous, pathetic Canadian 'eh?' was usually tacked on, to further soften it ... 'eh?' This was not a nation poised to shake the world.

Nobody seemed to have big dreams. Nobody wanted to stand out. Save for the annual wheat-bushel quotas and the snowfall records, excess might as well be legally outlawed. There wasn't a glamorous public figure in the entire dominion, and 'Canadian style' was an oxymoron ... The Americans grabbed off many of the best and the brightest to feed their voracious appetite for excellence. The immediate question attached to almost any halfway famous Canadian was 'Not good enough to make it in the States, eh?' ... In the end, I could find no reason to think of Canada as any different from what it had been in school geography books since time immemorial: a giant wheat-farming, ore-mining enterprise perched on the cusp of greatness since confederation almost a hundred years before, but in no particular rush to arrive there. As far as I was concerned, the sleeping giant had slept in. And it was time I tiptoed away.

Seated in his Central Park West apartment, McCall marvelled at how all his stereotypes about the American Dream seemed to be true.

"It's one of those things that I'm still rather boggled by—everything went just as I hoped it would. The minute I got to the United States, I walked into a much-better-paying job in a much-more-go-ahead climate with more interesting people. Obviously I was accepted and was successful, so I felt pretty good about myself.

"I had a car and a penthouse apartment. I met a girl the third day I was here. I was on my way ... It was a great start and it never stopped really. I moved to New York [from Detroit] after two and a half years, got a marvellous job with the best agency in town."

A few blocks away, at his writing studio on Central Park West, Robert MacNeil, broadcaster and author, echoed McCall's memory of arriving in the United States from the stultifying Canada of the 1950s. "I loved it here," MacNeil said. "I loved the ambience. I mean coming from Ottawa in 1953 to New York where there were bookstores everywhere and newsstands and Sunday papers and bars that were open. The contrast was so much more dramatic then. In Canada, everything interesting seemed to be happening somewhere else. And Canadian politics had absolutely no interest at the time."

And yet, successful as McCall and MacNeil have been in the city that so captivated them, they remained, through it all, Canadian citizens.

"There was this tug," McCall explained. "And I can only explain it by saying that there was this deep imprint on me in those early years and an abiding sense that there are aspects of the Canadian 'character' and society that are superior to this one. Part of me is proud of that, and part of me is a little abashed that I was so quickly willing to rid myself of all that. It's not a complete win. I go back to Toronto these days and it's a wonderful place. It's far more humane than New York. The medical system is so much fairer."

Says MacNeil, who bought a summer home in Nova Scotia in the early 1990s: "I would be introduced here in [giving] talks, of which over the years I did hundreds, and they would say 'originally from Canada.' And I would say 'but I'm still from Canada'." For thirty-five years he lived in the United States and as a correspondent in Britain, but did not take out U.S. citizenship until 1997. He had left Canada, but somehow Canada never left him.

"All those years, I kept wanting to write, apart from the non-fiction stuff, and I kept coming up with ideas for plays or novels that would get halfway or stalled. And usually I was setting them in Britain or here among people I thought I knew but really didn't," he said.

"It wasn't until I did a little book, a memoir about growing up in Nova Scotia, that suddenly the truism that you have to write what you know about opened things up for me and released whatever talent there was … I think that people have a sense of early place. Like animals, there's a territorial sense of place where they came from. I know I feel that in Nova Scotia. On a summer morning, when the chickadee is singing in a particular way through a particular thickness of the air in the morning—the smells and feels of the place—it's very, very evocative to me." Then, like a good journalist, he listened to himself and offered a correction. "I've seen it said in the past that people who are most Canadian are the people who don't live there any more. There's an obvious nostalgia and exaggeration."

As the Canadian author Elizabeth Hay, who spent many years in New York, wrote in *Captivity Tales*: "It's not that one place spoils the other, but that it becomes easier to hold a place in your mind if you're living somewhere else, and it becomes more important to hold the place in your mind than to be there."

I feel some guilt that I have not confessed to Chance that he is seeking help for making the great American film from a Canadian. But there is the question of money, and I have found that Americans, by and large, recognize no distinction between us. Why should I? — Guy Vanderhaeghe, The Englishman's Boy

ENTERTAINMENT, JOURNALISM

RACHAEL Wilson came to Los Angeles from a small Ontario town at twenty-one years of age. Blonde, ebullient, articulate, and attractive, she was willing to start at the very bottom in her quest for Hollywood stardom, the apex of the American Dream.

"I talked recently to my manager. It's been nine months and I've worked once. He said we believe in you and it's a matter of you believing in yourself," Wilson said.

"But that is the ultimate hardest thing to do, because no matter how much confidence you have, one day when you think you've done a great job in an audition it's shattered. Up–down. Up–down. It's a matter of keeping something solid inside that you can lock up and not let anything get at it. That's what propels you."

We were seated, on a November 1998 morning, in Wilson's small but pleasant one-bedroom apartment on the fringe of Beverly Hills, an apartment whose rent Wilson's parents subsidized while their daughter struggled for a toehold in the U.S. entertainment industry. That afternoon, Wilson would audition for the umpteenth time, hoping for a break that might lead to a bit part that might, if she were lucky and caught the attention of the right person, nudge her towards another part, and then another and another, until something big came along. She would then be on her way to the ultimate American Dream: movie or television stardom.

"The image. The cars. The clothes. It all hits you in the face and you say, 'Why can't I have those clothes?' The intense want is enveloping and you have to fight it off with all your being," Wilson continued.

"Everyone is here basically to make it in whatever way and they're coming from different places. They're all pretty young. You see people who are successful, even heads of studios, at twenty-eight years of age. If you really want to make it, you come here. The opportunity is here for the taking, even though you have to cut people's throats to get there.

"But that's not my way. For me success would be to choose to do a great film. Success for me isn't a house in the Hollywood Hills. Maybe that comes with it, and who's going to complain? But that's not my ultimate goal. I couldn't care less really if I made it on to the cover of *Vanity Fair*, if that's the pinnacle of L.A.'s definition of success.

"We're not given the opportunity as actors on a scale in Canada that allows you to survive financially. There's great independent work in Canada, if you can find it, but you are not going to pay the rent. You're going to be struggling for a long time to produce what you want to produce."

In nine months, Wilson said she had done more than 100 auditions. Like thousands, of young actors from across the United States and Canada searching for a break, Wilson got fixed up with an agency.

"You don't pay the agents until you work. They are working for you, however. Their job is to get you circulated. The manager guides you, establishes a game plan, sets up 'general' meetings with important people and half the time they don't even remember afterwards who you are," she recounted.

"'There's a definite superficiality in Los Angeles. No matter how much you might think people like you, it's always going to be exactly the same when you come in. There's a barrier and it's full of niceties, 'Hi, how are you? It's so nice to meet you.' You wish they'd say, 'Hi, I'm having a really bad day.' But there's definitely a thing that you have to be 'on' all the time."

The pressure to be "on all the time" extends to everyone dreaming of catching that one break that could lead to stardom in the entertainment capital of the world, but the pressure is especially intense for the young Canadians, who fear for their legal status in a city swarming with wannabe stars. Nobody knows how many young Canadians actors are scrounging around Los Angeles, because they come and go, hopping back and forth across the border to renew their visas, going underground as illegal immigrants waiting on tables or driving taxis, scratching to make ends meet while they struggle for that one big break. They wrestle with the reality of their initially precarious status, but they are fired by the dream that some day they, too, can be Jim Carrey or Mike Myers or Neve Campbell or Wendy Crewson or Gloria Reuben or Jason Priestley — some of the Canadians stars that light up Hollywood.

Jaelen Petrie, seated that Saturday morning in Wilson's living room, came from Cardston, Alberta, to L.A. to study drama. His courses completed, Petrie's student visa enabled him to remain for a year, and the clock was ticking on that visa.

"I don't have an agent. So I'm just hitting the streets myself. I talk to people. I read the newspapers. There's a specific newspaper for actors called *Backstage West* that has lots of the auditions. I went to four of them last week. To have four auditions in one week without an agent is actually quite a feat," he said.

"Everyone here is out for themselves. To go to an audition, you have to hope for the best but expect the worst. That's what it's all about. You can't take things personally. You hope you're in the right place at the right time.

"You come to L.A. and you hope for the best but expect the worst, especially as a Canadian, because you don't know if you can work. It's always on your shoulder. It's always there. The IRS [Internal Revenue Service] is going to get you. Or you're going to get deported. You've got to get a job within a year."

Petrie knew one person when he arrived in L.A. "He came down here and he had a hundred bucks to his name," Petrie recalled. "He got a job with MGM in the mail room, because he had the one year to work. From there he went on to work for Disney on an animated film ... I came here and I just barely had a bed. I slept on a foam mat we found by the side of the road ... I now live with four other guys. The rule here is basically: Be nice to everybody. Don't cross anyone's path."

The most critical time for the Rachael Wilsons of Hollywood is the three-month "pilot" season every spring when single episodes of hundreds of potential shows are filmed for the fall television season. Only a handful of these pilots will enter into production for a series lasting thirteen or twenty-six weeks, and of these only a couple will become long-running fixtures on the U.S. networks. These are the programs so eagerly coveted by Canada's private television networks, which make their profits by importing U.S. material into Canada. Indeed, the most important yearly decisions by CTV and Global executives in Canada are which U.S. programs to buy; the bottom-line results that owners and shareholders crave hang on these decisions, more than on any other. Canada, the ultimate cultural colony, not only sends most of its aspiring and realized entertainers to Hollywood and New York, but sucks back from the Mother Country, culturally speaking, what Canada's capitalists in film distribution and television programming believe Canada's mass audiences desire. For American movie and television moguls, Canada is merely a convenient appendage to the U.S. market, near and culturally assimilated; for Canadian mass-entertainment moguls, the United States is the lodestone of popular taste and profits.

The "pilot" season is all about contacts, luck, dreams for the young Canadian wannabe stars. "If you can get a pilot, everyone gets excited and thinks they might get a year's contract," Wilson explained. "But most pilots don't make it. And you can't really negotiate. Sometimes they say, 'Take it or leave it. This is the deal. There are ten other kids who want it, and we have five people we're offering it to. This is what you get, and if you don't want it, see you later'."

Visa status forces some Canadians to hide their national identity; others wear it as a badge.

"Being a Canadian? It's definitely an asset," Petrie said. "The Canadians are very well respected. They're good at what they do. There's a little network. Canadians are such a different mindset. It's about art. The country's mindset is that we're not out for the money. We talk to people. We're nice."

Maybe Canadians are nice. Maybe they do talk to people. And maybe young Canadians can benefit from the reputation for excellence that so many Canadians have earned previously in Hollywood. But it's hard to make that case a compelling one, since Canadians do not orient Hollywood to whatever different values they might bring to the place. Everyone, Canadians included, adjusts to Hollywood, not the other way around.

They can, like Rachael Wilson, cling internally to their identity, if that is what cheers them, but it does not change Hollywood, crucible for the American Dream.

"They don't have the same threat of losing their identity. Canadians are scared to bring Americans in because, Good God what would happen to our Canadian actors, whereas in the States there's never a worry about American actors not having work," Wilson said.

"So they say, 'You're from Thailand or you're from Canada. Yeah, come on in and make us some money. Give to the big machine.' The longer you're here, the harder it is to distinguish where you're actually from, but Canadians have within them something that is unique. I think that Canadians are very direct, very honest. This is a generalization, but there's no bullshit. We didn't grow up here."

Wilson's perseverance and talent paid off. Within eighteen months of our conversation, she landed a cameo appearance in *Austin Powers: The Spy Who Shagged Me* and larger supporting roles in *Mystery, Alaska,* and *Anywhere But Here,* small but important steps for a Star-Spangled Canadian actor bent, like so many others, on a career in Hollywood.

Wannabe Hollywood stars must try any and all methods of catching the eye of those who dole out parts. Every little job winds up on the résumé; every bit of income helps to pay the bills while actors wait for fatter paycheques and residuals. For every bona fide star, no one knows how many actors in Los Angeles (and New York) are scraping by, living in small apartments, trying to make ends meet between contracts, often working as waiters or bartenders or production-house assistants while they try to become better known in the film and television worlds. There are multiple entry points into the entertainment business, but each is clogged with actors young and old trying to squeeze through the door. Which is why one midweek evening I sat in a small theatre seating no more than fifty people on a nondescript street in North Hollywood lined with a gay bar, a bartending school, an appliance store, a liquor outlet, and a couple of fast-food joints. With me was Wendy Philpott from Orillia, Ontario, who, with a dozen other actors, listened to casting agent Maggie Fulford.

"We always accept mail, so don't hesitate to write," the beautiful, polished Fulford told Philpott, Philpott's actor-husband, and fifteen or so other L.A. actors, including one other from Canada. "Tell us right away about any change in agents," Fulford continued. "Make sure you know the nature of the show you're applying for. And remember," Fulford cautioned, "the show will not be about you. If the script calls for you to walk on and say nothing, or just provide a reaction shot, don't ham things up trying to impress somebody. Never lie on your résumé because you'll inevitably be caught. Don't exaggerate what you have done. Stay in touch. We read everything."

On the table in front of Fulford, the actors had laid their photos and résumés. She spent a while shuffling the photos around, trying to match pairs of actors to read the script she would hand them. After being paired, the actors retired to another room for ten or fifteen minutes to study the script, before returning to perform the brief skit while Fulford took written notes and, they hoped, made favourable mental notes so that she would call when her casting agency needed an actor.

The neighbourhood was down at the heels, and the theatre cramped and somewhat dingy, but, explained Philpott, this little operation, appropriately called "Seenwork," was well known to the casting agencies. Representatives such as the luminous Fulford showed up every week. Not just anyone could audition here. The organizers had prescreened the actors. Amateurs and starters had already been weeded out, meaning presumably that, despite superficial appearances, this was not rock bottom for the actors.

Wendy Philpott was working in a restaurant to earn money, sometimes opening it at 6:30 a.m.; her husband, an American, was selling automobiles on the side. They were both actors, had worked in commercials and live theatre and television shows, but were waiting for that elusive big break. "I am right on the brink," Philpott said, with a fire in her eyes and a confidence in her voice that made her helpless listener want to rush out and do something to give her a small push that might indeed take her over that "brink."

Philpott and her husband performed a skit they had worked up, then Philpott explained the source of her ambition to me, an ambition that fuels the dreams of hundreds of young Star-Spangled Canadians in Los Angeles.

"I wanted to be an actress ever since I can remember … When I was in high school I was part of a singing group that did really, really well. We travelled all over the place doing the whole resort circuit," she recalled. "When high school was coming to a close, I knew that, if I'm going to do this, I need to know exactly what I'm doing. Musical theatre from high school is not going to cut it on my résumé. I'll need to have training, know what I'm doing and be a professional.

"So I looked into all kinds of schools, and I did look into some in Toronto. But, for me, I felt that was playing it too safe. I really felt like, if I wanted to do this, I needed to move to L.A. So I did."

Philpott was good and fortunate. She auditioned in Toronto and was subsequently accepted into the American Academy of Dramatic Arts in Pasadena, one of the very best schools in North America. Remaining in L.A. for a year on a student visa, she worked in a bakery and got lucky with three parts. She won an award for the second play, critical acclaim for the third. She met casting agents, got a television commercial agent. She met her American boyfriend (now husband) and moved in with him. Things were going swimmingly. Philpott was up from the bottom rung of the ladder.

"But I got really homesick. I just really wanted to go home and visit. I flew back for a week, and at that point I hadn't had any problems. I knew I was going to have to take care of my papers at some point, and truth be known I had talked to lawyers and others and they had said it's next to impossible to get a visa unless you're an actor with a steady gig," Philpott said.

"It's really hard to do it by the book, unfortunately. I flew back for what was supposed to be a week's visit and, as I was getting ready to fly back, I got stopped. I don't know what tipped them off. Who knows?

"At that point it was a big mess because, in school, I had to lose my regional accent, so I had an American accent but I still had little hints of a Canadian accent, so I'm sure they had red flags that go up when they detect any kind of crazy combination like that. Who knows? They went through all my stuff. I had my Day Timer and I had play schedules, addresses, work schedules. I mean it was pretty obvious I was living there.

"So they said, 'You're not going back until you can show us that you have been living and working here for at least six months.' I had a home and a car and my boyfriend, my job, my life, my training; everything I'd worked for was there. I didn't know what to do. I was in a horrible position."

What to do? Philpott flew to Vancouver, where her sister lived, figuring she could head south from there. Philpott bought a plane ticket with cash from Bellingham, Washington, to Los Angeles. With her sister, Philpott headed to Vancouver from Bellingham in a rental car.

"They stopped me at the border at Bellingham. Two customs agents walked up to me and said, 'We're going to have to talk to you for a second'," she remembered.

"It was just a big mess. I've never been in trouble like that in my life. It was horrible. It was scary, terrifying, just terrifying. They put me in the back of a cop car and took me to the station. They interrogated me. They took my mug shot. They called my parents to verify who I was. They asked for any identifying birthmarks. You would have thought I was smuggling who-knows-what across the border."

Philpott was smuggling herself across the border, and she got caught for the second time.

"They dropped me off on the other side. I had no idea what to do. I phoned my sister and wound up staying with her for three months."

The cliché that love conquers all worked for Philpott. She and her American boyfriend had been contemplating marriage, so they accelerated those plans, tying the knot at Whistler during Philpott's forced sojourn in British Columbia. Now married to a U.S. citizen, Philpott resumed her life in Los Angeles, chasing the American Dream, working in the restaurant while he sells cars, doing commercial work, receiving a small residual each time the commercial is aired, performing whenever work becomes available, and turning out with other hopefuls on a weekday night in Los Angeles, giving it her best shot hoping that Maggie Fulford will remember Wendy Philpott's name when a part crops up for young, talented, enthusiastic actor from Orillia who thinks herself "on the brink."

Canadians fell in love with U.S. mass culture in the nineteenth century when most of the best-selling magazines in Canada were American. As for the movie business, Canadians were entering it even before there were movies. At the turn of the twentieth century, the leading light of the pre–motion picture pictograph era was Florence Lawrence, a young woman from Hamilton, Ontario.

Lawrence starred for a company called Biograph, where another young Canadian named Mary Pickford got her start.[1] Fans called Lawrence "The Biograph Girl" before she became the leading lady for the Independent Motion Picture Company. Her reputation flourished from about 1905 to 1915, when she was partially, although temporarily, paralysed after running into a burning studio to save friends. Her career, sadly, never recovered. Lawrence tried and failed to make a comeback in the eras of the "talkies," then tried her hand at journalism, interviewing other stars. In 1938, Lawrence killed herself.

Behind Lawrence arrived the greatest Canadian star of them all, Gladys Smith, the Torontonian who changed her name to Mary Pickford, "America's Sweetheart." From age eight to fifteen, Pickford was part of a theatrical touring group that played across the eastern United States and in Canadian cities. She then joined Biograph as a teenager in the age of pictographs. Toronto, her home town, had no movie industry. Nor did Hollywood, a city that had not even been created when Pickford emerged as a star in New York before the First World War. A publicist for Famous Players dreamed up the nickname "America's Sweetheart," and it stuck, not just for her roles in early movies but for her efforts to sell war bonds to finance U.S. military participation.

Pickford spoke at so many rallies, and her picture graced so many posters encouraging Americans to buy bonds, that a U.S. journalist wrote at the war's end, "If all the world were gathered in one huge, darkened auditorium and a portrait were to be flashed upon the screen which would be recognized by the greatest numbers, whose would it be? Would it be the picture of Woodrow Wilson, of Lloyd George, or even of the late Kaiser? No, indeed. It would be wee Mary Pickford ... for world popularity, she is the greatest American, the greatest world citizen."[2]

Allowing for some American chauvinism, Pickford, the "greatest

American," nonetheless was then, and would remain for a long time, one of the best-known and loved movie stars in the United States. She starred in dozens of films at a time when movies became all the rage, and made the trek with the rest of the industry to Hollywood. Her marriage to another star, Douglas Fairbanks, provided the grist for a thousand gossip columns, although that marriage ended in divorce. Occasionally, Pickford returned to Toronto, where she basked in celebrity status and received the keys to the city, but her Canadian roots, whatever they meant to her, did not stunt her U.S. fame. She died still known as "America's Sweetheart," the first but by no means the last ex-patriate embraced by U.S. popular culture whose appeal extended throughout Canada.

No one blamed Pickford for heading south. How could they when Canada before and after the First World War had no film industry at all? Hollywood studios vertically integrated production, distribution, and marketing in the 1920s and gobbled up Canadian independent producers. The Hollywood studios, then as now, considered Canada part of the U.S. domestic market, and bought distribution and marketing networks in Canada to integrate them with those in the United States. From the earliest days of U.S. motion pictures, the great sucking sound was of Canadians heading south. Jack Warner, born in London, Ontario, and Louis B. Mayer, whose parents emigrated to New Brunswick from Russia, became legendary producers in early Hollywood. The Canadian actors who went south from 1910 to 1940 are too numerous to list here, but among the names were: Pickford and Lawrence, Marie Dressler, Lew Coady, Walter Pidgeon, Walter Huston, Beatrice Lillie, Norma Shearer. (Dressler, from Cobourg, Ontario, and Shearer, from Westmount, Quebec, won the first two Academy Awards for best actress.) Directors included Sidney Olcott, and Allan Dwan, who did many classic Douglas Fairbanks films.[3]

The next generation of stars would include Raymond Burr (*Perry Mason*), Hume Cronyn, Glenn Ford, Lorne Greene (*Bonanza*), Raymond Massey (arguably best known for his portrayal of President Abraham Lincoln), Christopher Plummer, William Shatner (*Star Trek*), Jay Silverheels (*The Lone Ranger*). Their stories varied in the particulars but shared the same plot line: the United States offered creative and financial opportunities beside which Canada offered the Canadian Broadcasting Corporation, then as now a thin reed upon which to build a career. Canada, with its small market and limited creative outlets, simply could not compete with Hollywood or New York, so that many Canadians with ambition and talent gravitated south. And since, courtesy of television and movies, Canada's popular tastes became largely those of mass-market America, whatever compromises and adjustments Canadians made in the U.S. entertainment industry were minimal and inconsequential when placed beside the financial gain.

Only those with a taste for history among the young Canadians yearning for a place in Hollywood would know of Pickford or Massey or Pidgeon or Ford, but few of them are unaware of the recent generation of actors, writers, directors, producers, cameramen who have struck Hollywood gold. Today's Star-Spangled Canadian stars twinkle in a mental firmament that keeps the young aspirants heading for another audition, another meeting with an agent, another session with a casting director, another restaurant job while waiting for the bit part that might just lead to the first steps to fame or, at least, to steady work.

Mike Myers, Michael J. Fox, Martin Short, Jim Carrey, Jason Priestley, Neve Campbell, Gloria Reuben, Leslie Nielsen, Matthew Perry, Julianna Margulies, Keanu Reeves, Dan Aykroyd, Donald Sutherland, Christopher Plummer ... these are among the Star-Spangled Canadians whose stars shine brightest in the minds of those Canadians who moved to L.A., hoping for a break. Canadian actors also abound in second-tier films, sitcoms, soap operas, serialized television dramas. Their names are not yet of the household variety, and may never be, but are known by the aspirants: Wendy Crewson, Caroline Rhea, Terri Hawkes, Scott Bairstow, Allison Hossack, Joshua Jackson, Gary Basaraba, Klea Scott, Jill Hennessy, Gil Bellows, Cameron Mathison, Ryan Reynolds, Eric McCormack.

Then there are veteran third-tier actors such as John Kapelo, far from stardom but also far from the hand-to-mouth existence faced by most screen actors who remain in Canada.

"I couldn't go back to Toronto and make the same living. I'd like to work in Toronto and Vancouver as much as possible, but there just aren't the financial incentives," Kapelo said. "I was up for two or three movies and they wanted me, but we just couldn't make it work. There's just not the money available to pay. If you work for $75,000 or $150,000 a movie, the Canadians are offering $20,000 for a second or third lead. The last two or three times it's been that way."

If Mary Pickford was "America's Sweetheart," Pamela B. Anderson is America's sex symbol. Canadians may be known as nice, honest, decent, even straight-laced and, to many Americans, irredeemably boring, but they can also hawk sex with the best of them south of the border. A sprinkling of Canadians star in the U.S. hard-core porn industry, and the more genteel pornography of Playboy has never lacked Canadians.

Several of Playboy founder Hugh Hefner's girlfriends have been

Canadians, including one (Kimberley Conrad) he married and another who later committed suicide. It did not take long for the magazine to discover the reputation and curvaceous anatomy of Danielle House, the Miss Canada from Daniel's Harbour, Newfoundland, who was stripped of her title for slugging an ex-boyfriend's girlfriend in a St. John's bar. *Playboy* got House on its cover fast, wearing a tiara and boxing gloves. House moved to Los Angeles, hooked up with an ex-patriate Canadian agent originally from Edmonton, and tried unsuccessfully to parlay her brief moment of fame and her physical attributes into a career.[4]

Shannon Tweed, another native Newfoundlander, and Miss Ottawa Valley in 1977, first appeared in *Playboy* in 1981 as Miss November. She shacked up with Hefner for two years thereafter, split from him, and formed another relationship that has lasted ever since. The mother of two children, Tweed returned to the magazine's cover at the age of forty in 1998. Her would-be acting career did not exactly thrive through such forgotten films as *Assault on Devil's Island*, *Bimbo Movie Bash*, and *Human Desires*, although she did earn the title "Queen of the Erotic Thrillers" for her performances in such epics as *Indecent Behavior*, *Hard Vice*, and *Lethal Woman*.[5]

These Canadian sex symbols paled by comparison with Anderson, whose distinctly limited acting abilities, first displayed in *Baywatch*, hardly mattered, given her other attributes, two of which received implants presumably to enhance their appeal. With suitable fanfare—Anderson has always marketed herself cleverly—the implants were later removed.

Very few Americans knew of Anderson's Canadian heritage, but in one sense she could not be topped as an All-Canadian girl. Anderson was the first baby born in British Columbia in Canada's Centennial year, arriving just after the stroke of midnight on January 1, 1967. Originally from Ladysmith, Anderson was "discovered" by a talent scout when she appeared on the Jumbotron screen while a cheerleader for the British Columbia Lions football team.

Baywatch made no pretence of striving for artistic merit or interesting plot lines. It focused on a group of lifeguards and their daily efforts to pluck struggling swimmers from the surf, but what it really featured was a cast of women in revealing bathing suits, the tightest of which belonged to Anderson. Denigrated by critics, *Baywatch* nonetheless became an international television winner by virtue of the women who poured themselves into those suits. In 1994, *Baywatch* boasted a worldwide audience of 1 billion viewers in 128 countries.

Anderson's much-publicized troubled marriage to Tommy Lee,

drummer for the rock band Motley Crue, made even more headlines. So did a home video of the couple while on their honeymoon, engaging in a variety of sexual acts, including fellatio, a film presumably intended for private consumption that somehow made it into the public domain and became a staple of the late-night porn-movie schedule in hotel rooms across North America. Convicted of physically abusing his wife, Lee served time in prison, then emerged to be reconciled with Anderson and their two children, adding further grist to Anderson's publicity machine. Later, Anderson resumed her "acting" career with a program of her own inspiration, *V.I.P.*, in which she plays the head of a private investigating firm, again with clothes noticeable more for what they reveal than what they cover.

Sexual appeal also underpins the entire modelling industry, and it, too, has drawn Canadians to the United States like moths to a flame. Linda Evangelista, of course, became one of the world's most photographed models, but behind her were dozens of teenage and twenty-something Canadian women with the apparently prerequisite pouty lips, cascading blonde hair, sultry eyes, and barely post-pubescent bodies favoured by those peddling the sexual illusion that clothes make the woman rather than the other way around. Estella Warren of Peterborough became Chanel No. 5's new face in 1998. Rachael Roberts of Vancouver nabbed a spot in *Sports Illustrated*'s swimsuit issue and a Ralph Lauren undergarment campaign. Tricia Helfer from Donalda, Alberta, was named Ford's Supermodel of the World at age seventeen, then appeared on the cover of U.S. *Elle* and *Bikini* magazines. Hollyanne Leonard from Gloucester, Ontario, graced the cover of *Flare* but worried her Hollywood agent because "she likes to read too much." Lisa Winkler from Belleville, Ontario, became Gucci's "it girl" in February 1999.[6]

In the early weeks of 1999, New York's famed 92nd Street YMCA asked the question "Why are Canadians so funny?" and invited four of the most famous Star-Spangled Candian comedians to reply. Michael J. Fox, the host of the evening event held before a capacity crowd, framed the YMCA's question a different way in his opening remarks: "How is it that a country with a reputation for being inward-looking and polite could produce a seemingly disproportionate number of comedians, comedy writers, directors, and actors?" He reeled off quite a list: Mike Myers, John Candy, Wayne and Shuster, Catherine O'Hara, Norm Macdonald, Dan Aykroyd, David Steinberg, Phil Hartman, Rick Moranis, Ivan Reitman, Leslie Nielsen, Kids in the Hall, "various" Barenaked Ladies. Then

Fox, originally from Edmonton, introduced three others, his panellist colleagues: Martin Short, Eugene Levy and Lorne Michaels. "Can you hum the theme from 'Hockey Night in Canada,'" Fox asked. They started before collapsing in laughter.

Through ninety minutes of gags and repartee, the quartet circled the question "Why are Canadians so funny?" as if unsure of the premise. "So what is it, hockey?" jibed Eugene Levy, the sardonic writer and actor ("Second City TV," *Father of the Bride, Armed and Dangerous*). "Is it beer? Canada doesn't drink as much beer as Germany, so that's not it."

Maybe, speculated "Saturday Night Live" founder and executive producer Lorne Michaels, Canadians peering across the U.S. border think they know all about the United States and fulfil some inner need to offer free advice. "There's this feeling," he said, "that if we could only take Americans aside and in a polite way explain to them the things they were doing wrong—in a neighbourly way, in the sense that it just seemed so obvious. The whole country has this feeling that it was just so clear what America was doing wrong in the world."

Fox mentioned only the best-known Canadian comedic talents of recent years. He could have reached into history for Mack Sennett, the Canadian who created the Keystone Cops. Or Saul Ilson, Ron Clark, and Allan Blye, chief gag writers for "The Smothers Brothers Comedy Hour" in the 1960s and 1970s, the so-called Canadian Mafia whose numbers led an outnumbered U.S. writer to quip: "People say, 'Why don't you go back to Canada?' How can I? I'm from New Jersey."[7] Or Rich Little, the brilliant impersonator from Ottawa. Or Tim Long, who moved from being David Letterman's chief gag writer to executive director of writing for *The Simpsons*. Or the Second City graduate Dave Thomas, a brilliant comedic writer in Los Angeles. Why did they and others succeed in the United States?

Martin Short (*Father of the Bride*, "Saturday Night Live") took a stab at answering. "There's a drain to the United States. If you write a great comedy script, within a very short time you're lured with an enormous amount of money to do that same work for NBC, CBS, or ABC, and unless you were a devout patriot—with obviously an inheritance—you'd leave, because usually artists don't feel that boundaries are necessary." Later, Short tossed off a joke with a bitter truth: "I got a green card and I'm proud to call America the land where I take the money."

Money lures them south, but it does not guarantee lasting success. Other factors—especially great talent—explain that success. An inner distance, noted by so many Star-Spangled Canadians in other walks of

American life, may help. As Short remarked, "We can satirize because we have a different point of view."

Fiction writers probe what they know, as the celebrated Canadian literary critic Northrop Frye has explained. They observe the human condition through the prism of their own experience and surroundings. Almost by definition, an ex-patriate would have difficulty capturing the essence of the inner American experience rooted in place, time, and idiom. Canadian comics in the United States, like Canadian journalists there, can combine their own talents with the greater money and opportunities offered while still retaining, if they choose, the observer's sense of psychological distance. Canadians are, if the comics are to be believed, a kinder, gentler group of Americans, because of what Lorne Michaels described as the Canadian character, which is "cautious and risk-adverse." Michael J. Fox (*Back to the Future*; *The Hard Way*; *The Secret of My Success*; *Bright Lights, Big City*; *For Love or Money*; "Spin City") commented that "growing up, I was considered a bit strange. When I moved to the States I was celebrated for everything I was ostracized and ridiculed for at home. I felt like, 'Wow, I'm on to something. Whatever I couldn't do at home, I do here and they give me money'."

Laughs mask comedy's serious business, and not only the making of money. Satirical comedy, which Canadian ex-patriates do splendidly, makes a point. Perhaps Canadians are "so funny" because their country is really quite serious and sober and orderly. The greater the number of rules and conventions, legal or social, the more urgent the need to subvert them by laughter. As Fox quipped, "My wife is always giving me a hard time about—and she attributes it to being Canadian—a deep and abiding respect and fear for rules, authority."

Or, as Lorne Michaels said, "In terms of things that are considered serious, I think Canadians always felt proud that they could more than hold their own—and still do. In popular entertainment, however, the country was ambivalent about it, particularly at the state-sponsored CBC. Doing something popular and funny? Well-behaved was much better. The idea that you were going to pay good money to people who were just going to misbehave just wasn't going to happen."

Michaels's comments might have reflected his own disappointing experiences with the CBC that drove him from Canada in the late 1960s. That Canada, including its public broadcaster, is unwilling to pay good money for misbehaving comics belies the popularity of "The Royal Canadian Air Farce" and "This Hour Has Twenty-Two Minutes." But Michaels remembered what eventually caused him to leave.

"When I was at the CBC, I had a conversation with someone—I'd been trying to stay in Canada and I'd turned down a job here—and I went in to talk to the person responsible for 'light entertainment,' as it was called. I told him I was turning this thing down because I really wanted to stay and because there was this show I believed in," he recalled. "And he said to me, 'If you're that good, why are you here?' I really didn't have an answer. The idea was that it was going to be like a school that trained you but that, if you wanted to work on any other scale, then you were in the wrong place, because there wasn't the audience to support it or the economy to support it. But there was also a kind of inferiority that I am not sure is there in the present generation."

Michaels, like other Star-Spangled Canadians who left more than a quarter of a century ago, reflected on a Canada that remains but a memory.

"In a country where civility and modesty are celebrated, show business seemed like showing off. The thing I got from American television was that they had no problem showing off," he said. "What was called flag-waving in Canada was called patriotism here.

"Particularly when I was growing up, there was a very big distinction between American and Canadian culture. In the period before I left in the late 1960s and early 1970s, there was an attempt to become more like Americans in the sense of yearning to become part of North America.

"The voices you would hear on Canadian television when I was growing up had markedly British accents and sounded a certain way. Canadian television had a look and feel that was different. It was more serious [and] prided itself on being more serious. It was the land of documentaries on the premise that a well-informed populace was a happier populace. The very first thing I started doing in comedy was to do mock documentaries simply because people were already used to the form."

Michaels, the ex-patriate Torontonian, became a kind of Godfather to U.S. comedy through "Saturday Night Live," the late-night show that has survived for twenty-five years with its zany, satirical sketches about every aspect of U.S. life, especially politics. The night he invited me to watch the show, Michaels circled the edges of the set like a kind a paterfamilias, seldom saying anything, but surveying everything since the producer's role is finished in live television once the red light flashes. He can only hope for the best, and more often than not "Saturday Night Live" has delivered among the best of U.S. comedy, sometimes with Canadians whom Michaels recruited. Whenever critics complained that "Saturday Night Live" was becoming stale, Michaels displayed an ingenious ability to freshen it up with new talent.

Success does tend to breed success, and reputations do build upon each other, so that the successful recruitment of Canadians to "Saturday Night Live," a recruitment made possible by Michaels staying in touch with the Canadian entertainment scene, continues apace. The night I watched the show in New York, Michaels featured the Canadian band Crash Test Dummies.

The original team on "Saturday Night Live" included Dan Aykroyd, with whom Michaels had worked in Toronto; musical director Howard Shore; and Rosie Shuster, Michaels's wife (now ex-wife), who worked as a writer. Passing through later would be such Canadian talents as Phil Hartman, Martin Short, Norm MacDonald, Mike Myers, and Kids in the Hall.[8] Jim Carrey, arguably the most prominent Canadian comedic actor in the United States, has played host to the show.

Canada's comedic talent sometimes got started at the CBC; more often comedians honed their talent at Toronto comedy clubs, the most famous of which were Yuk Yuk's (where Jim Carrey performed his first amateur nights, commuting from his home in Jackson's Point) and Second City, the offshoot of Chicago's original troupe. Second City's mixture of improvisation and satire, which later was channelled into "Second City TV," allowed a generation of Canadian comedians to hone their talent before going south.

John Candy, until his death of a stroke in 1994, became one of the biggest stars in Hollywood. Catherine O'Hara played in various Hollywood films, as did Martin Short. Rick Moranis starred in various films, including *Ghostbusters*, produced by ex-patriate Ivan Reitman. Dave Thomas found work in sitcoms and as a successful writer.[9]

Andrew Clark, the best chronicler of Canadian comedy, provided a lengthy snapshot at the end of 1996 of Canadian comedic penetration of the United States, a description worth reproducing in full because it shows the staggering drain of talent south.

In New York: Norm MacDonald, a former Yuk Yuk's stand-up, and Mark McKinney, formerly of Kids in the Hall, were part of the *Saturday Night Live* cast. Norm Hiscock, an ex-writer for the Kids, and Lorri Nasso, a Second City alumnus, were SNL writers. It was produced, of course, by Canadian Lorne Michaels. John Rogers was in New York writing for Bill Cosby's new sitcom. Ex-Vacant Lot members Vito Visconi and Mick McKinney were producing an on-line comedy Web site for Microsoft. *SCTV* star Rick Moranis lived in New York but spent most of his time making movies. Fellow *SCTV* alumnus Andrea Martin was big on Broadway and had spent the summer touring her one-woman show. Vancouver stand-up Ian Bagg was working the clubs; he had management and an agent.

In Los Angeles: Brian Hartt, an ex-Kids writer, was head writer for the Fox-TV series *Mad TV*. Also on *Mad TV* were ex-Kids writer Garry Campbell, Martin Short's brother Mike Short and Chris Finn, a former Yuk Yuk's stand-up. Toronto stand-up Frank Van Keeken was making features and had a major role in a David Lynch film. Jeremy Hotz, a Yuk Yuk's stand-up, had landed a role in *Speed II*. Dan Redican, the ex-Frantic and former writer for the Kids, had become producer for *The Jenny McCarthy Show*, a variety show built around a former *Playboy* centrefold. Peter Johanson, a Montrealer, was booked into a development deal with CBS. Ex-*Vacant Lot* members Paul Greenberg and Rob Gfroerer were working on Redican's show. Canadian sketch comic Don Lake, another Second City alumnus, was working as a character actor. Former Kids Kevin McDonald and Scott Thompson were also in L.A.: McDonald shopping scripts and Thompson playing a recurring character on HBO's *The Larry Sanders Show*. Dave Foley was a star in the NBC sitcom *NewsRadio*. David Steinberg was now directing TV, his most noted work being a few episodes of *Mad About You*. Former *SCTV* member Dave Thomas was a regular on the sitcom *Grace Under Fire* … *SCTV* alumnus Catherine O'Hara was a well-respected character actor. Dan Aykroyd continued to churn out films, between entrepreneurial projects such as his House of Blues bar chain. Harland Williams had two movies and a sitcom deal. Mike Myers had a new movie, *Austin Powers*, due for a spring 1997 release. Jim Carrey had wrapped up his comeback film *Liar, Liar*, also due out in the spring.[10]

The reputation Canadians have established for comedic talent has made it easier for Canadians to get their videos watched and scripts read by agents. As in so many other areas of Canadian life, when Canadians excel, Americans do take notice and try to lure them to the big stage of the United States. American talent scouts therefore cruise Canadian clubs and scour Montreal's Just For Laughs annual comedy festival looking for fresh talent. Canadians in comedy—indeed, throughout the entire entertainment industry—long ago learned that North America, not Canada, is their market, a lesson now being learned by Canadians in fields as disparate as computer-software design and computer animation, banking and finance, law and medicine, academic life and scientific research, television and magazine journalism, marketing and architecture. If Canada cannot provide opportunities for the ambitious and talented in these and other fields, they will venture outside Canada, and will not be swayed to remain by fellow citizens who brag about their "kinder, gentler" country.

Well trained in Canada, comedic talents land in a harsh but risk-taking entertainment environment. Having peered across the border, they know lots about the United States, and therefore the acculturation process is easy. From a country that prizes irony—the classic pose of the detached critic—the Canadians cast an ironic eye on the country of green cards, money and opportunity, not completely succumbing to the American Dream. They are the classic outsiders inside: in but not of America—a useful position for social critics such as comics and journalists.

Joe Medjuk, an associate of producer Ivan Reitman's, captured the "in but not of" positioning of Canadians when we had lunch at a restaurant near Universal Studios.

"Being an ex-patriate gives you a sense of irresponsibility about both countries. Anything I didn't like going on in Canada, I could say, 'Well, I'm not part of that any more.' Anything I didn't like going on in the States, I could say 'I'm not an American so I don't care'," he said.

A Jew originally from Fredericton but a long-time resident of Toronto before moving to Southern California, Medjuk thinks being a Canadian gives him and others the outlook of the outsider when observing American life.

"I think it's a bit of an asset. I think that's why you've had all those Canadians in comedy. You're a little bit of an outsider. Why are Jews comedians? Why are Canadians comedians? Jewish Canadians are really comedians. There's a little bit of distance. I don't think it's a myth. It's been going on too long."

The Canadian comedic flight south continues in the wacky, weird talent of Canadian Tom Green. Trashed by Canadian television critics but adored by a coterie of young fans, Green left his show on the Comedy Network in Canada for his own program, "The Tom Green Show," on the MTV network in the United States. It quickly became one of MTV's most popular programs, with off-the-wall, outrageous stunts. Pitching his show to assembled MTV executives in Los Angeles, Green finished his presentation by covering himself in shaving cream and shouting "I want to be on MTV!" He was signed the following day.[11]

Green's humour is not for everyone, although MTV signed him to a two-year contract and Disney has offered him a film. Green's is a long way from John Candy's gentle humour or Mike Myers's harmless spoofs, or

Michael J. Fox's Middle American gags. Green has drunk milk directly from a cow's udder, brought along a dead raccoon as a prop, and tormented his parents in Ottawa. He turned their living room into a petting zoo, with sheep, goats, llamas, and geese, while they were away. He specializes in manic, provocative humour, or what his critics would call puerile, insulting insanity. It's hard to be neutral about Green's humour.

"The Tom Green Show" mixes in-studio segments, during which Green plays off two Ottawa friends who have been with him since he first began in Canada, and segments shot in the field, in which the camera records Green interacting with civilians in a variety of bizarre encounters. The day I met him, Green had just returned from five days of shooting in California, including a segment in which he purportedly followed his mother's instruction to carry a chest of drawers across the United States, ending with a triumphant walk over San Francisco's Golden Gate Bridge. Zany and unpredictable on-air; Green is surprisingly shy and soft-spoken in person.

Born in Pembroke but raised in Ottawa, Green was the class clown early on. He did stand-up comedy as teenager, then open-line radio, before getting a show with a shoestring budget on Rogers Cable. Then came his Comedy Network show which eventually brought him to the attention of MTV, at first temporarily in New York, then on a two-year contract in Los Angeles. Praised in the United States, Green was savaged in Canada.

"[The critics] were brutal at home. It's kind of upsetting in a way. I've got a lot of theories about it," he said.

"It's frustrating, to be honest, because I came down here not as any sort of disrespect towards Canada. We'd been working on this show for ten years. We had the opportunity—I'm twenty-eight years old—to take it to the next level from a very small network that was great in Canada, the Comedy Network, to go to a much bigger network ... I came down here with a very proud sort of nationalistic attitude. When I go on talk-show appearances, I always say I'm from Ottawa and talk about Canada."

Green's Canadian comedic heroes were the SCTV group and Kids in the Hall; others included Monty Python and U.S. late-night-show host David Letterman.

"When I went on 'Letterman' I was by no means embarrassed. I wasn't trying to hide my Canadianism at all, even though I'd only been in the States for a few months. I was talking about Ottawa and Algonquin Park and all these things. I thought it was kind of funny to do that.

"It is frustrating when you go on the Internet or read the hometown paper or *The Globe and Mail* or a lot of these national papers. There's definitely a negative spin on a lot of the articles up there, which for the most part doesn't exist down here. When people down here write articles about the show, they tend to just say it's funny."

Green's arrival in the U.S. market derived from the same forces that have pulled so many Canadian comics—and other performers and writers—to Los Angeles and New York: more income, a larger market, a bigger audience, more resources.

"The goal was never: I want to go to the States. That wasn't the first sentence that would pop up in my brain when I was trying to describe my dream in life. It was that I'd like to be able to make my living as a comedian," he said.

"I don't think I ever really thought about it ... concretely until I was about fourteen or fifteen, when I actually began doing stand-up comedy. But once I thought of that and began to think of it as a possible job or potential career, I don't think I was saying, 'I want to do this so I can move to the States.'

"It was frustrating when we were on Rogers Cable and not getting paid and working eighty hours a week on the show and having to live in your parents' basement and not being able to live a normal life for a twenty-three-year-old who's finished school. I just wanted to move into the professional ranks."

Green put his show together for the Comedy Network with five people, including himself. They worked, he recalled, every day of the year, often sixteen hours a day. "Here, it never really sort of ends, but you have two editors, a dozen production assistants. You end up having ten times the personnel."

Canada, already acculturated to things American, acts as a kind of farm team for the big leagues of U.S. entertainment. Farm-team training helps explain why some Canadian comics and other entertainers succeed when they hit the United States.

"I don't think there's one reason why we have this large amount of successful Canadian comedians. I think there are lots of reasons, including the national-insecurity angle of growing up next to this huge country and feeling, 'Hey, look at me. We're over here too.' That might go into people's individual psyche and make them act a little more extroverted. That might be one thing.

"I personally believe it's not so much that. That's the thing I always hear when I read an article or interview with a Canadian comedian ... But I feel because of the way it happened with me, it's because we have a sort of isolated chain of national media.

"You can start out local. We have this sort of breeding ground where you can really sort of develop your craft in isolation of the American market … I'd been doing my show for six years before anybody in the United States had ever even heard of me. Or heard of "The Tom Green Show" or seen it or had any idea of what it was. That's a lot of time to make mistakes, learn your craft, figure out how to do things properly, how to make people laugh, how to perfect what it is that you do …

"If we had started the show on MTV six years ago, I don't think it would have been as successful. I had to figure out just the right amount of dead-animal jokes that are acceptable within half an hour. In the two years on the Comedy Network, we came to the conclusion that you only want to do one dead-animal joke per half-hour, maybe not five. Which is the other thing about the critics in Canada versus the critics in the States. They saw a lot of that experimentation that nobody down here has seen. People in Canada saw me throw a dead raccoon at Mike Bullard. I haven't thrown a dead raccoon at anyone here yet."

"Big leagues," a cliché to be sure, is precisely how Tim Long described the U.S. entertainment world compared to the Canadian. Long, born in Brandon, Manitoba, could not wait to head for New York after graduating from the University of Toronto. His career there was meteoric: *Spy* magazine, freelance writing for *Vanity Fair* and *The Village Voice*, nine months at "Politically Incorrect," and three years at "Late Night with David Letterman." He ended up as Letterman's chief gag writer at the age of twenty-nine. Now in Los Angeles, Long has become co-ordinating writer for *The Simpsons*.

"I can't really say it was a Canadian–American thing that drove me from Toronto to New York. It's not like I split because Meech Lake failed," he recalled. "It was just that there was a need to play in the big leagues, and there was this horrible sense in Canada that you're not where the action is. Especially coming from a small town, I desperately wanted to get out of there, then I desperately wanted to get out of Toronto. I guess it's some kind of psychosis on my part, but I have this need to clear out once in a while.

"When I moved to New York, my mother was desperately worried and my friends thought I was crazy. But I never saw what was so risky. What were the chances I was going to die? Slim. So, what the hell? It worked out."

Working for the Letterman show was "unbelievably stressful": 9:30 a.m. to midnight six days a week, and daily pressure to deliver. By contrast, an episode of *The Simpsons* is nine months in preparation and production. Long works with fifteen writers, some of whom are graduates of Ivy League schools, including those who cut their comedic writing teeth at Harvard's

National Lampoon. Long quipped: "The two great comedy clichés in Hollywood are Harvard and Canada. If I'd gone to Harvard, I would have had the two of them."

Long describes himself as a "full Canadian citizen and a proud one." Hollywood may be brimming with Canadians, but he notices an enveloping ignorance of things Canadian. "There was a story when the dollar took a dive and somebody came in with a copy of *The New York Times* and said, 'Guess what they call the Canadian dollar'?" Long recounted. "He said the 'loonie.' No way, people said. It's not called the 'loonie.' They don't know a thing here. But it's hard to get worked up about it. When Quebec secedes, I think they'll get interested."

Would Long return some day to Canada? "I have this hopelessly naïve idea. Unlike almost anybody who writes comedy for a living, I've never had to work on a really embarrassing show, and I don't ever want to stop that. So if anything really cool came up in Toronto, I'd probably do it. But it's more important for me to work on a really good show than where I am.

"My sense, completely uninformed by any facts, was that the place [Toronto] was kind of hidebound and that the industry was very hierarchical and you had to work your way up … Here, for better or worse, there's this kind of loosey-goosey atmosphere where everyone admits that they don't know what they're doing, and if things don't work out in the next two weeks, you get fired. The guy who runs this studio has been hired and fired twice, and he's just been hired for a third time."

Nobody ever fired Monty Hall, not after he launched arguably the most successful game show in U.S. television history, "Let's Make a Deal." From 1964 to 1991, Monty Hall, a Jewish boy from Winnipeg, played host to about 4,700 episodes of "Let's Make a Deal." Although gone from the television screen for almost a decade, the show continues on the Internet.

Today, Alex Trebek, a native of Sudbury and a graduate of the University of Ottawa, is the best-known Star-Spangled Canadian playing host to a U.S. television game show. "Jeopardy!" reaches an audience of 17 million Americans and is widely watched in Canada. Trebek was host of CBC's "Reach for the Top" in the 1960s, but game shows on Canadian television have always paled beside those in the United States, the exception perhaps being CBC's long-running "Front-Page Challenge." Despite living in the United States since 1973, Trebek still identifies himself as a Canadian and injects Canadian content into some questions posed to contestants on "Jeopardy!"

When Trebek landed in the United States, Monty Hall had been a fixture on day-time U.S. television for almost a decade. "Let's Make a Deal" got short shrift from snobbish television critics, as most game shows do, but the audience loved how members of the audience dressed in outrageous costumes and wheeled and dealt for prizes. "People found it very attractive: buying, selling, trading, going for unknowns, winning prizes. It became a hit right away," Hall recalled.

Canadians and Americans seemed to react in the same way to "Let's Make a Deal."

"We made a deal with a Vancouver production house to do the show in Canada for airing in Canada and the United States. When I went up to Canada, my brother called me from Toronto and said, 'You'll find a different audience in Vancouver. That's not your Hollywood audience there. People will not come to the show dressed in costumes or whatever they do in the States, and you won't have success'," Hall said.

"After our second broadcast, I called him and said 'You're wrong on every count.' They came dressed as professors and pirates and sailors because they got into the spirit of the show ... And their reactions were the same. They reacted in the same way as when we did the show in Vegas or the streets of Norfolk, Virginia, or Saint Paul, Minnesota. People loved to play, to win, to take a risk, to gamble."

The audiences' reactions may have been similar, but Hall, echoing Tom Green's lament, remembered rougher treatment by Canadian critics.

"When we went up to Vancouver, before we did our first broadcast, a columnist had a scathing article: Who needs this show? Who sent for this show? Who cares for this show? Why should we have this show here? The audience didn't feel that way. They came the same way American audiences came. They won prizes and they lost prizes, and they hugged and kissed me, and everything was wonderful," Hall said.

"It's been like that from the beginning. The worst write-ups that Sammy Davis Jr. got were in Toronto. The worst write-ups that Lorne Greene got were in Canada. The worst write-ups Bill Shatner got were in Canada. The worst write-ups I ever got were in Canada. It was a way for reporters to vent their spleen somehow: 'Why should this man go to the States and be successful? Either he deserted us or his standards aren't as good as we have here' ... I don't think the general public thinks that way."

Monty Hall grew up in a proud, poor Winnipeg family but managed to attend the University of Manitoba. From his closely knit family and the mores of Winnipeg's Jewish community, Hall learned the virtues of helping others. Philanthropy has always been hugely important to Monty Hall. Wings have been named for him at Toronto's Mount Sinai Hospital, at hospitals in Philadelphia and Los Angeles, and at Johns Hopkins in

Baltimore. His secretary of thirty-two years standing calculated in 1990 that by then Hall had helped in raising $600 million for charity through more benefits, telethons, and more fund-raising efforts than he can remember. Winnipeg has named a street for him. Today, retired from television, Hall still does charity benefits. "My first impulse when people call me is to look at my book and, if I'm free, I say yes. Nancy Reagan had an old statement: 'Just say no.' I just say yes. I try to help as many people as I can for as long as I can," he said.

In his dining room, Hall showed me a painting of his old school in Winnipeg commissioned by his wife from a Winnipeg artist. Rifling through photographs, we found one of Governor-General Jeanne Sauvé presenting Hall with the Order of Canada. "I always identified as a Canadian. In every one of my television shows something came up that brought up the name Canada or Winnipeg or something like that," he said. Hall lived from 1955 to 1991 in the United States before taking out U.S. citizenship for estate-tax-planning reasons. His children are all U.S. citizens, so that his Canadian connection now consists largely of memories, not all of them pleasant.

Hall started his career in radio in Toronto, then switched to television at the dawn of that medium. His story of rejection at the CBC is one that wound its way through some of my conversations with other Star-Spangled Canadian entertainers and television news people. Before the advent of private television in Canada, there was only the CBC, hierarchical and bureaucratic, then as now. CBC was the only game in town, and if Canadian actors, writers, directors, producers, performers could not get through the CBC's door, then the escape route to the United States always beckoned. Today there are private Canadian television networks, but they make the minimum contribution to Canadian programming demanded as a condition of licence by the Canadian Radio-television and Telecommunications Commission (CRTC). They are the principal conduits for the importation of mass U.S. television into Canada, and their profits hang on that importation. Hollywood and New York are littered with Star-Spangled Canadians spurned or frustrated by CBC and the private television networks.

Film actors offer a slightly different story. Canadian television is required to provide at least some Canadian dramatic programming, but there are so few Canadian feature films that Canadian movie actors often have no choice but to try the U.S. market. The same goes for Canadian-born producer/directors from James Cameron (*Titanic*) to Ivan Reitman (*Ghostbusters*, *Meatballs*). Canadians have been almost completely colonized — or captured, to put it less pejoratively — by a U.S. movie industry that considers Canada the fifty-first state for marketing and a cheap place to produce films for the domestic U.S. market, courtesy of the weak Canadian dollar, lower wages paid Canadian technical personnel, and provincial tax breaks.

Foreign, overwhelmingly American, movies accounted for 98 per cent of the Canadian market in 1998, and that share did not change throughout the 1990s.[12] In home videos, foreign productions accounted for 99 per cent of the $812-million domestic market. Canadian home videos captured a piddling $7.3 million of that market. The same dominance was evident in both conventional and pay-television markets. Foreign productions represented 84 per cent of the $340 million paid for distribution rights in conventional television and 84 per cent of the $60-million pay-television market.

Today an actor or performer might get lucky and find temporary work on Canadian private television. His or her chances are only slightly better on CBC, but at least the CBC no longer has a monopoly of the kind that frustrated so many Canadian aspirations decades ago.

"I knew television was the future. My television show went off the air and we couldn't get it back on the air again," Monty Hall recalled. "I went to my friends at the CBC and asked them what was holding me back in my career since I had been rather successful in the first year or two of television. I got different kinds of excuses. I was diverted from certain questions and answers, and I realized then that I had to leave the country. So I went to New York without any contacts at all."

Hall departed after developing a show for CBC only to find the idea stolen by someone else.

"After I developed the show, we did a pilot and I was called in and told they liked the show and the musical group that I used and the announcer I used, but they were going to replace me with somebody else, somebody who worked at the CBC," Hall said.

"I said, 'Wait a minute. That's my show, my creation. How can you take me out of my vehicle?' And the answer I got, believe it or not, was 'We at the CBC are free to cull from all ideas that come to us.' That was the turning point. That's when I realized that, if they could take my idea and replace me with someone else, I would leave ... I never had any idea of going to the States. Never thought about it for a moment. This pushed me over the edge. I came home and I said to my wife, 'I haven't got a show. I don't think I'm going to get a show. I've got to go somewhere and get some work, and I'm going to go to New York.' And my wife, God bless her, said,

'I'll stay here and be mother and father to these kids for as long as necessary, but you go'."

Hall met other Canadians aspiring to make it in New York. Many got discouraged and returned home. He stuck it out doing colour commentary for New York Rangers hockey broadcasts and small-time radio shows until eventually he became a regular on radio, then television. Forty-five years later, Hall has his name engraved on a plaque along the Boulevard of Stars at Hollywood and Vine; he also has a home near Palm Springs, and one in Beverly Hills.

"I had one good year and I made $48,000 in New York and I paid $16,000 in taxes. My father never made any money at all. I was talking to him on the phone and I said, 'How do you like that. I had to pay $16,000 in taxes!' And my father said, 'Listen, Monty. I didn't make aggregate $16,000 in three years. I always wanted to pay taxes. I didn't make enough money to pay taxes. So if I were you, I'd get down on my hands and knees and kiss the ground of the United States of America that gave you this opportunity," Hall said.

"So I never forgot that the U.S. gave me that opportunity. I hold the USA close to my heart for what it did for me, and Canada close to my heart because that's where I came from."

Canadian-content regulations have been only modestly successful in requiring Canadian television networks to produce dramatic programs Canadians will watch, and substantial Canadian subsidies for Canadian films have been completely unsuccessful in the same pursuit. Canadians will subsidize domestic film-making, but that does not mean audiences will watch the final product.

If Canadian governments' efforts in television and film have produced disappointing overall results, requirements imposed on radio stations to play Canadian-made music have produced some gratifying ones. A host of Canadian musicians found an audience at home because the CRTC requires radio stations to play a certain amount of domestically produced music. Powerful corporations that now control the bulk of Canadian radio stations periodically chafe at these requirements—they would play more music from the United States if they could—but they have to abide by the CRTC regulations. The happy result is that Canadian listeners can hear all the leading U.S. music *and* be exposed to the work of Canadian artists. Some of them would never have found an audience in Canada without those regulations. Their voices would have been overwhelmed by American ones, the same fate facing Canadian television and film artists. In some cases, success in Canada has remained just that; in others, domestic success has allowed artists to hone their talents before making the leap into the "big leagues" in the United States and, in a few cases, around the entire world.

Canadian singers Celine Dion, Shania Twain, and Alanis Morissette are international recording phenomena whose songs rarely fell off the Top Ten charts in the last half of the 1990s. Dion sang at the opening of the Olympic Games in Atlanta, a presidential inauguration, and, shortly before her self-imposed retirement, recelebrated her marriage vows in Las Vegas in one of the gaudiest, most garish ceremonies-cum-parties that jaded city had ever witnessed. A native Quebecker married to her long-time agent, another Quebecker, Dion built what passed for a home in millionaires' heaven: Palm Beach, Florida. Twain married a wealthy although reclusive American music producer from Lake Placid, New York, and they live some of the year in Switzerland. Morissette left her native Ottawa (and Toronto where she played host to a CBC show, "Music Works") and landed in Los Angeles in 1994 to begin laying bare her soul for millions of listeners from her new home. The trio of mega-stars eclipsed in worldwide renown the reputation previous Canadian ex-patriate singers, including Paul Anka, Neil Young, and Joni Mitchell, had established for themselves in the United States.

In clubs and recording studios across Canada, artists know all about the successful Star-Spangled Canadians. Some are content to remain in Canada, where they can do better in many instances than actors, script-writers, and directors courtesy of Canadian-content regulations that have spawned a modest domestic industry. Others dream of the "big leagues," which is definitely what Val Azzoli, the New York–based Canadian presi-dent of Atlantic Records, the largest recording company in North America, considers the United States to be.

"Eventually, they all do come down here. The successful Canadian acts—and there are lots of them—most of their time is down here," Azzoli said from his Rockefeller Plaza office. "Their living is derived from down here. My job is here at Rockefeller Plaza. A musician's job is in the studio or on the road. So where does a successful Canadian musician spend most of his time? On the road, not in Calgary but in the U.S.

"They happen to live in Canada when they are not deriving a living. In order to make it in Canada, you have to come to the U.S. If you really want world stature, you have to come to the U.S."

Does success in Canada count before coming to the United States? I asked Azzoli.

"No. It's absolutely necessary to demonstrate your ability to be success-ful here. Absolutely. And you don't have to make it in Canada to make it here. Shania Twain. No one knew who she was in Canada until she made it here," he insisted.

"It's sad but true. All the big Canadian artists who have lasted the test of time have made it here. The Anne Murrays, the Bryan Adamses, Rush, Celine Dion, The Guess Who. They were all big here somewhere along the line. There are a whole lot of Canadian artists who are stars in Canada that never made it here, but it's a different type of star."

Azzoli's curly hair cascades almost to his shoulders, hardly the standard haircut for a corporate executive commanding a palatial office with a sweeping view of central Manhattan. He still looks like a band manager and booker of musical acts, which is how he started in the music business before becoming a record-company executive in Toronto. Now Azzoli's West Coast tennis partner is the Star-Spangled Canadian who enjoys the most fame north of the border, Wayne Gretzky. A long way, in other words, for the son of Italian immigrants in Toronto. New York has tough-ened, shaped him, as it does to so many people who arrive there, especially from Canada.

"I couldn't have tested myself as much as I have if I had stayed in Canada … I want to play with the big boys. On any given day, especially in the entertainment business, it's all here. One block away is Viacom. Two blocks away is NewsCorp. ITT is down the street; ATT is over there. I'm going to go back to Canada somewhere along the line, maybe to retire or run a restaurant or something, but not to do what I'm doing now."

Azzoli dismissed my defence of Canadian-content regulations without which Canadian artists would be swamped by the U.S. presence. His is the classic view from New York, Hollywood, and Washington: make it here or else you really don't count—an observation, if the truth be known, that has lured Canadians of all kinds for decades to the United States.

"I'm not a big proponent of Canadian content. I think it's a false sense of security. I think songs should be played on the radio because they're the best songs," he insisted.

"When I was managing bands in Canada, the hardest thing was to find a band to go on the road because they'd all say, 'Man, I can make $300 a week playing at this place in Toronto.' That's not what we're talking about! I'm giving you the opportunity to make millions if you're good. 'But what if it doesn't work?' they'd say. 'What do I do about my gig here?'

"There's no net. They have to. When I was managing little bands in Canada, the club owners would guarantee you $3,000 a week. So I came down here when I was managing bands and was going to try to do the same thing. There's no such thing as a guarantee.

"You get the door. Whatever people pay, you get. The club owner says, 'Listen, man, I take the money on the beer. You take the money on the people who are coming in. We're partners.' This guarantee was unheard of. That's the difference. The bands down here are hurting. They're playing every night because they're hoping that, by word of mouth, more people will come in the next night and that's the difference between $20 and $50 ..."

And yet, even Val Azzoli, successful, competitive free-marketer in music, recognizes the limits of a dog-eat-dog world.

"This country is a great country. But because of the competition and competitiveness, there's this edge to it that there wasn't in Canada. I think the quality of life is much better in Canada as a whole," Azzoli said.

"It's funny. I had never complained about the taxes, because you know what? Being brought up in Canada, I never had a problem with the taxes in the sense that the roads were always good.

"To this day everybody is still bitching about the hospitals in Canada. I think the hospitals in Canada are pretty good. You walk down to the hospital here down on the Lower East Side and see all these people trying to get in. It's a whole different kind of atmosphere down here. So that edge isn't in Canada. That's worth a lot.

"I've been fortunate. I came down here and have been successful. My family and I lead a very happy, controlled existence. We're in a beautiful neighbourhood in a beautiful part of the country. But I tell you I've been fortunate to be successful down here to protect them from that. We have private health insurance, private this, private that. Whereas in Canada, there's this sense of security. You feel much safer."

You can live on the edge in Canada, too. Ask the graduating students in animation at Sheridan College in Oakville, Ontario. Perhaps 130 of them enter the community college's internationally recognized animation program, but on the day I arrived in the spring of 1998 only 39 remained of the entering class. Roughly half the first-year class did not make it to year two, and about half of that number fell by the wayside before year three.

In the three months before the day I spent with them, the animation students had worked seven days a week, often fourteen or sixteen hours a day, occasionally sleeping at the school on the floor or on couches. Their task: to prepare a short, uncompleted animated clip of perhaps thirty or forty seconds to show representatives of film studios, animation houses, and video-game companies from Canada and the United States. More than sixty representatives wandered around in the morning, checking out the students' sketches; in the afternoon, they gathered in the theatre to screen the students' clips.

At the end of this day, the representatives would tell Sheridan officials whom they wanted to interview the next day. Lists went up that evening of which company wished to see whom and when. A day full of half-hour interviews awaited the lucky ones; for the less fortunate, there would be perhaps only three or four interviews. One young woman I had chatted with the first morning failed to secure any interviews. I found her silently weeping at her desk while a colleague stroked her hair. She would eventually find work, her colleague told me later, probably in Canada. But for now the big dream they had harboured through all the back-breaking weeks, months, and years would not be hers. For many of them, that dream meant the United States.

Walt Disney Studios, Industrial Light & Magic, Golden Knight, DreamWorks, Sony, Silicon Graphics, and about thirty other U.S. houses had sent representatives to Sheridan. There were almost as many Canadian companies represented, including Nelvana, Softimage, Alias, Discreet Logic. Or perhaps it would be more accurate to say Canadian-based companies, because in 1994 Softimage of Montreal was purchased by Microsoft. The following year the American company Silicon Graphics bought Alias of Toronto.

The computer age and Hollywood's rediscovery of markets for feature-length animated films have spawned a boom for animators. Classical animation had been around for a long time, but computer animation allowed images, characters, and technical wizardry of breathtaking ingenuity. The demand for top-flight animators soared in the 1990s, and Sheridan College became one of the two or three most respected centres for animation training in North America, its graduates found in all the major production houses of the United States. In Canada, the National Film Board had done pioneering research in animation in the 1940s and established a worldwide reputation. Five of the NFB's Oscars have been for animation. The animation boom of the 1990s produced a few large private Canadian companies and a welter of smaller ones finding niches making children's cartoons, computer graphics, and piecework for the feature films of Hollywood. Softimage of Montreal, for example, did some of the spectacular computer animation for *Jurassic Park*.

It is possible for Sheridan graduates to find work in one of Canada's nearly eighty animation houses. Perhaps as many as half of Sheridan's graduates choose to remain in Canada, and their talents have contributed to the surge in Canadian animation. The desire of some Canadian graduates to remain at home, plus cheaper costs of production, convinced Disney to open animation studios in Toronto and Vancouver in 1996 from which work, mostly in television animation, was fed to Disney's mammoth Los Angeles operations. They were the classic branch-plants and they were both closed in 2000.

The animation market is completely North American. Sheridan might just as well be in Illinois or Georgia for all Hollywood cares. The demand for animators is so great and the supply so short that Canadians are whisked through immigration procedures. Many excellent Sheridan graduates have worked in Hollywood, or in the graphics companies around San Francisco, and the best U.S. companies continue to recruit heavily at Sheridan. The money available at U.S. firms, plus the sense of being at the centre of the world's animation industry, pulls many Sheridan College graduates south in the same way that software designers and high-technology entrepreneurs from Canada are drawn to Silicon Valley.

Mike Surrey graduated from Sheridan in the mid-1980s, when the college was just beginning to attract U.S. attention and the domestic industry remained fledgling. Today, Surrey is a senior animator at Disney, coordinating character development for such films as *The Lion King, The Hunchback of Notre Dame*, and *Tarzan*. He works in a tiny office in Disney's sprawling complex, which belies how well Surrey has done financially in southern California; testament to his success is his black Mercedes, in which we drive from the complex to lunch.

"When I first came down here, it was more a case of saying [that] every job I had had up to that point had been a couple of years, then you moved on to another job," Surrey said. "So when I first came down here, I thought I'd be down here for a couple of years, get my feet wet, get more experience, then keep an eye on the country to the north and figure out if there is something I could work on back there at the same quality level that I'm working on down here. But after five or six years, you begin to realize that I don't think I'm going back. It's kind of weird to think that I would actually be growing ever older here."

Surrey, from St. Catharines, Ontario, has now married an American woman and they have three children, so the chances of his returning to Canada are slim.

"The idea of going back to Canada? … What it would take to get me back there now would be if there was a top-quality project going on there," he said. "The great draw for a lot of us down here is the fact that we're working on projects that do allow us to be very creative and give us a chance to do what we've been trained to do, what we wanted to be."

Surrey came to southern California when the boom in feature-film animation was just beginning. In the 1980s, Disney had a near monopoly on such films, but the creation of DreamWorks and several smaller companies produced a more competitive market for animators. When Dream-Works tried to lure Surrey away from Disney, he parlayed that offer into a better salary. Young animators will earn $45,000 to $60,000 on arrival, and the top animators in Hollywood can earn at least several hundred thousand dollars a year, so much in demand is their talent. Surrey estimated that "in this building, I would have to say we're looking at maybe twenty to thirty Canadians that are working in the studio, and maybe half of them are in high positions as far as animation is concerned."

Sheridan grads are at the top of California's animation industry. Steve "Spaz" Williams was for almost a decade the chief animator at Industrial Light & Magic (ILM), producing ground-breaking computer animation for *Star Wars* and the facial contortions for Jim Carrey's *The Mask* that earned Williams an Academy Award nomination. James Straus, another ILM employee who is now animation director for Santa Barbara Studios, won an Academy Award nomination in 1997 and has worked on such films as *Jurassic Park*, *Forrest Gump*, and *Jumanji*. Eleven Canadians in the United States worked on the film *Dragonheart*, for which Straus won his nomination. These are Sheridan's Star-Spangled Canadian headliners in classical or computer animation, but there are dozens and dozens of Mike Surreys in senior positions at the other major production houses, and hundreds of others with fewer supervisory responsibilities scattered through almost every animation house in the United States. Only graduates from the California Institute of the Arts are considered on a par with Sheridan graduates for technical excellence. The result at Disney, as elsewhere, is a clustering of Canadians, a few of whom, such as Surrey, play hockey in a local league.

"Some manage to blend in, but it's interesting that, when we get to work or are walking the halls and go to the water cooler, before you know it, there's five or six Canadians all gathered around talking about whatever," Surrey said. "They find a way of getting a hold of each other. I don't know if it's ESP or something. I'm going to the water cooler. So am I. Everybody seems to have the same timetable where they go off and you find yourself eventually talking about hockey and other things from back home. 'Did you go back recently?' 'Was it cold?' It starts to get into that, and sure enough an American might come up and look at you and say, 'Oh, you guys are talking about Canadian things, right?' And they'll walk off."

Mike Surrey has been in the United States for a long time and is unlikely to return to Canada. But a few miles away from where he works at Disney, I spent time with sixteen Canadians, mostly Sheridan grads, who worked at Disney's competitor, DreamWorks. They were much more recent emigrants, and they universally said the money was better and the creative challenge greater than what they could find in Canada, although many of them did miss various aspects of Canadian life. Two of them even had Canadian symbols tattooed on their bodies to remind them of home.

"The opportunities with DreamWorks are longer term and more stable," said Charlene Logan from Amherst, Nova Scotia. "The pay is better here because the union has a minimum cut-off. In Canada, you always wind up fighting with other people so you wind up with a lower wage. Taxes are about the same … I'm working with people who had been in the industry for thirty years and had worked on the effects for the original *Fantasia*. They learned from those people. You've got years and years of experience right here."

Dimos Vrysellas from Mississauga worked on *The Prince of Egypt* and marvelled at the "experience working here [and] learning from the great animators who have been doing this for twenty-odd years." His interest in returning? "I'd like to stay here as long as possible. I've got a life here and I love it." What did he miss? "Tim Horton's, Harvey's, Sleeman's beer, and Coffee Crisp."

Craig Whittaker from St. Mary's, Ontario, thought he would "only be down here for a couple of years, but I'm not going to make any more plans like that." Curiously, Whittaker found that living in Los Angeles, a city he has come to enjoy, tapped into his sense of being a Canadian. "I wouldn't have said I was a proud Canadian until I moved down here. We started playing hockey. I never played hockey in Canada — kind of a strange thing considering how popular it is in my home town," he said. "When we came down here, there was a bunch of us who had never played. We put together a road-hockey team. We sort of felt it was our patriotic duty. It's strange. You start pointing out who's Canadian among the celebrities. You go out with somebody and bring up Jim Carrey, Mike Myers, and you feel you have to point out that they're Canadian."

Irene Parkins, from London, Ontario, was apprehensive about Los Angeles when she first arrived, but quickly came to appreciate the hills, beaches, and sun. The prospect of her returning to Canada is distant, given how she enjoys her work at DreamWorks. "I'd like to retire there, but I don't know if I would go back any time soon unless they got rid of the PST, GST, the whole works. We're taxed heavily here but nowhere near as heavily taxed as in Canada. It's crazy," Parkins said. "Compared to what my friends earn in Vancouver, they're still living in apartments and can't afford to buy a house [although] we're doing the same job."

Robert Weaver, from Brampton, Ontario, put his finger on the competitive disadvantage Canada faces: No country can compete with the United States in producing animated feature films. "Canadian work tends to be in television pick-up work for larger studios," he said. "At this point I don't see myself going back. The industry I'm in is located around here, so going back doesn't really seem to be an option … Financially, it's a bit more secure than it would be in Canada. In Canada, you do a lot of work for a lot of different companies. You're bouncing around. It's more a freelance style. You're working for a couple of months and the pay may be very good, but then you go for a couple of months without work, then a couple of months with work, but here the work is fairly constant."

And so the conversations went: a mixture of nostalgia for home and excitement, or at least satisfaction, with the animation work at the world's leading studios. The Star-Spangled Canadians I spoke with reckoned they were being better paid, although they were divided on whether more of their money disappeared in California, a high-tax U.S. state, or in Canada. Opportunity in this specialized field, especially in animated motion pictures, knocked more clearly in the United States than in Canada, and the reputation of Sheridan College guaranteed that its graduates would at least receive serious consideration from these great U.S. firms.

Sheridan's success creates a dilemma for Canada. The Ontario government has poured money into Sheridan to maintain its cutting-edge reputation. The programs there could scarcely be more rigorous; the instructors are among the best in the world; the facilities are excellent. All this investment produces among the continent's, even the world's, best animators. And yet it is an observable fact for Canada that many of these outstanding young talents migrate south, and few of them return home, if my soundings offer an accurate portrait. Why, it might be asked, does Canada so heavily subsidize this kind of education when the history of Sheridan's animation program suggests the country is de facto subsidizing California's graphics and animation industries? Is it Canada's fate, in animation and other industries, to produce people of outstanding, specialized talent, only to see them disappear south in a North American labour market?

The answer is partly yes. That is the Canadian condition: some of the best in a continental labour pool will find the opportunities larger, the creative drive greater, and the monetary rewards richer at the pinnacles of

U.S. industry, against which the tug of home and roots and identity struggles to compete. But it can also be the Canadian condition—and Sheridan demonstrates this—that, by striving for domestic excellence in education, clusters of talent, drive, and money can form in Canada to produce companies and encourage creativity so that Canadians can achieve outstanding results, locate jobs at home, and offer for those who want to remain at home an opportunity to do so. Without Sheridan, it is highly unlikely that the current plethora of domestic animation companies would exist. Even if the biggest companies producing full-length feature films and snazzy computer graphics are in the United States, Canadian animation does excellent work in other fields and, within the North American animation industry writ large, punches above the country's demographic weight. Not a bad result, all things considered.

Peter Jennings earns vastly more money and reaches a nightly audience many times greater than any in Canada as anchor for "ABC World New Tonight," but he left his reporting and anchoring job at "CTV News" to earn less money in the United States.

"I decided, ironically enough, that I was tired of being an anchorperson. I was too young and too ill equipped, and America I perceived as this great new canvas on which to paint, to use the cliché. I was also aware that neither CTV nor CBC could afford to send me anywhere. I came to the U.S. and made less money than I was making in Canada, but the Americans had the money to send me around the world. So I saw the world on somebody else's money and it happened to be American," Jennings said.

We were sitting in Jennings's surprisingly small office adjacent to the ABC news desk, where the national editor is a Canadian, one floor beneath the studio from which Jennings reads the news and anchors special broadcasts. At that moment, ABC had seven Canadian news correspondents, excluding Jennings, plus Canadian producers scattered across its bureaux in the United States and abroad. It used to be joked that so many Canadians worked for ABC, some of them lured there by Jennings himself, that ABC stood for the "American Broadcasting Company of Canada." CBS had six Canadian correspondents, NBC five, and CNN three at the end of 1999, and Canadians were also reading the news for all the networks in regional markets across the United States.

These days, the big money available to successful U.S. television journalists provides a powerful incentive for Canadians to try their hand in U.S. television news. (A handful such as Global Television's Peter Kent returned to Canada from a successful stint in U.S. television.) As in so many other occupations, the success of some paved the way for the success of others. But when Jennings made the leap in 1964, the Canadian movement to U.S. television news was a trickle.

Jennings, while employed by CTV, had done a report for ABC about a North Atlantic Treaty Organization (NATO) conference in Ottawa, which the network liked. Some time later, an ABC executive contacted him.

"I got offered a job at ABC and I turned it down," he recalled. "I was scared. I was frightened of coming to New York, which I thought was too big, beyond anything I could manage. I woke up six months later and thought I'd made a terrible mistake. I wrote a letter to the then-president of the ABC news division and said, Could I change my mind?"

Writers, editors, and comics observed that being Canadian assisted them in the United States because it gave them a certain dispassion with which to observe U.S. life. Jennings is an enormously polished anchorperson, and he has been a first-rate correspondent in the United States, London, and the Middle East. He did not rise to the pinnacle of U.S. television journalism just because he came from Canada. His multiple talents give the lie to that assumption, but the Canadian perspective, which he carries still, did apparently help.

"This is the most magnificent country and there's nothing any reporter likes [better] than to come to a magnificent story—and America is replete with magnificent stories—with fresh eyes," he said.

"So Canadians bring a fresh set of eyes. This is a nation [the United States] which understands the rest of the world in terms of power, and has always had, as we Canadians know better than anyone—immense power and has never been reluctant to use it.

"Canadians, I think, grow up to understand and appreciate influence to a greater degree. So a Canadian seeing America in terms of the rest of the world, and appreciating nuance to a greater extent, and appreciating the value of nuance, is able to report to America about America's relationship with the rest of the world in a more nuanced way."

Jennings's father worked for the CBC, as did Jennings at the beginning of his career. He thus joins a large group of television journalists and entertainers who either could not get a job at CBC or got turned off working there, or simply found the opportunities and money in the United States irresistible.

One of those is Ashleigh Banfield, who was a news anchor at Fox-TV in Dallas at the time of our interview. Banfield, beautiful and articulate, has energy and ambition to burn. The combination was not enough for the CBC. She had worked in Winnipeg, Edmonton, and Calgary, and a year abroad, but she could not get anyone at CBC in Vancouver to shake her hand or watch her tape. She did reach someone in the CBC bureaucracy who said it would be acceptable to phone back. She did three or four times, then received a letter, the words of which Banfield has committed to memory: "while persistence is often the hallmark of a good reporter, I must ask you to stop calling me."

Fox-TV did not agree. They hired her for a job in Dallas, the seventh-largest market in the United States, where her newscasts vied for second place in the local ratings on which journalists' careers wax and wane in U.S. private television. She won an Emmy for anchoring four hours of daily live coverage of a murder trial in Forth Worth. She went back frequently to Canada on holidays, kept a small Canadian flag and a framed copy of her Queen's University degree in her office, but only the United States lies in her professional future. When we spoke, Banfield did not hide her passion for getting into one of the top-three American markets: New York, Los Angeles, and Chicago. A year later she made it, securing a New York job with MSNBC.

"There are so few jobs in Canada for me to be nailing one," Banfield said. "I'm making four times what I made in Canada, and that doesn't take into account the exchange. Remuneration for good jobs in Canada is often lower than the little jobs here ... In Calgary, I was making $54,000 a year as the sole female anchor for that station. An anchor in a top-ten market in the U.S. can easily secure six figures ... In Canada, there are three big markets—Toronto, Vancouver, and Montreal. In the U.S., the top ten markets are massive, the top twenty are still very big, and the next thirty aren't too bad. There's lots of room at the top."

How about returning to Canada? Banfield's answer might stand in for one many Canadian television journalists in the United States would offer.

"Why would I go back and work for the CTV morning news for maybe $100,000, or if they were feeling really generous $150,000?" Banfield said. "That's less than I'm making now as a local news anchor and a lot less than I'd be making at CBS "This Morning." It would be a huge cut. I'm not talking about a little change in my lifestyle, but less than half."

Keith Radford, WKBW anchor in Buffalo, has worked in local U.S. news since 1983. He's very happy and well paid, lives in the pleasant town of Lewiston north of Buffalo, but comes across as someone who has seen it all in U.S. television news, for better and worse.

"I always wanted to go to the States. I grew up in Windsor, and you can't get any closer to the States," he said. "When I started to move around in television, I realized the opportunities in the States were a hundredfold what they were in Canada. We're talking about a market that's ten times the size. Hundreds of television stations, and generally they paid a lot more money than Canadian stations. And the taxes were a huge factor. The taxes here are a fraction of what they are in Canada if you're working for a paycheque."

In the early 1990s, Radford was briefly tempted by an offer to return to Canada at CTV's Toronto station, CFTO.

"I was very interested and they were offering very good money compared to what I thought I could make in Canada. More money than I was making here," he recalled. "But I was sitting in the news director's office, and I said, 'Well, how much would I actually take home?' They dialled up the accountant upstairs and he reported that the tax rate would be 52 per cent, while here I pay 20 per cent after deductions, so it was more than double. Also, they make it hard to leave here by the way they structure contracts. We're number one so they don't want anybody to leave."

Local television news in the United States is characterized by a fascination with crime. "Blood sheets" are what local newscasts use to jack up ratings, even though U.S. violent crime rates declined throughout the 1990s. Conglomerates have gobbled up local stations with deleterious effects on news quality.

"In the last few years, salaries have gone right down the toilet, not just here but all over the United States, in local television," Radford said. "The stations used to be a licence to print money. They're not any more. There have been amalgamations, with huge companies buying up companies because they've eased the federal restrictions on how many stations you can own.

"Cut costs. Cut costs. Cut costs. Personnel is the big thing. They'll spend money on equipment and satellites. But when it comes to hiring a full-time person and having to pay benefits, they won't do it. All three stations in Buffalo have been sold twice in the last three or four years, and they're now owned by highly leveraged companies with debt up to their eyeballs. They have to squeeze as much cash out of them to pay the debt as fast as they can, and then they dump them as fast as they can.

"We've lost one-third in total numbers. Not just numbers but quality. We used to get people from Salt Lake City, Detroit, Boston—people with some experience. Now we get people from Binghamton, Ithaca, Syracuse, Rochester, because they won't pay any money to get anybody other than a kid who's just got out of school and who's got a year's experience in a tiny market, and if you look at our staff of reporters, that's what you'll see."

Radford began his career in Salt Lake City before joining WKBK in Buffalo. His co-anchor in Salt Lake City left a year after he arrived and landed a $750,000-a-year job as an anchor in Chicago, a sum twice what the best-paid Canadian television journalist might earn, although only a fraction of Peter Jennings's multimillion-dollar salary. Living on the Canadian border, Radford watches Canadian local news and draws a comparison favourable to Canada.

"There's less crime and more political stuff in local news in Canada. There are a lot of national stories we don't do. We have the network to do that," he said. "The quality in Canada seems to be better than it was a few years ago, while our quality has gone the other way."

Radford may be excessively generous to Canada. The CBC and CTV have cut back their news operations, and Global Television has always been a cheapskate affair. Government cutbacks have hurt the CBC badly; profit squeezes have done to CTV news operations almost precisely what Radford described happening in the United States.

"I cringe at a lot of the stuff we do. I just cringe. When you're young and coming up, it doesn't bother you so much. But then, after you've been doing it for a while, you think, 'Jeez, do people out there really know that we have one reporter on Saturday and Sunday who works from 2 to 10 p.m.," Radford said.

"I'm on my fifth news director in eleven years. The current one we have, he's into the flash ... They don't care about substance. They don't care about quality. They care about the physical presentation.

"Canadians are much more staid and formal and conservative. I still have lots of friends there, at places like CFTO, and they tell me they're being told to be more smiley, warm on the set ... Canada always does everything the States does sooner or later. It always comes around. In the broadcast business, they seem to be starting to do things that have been old hat in the States for a long time.

"The networks, I think, still do a very good job. But the locals. They'll do anything for ratings, anything ... Luckily, I'm the last link in the chain and can change things and they can't stop me, so they can only get mad later. Everything here is 'the cops,' 'the slammer.'"

Canadians populate U.S. television news at every level. They anchor newscasts in Buffalo, San Francisco, Dallas, Chicago, New York; they span the world as foreign correspondents; they work as producers at the major networks; they play host to national news programs; and for many years two of the United States' leading national news anchormen in the United States were Star-Spangled Canadians: Robert MacNeil at PBS, and Peter Jennings. If discerning Canadians are often struck by the jejune and inexperienced television reporters barking at them from CBC, CTV, and Global, one reason is obviously the brain drain of television talent from the Canadian to the U.S. networks: Mark Phillips, John Blackstone, Kevin Newman, Johnathan Mann, Sheila MacVicar, Morley Safer, Bob McKeown, Richard Gizbert, Gillian Findlay, J.D. Roberts, Allen Pizzey, Thalia Assuras, Keith Morrison ... the list of on-air Star-Spangled Canadians runs on and on and on. The Canadian accent elides easily into that of Middle America. The Canadian passport is occasionally a ticket into places closed to Americans. Canadians have that tendency to remain slight outsiders in American society, the correct position for journalists anywhere. And Canada has provided many journalists with the same farm-team training for the big leagues of U.S. television that it offered comedians, singers, actors, writers, directors. Talk to any Canadian television news director about talent slipping south and invariably the answer is the same: salaries are vastly greater south of the border because of the star syndrome in U.S. private television and the intense, incessant, demanding race for ratings.

"I think we take broadcasting seriously," Peter Jennings insisted, using the "we," as he often does, to describe Canadians. "Growing up in the CBC system, and laterally in CTV, young men and women believed that, in broadcasting news, you put the capital on 'n'. But you also appreciate, because we have a long tradition of public broadcasting in Canada, that even in the private sector broadcasting is a public service ...

"You also get pretty well trained in Canada ... I think the thing I learned more than anything else from the CBC, and from my father, was having respect for the audience ... As a Canadian I believe—it doesn't make it exclusively Canadian—[it is important] to have respect for all the components of the audience, which comes from the CBC notion that everybody in the country has a right to hear themselves represented somehow on the national broadcasting system. It's just something that is ingrained in me."

That said, add Peter Jennings to the list of people who would have worked for the CBC but for the corporation's chronic bureaucracy and high-handedness, characteristics that have driven away so much talent.

"I once thought I was coming back to Canada in the early 1980s. I'd always had the notion that I would come home," he said. "When I left Canada as a young man, Pierre Berton bet me $2 that I'd never come home. I said, 'That's an easy bet. I'll be home in two years.'

"Then two years led to five years that led to ten years. Then, in the early

1980s, my father died. He had a long history in Canadian broadcasting, and I thought maybe I should go home. I got what I thought was a job to come back and work on "The National" or "The Journal."

"The executive said to me, 'We'll be in touch tomorrow.' They never got back to me for about eleven months, and by that time I decided they weren't serious about it and I signed another contract."

Jennings is one of the most recognizable figures in the United States. In addition to his television work, he co-authored a best-selling and well-reviewed book about the twentieth century in the United States that accompanied a television series he developed on the same subject. The vast majority of his U.S. audience would not know he was Canadian, but he has never hidden his Canadian identity and has never taken out U.S. citizenship.

"There has been pressure on me over the years to become an American citizen. One of my bosses was so insistent at a particular time that I become an American citizen that I said he should back off or I'd become Vietnamese, which backed him off," Jennings said. "In the main, I don't think anybody has ever cared to the degree that they gave any thought to the fact that a Canadian shouldn't have the job ...

"I think it means that, when I was a child, and certainly as an adult, I have felt that to be Canadian ... is in some measure how I am defined as an individual. And it doesn't always make sense. So I love the uncomplicated daily life of the Ottawa Valley. Now you can have an uncomplicated daily life in the valleys of Vermont, New Hampshire, and lots of other places. But it just happens to be that it was the Ottawa Valley in which I grew up and which imbued me with a sense of place, which I can hang on to emotionally and to some extent ideologically as I wander around the world."

Jennings lives, of course, in New York, has a spacious home on Long Island filled with Inuit art, but also retains ownership of an apartment in Ottawa.

"When Americans go to Ottawa, they think it's the sweetest city of its size in all of North America because its access to the out-of-doors is so wonderful. It has a good national theatre. It has a good orchestra. You can have everything now except the Chinese food, which is still freeze-dried from the 1950s. But it's this wonderful, sweet city in which I cannot imagine not spending time, when I retire, for several months a year."

The city requites his affection. Carleton University bestowed upon Jennings, who never attended university, an honorary degree. The mayor gave him the keys to the city. Upon the death of a famous but quirky local merchant in the Byward Market, Jennings wrote a touching letter in memoriam to *The Ottawa Citizen*. He spends several weeks each summer, if he can, at a family property in the Gatineau Hills.

So Jennings, unlike so many other Star-Spangled Canadians, keeps his Canadian connections alive rather than merely familial. Crossing the border frequently, and possessed of the good journalist's observant eye, he notes how differences between the two countries are shrinking.

"I've always thought there was something quite fundamental, and yet as I talk to Canadians today, as I see the border less distinctive and more blurred, as I read about Canada today, it seems there is far less reluctance in Canada to be like Americans," Jennings said.

"In my generation, and certainly in my parents' generation, there was great reluctance to be like Americans … Part of being Canadian when I was growing up was not to be American, not necessarily to be anti-American, but not to be American. That seems to be a less urgent notion today. The slogan for Ontario for many years was 'Friendly, Foreign, Far and Near.' It's certainly still friendly, but it's far less foreign, and it doesn't seem very far. It just seems nearer …

"I think the countries are getting closer together, and I'm not sure I'm thrilled about that, to be perfectly honest, because I am one of those Canadians who continues to be fortified, to some extent, that we are different and that we benefit from our differences and that we contribute to other people because we are different. But I'm not sure it's going to be true of my children's generation."

*Alice rocked. I saw in her fragile-boned, serene demeanour the not
quite tragic flaw of English-Canadian society. Niceness. A fine
word for our compulsively tidy state of mind, all the dreams and
dust and unpleasant bits thrown away or swept under ... history
forgotten, pangs of longing for a brighter horizon ignored. Not
even here, so close to the Americans, was this niceness tainted with
exuberance or vulgarity or imagination, the things that I think of
as American. Another country, another culture, just a breath away,
but the lace curtain was neatly drawn.* — Marion Botsford Fraser,
Walking the Line

CONCLUSION

NOT all Canadians have wanted the lace curtain drawn between their
country and the United States. There is no way of knowing what the hundreds of thousands of Canadians whose tombstones dot the American
landscape thought of the utility or desirability of Canada retaining a separate political identity within North America. They left to pursue the American Dream, however they conceived of it. Whether they cared if Canada
remained an independent country or folded its future into the U.S.
Republic, as they themselves did, cannot be known.

Those who remained or arrived from abroad to build Canada may have
envied certain elements of the American Dream, but the vast majority
never favoured annexation or union. Canadian confederation arose
between 1864 and 1867 for many reasons, but one most certainly was fear
of the United States. As George-Étienne Cartier put it during the Confederation debates, "The matter resolved itself into this, either we must
obtain British North American Confederation or be absorbed into an
American Confederation." Even those who admired much about U.S.
institutions and preached for their incorporation into the Canadian way of
doing things opposed union and feared annexation.

Only scattered voices dissented. The most prominent in the late nineteenth century belonged to Goldwin Smith — professor, man of letters,

political critic—who left the Regius chair at Oxford to emigrate to Toronto around the time of Confederation. (He later taught at Cornell University in Ithaca, New York.) Smith coined the celebrated truism, whose echoes remain with us today, that even if the United States was not annexing Canada, it was certainly annexing Canadians.

Smith favoured Confederation but believed that commercial and political union with the United States was both inevitable and desirable. Several years after arriving in Toronto, he returned from visiting cousins on the shores of Lake Simcoe and observed that they were "intensely loyal and exaggerate all English habits and prejudices. The thought of union to America is hateful to them … but it must come in time. All the commercial forces pull so strongly in that direction. I do not wish to see it hurried, however. It is better that all the eggs of this Continent should not be put at once into one basket."[1]

A decade later, in 1877, Smith was debunking the idea of an Imperial union, mocking Canadian nationalism as a lost cause and insisting that union with the United States represented a moral imperative. As his biographer wrote, "to him, the schism between the Anglo-Saxon peoples of the continent seemed an unfortunate accident of history. Hence he thought of the union between Canada and the United States as a desirable reunion of like-minded peoples, the undoing of a historical wrong."[2]

Smith argued his case a final time in *Canada and the Canadian Question*, published in 1891: "Annexation is an ugly word; it seems to convey the idea of force or pressure applied to the smaller State, not of free, equal and honourable union, like that between England and Scotland. Yet there is no reason why the union of the two sections should not be as free, as equal, and as honourable as the union of England and Scotland." Union, Smith insisted, would raise the value of property in Canada, increase general prosperity, eliminate the possibility of war. Union would eventually eradicate the French fact in North America for once and for all, "since it is perfectly clear that the forces of Canada alone are not sufficient to assimilate the French element or even to prevent the indefinite consolidation and growth of a French nation."[3]

Samuel Moffett, an American social scientist and journalist, took up where Smith left off, publishing a thesis in 1901 that became a book in 1907: *The Americanization of Canada*.[4] Although pockmarked by small factual errors, and obviously wrong in its prediction, this book of Moffett's outlined the economic and cultural factors pulling Canada towards union with the United States. Canada on the surface seemed attached to the British Empire at the turn of the century, Moffett observed, but in many practical matters of daily life, to say nothing of transportation and economics, Canadians had become ersatz Americans. He noted the prevalence of American spelling, U.S. service clubs and university fraternities, U.S. news in Canadian newspapers and magazines, Canadians' membership in U.S. unions, the attachment of Canadians to U.S. sports teams, the decimal system, driving on the right-hand side of the road. None of these strike Canadians as odd today, but they suggested to Moffett at the turn of the century that, while Canadians nominally favoured the British connection, they were in fact becoming Americans. Political integration, he suggested, was just a matter of time. "The English-speaking Canadians protest that they will never become Americans—they are already Americans without knowing it," he concluded.

Canadians today are vastly more "American" than in Moffett's time, and yet the inevitability of union with the United States predicted by Smith and Moffett never materialized. Nor will it any time soon, although, when asked an abstract question in a 1990 survey about abolishing the Canada–U.S. border, one in four Canadians supported the idea. One in three Quebeckers favoured the border's elimination, compared with one in five in the rest of Canada.[5]

Liberal leader John Turner expressed the classic Canadian opposition to reciprocal-trade deals as a slippery slope towards integration when he declared in the 1988 televised debate with Prime Minister Brian Mulroney, "With one signature of the pen you've ... thrown us into the north–south influence of the United States and will reduce us to a colony of the United States, because when the economic levers go, the political independence is sure to follow." A majority of Canadians voted for parties opposed to the deal, but the pro–free trade Conservatives won a handsome majority of seats in the 1988 election. Today, the debate over free trade, per se, is dead. No party favours revocation. Protectionism as trade policy is passé, although clusters within the Canadian economy, such as dairy farmers and producers of cultural products, still live under it. Those who opposed the Canada–U.S. deal accept, however reluctantly, that what is done cannot be undone. The Liberal party, so hostile to bilateral free trade in the 1980s, has swung completely around, negotiating bilateral deals with Chile and Israel, extending the Canada–U.S. agreement to include Mexico, urging hemispheric free trade, pushing for trade liberalization with Pacific Rim countries and even proposing a North American–European Union free-trade agreement.

Liberals who defend themselves against the charge of intellectual hypocrisy, admittedly not something supporters of such an elastic political party fret much about, might insist that these various trade initiatives were designed to diversify Canada's trade opportunities, thereby reducing reliance on the U.S. market. Canadian governments have periodically dreamed of such diversification. Prime Minister John Diefenbaker decreed at one point that 30 per cent of Canada's trade should revert to Britain. Prime Minister Pierre Trudeau chased the "Third Option," a foreign policy that included the dream of trade diversification. Advocates of the Canada–U.S. trade deal claimed that Canadian companies, having enlarged themselves through expanded trade in the U.S. market, would then use their longer lines of production and fatter balance sheets to conquer other markets. Prime Minister Jean Chrétien hit upon Team Canada missions to China, Japan, India, and Latin America, replete with provincial premiers and legions of business people, to open up new avenues for Canadian trade.

All trade diversification policies failed. Canada's trade moved steadily into a bilateral north–south pattern, from 70 to 75 to 80 per cent and, in 1999, to 84 per cent dependence on the U.S. market. In one sense, advocates of the 1988–89 free-trade deal were prescient. Bilateral trade did boom, and in the economically indifferent decade of the 1990s for Canada, the brightest spot remained exports to the United States, on which so many Canadian jobs depended. The trade deal, per se, had less to do with these booming exports than with other powerful factors. The Canadian dollar hit $0.89 (U.S.) when the trade deal entered into force in 1989 and declined steadily thereafter into the $0.65–$0.70 range, thus making Canadian products and services cheaper in the U.S. market. With that advantage, it struck Canadians as sensible to concentrate on exporting goods to the familiar, next-door market of the United States rather than the unfamiliar, complicated (and, in some instances, corrupt) markets of Asia and Latin America. The tremendous, even unprecedented, boom of the U.S. economy throughout the 1990s—the longest, sustained period of uninterrupted postwar growth in the United States—made its market even more attractive. The United States continuously ran huge trade deficits with the rest of the world, including Canada, but the protectionist reaction to those deficits in the United States focused on Japan, China, other Asian countries, and the European Community. Particular U.S. interests targeted trade in a few Canadian products such as softwood lumber and wheat, forcing Canada to negotiate export-limitation arrangements, but the bulk of Canadian exports entered the United States free of hassles.

Other developments also increased Canada's economic dependence on the U.S. market. The 1990s featured a push to size. Mergers and acquisitions became the orders of the day for companies seeking to compete internationally, and companies already large by domestic standards sought room for growth through foreign expansion. In Canada, that meant invariably looking for expansion in the U.S. market. Canadian National, for example, switched from being a Crown corporation to operating as a privately owned railway company with a majority of its shareholders in the United States, its future growth in that market facilitated by its take-over of the Illinois Central and a merger with the Burlington Northern Santa Fe. The first of the unsuccessful bank mergers proposed in the 1990s—the one between the Bank of Montreal and the Royal Bank—was designed almost exclusively to allow the new bank to expand into the United States. The federal government rejected this merger, but the fact that Canadian banks need to grow internationally suggests that other merger plans will evolve in the years ahead. Canadian high-tech companies such as Nortel Networks and Newbridge gobbled up U.S. firms and JDS Fidel merged with Uniphase, but U.S. capital from that sector was just as busy in Canada. In 1999, the equivalent of 8 per cent of the asset value of companies on the Toronto Stock Exchange was purchased by American companies, the most spectacular take-overs being those of MacMillan Bloedel by the U.S. giant Weyerhaeuser, and of Newcourt Credit Group by CIT Group Inc. In corporate boardrooms, and among the highly mobile and best-educated of Canada's population, Canada began to seem too small a place, a pleasant-enough country on the edge of the action, but not one central to it. A tell-tale sign of Corporate Canada's fixation with the United States was revealed when company after company began reporting financial results in U.S. dollars. One-quarter of the TSE 100 Index companies report in U.S. dollars despite being headquartered in Canada, because these companies do a majority of their business in the United States. Some of these include: Alcan, Barrick, Inco, Ipsco, Laidlaw, Nortel, Placer Dome, Quebecor, Seagram, Teleglobe, and Thomson.[6]

The original Canada–U.S. free-trade deal in 1989, later expanded to include Mexico, left off the table certain knotty issues neither side was willing to concede. Both sides agreed to negotiate subsequently a subsidy code regarding government help for companies, but nothing ever came of that agreement. That certain Canadian practices were excluded from the deal did not mean that the United States agreed to cease and desist from opposing them. The U.S. government kept up a steady barrage of opposition against certain irritants, as the U.S. considered them, that were not addressed under the terms of the deal, including the Canadian Wheat Board, provincial stumpage fees, certain Canadian cultural policies, and supply-management in agriculture. The United States took its complaints about Canadian magazine policy to the World Trade Organization (WTO), won the case, and eventually forced changes to that policy through hard bilateral negotiations. Import-quota protection for supply-managed agricultural products was knocked down by the WTO, only to be replaced by high Canadian tariffs, but these, too, faced opposition and would eventually have to be reduced under U.S. pressure in international-trade negotiations.

In the 1960s, Canadian nationalists blamed U.S. capitalism for the "Americanization" of Canada. High levels of foreign ownership. The ubiquity of Hollywood and U.S. television. Integrated continental defence and military treaty alliances abroad. These integrative forces, all originating in the United States, had somehow to be resisted. Not much, if anything, is left of the policies that flowed from this concern. Crown corporations have been privatized. Foreign-investment screening mechanisms now encourages U.S. investment. The National Energy Policy is but a bad memory. Trade diversification flopped. Canada remains in continental and overseas military alliances. Liberalized trade is enshrined in North American and world agreements.

Canadians, responding to a poll for *Maclean's* magazine in 1999, believed by an almost 4–1 margin (63 to 17 per cent) that the United States had gotten the better of the free-trade deal, but that has not stopped them from apparently accepting the logic of continental economic integration.[7] According to an Angus Reid poll conducted in August 1999, 77 per cent of Canadians believe the two countries will have a common currency within the next twenty years, and one of every two people think it will occur within a decade. A majority—58 per cent—considered a common currency a "bad thing," but the majority also appeared to believe it likely or inevitable. As for reducing Canada's economic links with the United States, only 16 per cent were in favour, while 45 per cent favoured keeping the relationship as it is, and 37 per cent supported closer economic ties.[8]

Whatever Canadians may think of their American neighbours, they have never been more like them. And not because Americans have changed to become more like Canadians, but the other way around. The imperatives of economic integration and the enveloping embrace of U.S. mass culture in the era of modern communications have shrunk the attitudinal and institutional differences between the two countries, which means in every sense that Canadians have become more American in their outlook, values, and structures—an exception might be moral and religious issues, where significant gaps divide the two nationalities.

Of all the "Americanizing" influences on Canada, the most consequential is one Canadians imposed upon themselves. Canadians had a choice not to follow the United States, with its constitutionally enshrined Bill of Rights, but in the constitutional debates of the early 1980s Canadian politicians decided—the people were not consulted except through opinion polls—that Canada would have a Charter of Rights and Freedoms. Even Seymour Martin Lipset, the distinguished sociologist who has argued that fundamental differences do exist between Canadians and Americans, acknowledged that those differences might shrink, in the new age of the Canadian Charter. And he was right.

The Charter has quite fundamentally changed the nature of political discourse in Canada. Ever since the great U.S. jurist John Marshall ruled in the early nineteenth century that U.S. courts could review legislative initiatives and find them unconstitutional, the so-called third branch of the U.S. government, the judiciary, has played a cardinal role in U.S. society, not just in ruling on narrow legal cases, but also in defining public policy in terms of its adherence to the text and spirit of the U.S. constitution. A cynic would say, as a New York governor once did, that constitutional interpretation is the vaguest of arts since "the Constitution is what the judges say it is." Nonetheless, judicial interpretation of the written constitution and concomitant power to accept, alter, or overturn legislative initiatives have been central to the U.S. political process as it never was in Canada until the Charter of Rights and Freedoms.

Canadian constitutional law in the pre-Charter era usually concerned jurisdictional disputes between the federal and provincial governments. These disputes were sometimes of considerable moment, granting authority over areas of public policy to one level of government or the other. But these rulings dealt with who had the power to set public policy, not the substance of that policy. If plaintiffs asserted that somehow their "rights" had been infringed upon, the courts politely steered them to Parliament or the legislatures, or ruled on the basis of common- or civil-law precedents. If various interests tried to piggyback their concerns onto the case at bar, the courts sternly told them to get lost. Only the plaintiffs and defendants could speak to the case.

No longer. The Charter has fundamentally altered the role of the courts, and especially the Supreme Court of Canada. The courts are now invited, as are their U.S. cousins, to alter or strike down legislation. Parties not directly involved in a particular case, but which can demonstrate some policy interest, are invited to make presentations to the courts. Foreign precedents, when cited, are invariably American rather than British. More profoundly, Canada has moved far away from the earlier British conception that "rights" are protected by the Crown through Parliament and common-law precedent to a U.S. conception that rights are inherent and inalienable, held by individuals or collectivities (as, in the Charter, references to linguistic minorities and aboriginals, for example) who can argue by reference to the written Charter than their rights have been either abridged or not recognized.

The political roots of the Canadian Charter are many and varied but largely American. Canada would certainly never have accepted a Charter without the abiding determination of Prime Minister Pierre Trudeau, who, fiercely opposed to nationalism in general, and French-Canadian nationalism in particular, began calling for a written bill of rights while teaching in Montreal in the 1950s. Trudeau had been deeply influenced by U.S. constitutional practice during his years of study at the Harvard Law School. In one of his first set of public remarks after being named Minister of Justice by Prime Minister Lester Pearson, Trudeau called for a written charter. His reasons were many, and included a deeply held liberal view of the sanctity of the individual, but he also believed a charter would wrench French Canadians in Quebec from their belief that only the Quebec state could protect the French fact in Canada. Rebuffed throughout the 1970s in attempts to affect constitutional change, Trudeau returned unexpectedly to office in the 1980 election and resolved to achieve what his biographers called his "magnificent obsession." The Charter that emerged from those years was not precisely to his liking, especially the "notwithstanding" clause insisted upon by recalcitrant premiers, which gave legislatures the right to stay certain court rulings for five years. Trudeau was correct, however, when he predicted that the Canadian public would not support the clause either, and the "notwithstanding" clause has seldom been used.

There was more behind the drive for a Charter than Pierre Trudeau. If he had not succeeded, it is still likely that the demand would have continued for some sort of written constitution, rather than the statutory Bill of Rights passed under Prime Minister John Diefenbaker. The rulings on desegregation and civil rights of the U.S. Supreme Court had greatly impressed legal scholars and social activists in Canada. Here was a court striking out against the most egregious infringement on human rights in a country where the slavery and subsequent plight of black Americans mocked the U.S. credo of "liberty and justice for all." In Canadian law schools of the 1970s, and in certain Canadian judicial circles, a deep admiration developed for the U.S. Supreme Court, and more generally, for the

U.S. method of protecting human rights. Diefenbaker's Bill of Rights had initially seemed promising, but it was only a statute of Parliament with the same status as other bills, not a constitutional document standing above legislatures. This admiration arose simultaneously with the rise of organized groups pressing the concerns of particular groups of Canadians: aboriginals, women, multicultural organizations, and linguistic minorities who saw considerable advantages in asserting their "rights" through the courts instead of male- and white-dominated legislatures. When Trudeau began insisting after his election of 1980 on another round of constitutional reform, including a written Charter, these groups became his most ardent supporters. He, in turn, used their political support to mobilize the Canadian population as part of his campaign to appeal, as he put it, "over the heads" of the provincial premiers. Not surprisingly, when the Charter emerged in its final form, it provided specific "rights" for these designated groups under the so-called equality rights clauses of the Charter. These "equality rights" for particular groups and the "notwithstanding" clause are the two most significant differences between the Charter and the U.S. Bill of Rights. The Charter itself, however—if not in each of its particulars— was heavily influenced by the American example.

Intended or otherwise, the Charter has made Canadians more "American" in the sense of rendering them more sceptical of legislatures and the political process since their "rights" are now protected elsewhere. Canada has moved, in the words of political scientist Peter Russell, from a parliamentary democracy to a constitutional democracy, a move paralleled in other countries too, but rejected by Britain and Australia.[9] The adoption of the Charter of Rights and Freedoms was extensively and intensely debated in political circles in the early 1980s. The Western Canadian premiers of the day—Peter Lougheed, Allan Blakeney, Sterling Lyon—all outlined the perils, as they saw them, of weakening legislatures at the expense of courts. The Charter, they said in so many words, would make Canada more like the United States. Their arguments did not effectively prevail. Public-opinion polls showed then what they do now: the Charter of Rights and Freedoms is popular, more popular today indeed than any other national symbol, including the monarchy, bilingualism, the Royal Canadian Mounted Police, the military, the flag, or the anthem. And of all these symbols, the Charter is by far the most American in its roots and reality.

Political and social differences remain between Canada and the United States. There is a substantially lower degree of religiosity and higher union membership in Canada. More Canadians live in cities as a share of total population than do Americans. The parliamentary system. The flag. Gun control. Regional equalization payments enshrined in the constitution. The French fact. The U.S. black population and the legacy of slavery. The monarchy, an institution valued by only a minority of Canadians. A somewhat less unequal distribution of income in Canada, although the smaller income differences are less than one might expect listening to Canadians bragging about them and also less than they should be, given higher Canadians taxes, massive spending on regional equalization programs, and somewhat more generous social programs. In terms of attitudes and values, however, Canadians and Americans are about as close as any two peoples in the world. What Freud called the "narcissism of small differences" may fairly describe what separates Canadians from Americans, and yet, for those who hew to them, these "small differences" matter. Beyond political institutions and flags, despite north–south economic links, and notwithstanding the lure of the American Dream that pulls Star-Spangled Canadians south, there remains what the writer Benedict Anderson has called the "imagined community" of the nation, weaker to be sure in Canada than in the United States, but nonetheless an animating force in Canada to ensure, within the limits of the possible, that the "small differences" persist and remain present in the daily lives of Canada's citizens.[10]

William Watson, the Canadian economist and writer, offered an intriguing illustration of Anderson's point about an "imagined community" existing in the mind. He listed 229 phrases, institutions, personalities, geographical places ("... the Calgary Stampede, Hudson's Bay Company blankets, the beaver, Pierre Berton, Bob White, Peggy's Cove, cod tongue, fiddleheads, pogy, muskeg ...") that would mean something to Canadians but nothing to Americans. Most of Watson's place names, institutions, and people would have meant little to French-speaking Canadians, too, but that is another story. Watson concluded that, "despite eighty years of radio and almost half a century of television, we Canadians also have hundreds of cultural references that mean more or less nothing even to very knowledgeable Americans."[11] A nation, in other words, is also a matter of the mind. Even if, as the Canadian ex-patriate broadcaster Robert MacNeil remarked to me, Canadians are programmed from birth with gigabytes of information about the United States, there still seems room for distinctively Canadian cultural signposts that signal a trail close to but not identical to the American one.

It has been often asserted, and it was repeated in my interviews with Star-Spangled Canadians, that Canadians are more "deferential" to the state, more sceptical of the free-enterprise system, more "collectivist" in outlook than the "individualistic" Americans. These beliefs also form the thesis, broadly stated, of Seymour Martin Lipset's book comparing the two societies, *Continental Divide*.[12] The thesis has a long history grounded in the argument that the U.S. democracy sprang from revolution, whereas Canadian democracy evolved slowly. "Life, liberty and the pursuit of happiness," the U.S. credo, expresses fundamental scepticism about the state, whereas Canada's "peace, order and good government" reflects a more statist view. After all, "peace" and "order" and "good government" depend axiomatically upon government, good or bad, whereas "life, liberty and the pursuit of happiness" do not. An explanation for the fundamentally different natures of Canada and the United States was ventured in Louis Hartz's seminal "fragment" theory, and later elaborated upon by political scientist Gad Horowitz. The "fragment" theory emphasized the importance of the Loyalists, the anti-revolutionaries who left the United States during the Revolution and brought north to Canada quite different conceptions of how best to protect liberty from those inspiring the rebelling colonists. From that early "fragment" grew Canada's differences from the United States. The thesis has enjoyed a long and durable history, if a somewhat dubious one, since the number of Loyalists and their descendants was small relative to Canada's nineteenth-century population. In any event, neither theory has ever had less explanatory power in examining the two countries, because contemporary Canada has never been more like the United States, whether Canadians like to acknowledge that observation or not.

George Perlin, a leading analyst of public opinion in Canada, has compared dozens of polls over several decades in which Canadians and Americans were asked similar questions. In particular, he wanted to discover whether Canadians display a weaker commitment to capitalism, a greater emphasis on social order, and a stronger commitment to equality of condition.[13] If so, it would tend to underscore the theses about the fundamental differences between the two peoples. Instead, he found that the "level of commitment to the culture of capitalism in the two countries is essentially the same." Canadians and Americans show similar support for "the virtues of competition, individual self-reliance, hard work and the profit system." As for "collectivism," Perlin found that "Canadians as a whole seem to be slightly more collectivist than Americans, but the differences are small." As for "equality of condition," the evidence is "mixed." In one only area—albeit an important one—did Canadian attitudes differ appreciably from American ones. Canadians seemed somewhat more prepared to use to the state to create greater equality of opportunity. Perlin's general conclusion: "We have seen little evidence of differences either in underlying values or approaches to public policy— with one significant exception. Canadians, collectively, seem more willing than Americans to use government in an active role to pursue both economic and social objectives. This difference persists, even though there is evidence that a majority of Canadians have been willing to support some curtailment of government's role."[14] French Canadians were most supportive of state activity. The gap was narrow between English-speaking Canadians and Americans.

Neil Nevitte of the University of Toronto has done the most exhaustive research yet into the values and attitudes of Canadians and Americans based on data from the World Values Survey.[15] That survey has tracked values and attitudes since 1970 in a group of advanced industrial democracies, allowing changes to be analysed over time. Nevitte concentrated on the 1980–1990 period and asked, "Did Canadian and American 'main values' converge over that period?" His broad answer: "On balance, the answer is that they did." Of all responses from the countries included in the World Values Survey, those of Canada and the United States were generally the closest. The largest differences arose in attitudes towards religion, as Canadians are much less religious than Americans, and in broadly defined "moral" issues, as Canadians are more tolerant on such issues as gay rights, divorce, and abortion.

Are Canadians are more "deferential" to authority than Americans, a lynchpin of Seymour Martin Lipset's thesis? Perhaps at some point, but not any more, according to the World Values Survey. "On this indicator," concluded Nevitte, "there is no evidence that Canadians lag behind the United States." Confidence in government institutions fell in both countries in the 1980s so that, by 1990, almost no difference existed in the number of Canadians (29.4 per cent) and Americans (31.8 per cent) expressing a "high" degree of confidence in government. (This finding may have been skewed by Canadians' distaste for the government of Prime Minister Brian Mulroney.) Canadians, it turned out, were less reluctant than Americans to engage in forms of political protest in this period, hardly an indication of a "deferential" people. As for supporting state activity in the economy, Canadians were no more likely to favour it than were Americans. Nevitte discovered: "Canadians do not fall short on some key entrepreneurial values ... Americans *and* Canadians are more likely than Europeans to believe that competition is good, individuals should take responsibility for themselves, and there should be greater incentives for individual effort."[16] He added: "The general economic orientations of

Canadians—their views about free markets and meritocracy—differ less than those of their American counterparts than is sometimes implied."[17] Nor would Nevitte agree with what some Star-Spangled Canadians told me—that Americans, on balance, work harder than Canadians. Nevitte found attitudes towards work and meritocracy quite similar in both countries. Only 1 per cent of Americans and 2 per cent of Canadians agreed with the statement that, in business and industry, "the state should be the owner and appoint the managers."[18]

Seventy-three per cent of Americans and 70 per cent of Canadians agreed that "private ownership of business and industry should be increased."

For a variety of reasons, Canadian and American attitudes in the 1981–90 period converged on economic values, but they actually widened on what are called "social values," such as attitudes to the traditional family, the role of religion, and moral permissiveness. Canadians became more American in their economic values, but less like Americans on social and moral questions. Nevitte's analysis ended in 1990, but nothing suggests that, in the economic domain, Canadian attitudes in the 1990s reverted back to pre-1980s attitudes. Canadians did organize in unions more successfully and more often than Americans, although outside the union movement itself trade unions were as unpopular in one country as in the other. Canadian laws are more favourable to starting and maintaining unions—the Canadian public sector is heavily unionized, whereas the U.S. public sector is not—and nothing equivalent exists in Canada to the U.S. "right-to-work" laws that prohibit labour-management agreements for deducting dues from non-union members.

Ekos Research, an Ottawa-based company specializing in public opinion, provided further evidence that Canadians were becoming more like Americans on economic issues.[19] Ekos conducted a major survey of Americans, compared their responses to those of Canadians, and found that although Canadians were more "liberal" in social and political values, "it is equally clear that many of the supposed areas of difference between the U.S. and Canada are more imagined than real." Ekos continued: "We appear no more compassionate (arguably less so), reveal similar levels of trust in governments as an institution and endorse the same broad policy choices and tradeoffs. Moreover, our value orientations, while still different, are blurring under common forces of technology, globalization and post-modernism."

Canadians felt themselves becoming more American, but they disliked the trend. Fifty-five per cent of Canadians in a December, 1999 sample said yes to the question "Is Canada becoming more like the U.S?" compared to only 10 per cent who said the countries were becoming less alike. A majority believed Canada was becoming more like the U.S. in both economic and cultural terms. And yet, by a 47 to 14 per cent margin Canadians said they would like Canada to become less like the U.S. (Thirty-eight per cent said Canada should remain the same.) In these and other polls, it would seem that Canadians are accepting, however grudgingly, the imperatives of globalization and free-trade, and coming around to a more traditional U.S scepticism about the role of government, while simultaneously regretting the trends. That margin of Canadian difference—Benedict Anderson's "imagined community"—nonetheless retains its grip on the Canadian psyche, since Ekos reported finding "a profound public consensus on the importance of maintaining a unique and distinct identity." Ekos got it precisely right when it concluded, "the themes of globalization and identity will emerge as the dominant national debate over the next five years."

The 1990s in Canada featured the struggle against deficits, government cut-backs, and, as the country entered the twenty-first century, a growing call for lower taxes. Continental free trade, globalization, and the extraordinary economic boom in the United States in the 1990s put the whip to Canadian companies and workers. They may have groaned under the intensified competition, and they were somewhat cushioned from the full effects of that intensified competition by a steadily depreciating currency, but Canadian attitudes did reflect greater scepticism towards government involvement in the economy and more openness to free markets and private-sector competition—a more American approach, in other words. Canada was not alone in that shift. The Asian economic crisis revealed the weaknesses of statism and crony capitalism. British Prime Minister Tony Blair led the Labour Party to electoral triumphs with a Third Way that emphasized markets, personal responsibility, and help for the disadvantaged to improve "equality of opportunity" rather than "equality of results." The world might not be headed conclusively towards the End of History, the definitive triumph of free markets and democratic institutions prophesied by Francis Fukuyama, but as the twenty-first century opened, that formula, and especially the American version of it, was the comparative standard for other advanced industrialized countries.[20] Geography, history, communications, interfamilial ties, trade, investment—and the loss of people who become Star-Spangled Canadians—meant that, for Canadians, the U.S. model would be the one against which the country would continue to judge itself, a model not necessarily to be copied slavishly, but one inextricably entwined with how Canadians viewed their own progress.

Sir Wilfrid Laurier, Canada's prime minister at the turn of the last century, predicted in a fit of hope over prescience that the twentieth century
would belong to Canada. Canada turned out to be a decent, civilized,
prosperous country, with nothing for which to apologize to itself or anyone else, but Walter Lippman, the American columnist and author, was
right. The twentieth century, he wrote, was "the American Century."

It did not begin that way, but it so ended. Isolationist in foreign policy
and possessed of a vast internal market, the United States remained pre-
occupied with domestic matters for much of the first half of the century.
The country entered the First World War belatedly, and shortly after that
war's end it became conventional wisdom in the United States that participation had been a mistake. It was against that backdrop that the Americans witnessed the first stages of the Second World War. Constrained by
public opinion, President Franklin D. Roosevelt could not convince his
country to enter the war until bombs dropped on Pearl Harbor.

Half a century later, the United States had become incontestably the
planet's only superpower, its attention sought in every corner of the world,
its decisions, or lack thereof, consequential far beyond its borders. Its cultural products, mass or specialized, penetrated homes everywhere; its economic might, although marred by social disparities at home, extended to
every continent; its diplomatic ear was sought by friend and potential foe.
Under these circumstances, Canadians could not help but be influenced,
and even shaped, by the United States towards the end of the American
Century in ways that would have surprised even Samuel Moffett.

And yet, apart from a few dissenters who said it was inevitable or would
be beneficial for the country, Canadians have never wanted to join the
United States. Maybe today's border, from an economic point of view,
makes less sense than ever, although the intensity of trade within Canada
remains robust when factors of distance and density of population are considered. The lace curtain of the border, a line on a map and a demarca-
tion of the mind, has endured and no one of consequence wants to erase
it even if Star-Spangled Canadians hopscotch it every year, and in recent
years in somewhat larger numbers.

One scenario, however, could cast in doubt the border's existence. If
Quebec were to secede from Canada, the rest of Canada would face a
future quite unlike anything it had ever known. It would obviously and
painfully be geographically divided. The United States is also geographically divided, but Hawaii and Alaska are appendages to the United States,
not large chunks of territory in the middle containing roughly a quarter of

the population. There are countries-as-archipelagos—Indonesia, the Philippines, New Zealand, Japan—but no separate country speaking another language lies in their midst. A successful but geographically divided country such as Canada without Quebec would be a historical curiosity, a possible but not guaranteed survivor.

No one can predict Canada's future without Quebec, and it is painful in the extreme even to contemplate one. The disruptions and animosities surrounding secession would be complicated enough, but even after (if?) disputes were resolved and animosities calmed, the future for the rest of Canada would be an uncertain one, for reasons relevant to the new situation within Canada and the overwhelming, neighbouring presence of the United States.

A few possibilities suggest themselves. The secession of Quebec would eliminate the "Quebec problem" only to replace it with the "Ontario problem." Ontario would so dwarf the new country that people everywhere else in Canada would feel even more uncomfortable with Ontario's power than they already do. The West—in particular, Alberta and British Columbia—would demand, and rightly so from their perspective, that something be "done" about Ontario. These provinces might not wish to live within a lopsided country wherein one province, Ontario, contained half the seats in Parliament, and more than half the country's gross domestic product and tax revenues. If people in Calgary and Vancouver are bred to believe Toronto already calls too many shots within Canada, think how they might react in a Canada-without-Quebec country. If they could not somehow fetter Ontario's power within the new Canada—say, by an American-style Senate: powerful with equal representation from all states—then some voices might suggest other political arrangements, with governors at home and congressmen and senators in Washington. If my Star-Spangled interviewees in the Pacific Northwest are correct, adjusting to living in the same country with Oregon and Washington would not be too wrenching for British Columbians, nor finding new links with the Rocky Mountain states and Texas for Albertans. As for Ontario, Premier Mike Harris has already bragged on U.S. soil that his province in some key respects has more in common with U.S. Great Lakes states than with far-away Canadian provinces.

These speculations assume that, even if parts of Canada wanted to join the U.S. union, the Americans would have them: a completely untested proposition. The occasional proponents of Manifest Destiny, or scattered voices among U.S. writers, suggested the United States should envelop Canada within the union, but the idea has never been seriously pursued except when, during the American Revolution, troops marched north to spread the good word, only to be given a licking. It would be for Canadians to propose, and for Americans to dispose, terms and conditions to be negotiated. And it might never happen if Quebec seceded, because the first instinct of Canadians would be, as always, to carry on as before. Except that those who believe that the secession of Quebec would be like travelling over an irritating rut in the road are wrong. Quebec's secession would be hugely unsettling, and in unsettled times previously discarded possibilities no longer seem axiomatically impossible.

Assuming Canada remains one country, which every sensible Canadian desires, there is no reason for anyone to want to join the United States, unless of course citizens in large numbers felt, as many Star-Spangled Canadians do, that the gap in living standards and opportunities had become so unbearably large that patriotism must yield to completely utilitarian behaviour. Even then, the chances are that the majority of Canadians would insist upon their own country. From the U.S. perspective, as journalist and author Richard Gwyn quipped, the Americans already have everything they want from Canada. From the Canadian perspective, joining the United States would be the end of the Canadian Dream of building a somewhat different society beside the U.S. colossus. The Canadian Dream, like all dreams, including the American, has had its trying moments of internal strife, but, all things considered, it has been a worthy one for a majority of Canada's citizens and for those who joined the country from abroad. Canadians want the "lace curtain," or Robert Frost's "good fences" between "good neighbors."

It is not always easy to carve out a distinctly Canadian Dream when living beside one so powerful as the American Dream, as the loss of so many Canadians to the United States has often reminded Canadians. Journalist and author Peter Newman once said people in Canada wanted to be "as Canadian as possible under the circumstances," and there is much wisdom in that phrase. Prime Minister Lester Pearson observed that Canadians and Americans are each other's best friends, whether they like it or not.

Canadians have never been so similar to Americans in values, assumptions, and economic organization, but differences remain, as most of these Star-Spangled Canadians have noted in interviews, although these have narrowed over time. Even Canadians themselves agree that they are changing. In the *Maclean's* survey, 50 per cent of Canadians agreed with the statement that "Canadians are becoming more like Americans," as opposed to 18 per cent who disagreed.[21] The challenge for Canadians in this American Century is to maintain those differences in ways that make economic, cultural, and political sense in a world, and specifically a North American continent, more integrated than ever with heightened pressures to compete.

Anti-Americanism has never been less apparent in Canada. Canadians may find disagreeable certain aspects of the United States, but their over-all impression is positive. Environics Research has been doing its Focus Canada surveys since 1981, thereby making it possible to trace attitudes over many years. In Environics's 1999 survey, 71 per cent of Canadians said they had a "favourable" view of the United States, compared with 24 per cent holding an "unfavourable" one. The "favourable" view had been holding steady since 1981, although it reached as high as 82 per cent in 1995, but the "unfavourable" opinion has inched up almost each year, to 24 per cent from 8 per cent in 1981. Still, by about a 3–1 margin, Canadians hold "favourable" rather than "unfavourable" views of the United States.

The most enthusiastic views about the United States, perhaps not sur-prisingly, are found among more affluent and better-educated Canadians, private-sector union members, and the Reform Party, according to Envi-ronics's research. The most unfavourable views were found among young people (aged eighteen to twenty-nine), non-British European immigrants, the unemployed, and NDP supporters. Atlantic Canadians held the most positive views of the United States (84 per cent), followed by Albertans (78 per cent). Montrealers and residents of Saskatchewan expressed the least positive views.

"Favourable" attitudes towards the United States have not led, accord-ing to Environics's findings, to any upsurge in support for even closer ties between the two countries. But those who want "somewhat distant" ties represent only 12 per cent of Canadians, and those who want "very distant" ties represent only 4 per cent. Canadians know who their best friends and closest neighbours are, and by far the largest number of them (58 per cent) wanted "somewhat close" ties—close but too close—and 23 per cent pre-ferred "very close" ties. The margin of Canadian distinctiveness, in other words, is what Canadians want preserved, even if the margin is smaller and more difficult to maintain.

The loss of Canadians to the United States has been going on for a very long time, as this book has shown. The numbers have ebbed and flowed. They ebbed in the 1970s and 1980s, but began modestly to flow again in the 1990s, in part because of continental economic integration and the gaps that emerged between Canadian and U.S. economic performance. Comparing recent losses to those a century ago is an interesting contextual exercise, but not terribly comforting. The border was then a permeable line on a map for people wanting to emigrate. Immigration policies in both countries were completely different. Brawn power not brain power accounted for economic growth. Public-sector employment was tiny. English Canada aped things British; French Canada remained a Catholic enclave. Taking comfort from the statistical fact that today's losses pale by comparison to those at the start of the twentieth century is akin to an aircraft manufacturer bragging that his machine goes faster than a train while his competitors build a better plane. Today's situation and tomorrow's challenges should preoccupy Canadians, not comparisons with yesterday.

Something similar can be said about the argument that, even if today's losses through emigration are rising, they are dwarfed by Canada's immigration of talent from abroad. Canada has been attracting 175,000 to 225,000 immigrants in recent years, and a good thing it is that so many immigrants are coming to Canada. Happily, in the last half of the 1990s, Canada's immigration policy tilted towards independent immigrants and slightly away from family-reunification immigrants, since every study has shown that the first generation of independents adds more to the country's skill levels. A "brain gain" for Canada is other countries' "brain drain," and hard as it may be for other countries, Canada clearly emerges from this flow a winner on every count. If Canadians are determined to be the world's largest per-capita importers of immigrants, as they are, then at least Canada should try to make immigration contribute the maximum to the country's short- and long-term well-being, without forsaking the country's honourable tradition of importing genuine refugees.

To leap from pats on the back about immigration to dismissal of losses to the United States would be to slump into the pillow of self-congratulation. Gains from abroad coupled with complacency about losses to the United States—even if numerically the gains exceed the losses—might be described as a typically, if regrettably, Canadian preference of settling for second best. The optimal question is: How can Canada continue to attract skilled people from abroad *and* create domestic conditions to reduce the pull for people leaving to become Star-Spangled Canadians? The people who are leaving, and in somewhat larger numbers in recent years, are among the "best and the brightest" with better-than-average, and often superior, educational qualifications and skills who wish to test themselves in a larger country with more cutting-edge challenges, wider opportunities, and potential economic rewards. Their numbers may be small by the standards of a century ago and be dwarfed by total immigration, but their potential contribution to Canada's well-being eclipses their numerical size. Independent immigrants, according to most studies, earn incomes at or above the Canadian average over time, but not right away. Star-Spangled Canadians tend to earn high incomes throughout their lives, so the aggregate trade-off between losing these workers while attracting the same number of skilled immigrants from abroad would represent a net loss for Canada.

The work of Star-Spangled Canadians in the United States may indeed contribute to greater progress for humankind than if they had remained at home. If their research produces medical or scientific breakthroughs that they could not have achieved in Canada, or if they make a film giving pleasure and enlightenment to millions that could never have been made in Canada, or if they create a computer company whose services reach into Canada but could never had been created in Canada, then the loss to Canada can perhaps be justified, not only by their own personal success, but because Canadians, too, will benefit, directly or indirectly. Whether Canada itself benefits, however, is another matter since the spin-offs from their success—in jobs, taxes, further innovation, bigger deals, or whatever—remain largely in the United States.

What I would describe as a worrisome trend of more Canadians emigrating to the United States, Professor Johnathan Kesselman, a level-headed student of the "brain drain," calls an "ominous trickle." Kesselman lines up neither with the blind "cut taxes and they will stay" school nor with the ostrich school that pooh-poohs the idea of a "brain drain." He writes: "What's at stake for Canada from any brain drain—actual or potential—is not only the individuals departing each year or even their cumulative numbers of a longer period. When we lose the elite of our artistic, scientific, technical, managerial and entrepreneurial classes, Canada does not simply lose prosperous workers who take with them all their earnings. Highly productive and creative workers create significant positive externalities that benefit society generally. The external costs imposed on Canada by brain drain arise in three areas—economic, fiscal and civic."[22]

Kesselman notes that a loss of talented people inhibits firms' ability to innovate and prosper. Their departure deprives governments of above-average tax sources that put below-average burdens on public services, which leads to a lessening of "the ability of governments to finance important social investments." Their departure also removes some of society's most active "civic" members: participants in community and political organizations, philanthrophy, and the ongoing social dialogue that defines a "distinct national culture and identity."

Twenty-five years ago, the Canadian dollar traded at or above par with the U.S. dollar. Canada's unemployment rate curled around the U.S. rate, sometimes higher, sometimes lower, but for the last twenty years it has been two to four points higher. Canada's tax load—once only slightly higher as a share of GDP—is now eight or nine points higher, although the February 2000 budget began a five-year plan to reduce personal income taxes modestly. Taxes rose faster in Canada in the 1980s than in any other member country of the Organisation for Economic Co-operation and Development, and they continued to rise throughout the 1990s. Canada's productivity has held its own across many sectors of the economy, except in two critical areas—industrial machinery and equipment, and electronics, which includes computers and related industries. Trailing badly in electronics and computers entering the twenty-first century is akin to having trailed in railways and manufacturing at the beginning of the twentieth. Of critical importance to ordinary Canadians, aggregate personal disposable income did not grow at all in the 1990s, while it increased in the United States. This gap in personal disposable income, courtesy in large part to higher unemployment and higher taxes in Canada, underpinned much of the unease about the "brain drain." But even without the "brain drain" debate, it would have been worrisome enough that Canadians' personal disposable incomes had stagnated and that the Canadian economy simply could not keep up with the U.S. economy. The impact of that failure was felt by Canadians in their pocketbooks and "life chances."

How dramatic has been the relative decline? In 1970, Canada's purchasing power of real private disposable income per adult stood at 64 per cent of its U.S. counterpart. Rapidly, the gap narrowed to 78 per cent in 1980, but since then it has fallen back to 66 per cent—almost the 1970 level![23]

In purchasing power, which includes public and private real incomes, the same rise and fall occurred: from 72 per cent in 1970 to 83 per cent in 1980, to 73 per cent in 1998. Of twenty-five OECD countries from 1988 to 1998, Canada's real gross domestic product per capita grew the second slowest, at only 5 per cent, compared with 18.5 per cent for the United States, which ranked twelfth on the list. These figures, dry on their face, trace a story of a country not fully realizing its potential both in absolute terms and relative to the United States. Properly understood, they reinforce the observation previously advanced that better public policies are needed for the sake of Canadians, and if those policies encourage, as they might, at least some people not to become Star-Spangled Canadians, then so much the better.

To be sure, many Americans were left behind as personal disposable incomes rose, and indeed some Americans witnessed their real incomes decline. The aggregate U.S. numbers were inflated by the huge gains a relatively small number of Americans made as the stock market soared and high-technology industries flourished. The Dow Jones slightly trailed the TSE Index in the early 1990s, but roared ahead of the major Canadian exchange throughout the rest of the decade. The stock market merely reflected that the U.S. economy had grown faster and outperformed the Canadian economy on every level during the 1990s. The result was that, after a slight narrowing in the 1980s, Canadians' per-capita income at the turn of the century had returned to its level of a quarter of a century ago — 25 per cent below that of Americans.

Gaps such as these, if left unattended, will continue to produce even larger numbers of Star-Spangled Canadians. The "brain drain," however, is not the principal reason why these gaps need attention. Indeed, no one should seek out macro-economic policies whose objective is to stop or significantly slow down emigration, per se. The "brain drain" is one effect of these gaps, but the more consequential problem is the Canadian economy's inability to produce enough opportunities for go-ahead people who remain in Canada. If these gaps are attended to over time, Canadians' own living standards will improve, and at least some of those who might otherwise have felt compelled or enticed to become Canadians of the Star-Spangled variety will remain Canadians, at home.

It is hard to know what is more misleading: the argument that the "brain drain" is a myth, or the one that proposes a magic bullet — as in, slash taxes and the "brain drain" will evaporate. Regrettably, at the political level this seems to be about the level of discourse. The Chrétien Liberals have banished any official mention of the "brain drain." It is *verboten* among them even to utter the phrase. The Reform Party (and its successor, the Canadian Alliance) and like-minded prophets in the media and think-tanks simplistically believe that the push–pull dynamics that cause emigration would largely evaporate if Canadians just paid much lower taxes. As this book has tried to explain, emigration is real and does represent a challenge to Canada, but the reasons for emigration are multiple, and taxes are only part, albeit an important one, of the equation.

If we have learned anything about the modern economy, it is that progress depends upon human skills. A country that loses them, even while gaining them from elsewhere, is not maximizing its own potential. It is settling for second-best solutions, comforting itself with a lazy moral superiority. It is also fooling itself, because, by failing to maximize its potential, it slowly declines relative to others that are maximizing theirs. A declining dollar, lower productivity in crucial economic areas, a battered social safety net, higher structural unemployment, and a rising tax-to-GDP ratio are surely sufficient signals to Canadians that their country has not been maximizing its potential, with important consequences for those who live in Canada, let alone those who have decided to leave.

Disgrace does not lie in borrowing and then adjusting, for Canadian circumstances, policies that work in the United States while maintaining a healthy scepticism about those that fail. Canadians, whether they admit as much or not, have always borrowed from the United States through a kind of filtering process whereby what happens south of the border is analysed to determine its potential for adaptation to Canadian circumstances. The latent fear within Canada is that in borrowing from the United States, Canada will lose its identity, forfeit its soul, and otherwise dilute that margin of distinctiveness Canadians insist upon. To some extent, whether Canadian governments consciously borrow and adapt successful American approaches, the filtering goes on anyway in companies, industries, universities, unions, media—indeed in almost every aspect of everyday life in Canada. Canadians borrowed and adapted labour laws and social security from the New Deal, government anti-poverty efforts from the War on Poverty, environmental awareness from the Clean Air Act, the Charter of Rights and Freedoms from the U.S. Bill of Rights, the legislative fight for equality from the civil-rights movement, affirmative-action programs from U.S. examples. Canadians adapted initiatives to their own circumstances, and added their own initiatives, from equalization to Medicare, to children's bonuses, to Child Tax Credits, to regional-development programs, to public broadcasting.

Canadians should insist that their governments' priorities be those of tomorrow and not those of yesterday. Examine any government's budget, and what leaps to the eye are spending priorities dictated by the decisions of long ago or by the politics of redress lobbied for by particular groups. The biggest single item in the federal government's budget is interest on the public debt—$42 billion in 2000—yesterday's obligation if ever there was one. Around every cabinet table, and from every concerned citizen, a new standard of inquiry is needed to judge every public policy: Will this or that decision help tomorrow's Canada become a prosperous country, enhancing the "life chances" of its citizens, or are we just paying yesterday's debts?

Universities are the classic institutions to prepare citizens for the future, because they are incubators for the skills and innovations of tomorrow, and yet they have been short-changed for research monies and per-capita student allocations. In the battle for public funds, universities have lost—and lost badly—against health care, pre-university education, and social programs. The Americans, by contrast, have properly financed their public universities, and that financing has been a key to the country's economic success and prosperity. It's sensible Canadian public policy to provide more funds for universities to better prepare citizens for the challenges of tomorrow, a reality the federal government has belatedly recognized.

Whether universities, or almost any other spending directed at the new priorities of tomorrow, can compete with the voracious health-care system of which Canadians are so proud is an open but vital question. Medicare is a program designed in the 1960s, fully implemented in the 1970s, with almost open-ended spending commitments that governments have tried to meet with an assortment of command-and-control measures. These are almost certainly going to be insufficient to cope with soaring costs as the population ages, health-care technology and pharmaceuticals become more expensive, and demands continue to escalate. After a period of restraint in the mid-1990s that brought health-care spending as a share of gross domestic product down, from 10.0 to 8.9 per cent, the share began to rise again in 1998 and 1999. By 2003, Canada will be spending over $100 billion on health care—and this before the portion of the population over 65 years of age begins to take off in 2010. The Canadian health-care system, in other words, cannot endure, even if the broad Canadian public does not yet understand or accept that reality. Despite some excellent aspects, the U.S. health-care model is certainly not one Canadians should borrow and adapt because it is fundamentally flawed. But other health-care models that provide a basic publicly financed system with some private add-ons exist in Scandinavia, Europe, and Australasia from which Canadians can learn—indeed, must learn—if money will be found for other pressing public concerns.

Taxes are an influential factor for some Canadians who leave for the United States, and they do become a determining factor for some Star-Spangled Canadians who might consider returning. But that is not the driving reason why taxes are too high. Instead, the widening economic gaps between Canada and the United States coincided with several decades in which the two countries' tax rates sharply diverged. The U.S. economy has outstripped the Canadian since the late 1970s on almost every aggregate economic indicator while taxes have risen much faster in Canada than the United States. There is a link here between the superior performance of the United States and a lower tax rate. If Canadians want to retreat to the high ground of moral superiority, or content themselves with sterile parlour games over national unity and federal–provincial bickering, while watching the U.S. economy grow faster, innovate better, and increase more rapidly the "life chances" for the vast majority of its citizens, then they are welcome to those recipes for Canada's relative economic decline. Canada does not need the same tax rates as the United States, for there are elements of Canadian society that are worth financing publicly that the Americans have chosen to finance privately. But Canada cannot be as competitive as it needs to be in the restless, demanding economic world of tomorrow, lumbered by taxes on labour and capital so much higher than those of their principal trading partner and hugely attractive alternative for investment.

What Canada needs are more successes. Not that Canada is without them. Far from it. Indeed, hiding your light under a bushel is a Canadian pastime. But Canada needs more discoveries, more cutting-edge research, more cultural accomplishments, more business triumphs, more innovation, more head offices—all in an age of more continental integration— to accompany its somewhat more egalitarian ethos. Protectionist policies are now behind Canada, either because they did not work or because they have become illegal under trading treaties. The competitive world Canadians now face is a very different one from that of a decade or more ago. The demand for labour in certain highly skilled industries is now continent- or worldwide. Capital ranges the globe looking for the best return on investment, and as the twenty-first century opens the United States, unfortunately for Canada, has the international brand name for the world's most dynamic, innovative, tax-friendly economy. Canada's best are no longer restricted to Canada. The world is their oyster, with the biggest pearl being the United States. Young Canadians, especially the educated ones, grow up in the world of the Internet that respects no international barriers. If they cannot be stimulated at home, some of them will search for excitement and rewards abroad, especially in the United States.

There is no reason why Canada cannot succeed. Living beside the United States is both a challenge and an opportunity—a challenge to preserve Canadians' margin of distinctiveness, an opportunity to examine what the Americans are doing and adapt the successful aspects of American society for Canadian purposes. Star-Spangled Canadians repeatedly told me they felt favoured by their Canadian upbringing because they had lived in a more outward-looking country. Learning other languages, which Americans seldom do, could be a significant Canadian advantage, and school systems should insist upon it. Properly financing a public broadcasting system that brings Canadians to each other—and the best of the world to Canada—helps open minds and broaden understanding. It is ludicrous that those who have managed the CBC have closed foreign news bureaux while refusing to pull the plug on local newscasts that are systematically clobbered by private broadcasters. What sets these cultural industries apart from others is their traffic in ideas—Canadian ideas. If Benedict Anderson is right that a nation exists in the mind, and he is, then the traffic in ideas will continue to merit the investment of public money because, however open Canadians are to things American, Americans will remain indifferent to things Canadian unless they have been Americanized. A free market in communications within North America would inevitably produce an even further blending of Canada into the United States. If Canadians want to preserve, as they should, some margin for cultural distinctiveness, it will cost them public monies. And public monies, properly directed, can lead to successes of the kind Canada also needs in culture, research, innovation.

The twenty-first century will not belong to Canada, just as the twentieth century did not. Belonging suggests ownership, and no country will own the world, not even the United States. That the United States will be the world's dominant country is likely for many decades; that it will always be the dominant country for Canada is a fact of life. Behind the lace curtain that Canadians insist upon, they can build a more prosperous, economically dynamic country—that will incidentally produce fewer Star-Spangled Canadians—if they shuck off their moral superiority about the United States, the outgrowth of a sense of needless inferiority, and enter the modern, global world equipped to compete, innovate, create, and succeed.

NOTES

History

1 The biographical information about Lavallée comes from his entry in volume 12 of the *Dictionary of Canadian Biography* (Toronto: University of Toronto Press, 1990), and Eugène Lapierre, *Calixa Lavallée: Musicien National du Canada* (Montreal: Fides, 1966).

2 Robin W. Winks, "The Creation of a Myth: 'Canadian' Enlistments in the Northern Armies during the American Civil War," *Canadian Historical Review* 39/1 (March 1958), pp. 24–41. Winks makes the point that French Canadians were much more pro-Union than English-speaking Canadians. He notes "that a large number of Canadian youths entered the Northern armies in March, 1865, when it was obvious to all that the war soon would be over" (p. 37).

3 Lapierre, *Calixa Lavallée*, p. 175.

4 John Herd Thompson and Stephen J. Randall, *Canada and the United States: Ambivalent Allies* (Kingston and Montreal: McGill–Queen's University Press, 1994), p. 11.

5 David Staines, *Beyond the Provinces: Literary Canada at Century's End* (Toronto: University of Toronto Press, 1995), p. 43.

6 Marcus Lee Hansen and John Bartlett Brebner, *The Mingling of the*

Canadian and American Peoples (New Haven, CT: Yale University Press, 1940), p. 27.

7 Staines, *Beyond the Provinces*, p. 45

8 Thompson and Randall, *Canada and the United States*, pp. 27–29.

9 These estimates are drawn from Thompson and Randall, *Canada and the United States*; and from R. K. Vedder and L. E. Gallway, "Settlement Patterns of Canadian Emigrants to the United States, 1850–1960," *Canadian Journal of Economics* No.3 (August 1970); and the classic study by Leon Truesdell, *The Canadian-Born in the United States: An Analysis of the Statistics of the Canadian Element in the Population of the United States* (New Haven, CT: Yale University Press, 1943).

10 Thompson and Randall, *Canada and the United States*, p. 55.

11 Ibid. p. 81.

12 Jack L. Granatstein, *Yankee Go Home?: Canadians and Anti-Americanism* (Toronto: HarperCollins, 1996), p. 74.

13 These and subsequent figures up to 1923 come from Department of Immigration and Colonization reports in *Canada Year Books*, 1915–24, and from Commissioner-General of Immigration, Washington, *Annual Reports*, 1914–23.

14 A. W. Carlson, "One Century of Foreign Immigration to the United States: 1890–1979," *International Migration* 23/3 (September 1985), pp. 310–11.

15 This quotation and those that follow are all taken from House of Commons debates in 1922, 1923, 1924, and 1925. They represent but a small fraction of the comments made by MPs from all parties about emigration.

16 *MacLean's*, February 15, 1922.

17 Thompson and Randall, *Canada and the United States*, p. 114.

18 Ibid, p. 129.

19 "What's the Bait Across the Border?" *Canadian Business*, March, 1955, p. 46.

20 H. G. Grubel and A. D. Scott, "The Immigration of Scientists and Engineers to the United States, 1949–1961," *Canadian Journal of Economics*, Vol. II, No. 3, 1976.

21 T. J. Samuel, *The Migration of Canadian-Born between Canada and the United States of America, 1955 to 1968*. (Ottawa: Research Branch, Department of Manpower and Immigration, 1969), pp. 11–12.

22 Quoted in C. Hesse and D. G. Fish, "Canadian-Trained Medical Scientists View Canadian Academia from Their American Laboratories," *Canadian Medical Association Journal*, November 5, 1966.

23 Samuel, *The Migration of Canadian-Born*, p. 31.

24 See, for example, K. V. Pankhurst, "Migration between Canada and the United States," *The Annals of the American Academy of Political and Social Science*, September 1966, pp. 53–62.

25 *Maclean's*, July 27, 1963.

26 *Migration between the United States and Canada*, published jointly by the U.S. Department of Commerce and Statistics Canada, 1990.

27 Granatstein, *Yankee Go Home?*, p. 185.

28 David D. Harvey, *Americans in Canada: Migration and Settlement since 1840* (Lewiston, NY: Edwin Mellen Press, 1991), pp. 20–21.

Differences

1 Joel Garneau, *The Nine Nations of North America* (Boston: Houghton Mifflin, 1981).

2 Ibid., p. 6.

3 Sam Roberts, *Who We Are: A Portrait of America* (New York: Times Books, 1993), chapter 6.

4 Jeffrey Simpson, "A Visitor's Guide to the American Century," *Queen's Quarterly*, 102/3, Fall 1995, p. 581.

5 *Research Perspectives on Migration* 22, guest editors Miriam Feldblum and Douglas Klusmeyer.

6 *Migration between the United States and Canada* (Washington, DC, and Ottawa: U.S. Department of Commerce and Statistics Canada, 1990), p. 30.

7 U.S. Bureau of Census, *Selected Characteristics of the Foreign-Born Population by Citizenship and Selected Countries of Birth*, 1996 (Washington, DC, April 8, 1997).

8 Ronald Englehart, Neil Nevitte, and Miguel Basanez, *The North American Trajectory* (New York: Aldine de Gruyter, 1966), p. 8.

9 Sage Research Corp., "Focus Groups with Politically Active Americans on Their Views of Canada," March 31, 1999.

10 For an excellent analysis of relations between U.S. and Canadian political leaders, see Lawrence Martin, *The Presidents and the Prime Ministers: Washington and Ottawa Face-to-Face, The Myth of Bilateral Bliss* (Toronto: Doubleday, 1982).

11 "How the World Sees Us," *The New York Times*, June 8, 1997.

12 Bruce McCall, *Thin Ice* (Toronto: Random House, 1997).

13 John Kenneth Galbraith, *The Scotch* (Toronto: Macmillan, 1964), p. 84.

14 Jack L. Granatstein, *Yankee Go Home? Canadians and Anti-Americanism*, (Toronto: HarperCollins, 1996), p. 286.

15 Seymour Martin Lipset, *Continental Divide: The Values and Institutions of the United States and Canada* (Toronto: C. D. Howe Institute, 1989).
16 Fraser Forum, April, 1996.

Race, Ethnicity
 1 The literature on the impact of black people, or African Americans as they are called more frequently now in the United States, on aspects of American politics, urban growth, economics, universities and so on is vast. Some of the recent studies include: David K. Shipler, *A Country of Strangers: Blacks and Whites in America* (New York: Knopf, 1997); Stephan Thernstrom and Abigail Thernstrom, *America in Black and White: One Nation, Indivisible. Race in Modern America* (New York: Simon & Schuster, 1997); Thomas Byrne Edsall, *Chain Reaction: The Impact of Race, Rights and Taxes on American Politics* (New York: W. W. Norton, 1992); Andrew Hacker, *Two Nations: Black and White, Separate, Hostile and Unequal* (New York: Ballantine, 1995); William Julius Wilson, *When Work Disappears: The World of the New Urban Poor* (New York: Knopf, 1996); William Julius Wilson, *The Truly Disadvantaged: The Inner City, the Underclass and Public Policy* (Chicago: University of Chicago Press, 1987).
 2 Quoted in George Elliott Clarke, "Contesting a Model Blackness: A Meditation on African-Canadian African Americanism, Or the Structures of African Canadianité," *Essays on Canadian Writing* 63/3 (1998).
 3 See Gladwell's article "Black Like Them," *The New Yorker*, April 29/May 6, 1996.
 4 *The Globe and Mail*, August 30, 1997.
 5 Michael Lind, *The Next American Nation: The New Nationalism and the Fourth American Revolution* (New York: The Free Press, 1995), p. 80.
 6 Jeffrey Reitz and Raymond Breton, *The Illusion of Difference: Realities of Ethnicity in Canada and the United States* (Toronto: C.D. Howe Institute, 1994), p. 125.
 7 Irene Bloemraad, "The North American Naturalization Gap," unpublished paper, quoted by permission of the author.
 8 George Perlin, "A Changing World," in *Degrees of Freedom: Canada and the United States in a Changing World*, ed. Keith Banting, George Hoberg, and Richard Simeon (Montreal and Kingston: McGill–Queen's University Press, 1997) p. 146.

Crime

1 *The Globe and Mail*, November 16, 1999.

2 I am indebted to Professor Rosemary Gartner, director of the Centre of Criminology at the University of Toronto, for this information.

3 "Curse of the South: Behind American homicide," *The New York Times*, July 22, 1998.

4 Gary Mauser, "A Comparison of Canadian and American Attitudes towards Firearms," *Canadian Journal of Criminology*, 32/4 (October 1990), p. 586.

5 See George Perlin, "The Constraints of Public Opinion," in *Degrees of Freedom*, ed. Keith Banting, George Hoberg, and Richard Simeon (Kingston and Montreal: McGill-Queen's University Press, 1997), p. 116.

French Canadians

1 Roch Carrier, *The Lament of Charlie Longsong*, (Toronto: Viking, 1998), p. 72.

2 The information about Ernest Dufault comes from Jacques Godbout's 1993 National Film Board documentary *Alias Will James*.

3 Among the many demographic studies of French-Canadian migration, perhaps the most detailed is Yolande Lavoie, *L'émigration des Canadiens aux Etats-Unis avant 1930* (Montreal: Les Presses de l'Université de Montréal, 1972).

4 Some of this information comes from *La Survivance*, an excellent forty-three-page publication produced by the Museum of Work and Culture in Woonsocket. Another source is Bessie Bloom Wessel, *An Ethnic Survey of Woonsocket, Rhode Island* (Ayers Company, 1970).

5 Lavoie, *L'émigration des Canadiens*, p. 39.

6 Gerard J. Brault, *The French-Canadian Heritage in New England* (Hanover and London: University Press of New England, 1986), p. 65.

7 See David M. Hayne, "Emigration and Colonization: Twin Themes in Nineteenth-Century French-Canadian Literature," in *The Quebec and Acadian Diaspora in the United States*, ed. Raymond Breton and Pierre Savard (Toronto: Multicultural History Society of Ontario, 1982) pp. 11–22.

8 A copious literature exists on the economic problems of rural Quebec and the demographic and political consequences that flowed from it. The best volume is arguably Fernand Ouellet, *Le Bas-Canada, 1791–1840: Changement structuraux et crise* (Ottawa: Editions de l'Université d'Ottawa, 1976).

9 *Report of the Commission to Study the Development of Maine's Franco-American Resources*, December 1997, p. 5.

10 *La Survivance*.

11 Emily Toth, "Fatherless and Dispossessed: Grace Metalious as a French-Canadian Writer," *Journal of Popular Culture*, 15/3 (1981): pp. 28–38.

Brain Drain

1 "Chrétien Dismisses 'Tax Rage' Reports," *The Globe and Mail*, July 22, 1999.

2 Office of the Leader of the Opposition, "Heading South: The Problem of the Brain Drain," June 1998.

3 Branham Group, "IT Skills Shortage in Canada—a Snapshot," February 1999.

4 U.S. Bureau of the Census, "Selected Characteristics of the Foreign-Born Population by Citizenship and Selected Countries of Birth," April 8, 1997.

5 Provided to author by Statistics Canada, but also based on U.S. Department of Justice, *Statistical Yearbook of Immigration and Naturalization Service*, various years. See also papers delivered at Fraser Institute conference, Nov. 13, 1998, by Steven Globerman, "NAFTA and Labour Markets," and Don DeVoretz and Samuel Laryea, "Canadian Human Capital Transfers: The United States and Beyond." Also important is John Helliwell's "Checking the Brain Drain: Evidence and Implications," paper for the Advisory Council on Science and Technology's Export Panel on Skills, March 1999.

6 For a list of the groups, see form M-316, published by the Immigration and Naturalization Service and the U.S. Department of Justice.

7 Statistics Canada, "South of the Border," 1999, fig. 3–10.

8 U.S. Immigration and Naturalization Service, "Illegal Alien Resident Population," October 1996.

9 Helliwell, "Checking the Brain Drain: Evidence and Implications," *Policy Options*, September 1999, pp. 6–18.

10 These and other comparative unemployment statistics come from Statistics Canada, *Labour Force Update: Canada-U.S. Labour Market Comparison*, Autumn 1998.

11 Bruce Little, "Americans Have Bragging Rights," *The Globe and Mail*, November 23, 1998.

12 Michael Wolfson and Brian Murphy, *New Views on Inequality Trends in Canada and the United States*, (Ottawa: Statistics Canada, 1999). Also "Gap between Rich and Poor Found Substantially Wider," *The New York Times*, September 5, 1999.

13 Industry Canada, *Improving Productivity: The Key to High Living Standards*, May, 1999.

14 "Canada's economy in the '90s: 'Truly Ugly'," *The Ottawa Citizen*, July 15, 1999.

15 I am grateful to New Zealand High Commissioner Jim Gerard and his research staff for this information.

16 OECD Report on Canada, 1998.

17 OECD Report on Canada, 1996.

18 David Perry, "Fiscal Figures," Canadian Tax Journal, 46/2 (1998). Also Bruce Little, "Why the Taxman Loves Big Earners," *The Globe and Mail*, April 13, 1998.

19 These and subsequent figures are provided by the Canadian Department of Finance in personal correspondence.

20 David Card and Richard Freeman, eds., *Small Differences That Matter: Labor Markets and Income Maintenance in Canada and the United States* (Chicago: University of Chicago Press, 1993).

21 Mahmood Iqbal, *Implications of Taxes on Investment Decisions in Canada: Some Comparisons with OECD Countries*, Conference Board of Canada, October 1997, table 5, p. 19.

22 U.S. Bureau of Census, *Current Population Survey*, March 1996.

Health

1 See also Eva Ryten, A *Statistical Picture of Past, Present and Future of Registered Nurses in Canada*, a report prepared for the Canadian Nurses Association, Ottawa 1997.

2 Statistics Canada, *South of the Border: Graduates from the Class of '95 who moved to the United States*, 1999.

3 *The Future Supply of Registered Nurses in Canada*, (Toronto: Canadian Nurses Association, 1997).

4 Fact sheet from Health Human Resource Development, "Nursing in Ontario, 1997," published by the Ontario Ministry of Health.

5 Robert McKendy, George Wells, Paula Dale, Owen Adams, Lynda Boske, Jill Strachan, Lourdes Flor, "Factors Influencing the Emigration of Physicians from Canada to the United States," *Canadian Medical Association Journal*, 154/2, January 15, 1996.

6 "Medical Insurers Revise Cost-Control Efforts, *The New York Times*, December 3, 1999.

7 *The New York Times*, July 23, 1998.

8 Canadian Institute for Health Information, *National Health Expenditure Trends, 1975–1998*. Also, various OECD reports comparing health-care spending in the twenty-six member countries, the latest of which appeared in 1999.

9 Canadian Institute for Health Information, *National Health Expenditure Trends, 1975–1998*.

Academics

1 For these and other comparative statistics, see *The Canadian University in Profile*, published in 1999 by the Association of Universities and Colleges of Canada.
2 Canadian Association of University Teachers, *Have We Lost Our Minds?*, 1/2 (July/August 1999).
3 "Academic Brain Drain," study prepared by ARA Consulting Group.
4 I have lost track of many of my classmates, but I know that two others are also teaching at U.S. universities, one a mathematics professor at Dartmouth, the other a philosophy professor at Arizona.
5 For an accessible exploration of Rose's ideas on evolution, see his book *Darwin's Specter, Evolutionary Biology in the Modern World*, (Princeton, Princeton University Press, 1998).
6 Caren Heilberg, Marja Verheof, and Cheryl Wellington, "Finding Identity and Voice: A National Survey of Canadian Postdoctoral Fellows," unpublished, 1997.
7 Statistics Canada, *South of the Border: An Analysis of Results from the Survey of 1995 Graduates Who Moved to the United States*, 1999.
8 Association of Universities and Colleges of Canada, "Brain Drain," paper, 1997.

Entrepreneurship, Business

1 Branham Group, "IT Skills Shortage in Canada," February 4, 1999.
2 See also "Budding Business Migrates South," *National Post*, July 17, 1999.
3 "Cross-Border Firms Look North for Talent," *The Globe and Mail*, December 8, 1999.
4 James Fallows, "Billion-Dollar Babies," *The New York Review of Books*, December 16, 1999.
5 "Borderline Differences," *The Globe and Mail*, November 25, 1999.
6 Interview with John Roth in *Ivey Business Journal*, November/December 1999.
7 "Brain Drain Blamed on Pay, Not Tax," *The Globe and Mail*, December 2, 1999.
8 "A Tale of Two Valleys," *The Ottawa Citizen*, April 24, 1999. The Canadian cities selected for comparison were: Ottawa, Vancouver, Calgary, Toronto, and Montreal. The U.S. cities were: Raleigh, Austin, Seattle, San Jose, Boston.

9 *Statistics Canada Daily*, March 23, 1999, noted that "with annual mul-
tifactor productivity gains respectively of 5.7 per cent and 3.4 per cent
since 1986, these two industries [computers and computer parts] far
outperformed their Canadian counterparts."
10 "Ebbers Field," *The Wall Street Journal*, August 14, 1998.

Entertainment, Journalism
1 The information about Lawrence and Pickford comes from Eileen
Whitfield's excellent biography *Pickford: The Woman Who Made Hollywood* (Toronto: Macfarlane Walter & Ross, 1997).
2 Ibid., p. 180.
3 Peter Morris, *Embattled Shadows: A History of Canadian Cinema,
1895–1939* (Montreal and Kingston: McGill-Queen's University Press,
1978), p. 28.
4 "Power House," *Saturday Night*, June 1998.
5 "Shannon's Still Got it after 20 Years," *The Ottawa Citizen*, January 20,
1998.
6 "Legion of Supermodels," *Saturday Night*, November 1999.
7 "How Canadians Are Infiltrating Hollywood," *Maclean's*, January 1968.
8 Andrew Clark, *Stand and Deliver: Inside Canadian Comedy* (Toronto:
Doubleday, 1997), chapter 11.
9 Ibid. p. 224.
10 Ibid. pp. 251–52.
11 "Shocking Green," *Maclean's*, November 29, 1999, p. 90.
12 Statistics Canada daily, "Film and video distribution," February 3, 2000.

Conclusion
1 Elisabeth Wallace, *Goldwin Smith: Victorian Liberal* (Toronto: University of Toronto Press, 1957), pp. 254–55.
2 Ibid. p. 264.
3 Goldwin Smith, *Canada and the Canadian Question* (Toronto:
Macmillan and Co., 1891), p. 267.
4 Samuel Moffett, *The Americanization of Canada* (Toronto: University
of Toronto Press, 1972), p. 114.
5 Ronald Inglehart, Neil Nevitte and Miguel Basanez, *The North American Trajectory: Cultural, Economic and Political Ties among the United
States, Canada and Mexico* (New York: Aldine de Gruyter, 1996), p.
139.
6 "Reporting Results the American Way a Growing Trend," *The Globe
and Mail*, July 2, 1999.

7 *Maclean's*, December 20, 1999, p. 42.
8 "Canadians Expect Loonie to Disappear," *The Globe and Mail*, August 3, 1999.
9 Peter Russell, *Constitutional Odyssey: Can Canadians Be a Sovereign People?* (Toronto: University of Toronto Press, 1992).
10 Benedict Anderson, *Imagined Communities* (New York and London: Verso, 1991).
11 William Watson, *Globalization and the Meaning of Canadian Life* (Toronto: University of Toronto Press, 1998), pp. 220–21.
12 Seymour Martin Lipset, *Continental Divide* (Toronto: Canadian-American Committee, 1989).
13 George Perlin, "The Constraints of Public Opinion," in *Degrees of Freedom*, ed. Keith Banting, George Hoberg, and Richard Simeon, (Montreal and Kingston: McGill–Queen's University Press, 1997), pp. 77–149.
14 Ibid., p. 103.
15 Neil Nevitte, *The Decline of Deference* (Toronto: Broadview Press, 1996).
16 Ibid., p. 121.
17 Ibid., p. 148.
18 Inglehart et al., *The North American Trajectory*, p. 108.
19 Ekos Research Associates, "Exploring perceived and comparative differences in Canadians and Americans values and attitudes: Continentalism or Divergence?" presented to Human Resources Development Canada, May 3, 2000.
20 Francis Fukuyama, *The End of History and the Last Man* (New York: The Free Press, 1992).
21 *Maclean's*, December 20, 1999, p. 22.
22 Johnathan Kesselman, "Policies to Stem the Brain Drain—Without Americanizing Canada," paper presented at a Fraser Institute Conference, November, 13, 1998.
23 Pierre Fortin, "The Canadian Standard of Living: Is There a Way Up?" C. D. Howe Benefactors Lecture, 1999, p.7

BIBLIOGRAPHY

Benedict Anderson, *Imagined Communities* (New York and London: Verso, 1991).

Keith Banting, George Hoberg, Richard Simeon, eds., *Degrees of Freedom: Canada and the United States in a Changing World* (Montreal and Kingston: McGill-Queen's University Press, 1997).

Richard L. Barton, *The Ties that Blind in Canadian-American Relations: Politics of News Discourse* (Mahwah, NJ: Lawrence Erlbaum Associates, 1990).

Pierre Berton, *Hollywood's Canada: The Americanization of our National Image* (Toronto: McClelland & Stewart, 1975).

James Blanchard, *Behind the Embassy Door: Canada, Clinton and Quebec* (Toronto: McClelland & Stewart, 1998).

Gerard J. Brault, *The French-Canadian Heritage in New England* (Kingston and Montreal: McGill-Queen's Press, 1986).

Raymond Breton and Pierre Savard, eds., *The Quebec and Acadian Diaspora in North America* (Toronto: Multicultural History Society of Ontario, 1982).

David Card and Richard Freeman, eds., *Small Differences That Matter: Labor Markets and Income Maintenance in Canada and the United States* (Chicago: University of Chicago Press, 1993).

Roch Carrier, *The Lament of Charlie Longsong* (Toronto: Viking, 1998).

Andrew Clark, *Stand and Deliver: Inside Canadian Comedy* (Toronto: Doubleday, 1997).

Thomas Courchene, ed., *Room to Manouevre? Globalization and Policy Convergence* (Kingston, ON: Bell Canada Papers on Economic and Public Policy, 1999).

Gerald Craig, *The United States and Canada* (Cambridge, MA: Harvard University Press, 1965).

J. H. Dales, *The Protective Tariff in Canada's Development* (Toronto: University of Toronto Press, 1966).

E. J. Dionne Jr., *Why Americans Hate Politics* (New York: Simon & Schuster, 1991).

James Doyle, ed., *Yankees in Canada: A Collection of Nineteenth-Century Travel Narratives* (Saint John, NB: ECW Press, 1980).

Thomas Byrne Edsall with Mary D. Edsall, *Chain Reaction: The Impact of Race, Rights and Taxes on American Politics* (New York: W. W. Norton, 1992).

Marc Egnall, *Divergent Paths: How Culture and Institutions Have Shaped North American Growth* (New York: Oxford University Press, 1996).

Scott Eyman, *Mary Pickford, America's Sweetheart* (New York: Donald Fine, 1990).

Marion Botsford Fraser, *Walking the Line: Travels along the Canadian/American Border* (Vancouver: Douglas & McIntyre, 1989).

Earl Fry, *The Expanding Role of State and Local Government in U.S. Foreign Affairs* (Washington: Council on Foreign Relations, 1998).

Francis Fukuyama, *The End of History and The Last Man* (New York: The Free Press, 1992).

John Kenneth Galbraith, *The Scotch* (Toronto: Macmillan, 1964).

Joel Garneau, *The Nine Nations of North America* (New York: Houghton Mifflin, 1981).

Jack L. Granatstein, *Yankee Go Home?: Canadians and Anti-Americanism* (Toronto: HarperCollins, 1996).

Douglas Gray, *The Canadian Snowbird Guide* (Toronto: McGraw Hill-Ryerson, 1998).

Fredrick Philip Grove, *A Search for America* (Toronto: Graphic Publishers, 1927).

Herbert G. Grubel and Anthony D. Scott, *The Brain Drain, Determinants, Measurements and Welfare Effects* (Waterloo: Wilfrid Laurier University Press, 1977).

Richard Gwyn, *The 49th Paradox: Canada in North America* (Toronto: McClelland & Stewart, 1985).

——, *Nationalism without Walls: The Unbearable Lightness of Being Canadian*, (Toronto: McClelland & Stewart, 1995)

Andrew Hacker, *Two Nations: Black and White, Separate, Hostile and Unequal* (New York: Ballantine, 1995).

Thomas Haliburton, *The Clockmaker* (Toronto: McClelland & Stewart, 1971, originally printed 1871).

Monty Hall and Bill Libby, *Emcee Monty Hall: Star of Let's Make a Deal* (New York: Grosset and Dunlap, 1973).

Marcus Lee Hansen and John Bartlett Brebner, *The Mingling of the Canadian and American Peoples* (New Haven, CT: Yale University Press, 1940).

David D. Harvey, *Americans in Canada: Migration and Settlement since 1840* (Lewiston, NY: The Edwin Mellen Press, 1991).

Louis Hémon, *Maria Chapdelaine* (Paris: Grasset, 1924).

Victor Howard, ed., *Creating the Peaceable Kingdom* (Lansing, MI: Michigan State University Press, 1998).

Ronald Inglehart, Neil Nevitte and Miguel Basanez, *The North American Trajectory: Cultural, Economic and Political Ties among the United States, Canada and Mexico* (New York: Aldine de Gruyter, 1996).

David M. Kennedy, *Freedom from Fear: The American People in Depression and War, 1929–1945* (New York and London: Oxford University Press, 1999).

Eugène Lapierre, *Calixa Lavallée: Musicien National du Canada* (Montreal: Fides, 1966).

Yolande Lavoie, *L'Emigration des Canadiens aux États-Unis avant 1930* (Montreal: Les Presses de L'Université de Montréal, 1972).

Michael Lind, *The Next American Nation: The New Nationalism and the Fourth American Revolution* (New York: The Free Press, 1995).

Kenneth Lines, *British and Canadian Immigration to the United States Since 1920* (San Francisco: Rand Research, 1978).

Seymour Martin Lipset, *Continental Divide: The Values and Institutions of the United States and Canada* (Toronto: C. D. Howe Institute, 1989).

Andrew H. Malcolm, *The Canadians* (Toronto: Fitzhenry & Whiteside, 1985).

Marci McDonald, *Yankee Doodle Dandy: Brian Mulroney and the American Agenda* (Toronto: Stoddart, 1995).

Samuel Moffett, *The Americanization of Canada* (Toronto: University of Toronto Press, 1972).

Peter Morris, *Embattled Shadows: A History of Canadian Cinema, 1895–1939* (Montreal and Kingston: McGill-Queen's University Press, 1978).

Neil Nevitte, *The Decline of Deference* (Toronto: Broadview Press, 1996).

W. H. New, *Borderlands: How We Talk about Canada* (Vancouver: University of British Columbia Press, 1998).

Organization of Economic Co-operation and Development, *Canada* (Paris: OECD, 1997).

Jeffrey Reitz, *Warmth of the Welcome* (Boulder, CO: Westview Press, 1998).

Jeffrey Reitz and Raymond Breton, *The Illusion of Difference: Realities of Ethnicity in Canada and the United States* (Toronto: C.D. Howe Institute, 1994).

Sam Roberts, *Who We Are: A Portrait of America* (New York: Times Books, 1993).

Peter Russell, *Constitutional Odyssey: Can Canadians Be A Sovereign People?* (Toronto: University of Toronto Press, 1992).

David K. Shipler, *A Country of Strangers: Blacks and Whites in America* (New York: Knopf, 1997).

Allan Smith, *Canada—An American Nation?* (Kingston and Montreal: McGill-Queen's Press, 1994).

Goldwin Smith, *Canada and the Canadian Question* (Toronto: Macmillan and Co., 1891).

David Staines, *Beyond the Provinces: Literary Canada at Century's End* (Toronto: University of Toronto Press, 1995).

John Herd Thompson and Stephen J. Randall, *Canada and the United States: Ambivalent Allies* (Kingston and Montreal: McGill-Queen's Press, 1994).

Stephan Thernstrom and Abigail Thernstrom, *America in Black and White: One Nation, Indivisible: Race in Modern America* (New York: Simon & Schuster, 1997).

Leon Truesdell, *The Canadian-Born in The United States: An Analysis of the Statistics of the Canadian Element in the Population of the United States* (New Haven, CT: Yale University Press, 1943).

Elisabeth Wallace, *Goldwin Smith: Victorian Liberal* (Toronto: University of Toronto Press, 1957).

William Watson, *Globalization and the Meaning of Canadian Life* (Toronto: University of Toronto Press, 1998).

Eileen Whitfield, *Pickford: The Woman Who Made Hollywood* (Toronto: Macfarlane Walter & Ross, 1997).

William Julius Wilson, *The Truly Disadvantaged: The Inner City, the*

Underclass and Public Policy (Chicago: University of Chicago Press, 1987).

——, *When Work Disappears: The World of the New Urban Poor* (New York: Knopf, 1996).

S. F.Wise and Robert Craig Brown, *Canada Views the United States: Nineteenth-Century Political Attitudes* (Seattle, 1967).

ARTICLES

Irene Bloemraad, "The North American Naturalization Gap," Department of Sociology, Harvard University, unpublished.

James A. Brox, "Migration between the United States and Canada: A Study in Labour Market Adjustment," *International Migration*, 21/1, (1983).

A. W. Carlson, "One Century of Foreign Immigration to the United States: 1880–1979," *International Migration*, vol. 23/3 (September 1985)

"Education for Export?" Canadian Advanced Technology Association (April, 1997).

Donald DeVoretz and Samuel Laryea, "Are We Losing It? Canada's Brain Drain to the United States: New Evidence from the 1990s," paper presented to C.D. Howe Institute conference, October 1997.

Donald DeVoretz and Samuel Laryea, "Canadian Human Capital Transfers: The USA and Beyond," paper presented at Policy Research, Creating Linkages conference, Ottawa, 1998.

Pierre Fortin, "The Canadian Standard of Living: Is There a Way Up?" C.D. Howe Benefactors Lecture, 1999.

Steven Globerman, "NAFTA and labour markets," paper presented at Fraser Institute conference, Nov. 13, 1998.

Caren Helbing, Marja Verhoef and Cheryl Wellington, "Finding Identity and Voice: A National Survey of Canadian Postdoctoral Fellows," unpublished.

Herbert G. Grubel and Anthony D. Scott, "The Immigration of Scientists and Engineers to the United States, 1949–1961," *Canadian Journal of Economics*, Vol. II, No. 3, 1976.

David M. Hayne, "Emigration and Colonization: Twin Themes in Nineteenth-Century French-Canadian Literature," in Raymond Breton and Pierre Savard, eds., *The Quebec and Acadian Diaspora in the United States* (Toronto: Multicultural History Society of Ontario, 1982).

John F. Helliwell, "Comparing capital mobility across provincial and national borders," National Bureau of Economic Research, Canbridge, 1998.

John F. Helliwell, "National Borders, Trade and Migration," *National Bureau of Economic Research*, Cambridge, 1997.

John F. Helliwell and Ross McKitrick, "Comparing Capital Mobility across Provincial and National Borders," *National Bureau of Economic Research*, Cambridge, June 1998.

Harry Johnson, "The Economics of the Brain Drain: The Canadian Case," *Minerva*, III/3 (Spring 1965).

Yolane Lavoie, "Québécois and francophones dans le courant migratoire vers les états-unis aux XIXe et XXe siècles," *Critère* 27 (Printemps 1980).

David L. McKee and Henry Woundenberg, "Some Reflections on the Loss of Canadian Economists to the United States," *International Migration* 28/1, 2 (1980).

Robert J. R. McKendry et al., "Factors Influencing the Emigration of Physicians from Canada to the United States," *Canadian Medical Association Journal* 154/2 (January 15, 1996).

K. V. Pankhurst, "Migration between Canada and the United States," *The Annals of the American Academy of Political and Social Science*, September 1966.

K. V. Pankhurst, "Migration between Canada and the United States," in Carl Grindstaff et al., *Population Issues in Canada* (Toronto: Holt, Rinehart and Winston, 1971).

Policy Options, "The Brain Drain," 20/7 (September 1999).

T. J. Samuel, *The Migration of Canadian-Born between Canada and the United States of America, 1955 to 1968*. (Ottawa: Research Branch, Department of Manpower and Immigration, 1969).

Statistics Canada, *Migration between the United States and Canada*, jointly produced with U.S. Department of Commerce, Series P-23, February 1990.

George Theriault, "The Franco-Americans of New England," in Mason Wade, ed., *Canadian Dualism: Studies in French-English Relations* (Toronto: University of Toronto Press, 1960).

Emily Toth, "Fatherless and Dispossessed: Grace Metalious as a French-Canadian Writer," *Journal of Popular Culture* 15/3 (1981).

Calvin J. Veltman, "Le Sort de la Francophonie aux États-Unis," *Cahier québécois de démographie* 9/1 (avril 1980).

Robin W. Winks, "The Creation of a Myth: 'Canadian' Enlistments in the Northern Armies during the American Civil War," *Canadian Historical Review* 39/1 (March 1958).

Henry Woundenberg and David L. McKee, "American Economists in Canada: A reversal of the brain drain," *International Migration* 28/1, 2 (1980).

INDEX